BIRMINGHAM COLLEGE OF FOOD, TOURISM & CREATIVE STUDIES
COLLEGE LIBRARY, SUMMER ROW
BIRMINGHAM B3 1JB
Tel: (0121) 243 0055

Books must be returned by the last date stamped
or further loans may not be permitted

Consumer Psychology of Tourism, Hospitality and Leisure
Volume 2

Consumer Psychology of Tourism, Hospitality and Leisure
Volume 2

Edited by

J.A. Mazanec
G.I. Crouch
J.R. Brent Ritchie
A.G. Woodside

CABI *Publishing*

CABI *Publishing* is a division of CAB *International*

CABI Publishing
CAB International
Wallingford
Oxon OX10 8DE
UK

Tel: +44 (0)1491 832111
Fax: +44 (0)1491 833508
Email: cabi@cabi.org
Web site: http://www.cabi.org

CABI Publishing
10 E 40th Street
Suite 3203
New York, NY 10016
USA

Tel: +1 212 481 7018
Fax: +1 212 686 7993
Email: cabi-nao@cabi.org

A catalogue record for this book is available from the British Library, London, UK.
A catalogue record for this book is available from the Library of Congress, Washington DC, USA.

ISBN 0 85199 535 7

Printed and bound at Cromwell Press, Trowbridge, from copy supplied by the editors.

Contents

Contributors

Irena Ateljevic,
School of Business and Public Management, Victoria University of Wellington, PO Box 600, Wellington, New Zealand

Theo A. Arentze,
Urban Planning Group, Eindhoven University of Technology, PO Box 513, 5600 MB Eindhoven, The Netherlands

Jay Beaman,
Auctor Consulting Associates, Ltd., Ottawa, Ontario, Canada

Jeff Beaman,
Auctor Consulting Associates, Ltd., Ottawa, Ontario, Canada

Thomas Bieger,
Institute for Public Services at the University of St. Gallen, Varnbüelstrasse 19, CH-9000, St. Gallen, Switzerland

Mark A. Bonn,
Florida State University, College of Business Department of Hospitality Administration, Tallahassee, Florida, USA

Aloys W.J. Borgers,
Urban Planning Group, Eindhoven University of Technology, PO Box 513, 5600 MB Eindhoven, The Netherlands

Joseph S. Chen,
Department of Hospitality and Tourism Management, Virginia Polytechnic Institute and State University, 351 Wallace Hall, Blacksburg, VA 24061-0429, USA

Geoffrey I. Crouch,
School of Tourism and Hospitality, Faculty of Law and Management, La Trobe University, Bundoora, Melbourne, Victoria 3083, Australia

Alain Decrop,
Department of Business Administration, University of Namur, Rempart de la Vierge 8, 5000 Namur, Belgium

Sara Dolnicar,
Institute for Tourism and Leisure Studies, Vienna University of Economics and Business Administration, Augasse 2-6, 1090 Vienna, Austria

Stephen Doorne,
School of Business and Public Management, Victoria University of Wellington, PO Box 600, Wellington, New Zealand

Yüksel Ekinci,
School of Management Studies for the Service Sector, University of Surrey, Guildford GU2 5 XH, UK

H. Leslie Furr,
Georgia Southern University, Hotel and Restaurant Management, Statesboro, USA

Alexandra Ganglmair,
Department of Marketing, University of Otago, PO Box 56, Dunedin, New Zealand

John Y. Gountas,
School of Business, University of Ballarat, Mt. Helen Campus, Ballarat, Victoria, Australia

Sandra (Carey) Gountas,
School of Business, University of Ballarat, Mt. Helen Campus, Ballarat, Victoria, Australia

Tracey Harrison-Hill,
School of Marketing and Management and CTHMR, Griffith University, Gold Coast, PMB 50, GCMC. 4217, Australia

Angela Hausman,
Lewis College of Business, Management/Marketing Division, Marshall University, Huntington, West Virginia, USA

Simon Hudson,
Tourism Management Group, Faculty of Management, University of Calgary, Calgary, Alberta, Canada

Robert L. King,
University of Hawaii at Hilo, Hawaii, USA

Metin Kozak,
P.K. 27, 48000 Mugla, Turkey

Christian Laesser,
Institute for Public Services at the University of St. Gallen, Varnbüelstrasse 19, CH-9000, St. Gallen, Switzerland

Friedrich Leisch,
Department of Statistics, Probability Theory and Actuarial Mathematics, Vienna University of Technology, 1040 Vienna, Austria

Jordan J. Louviere,
University of Sydney, Sydney, Australia

Josef A. Mazanec,
Institute for Tourism and Leisure Studies, Vienna University of Economics and Business Administration, Augasse 2-6, 1090 Vienna, Austria

Robyn L. McGuiggan,
School of Marketing, University of Technology Sydney, Sydney NSW 2007, Australia

Manon van Middelkoop,
Urban Planning Group, Eindhoven University of Technology, PO Box 513, 5600 MB Eindhoven, The Netherlands

Joseph O'Leary,
Purdue University, West Lafayette, Indiana, USA

Tove Oliver,
Institute of Rural Studies, University of Wales, Aberystwyth SY23 3AL, UK

Richard R. Perdue,
College of Business and Administration, University of Colorado, Boulder, Colorado, USA

Michael Riley,
School of Management Studies for the Service Sector, University of Surrey, Guildford GU2 5XH, UK

J.R. Brent Ritchie,
World Tourism Education and Research Centre, University of Calgary, Calgary, Alberta, Canada

Peter Schofield,
School of Leisure, Hospitality and Food Management, University of Salford, Salford M6 6PU, UK

Stephen L.J. Smith,
Department of Recreation and Leisure Studies, University of Waterloo, Waterloo N2L 3G1, Ontario, Canada

Harry J.P. Timmermans,
Urban Planning Group, Eindhoven University of Technology, PO Box 513, 5600 MB Eindhoven, The Netherlands

Arch G. Woodside,
Carroll School of Management, 450 Fulton Hall, Boston College, 140 Chestnut Hill, MA 02647, USA

Ben Wooliscroft,
Department of Marketing, University of Otago, PO Box 56, Dunedin, New Zealand

Andreas H. Zins,
Institute for Tourism and Leisure Studies, University of Economics and Business Administration, Augasse 2-6, 1090 Vienna, Austria

Preface

This volume is dedicated to a series of research reports presented at the Second Symposium on the Consumer Psychology of Tourism, Hospitality and Leisure (CPTHL) in Vienna, Austria, during 6 and 9 July, 2000. It follows the tradition of the first Symposium held in Hilo, Hawaii, 1998 (see Woodside *et al.*, 1999). Like its predecessor the second Symposium aimed at soliciting multidisciplinary contributions from a broad social science background and from a variety of methodological origins. The underlying ideas are illustrated by quoting from the call for papers:

"The CPTHL Symposium comprises papers reflecting the progress in consumer psychology theory and research of tourism, hospitality, and leisure. This implies more than just transferring widely known theory or measurement technique to consumer behaviour in leisure, tourism, or hospitality. A multi-faceted product, a multi-stage decision-process, a fragmented service encounter, and a versatile consumer in an application domain such as leisure and tourism are particular challenges. The Vienna Symposium puts special emphasis on the consumers' decision making for evaluating choice alternatives in tourism, leisure, and hospitality operations. Coping with nonlinear utility functions, capturing highly emotional product attributes, incorporating non-compensatory decision rules, or accounting for unobserved heterogeneity in a consumer population are typical problems behavioural research and measuring methodology are facing in this industry."

The reports have been arranged into five major compartments. Part 1 deals with tourist destinations, their struggle for competitive advantage and its measurement. Part 2 goes into tourist decision processes and analyses some of the choice rules consumers exhibit in evaluating tourist products. Part 3 outlines several criteria for travel market segmentation while Part 4 discusses recent improvements in the methods that are instrumental in detecting or building tourist segments. Part 5 watches the tourist's consumption experience and reviews recent results in service quality and satisfaction monitoring.

The approaches practised in the empirical studies range from quantitative model construction to hermeneutical, interpretive research designs. The reports witness the vitality of 'tourism, hospitality and leisure' and its vigour of arousing highly original and imaginative research.

The Second CPTHL Symposium would have never become the stimulating and instructive undertaking, unless my esteemed colleagues Geoff Crouch, J.R. Brent Ritchie, Rick Purdue and Arch Woodside had volunteered to assist in evaluating the paper submissions, advising the authors and chairing the sessions. It is to them, to all authors, and to the faculty and staff of the Institute for Tourism and Leisure Studies of the Vienna University of Economics and Business Administration, where I want to direct my appreciation and gratitude. I am particularly indebted to my wife Gertrud, who undertook to polish the documents of 21 authors preferring many idiosyncratic formatting styles and finalized the manuscript with greatest accuracy. Rebecca Stubbs of CABI gave many hints and comments while the Second CPTHL and its associated Volume 2 were in preparation.

Vienna, November 2000   J.A. Mazanec

Reference

Woodside, A.G., Crouch, G.I., Mazanec, J.A., Oppermann, M., Sakai, M. (eds.) (1999) *Consumer Psychology of Tourism, Hospitality and Leisure*, CAB International, Wallingford, UK.

Chapter one
Developing Operational Measures for the Components of a Destination Competitiveness / Sustainability Model: Consumer versus Managerial Perspectives

J.R. Brent Ritchie
World Tourism Education and Research Centre
University of Calgary, Calgary, Alberta, Canada

Geoffrey I. Crouch
School of Tourism and Hospitality
La Trobe University, Melbourne, Victoria, Australia

Simon Hudson
Tourism Management Group, Faculty of Management,
University of Calgary, Calgary, Alberta, Canada

Introduction

'Without the consumer there can be no sustainable tourism.' (Sharpley and Sharpley, 1997)

The importance of understanding the factors that determine the ability of a tourism destination to compete effectively in the marketplace – and to do so in a sustainable manner – has been recognized from both theoretical and managerial perspectives. The recent special issue of *Tourism Management* on the theme of 'The Competitive Destination' represents a high point in this growing interest in the topic (Ritchie and Crouch, 2000). Despite the conceptual advances highlighted in the special issue, we are still some distance from achieving the in-depth level of understanding of destination competitiveness/sustainability (C/S) that will be required if the concept is to become truly operational from a management perspective.

As we work towards this goal, at least three additional milestones need to be passed. They are:
- Phase 1, the development of operational measures for each of the components of the Ritchie and Crouch C/S Model (see Figure 1);

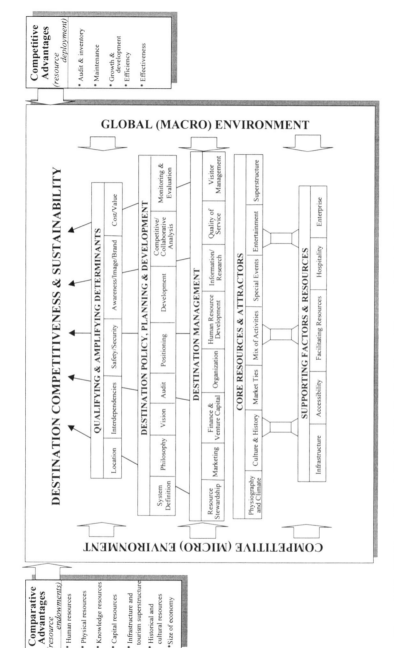

Figure 1 The Ritchie and Crouch Model of Destination Competitiveness / Sustainability (C/S)
Source: Ritchie and Crouch, 2000

- Phase 2, the use of these measures to develop an index of destination C/S in a manner similar to that currently used by the *World Competitiveness Yearbook* to describe the industrial competitiveness of nations;
- Phase 3, the development of a generic simulation model that will characterize and explain the behaviour of destinations with respect to C/S as the various determinants of C/S are varied by destination managers.

This paper seeks to address the first of the above milestones – namely, the need to develop operational measures for each of the variables in the C/S model. It does so however, only partially. As the task of developing operational measures of C/S gets underway, it is evident that these measures needed to be developed from two very different, yet highly complementary perspectives:

- Initially, it was proposed to use only the more traditional measures of C/S that reflected industry/managerial standards of performance regarding C/S. The advantages of these measures are that they tend to be more readily available and they tend to be better understood by members of the tourism sector;
- However, as we exposed these measures to peer review, it was brought to our attention that many important aspects of C/S are determined primarily by the degree to which the marketplace perceives C/S to be achieved. While 'waiting time' is one commonly used industry standard of quality of service (QOS), we have been reminded that absolute measures of waiting time are often perceived quite differently by different individuals. For example, a 15-minute wait for a skier in a lift line may be subjectively viewed as quite annoying by one skier; in contrast, the same 15 minutes in line may be considered to be quite enjoyable by another skier who derives pleasure from the social interaction with others in the line-up.

Given the foregoing reality, it would be a grievous error for both theoreticians and managers to rely solely on traditional industry-based measures of destination performance or destination appeal when attempting to establish measures of C/S. While this assertion is by no means innovative (for example, see extensive earlier works by Belk (1974) regarding the impact of objective/subjective measures – or situational factors, on consumer behaviour), it is nevertheless, a very fundamental premise that must be acknowledged before we proceed further with the development of our C/S model. As well, it was felt particularly appropriate to develop this important theme within the setting of a symposium on the Consumer Psychology of Tourism, Hospitality and Leisure (CPTHL). As such, in the subsequent discussions where we will compare and contrast industry/managerial measures of C/S with consumer-based measures, the emphasis will be on ensuring an in-depth understanding of the consumer side of the equation.

Competitiveness and Sustainability for What?

What is the meaning of success for a destination?

In all of our efforts to date in the development of the model of C/S, it has been implicitly assumed that C/S are good in themselves; that is that they contribute to the success of the destination. It may be useful at this point, in what is essentially a theoretical or conceptual paper, to further reflect on the very meaning of success itself. In **traditional industry terms**, success in tourism has meant attracting visitors and doing so at a profit. Therefore, it follows that the most successful destination is the one that most profitably attracts visitors. From a **consumer perspective**, it may be argued that success means providing satisfying experiences for visitors. Under this approach, the most successful destination is the one that provides the greatest satisfaction for the greatest number of visitors.

Our position is somewhat different. We define tourism success as the ability of a destination to enhance the well-being of the **residents** through tourism. Under this scenario, the most successful destination is the one that enhances the well-being of its residents to the greatest extent. For the moment, we will assert that economic well-being (as measured by income and employment) is the most relevant measure of success – although we recognize that this approach is not without its shortcomings.

The foregoing approach also implies that in absolute terms, the most competitive destination is that which brings about the greatest success; that is, the most well-being for its residents, on a sustainable basis. However, we shall also argue that competitiveness also implies a certain efficiency/effectiveness on the part of DMO[1] managers. As such, we further assert that: 'the most competitive destination is that which most effectively creates sustainable well-being for its residents.' By effectively, we intend to convey the idea that the level of sustainable success realized by a destination should be achieved with the least possible expenditure of resources.

In effect, we are arguing that the true measure of destination C/S must be a blend of two dimensions:

- the actual success of the destination as measured by the contribution which tourism makes to enhancing the sustainable well-being of destination residents; plus
- the extent to which the foregoing level of success has been achieved through an effective deployment of destination resources.

Destination versus DMO competitiveness

Finally, there is another important distinction that must be made in our efforts to understand C/S. This distinction is the difference between the C/S of the Destination as a whole, and the C/S of the DMO responsible for managing the Destination. This is a very critical distinction – and one that has not been clearly defined in much of the discussion to date. In brief, a destination may be highly successful due to:

- both its comparative advantages (its natural resources) and its competitive advantages (effective deployment of its resources by the DMO);
- a strong comparative advantage that offsets a poorly performing DMO;
- a weak comparative advantage that is overcome by a highly effective DMO, that through astute deployment of its resources, has unduly influenced the success of the destination.

In effect, we argue strongly that any measure of destination C/S must clearly distinguish between the overall performance (success) of the Destination and the specific performance of the DMO that seeks to enhance this success.

Similarly, DMO success is also more complex in that it may be viewed as consisting of:

- both **Industry Member** and **Competitor** views regarding the influence they believe the DMO has had in determining the success of the destination; and
- **Resident** views regarding the effectiveness of the DMO as a community-building organization.

A roadmap for the present discussion

Given the complexity of the model in Figure 1, there exists some difficulty in presenting the discussion in a manner that is logical and easily understandable to the reader. While the order we have chosen is somewhat arbitrary, it will hopefully be both comprehensive and comprehensible. More specifically, we will address the core components of the model that emphasize those areas of greatest interest to consumer researchers. More specifically, the major part of the discussion focuses on the CORE RESOURCES and ATTRACTORS component of the model, since these are the primary motivators that drive visitations to a destination. As such, consumer perceptions of the desirability of these components and their constituent elements are of primary concern to those responsible for destination C/S.

Core Resources and Attractors

Consumer vs. industry measures

The first critical step in this review and analysis was to identify the most significant elements of this component of the C/S model. The results of this process are summarized in Table 1. As shown, typical industry measures of a more objective nature for the component **Physiography and Climate** document such things as the annual amount of sunshine at the destination, the average temperatures throughout the year, and the amount of precipitation. This 'objective' measure also seeks to capture the physical characteristics of the destination; such as whether it is mountainous or prairie like, whether it is 'unspoiled' or undeveloped, and whether it is relatively pristine or is littered by human (or other) spoils.

From a psychological standpoint however, it shows how the visitor (or potential visitor) perceives those physiographic and climatic elements that determine the attractiveness of the destination and eventually its C/S. Furthermore, we know that there can be significant differences across individuals (Carroll and Chang, 1970; Wish, 1971) in the subjective manner in which they view the same 'objective' reality. Many destinations are visited primarily because of their 'scenery'. However, since 'beauty is in the eye of the beholder,' certain tourists may prefer the simplicity of a rural scene to the more dramatic mountains of the Alps or the North American Rockies. Many visitors find Switzerland to be a highly attractive, wonderfully maintained destination. At the same time, not an insignificant number of visitors to Switzerland are overwhelmed by the level of development in the mountain areas.

The **Culture and History** component of the model also contains many elements that demonstrate how traditional industry and consumer measures of competitiveness can differ substantially. Past research has examined how the many dimensions of culture enhance the attractiveness of a tourism destination (Ritchie and Zins, 1978). This particular study has not, however, distinguished between the way in which industry views the 'richness' of culture as opposed to how consumers perceive it. The mere counting of the number of museums and historical sites, while helpful in measuring competitiveness, may well mask the quality of these attractions – something that is often the primary appeal to visitors. Similarly, while a poor state of repair of cultural facilities within a destination may discourage visitation, the fact that these facilities may be truly unique can lead consumers to rate them as much more desirable from a tourism perspective. For example, the Winter Palace in St. Petersburg, Russia is in a declining state of repair. Despite this, the cultural and historical value of its contents make it an absolute 'must see' in the eyes of most tourists.

Other seemingly mundane elements of a destination's culture that can be enumerated, such as the number of different foods, further reinforce the thesis of this paper. Despite the existence of many dishes, it is frequently one distinctive type of food/meal that characterizes a destination's gastronomy. Swiss restaurants serve a broad range of high quality foods – and yet consumer demand for a single, very traditional meal – cheese fondue – is very instructive in our efforts to understand destination appeal. In this case, it is likely that the 'trappings' associated with this dish create an atmosphere that adds disproportionately to the value that consumers associate with this particular dining experience.

The model component **Market Ties** is much less complex. In this case, the traditional industry approaches primarily include such measures as the percentage of the host region population having strong ethnic or personal ties to key target markets. In terms of business travel, they include the extent to which there are strong commercial linkages due to common interests in certain industrial sectors such as petroleum, forestry, fashion, computers, banking, and even tourism itself. The consumer perspective in this case is essentially the degree to which employees in these common interest sectors consider these 'ties' with 'sister' destinations to be important to them.

The **Activities** component seeks, in the simplest sense, to measure the number of activities available at a destination. It may also seek to capture a particular manner in which a given activity is performed at the destination. As Table 1 indicates, swimming as an activity may be quite different in the consumer's mind when it is performed in a pool as opposed to occurring in an ocean/beach setting. This example demonstrates quite forcefully that we must take great care in interpreting reported measures of activities available at a destination. Clearly, in the case of swimming, the two consumer experiences described above are quite different – even though the hard statistics might fail to distinguish between them.

The measurement problems associated with the **Events** component are different again. Traditional industry measures frequently report the number and type of events available to visitors over the course of a year. Clearly, from a consumer perspective, all events are not of equal value. Even the timing of the event can significantly alter its utility, or appeal, to the visitor.

While event attendance figures is a traditional industry measure that may reflect an event's consumer appeal, they may also be misleading. Certain 'signature' events, even though they may not be categorized as mega-events, can generate substantial consumer interest in particular market segments. The 'once in a generation' Royal Coronation may not attract a large number of visitors, nevertheless, the extensive – and intensive – media coverage that is associated with this type of event can draw huge television audiences, that in turn create a certain aura or mystique around the destination as a whole – and particularly for the particular locale in which the event occurred.

The point to be emphasized from the foregoing is simply that the cold numbers describing events can greatly under or over estimate their contribution to determining the C/S of a destination. A complimentary in-depth look through the eyes of the consumer is clearly essential if we are to adequately measure their true significance.

Measurement of the **Entertainment** component of the model encounters many of the same challenges as discussed above for events. There are, however, some unique measurement issues. From a consumer perspective, the amount of entertainment available at a destination is probably much less important than its perceived uniqueness, or even more important, the degree to which it is 'appropriate' to the destination. The world famous Oberammergau Passion Play is uniquely associated in the consumer's mind with the destination – even though it could theoretically be staged anywhere. As such, the competitiveness value of this event far surpasses its entertainment value as a mere 'religious' event.

The **Superstructure** component of the model lends itself easily to traditional industry measures that include the number of attractions located at the destination, the level of total investment in attractions, and the range of different attractions. It also includes the number and the quality of lodging units as well as the existence and quality of a destination convention centre.

In this case, the consumer side of the equation might be measured by the reported preferences for different types of accommodations and the degree to which different types of attractions generate excitement due to the kinds of experiences they offer. As well, for any particular destination, it will be useful to determine the degree to which consumers prefer them for personal versus professional visitation.

Review and Discussion

To this point the present paper has focused our review on the contents of Table 1. This table presents a detailed comparison of the approaches that might be used to measure the various components of the Core Resources and Attractors of a destination from both an Industry and a Consumer Perspective. Given an unlimited amount of time and space, it would be useful to carry out the same detailed discussion for the other four major dimensions of the model outlined in the Appendix: Qualifying and Amplifying Determinants in Table 2; Supporting Factors and Resources in Table 3; Destination Policy, Planning, and Development in Table 4, and Destination Management in Table 5.

While such an in-depth examination will be necessary for the completion of Phase 1 of our programme, and for the eventual work on Phase 2 (Index of Destination Competitiveness) and Phase 3 (Simulation Model of Destination Performance), the present discussion has focused on providing the reader with a detailed insight into how the Industry and Consumer measures will be defined. While all the measures may not be necessary for all components (and indeed, may be too costly in realistic terms), we have attempted in this paper to demonstrate the scope and complexity of Destination Competitiveness/Sustainability, and the challenges that Policy Makers and Managers face.

Since it would be rather tedious to review all components of the model in the present context, we shall refrain from doing so. However, interested readers will hopefully be able to extract the essence of our arguments from the detailed contents of Tables 2–5.

Subsequent phases

In the remainder of this paper we shall briefly outline our vision for the remaining two phases of the model development process.

Phase 2 – Towards a blended Index of Destination Competitiveness / Sustainability (IDC/S)

Based on the foregoing discussion, and the detailed contents of Tables 1–5, we are now in a position to move towards the development of a 'Blended' Index of Destination Competitiveness/Sustainability. By blended, we mean an index that includes both objective industry measures of C/S, as well as consumer based measures of C/S.

Again, as Quality of Service (QOS) is one component of this index, we potentially envisage assembling the following types of data on which to base the Index:

- industry based judgements as to the relative importance of QOS in determining destination C/S;
- consumer based judgements as to the relative importance of QOS in determining destination C/S.

Again, once the Index has been developed, we may wish to obtain:

- some indication regarding the extent to which the context of visitor decision-making might influence each of the measures of C/S;
- some indication regarding the extent to which the measures of importance for QOS may vary among major market segments;
- for each destination of interest, the degree to which that destination is judged to be capable of providing the necessary QOS.

In an ideal world, the final Index of C/S would include measures for all the components of the model. In a more realistic world, we envisage that initial versions of the Index will focus on a 'reduced set' of the most important components of the model. Once measures are available for this reduced subset of components across a meaningful number of destinations, it will be possible to rate the C/S of each destination, in a manner similar to that employed by the World Competitiveness Index.

All of the foregoing assumes that an Index of Destination C/S will have some value. In attempting to respond to this assumption, we need to again ask:

- What is the ultimate measure of 'success' for a destination?
- How does the Index of C/S relate to this ultimate measure of success?
- Does competitiveness determine success – or does success define competitiveness?
- To what extent can a DMO influence the success of a destination?

- To what extent can a DMO influence the competitiveness of a destination?
- To what extent is a successful DMO and a successful destination the same thing?
- To what extent is a competitive DMO and a competitive destination the same thing?

Phase 3 – Development of a generic simulation of destination performance
Once measures have been 'perfected' for the key variables that are judged to determine destination C/S, we envisage the development of a generic model of Destination C/S. One possibility of operationalizing the vision may be through the 'i think' software purchase (High Performance Systems, 1994). This algorithm has been used by others to assess the manner in which the performance, or 'success', of a system can be examined in relation to the factors that are hypothesized to determine that success. Regardless of the actual predictive accuracy of the simulation model, it has still been found to be extremely valuable as a tool for management education and training. From a consumer, and visitor management perspective, such a simulation model provides a vehicle for assessing the desirability to potential visitors of a range of destination development options and visitor management programmes.

Concluding remarks

The constantly growing number of travel destinations, and the enhanced quality of existing ones, is putting great pressure on those responsible for a given destination to find better ways to compete in the tourism marketplace – and to do so in a sustainable manner. The first step in attempting to achieve this goal is to better understand those forces and factors that determine the C/S of major tourism destinations. One framework for achieving this understanding (Figure 1) has received general acceptance in the management community. However, in order to make this model more managerially valuable, there is a clear need to develop operational measures for each of its components. This paper has provided a detailed set of guidelines for this process. In keeping with the arguments presented, the process suggested includes a strong consumer orientation to complement the industry based measures that are traditionally employed. As a consequence, future development of the C/S model will draw heavily on the theories and skills of behavioural researchers. Regardless of the emphasis (industrial or consumer), we should consistently keep in mind that measurement is truly the key to strategic success (Schiemann and Lingle, 1999)

Appendix

Table 1 Consumer versus Industry Measures of C/S: A Comparison of Core Resources and Attractors

COMPONENT: Physiography and Climate	
Subjective Consumer Measures	**Objective Industry Measures**
• perceived comfort • aesthetics/'eye appeal' • variability of terrain • perceived 'majesty' of scenery • perceptions of 'appropriate' levels of development • perception of 'cleanliness' and 'unspoiled nature' • how values of different types of destinations change over time	• amount of sunshine • average temperature • amount of precipitation (snow, rain) • existence of mountains, sea • existence of wildlife • existence of unspoiled 'nature' • existence of facilities complementary to physiography and climate • lack of garbage/human spoils

COMPONENT: Culture and History	
Subjective Consumer Measures	**Objective Industry Measures**
• perceived 'richness' of the culture • perceived contributions to human development • extent to which culture has been studied • perceived 'exoticness' • consumer 'familiarity' with culture • perceived 'uniqueness' of the culture • perceived 'sophistication' of the culture • consumer 'liking' of different 'dishes' • consumer 'liking' of local music • perceived 'eye appeal' of distinctive architecture • consumer acceptance/fear of different religions • consumer acceptance/fear of different races • degree to which distinctive dress creates cultural identify of people • interest created by traditions • interest created by work habits/practices • interest created by leisure activities/behaviours • interest created by unique social/family structures • interest generated by educational system/practices • different perceptions of 'old world' and a new world	• age of culture • number of museums • number of historical sites • literary citations regarding culture • level of investment in cultural facilities • extent of historical documentation • state of repair of cultural facilities • number of identifiable historical 'stars' • extent of international 'duplication' of art/sculptures • level of media attention • different language • number of different foods • distinctive music • distinctive architecture • distinctive religion • dominant race within culture • distinctive mode of dress (everyday/special occasion) • number of distinctive traditions • distinctive work habits/practices • number of distinctive leisure activities/behaviours • unique social/family structures • distinctive educational system/practices

COMPONENT: Market Ties	
Subjective Consumer Measures	**Objective Industry Measures**
• importance that destination residents attach to maintaining family/ethnic ties • degree to which employees in key industry sectors attach to maintaining personal/business ties with colleagues in 'sister' cities • difference between past 'historical' and future 'emerging' ties	• percentage of population having strong ethnic/personal ties to key markets • extent of business travel in specific industries of importance to destinations (e.g. petroleum, computers, fashion, banking) • extent of 'sports' ties

Table 1 (Continued) Consumer versus Industry Measures of C/S: A Comparison of Core Resources and Attractors

COMPONENT: Mix of Activities	
Subjective Consumer Measures	**Objective Industry Measures**
• special appeal to the individual of available activities • individual preference for certain form of activity • perceived quality facilities for activities • liking for a mix of activities vs. individual activities • price sensitivity of individuals	• unique/distinctive activities available within the destination • particular way certain activities are performed at destination (e.g. swimming in a pool vs. an ocean) • number of different activities available • range of activities available • cost of activities

COMPONENT: Special Events	
Subjective Consumer Measures	**Objective Industry Measures**
• desire/ability to participate in multiple events during visit • importance visitor attaches to uniqueness • strength of desire to see mega-event • importance attached to having seen an event of international renown • desire to see an event that reflects nature of destination • extent to which visitor identifies event with destination (e.g. Boston Marathon)	• number of events per year • timing of events over the year • uniqueness of event(s) • annually re-occurring mega-event(s) • international reputation of mega-event(s) • local support for event • expenditures on site/facilities to host event(s)

COMPONENT: Entertainment	
Subjective Consumer Measures	**Objective Industry Measures**
• consumer preference for passive vs. active experiences • visitor desire to expand range of life experiences • values of visitor and resulting acceptance/liking of different forms of entertainment • desire to experiences entertainment first hand vs. indirectly • importance of seeing personalities 'live'	• amount of entertainment available • diversity of entertainment available • size and scope of entertainment • uniqueness of entertainment • 'appropriateness' of entertainment for destination • media coverage of destination entertainment • personality/reputation of entertainers

COMPONENT: Superstructure	
Subjective Consumer Measures	**Objective Industry Measures**
• consumer liking for built attractions • consumer preference for different types of accommodation • preference for professional vs. personal travel • perceived degree of 'maintenance' of superstructures	• number of attractions at destination • investment in attractions • range of different attractions • number and quality of lodging units • number of independent vs. chain units • existence and quality of convention centre • existence and quality of … • …

Table 2 Consumer versus Industry Measure: A Comparison of Qualifying and Amplifying Determinants

COMPONENT: Location	
Subjective Consumer Measures	**Objective Industry Measures**
• consumer perception of closeness/remoteness of destination • consumer perception of 'remoteness' may differ for different individuals and markets • consumer acceptance of/tolerance for distances to destination via land/air/sea • consumer perceptions of severity of barriers to reaching a given location/destination • consumer perceptions of ease of access/level of 'hassle' to reach destination	• absolute distances from key target markets • relative distances from key target markets, as compared to major competitor • possibility of land access by major target market groups • possibility of sea access by major target market groups • frequency/capacity of air access by major target market groups

COMPONENT: Interdependencies	
Subjective Consumer Measures	**Objective Industry Measures**
• likelihood of traveller diversion en route • consumer acceptance/ability to function using a foreign language/currency/reservation system • visitor acceptance of, or desire for local gastronomy • event (e.g. riots) in substitute or complementary destinations can effect visitation	• need to pass through/stop-over in another destination en route • domestic use of a foreign currency • use of an international reservation system (airlines/hotels) • use of outside travel statistics/research • need to use English (other foreign) language • need to import foreign foodstuffs

COMPONENT: Safety/Security	
Subjective Consumer Measures	**Objective Industry Measures**
• level of resident concern/discomfort re: personal safety • visitor perceptions regarding concerns for personal safety • perceived trust that visitors place with destination police/security forces	• crime statistics on local robberies, assaults, homicides, etc. • statistics re: attacks on visitors and foreigners • incidents of terrorism, hostage taking at a near destination • expenditures on anti-burglary equipment for local homes/businesses • number of guns in destinations • number of media stories on crime • existence of a state of war/insurrection • number of prison cells serving destination • number of police personnel in destination • number of inquiries received from potential visitors regarding safety of destination

COMPONENT: Awareness/Image/Brand	
Subjective Consumer Measures	**Objective Industry Measures**
• awareness levels re: destination • nature of perceived image of destination • strength of consumer image of destination • consumer attitudes towards destination	• relative level of awareness compared to competitors • accuracy of potential visitor image • relative level of knowledge of destination compared to competitors • relative liking of destination compared to competitors • positioning of destination relative to competitors

Table 2 (Continued) Consumer versus Industry Measure: A Comparison of Qualifying and Amplifying Determinants

COMPONENT: Cost/Value	
Subjective Consumer Measures	**Objective Industry Measures**
• consumer perceptions of value received for a range of travel products and services • consumer reactions to advertising messages on value for money spent	• price levels at destination as per TPI (Travel Price Index) • price levels at destination as compared to other destinations • exchange rates at a given point in time and over periods of time • advertising expenditures to convey message of value for money spent

Table 3 Consumer versus Industry Measure: A Comparison of Supporting Factors and Resources

COMPONENT: Infrastructure	
Subjective Consumer Measures	**Objective Industry Measures**
• consumer perceptions of the adequacy of each component of the infrastructure in relation to: a) their functional needs b) infrastructure at their place of residence	• extent and quality of road system at/in destination • extent and quality of airports at destinations • extent and quality of cruise boat harbours • extent and quality of modernity of telecommunications/media system • quality and safety of electricity, water, and waste disposal systems
COMPONENT: Accessibility	
Subjective Consumer Measures	**Objective Industry Measures**
• consumer perceptions as to how easy it is to gain access to the destination	• number of 'ports of entry' to destination (number of road entrances, number of airports) • number of airlines, flights serving a destination
COMPONENT: Facilitating Resources	
Subjective Consumer Measures	**Objective Industry Measures**
• consumer perceptions regarding the extent to which visitor's entry is made easy or difficult	• visa requirements (ease/cost of obtaining visas) • customs procedures, attitude of customs agents • 'red tape' re: entry/exit
COMPONENT: Hospitality	
Subjective Consumer Measures	**Objective Industry Measures**
• visitor perceptions as to 'friendliness' of destination residents • visitor sentiment that the region wants them to visit • visitor perception that destination is providing information services that reflects an appreciation for their visit	• resident acceptance of/support for tourism industry • extent to which residents welcome visitors • existence of resident hospitality development programmes (e.g. B.C. Superhost and the Calgary Way) • IRREDIX Index • resident reaction to requests for information/assistance • visitor usage of information/service centres

Table 3 (Continued) Consumer versus Industry Measure: A Comparison of Supporting Factors and Resources

COMPONENT: Enterprise	
Subjective Consumer Measures	**Objective Industry Measures**
• perceptions of an industry that truly wishes to satisfy the visitor • perception that facilities, services, and experiences have been adapted to individual preferences	• programmes to monitor/ensure high levels of visitor satisfaction • research to understand visitor likes and dislikes regarding destination • responsiveness to visitor needs/wants in the design and development of tourism facilities and experiences

Table 4 Consumer versus Industry Measure: A Comparison of Destination Policy, Planning, and Development

COMPONENT: System Definition	
Subjective Consumer Measures	**Objective Industry Measures**
• visitor perception that destination signage clearly identifies destination boundaries and membership	• system structure, boundaries and membership are well defined
COMPONENT: Philosophy/Vision	
Subjective Consumer Measures	**Objective Industry Measures**
• visitor perception that destination has a clear idea of the kind of destination it wants to be and the kinds of experiences it wants to offer	• existence of a formal vision for the long-term development of tourism in the destination
COMPONENT: Audit	
Subjective Consumer Measures	**Objective Industry Measures**
• consumer perceptions of the adequacy and desirability of current destination offerings • consumer appreciation for the efforts being made to assess and respond to their preferences	• existence of a formal audit that inventories and assesses the availability and quality of tourism-oriented resources and 'experiences' • inventory of most significant attractors, facilities, services, and experiences offered by a destination • quantitative and qualitative assessment of most significant attractors, facilities, services, and experiences offered by a destination • identification of most significant shortcomings (gap) in present offerings
COMPONENT: Positioning	
Subjective Consumer Measures	**Objective Industry Measures**
• consumer perceptions as to the 'evoked set' of destinations they view as primary alternatives when choosing a travel destination in a given set of circumstances • consumer definition of the 'ideal destination' for a given type of travel	• industry has a clear understanding of its position in the market (e.g. its strengths and weaknesses vis-à-vis its competitors) • existence of a formal destination vision • identification of major competitors and the experiences, attractors they offer

Table 4 (Continued) Consumer versus Industry Measure: A Comparison of Destination Policy, Planning, and Development

COMPONENT: Development	
Subjective Consumer Measures	**Objective Industry Measures**
• consumer perceptions of the on-going emergence of an exciting, high quality destination • consumer views as to type of development most needed to enhance the appeal of the destination • favourable consumer reaction to specific new facilities, services, and programmes	• existence of a coherent, long-term destination development plan flowing from destination vision • consistent, systematic translation of development plans into reality (e.g. 'on the ground' facilities, services, and programmes for visitors)

COMPONENT: Competitive/Collaborative Analysis	
Subjective Consumer Measures	**Objective Industry Measures**
• consumer perceptions regarding the desirability of visiting several complementary destinations during a single trip consumer preferences for the larger 'critical mass' of facilities, services, experiences available in a collaborating 'super destination'	• competitive; similar to positioning • collaboration; identification of other destinations whose attributes might justify/require a cooperative or 'co-opetition' strategy

COMPONENT: Monitoring and Evaluation	
Subjective Consumer Measures	**Objective Industry Measures**
• consumer desire/willingness to provide feedback via surveys and/or focus groups • consumer reactions to developments that have been undertaken and completed based on their input	• existence of a systematic, rigorous, and on-going monitoring/evaluation system to assess product performance and visitor satisfaction • concrete examples of how monitoring evaluation information is used to improve the quality of facilities, services, programmes, and experiences

Table 5 Consumer versus Industry Measure: A Comparison of Destination Management

COMPONENT: Marketing	
Subjective Consumer Measures	**Objective Industry Measures**
• favourable consumer reaction to destination 'brand' and supporting visual icons • consumer understanding and liking of the type of experience they can expect at the destination	• level of total marketing expenditures • clear definition of target markets • understanding of experiences desired by each target market • destination brand that conveys the essence of desired vision • high levels of brand recognition • effective packaging of destination experiences • strong relationships between destination and travel trade

Table 5 (Continued) Consumer versus Industry Measure: A Comparison of Destination Management

COMPONENT: Quality of Service/Experience	
Subjective Consumer Measures	**Objective Industry Measures**
• measures of consumer satisfaction regarding a range of major services • consumer perceptions as to major shortcomings in different types of services • consumer views on how best to overcome major shortcoming in service/experience delivery • consumer views on how best to deliver a quality 'experience chain'	• agreed upon, well defined measures if appropriate/expected standards for major types of services delivered to visitor • well defined quantitative and qualitative measures as to how well services are actually performed • measures of productivity regarding the delivery of services

COMPONENT: Visitor Management (VM)	
Subjective Consumer Measures	**Objective Industry Measures**
• views of visitor regarding the adequacy of VM programmes • views of visitors concerning the extent to which VM impacted (+ or -) on their enjoyment of destination	• well defined processes for ensuring fair and efficient allocation of access to destination facilities, services, programmes, and experiences

COMPONENT: Resource Stewardship	
Subjective Consumer Measures	**Objective Industry Measures**
• visitor acceptance of/liking for programmes to support destination stewardship • views of visitors regarding which approaches they prefer – and why	• measure of extent to which visitor behaviours impacts on environmental integrity at the destination • effectiveness of VM in minimizing negative environmental impacts, while enhancing visitor enjoyment • ability of tourism/visitation to enhance quality of environment

COMPONENT: Human Resource Development	
Subjective Consumer Measures	**Objective Industry Measures**
• employee perceptions as to the adequacy of their education/training • consumer perceptions regarding the extent to which front line staff and industry managers are well/appropriately trained	• number and quality of education and training programmes in support of tourism/hospitality • measure of employment, employment opportunities, front line/managerial shortages/oversupply • measure re: match between education/training capabilities vs. needs at destination • information on career paths in industry

COMPONENT: Finances/Venture Capital	
Subjective Consumer Measures	**Objective Industry Measures**
• n/a	• measures regarding adequacy of/access to venture capital for destination development • actual amounts of venture capital absorbed by tourism/hospitality industry at the destination

Table 5 (Continued) Consumer versus Industry Measure: A Comparison of Destination Management

COMPONENT: Information/Research	
Subjective Consumer Measures	**Objective Industry Measures**
• consumer willingness to serve as respondents in destination research projects	• amounts spent on research/monitoring • number of research projects • extent to which research findings are integrated into planning and decision-making • number of different types of methodologies employed
COMPONENT: Organization	
Subjective Consumer Measures	**Objective Industry Measures**
• consumer and community perceptions regarding the roles, visibility, and contributions of the DMO	• measures of community support for the DMO • similarity of DMO structure and roles to those in other destinations

Endnotes
[1] DMO = Destination Management Organization

References

Belk, R.W. (1974) An Exploratory Assessment of Situational Effects in Buyer Behavior. *Journal of Marketing Research* 11, 157.

Carroll, J.D. and Chang J.J. (1970) Analysis of Individual Differences in Multidimensional Scaling via an N-way Generalization of 'Eckart-Young' Decomposition. *Psychometrika* 35(September), 283-319.

High Performance Systems (1994) I think: From Strategy Design to Business Process Engineering (version 5.0). High Performance Systems, Inc., Hanover, NH.

Hu, Y. and Ritchie, J.R.B. (1993) Measuring Destination Attractiveness: A Contextual Approach. *Journal of Travel Research* 32(2), 25-34.

Ritchie, J.R.B. and Crouch, G.I.(2000) The Competitive Destination: A Sustainability Perspective. *Tourism Management* 21(1), 1-7.

Ritchie, J.R.B. and Zins, M. (1978) Culture as Determinant of the Attractiveness of a Tourism Region. Annals of Tourism Research 5(2), 252-267.

Schiemann, W.A. and Lingle, J.H. (1999) Bullseye! Hitting Your Strategic Targets Through High-Impact Measurement. The Free Press, New Jersey.

Sharpley, R. and Sharpley, J. (1997) Sustainability and the Competitiveness of Tourism-Chapter 16. *Tourism and Sustainability: Principles to Practice*. CAB International, Wallingford, UK, pp. 231-241.

Wish, M. (1971) Individual Differences in Perceptions and Preferences Among Nations. In: King, C.W. and Tigert, D. (eds.) *Attitude Research Reaches New Heights*. American Marketing Association, Chicago, pp. 312-328.

Chapter two
Destination Images and Consumer Confidence in Destination Attribute Ratings

Richard R. Perdue
College of Business and Administration
University of Colorado, Boulder, Colorado, USA

Abstract

The purpose of this paper is to propose consumer confidence as an intervening variable conditioning the effects of experience and knowledge on tourists' ratings of destination images. Specifically, this research proposes that experience and knowledge influence both destination attribute assessments and the tourists' confidence in making those assessments. Further, tourist confidence also moderates the influence of image on destination choice. In a study of ski vacation destination images, consumer confidence and enduring involvement in skiing were correlated with significantly more positive destination images. As confidence increased, the strength of the association between image and choice also increased.

Introduction

The mechanisms and processes by which tourists assess the attributes of alternative destinations is a major tourism research focus (van Raaij and Crotts, 1994; Ritchie 1996). Building primarily on cognitive psychology and information processing theories (Woodside and Lysonski, 1989; Kotler *et al.*, 1999), tourism researchers postulate: first, that tourists view alternative destinations as bundles of attributes that can be evaluated and compared; second, that an individual's perceptions of the attributes of a destination comprise the concept of destination image; and third, that destination images are a major factor influencing an individual's destination choice process (Murphy, 1999). Key research topics include the influence of attribute perceptions on destination choice (Sieakaya *et al.*, 1996), search strategies for destination attribute information (Vogt *et al.*, 1998), market segmentation and positioning on the basis of attribute preferences (Reich, 1999), and, perhaps most importantly, destination image measurement and management (Echtner and Ritchie, 1993).

Destination image research generally follows a two-stage process. First, a variety of qualitative techniques, including depth interviews (Lubbe, 1998), focus group interviews (Corey, 1996), and repertory grid techniques (Embacher and Buttle, 1989), are used to identify the attributes relevant to a particular decision, destination, and/or market segment (MacKay and Fesenmaier, 1997; Walmsley and Young, 1998). Second, a sample of potential tourists are asked to rate the destination on the identified attributes, generally using either a Likert or a semantic differential measurement scale (Echtner and Ritchie, 1993). Multidimensional scaling, canonical correlation, and factor analysis are typically used for analysis and presentation of the resulting image data (Murphy, 1999).

A key theoretical and methodological issue of this process is the accuracy of the destination attribute ratings (Dann, 1996). In a survey questionnaire format, respondents can and do provide attribute assessments based on varying levels of experience, knowledge, and expertise (Fakeye and Crompton, 1991). Destination-naive tourists often provide attribute ratings for a particular destination based on hearsay, experience at other destinations, and speculation (Snepenger *et al.*, 1990; Vogt *et al.*, 1998). As a result, destination image data often contain substantial variance that is only tangentially related to the actual attributes of the destination.

Two schools of thought and research exist concerning this image variance. First, research examining the influence of images on destination choice tends to view it as a natural condition (Kim, 1998; Kotler *et al.*, 1999). A consumer's choice is based on his/her images of the alternative destinations, regardless of the validity of those images. Understanding the relationship between images, regardless of accuracy, and destination choice is the key research question.

Second, research focusing on understanding destination images attempts to apportion the image variance into components based on both destination and respondent characteristics (Gartner, 1993; Milman and Pizam, 1995; Court and Lupton, 1997). The research on respondent characteristics has focused heavily on examining differences in attribute ratings associated with respondent experience and knowledge (Hu and Ritchie, 1993; Baloglu and Brinberg, 1997; Murphy, 1999). The purpose of this research is to propose an intervening variable, consumer confidence, that conditions both the effects of experience and knowledge on respondent ratings of destination images and, subsequently, the role of images in the destination choice process. Specifically, this research proposes that experience and knowledge influence both attribute assessments and the consumer's confidence in making those assessments. Further, it is also proposed that increasing consumer confidence will be correlated with more extreme, both higher and lower, destination attribute ratings. Finally, it is proposed that the strength of the effect of image on destination choice will increase with increasing levels of consumer confidence.

Conceptual Framework

Consumer confidence in destination attribute ratings

Consumer confidence is defined as the respondent's belief in his or her ability to accurately assess the attributes of a destination. This paper postulates that consumers have varying levels of confidence in their destination assessments as a function of the inter-related concepts of experience, destination familiarity, knowledge, and expertise.

As these factors increase, the consumer is increasingly confident in his/her ability to describe the attributes of a specific destination. Conversely, a consumer who lacks confidence will recognize his or her lack of information and knowledge about a specific destination and will, consequently, use a variety of similarity or difference-reduction judgments to rate the destination's attributes (Anderson, 1990). Specifically, this individual will tend to assume that the targeted destination is essentially similar to other destinations. Thus, a 'regression to the middle' bias is expected, wherein the respondent lacks the confidence to assign either extremely high or extremely low attribute ratings.

Consumer experience and involvement

Destination and product attribute assessments as influenced by consumer experience and the related concepts of knowledge, familiarity, and expertise have been extensively studied by both consumer behaviour researchers (Alba and Hutchinson, 1987; Gregan-Paxton and John, 1997) and tourism researchers (Fakeye and Crompton, 1991; Hu and Ritchie, 1993; Milman and Pizam, 1995). The consumer behaviour research has focused more extensively on the influence of experience on an individual's processing of product information. As experience increases, it is postulated that the individual has greater ability to utilize his or her existing knowledge structures to interpret and elaborate on new product information (Alba and Hutchinson, 1987), resulting in increasingly specific and precise product images and preferences (Coupey *et al.*, 1998). This research proposes that 'experienced' consumers not only have a greater ability to process product information, but also greater confidence in their ability to evaluate products, thereby resulting in a greater willingness to assign extremely high or low attribute ratings.

The tourism research on destination experience and images has tended to focus on comparing tourists who have, versus have not, previously visited a destination. This research has consistently found that previous visitors have more positive destination images (Fakeye and Crompton, 1991; Hu and Ritchie, 1993; Milman and Pizam, 1995). However, the causal direction of this relationship has not been established. Visitation may result in greater appreciation of a destination's unique characteristics and, consequently, a more positive image. Alternatively, a more positive image may have existed prior to and been the proximate cause of the initial visitation.

In addition to experience, enduring involvement is also proposed as contributing to a tourist's confidence in rating destination attributes. Enduring involvement is defined as the degree to which tourists perceive a product or behaviour to be self-related or instrumental in achieving their personal goals and values (Havitz and Dimanche, 1990). As enduring involvement increases, on-going information search, defined as activities aimed at acquiring information both to build a bank of information for future decisions and for the pleasures derived from the search and consumption of the information itself (Bloch *et al.*, 1986), also increases (Perdue, 1993). Thus, with increasing enduring involvement, consumer confidence in destination attribute ratings is also expected to increase.

Defining destination images as a form of consumer attitudes further supports consumer confidence as a potentially important factor influencing destination choice. Building heavily on Howard and Sheth's Theory of Buyer Behaviour (1969), a substantial body of attitude–behaviour research exists assessing various moderating variables, including 'attitude certainty' (Fazio and Zanna, 1978a; Antil, 1983) and 'attitude confidence' (Sample and Warland, 1973; Fazio and Zanna, 1978b; Berger and Mitchell, 1989; Berger, 1992). Additionally, a variety of researchers have examined subjective product knowledge, the consumer's perception of his/her knowledge, as an attitude–behaviour moderator (Berger *et al.*, 1994). Each of these studies has found increasing attitude-behaviour consistency with increasing levels of certainty/confidence/subjective knowledge. Thus, with increasing levels of consumer confidence, the effect of image on destination choice should also increase.

Figure 1 summarizes the conceptual framework of this study. Consumer information processing is positioned as a filter between the actual attributes of a destination and the consumer's perceptions of those attributes. It is important to recognize that the primary factor influencing the image of a destination should be the actual attributes of that destination, particularly for factual attributes such as size and facilities. Evaluative attributes are filtered through some perspective of what the consumer wants or needs, e.g., high quality skiing may be associated with extremely steep, ungroomed slopes by one consumer and with moderate, well-groomed slopes by another. Still, with increasing knowledge and experience, the consumer's destination image should increasingly reflect the actual destination.

Figure 1 Model of Consumer Confidence and Destination Attribute Ratings

Experience, involvement, and confidence are articulated as primary factors involved in the consumer's processing of destination attribute information. Experience is divided into destination experience (at the specific destination being rated) and behavioural experience. The destinations included in this research were ski resorts in the United States. Thus, behavioural experience was defined as downhill skiing experience.

Methodology

The data reported in this paper were collected as part of a study of ski resort destination selection and behaviour. The study population was comprised of individuals who requested information from a major resort corporation, excluding local residents who lived within the state. A stratified random sample was selected based on inquiry media source (ski magazines vs. general media) and inquiry form (telephone, business reply coupons, and reader service cards).

Instrumentation

As in the process described earlier, destination (ski mountain) attributes were identified using a combination of previous research, focus groups, and pre-test surveys. Specifically, a preliminary list of attributes was developed using both the existing research and focus group interviews with resort guests. Survey pre-tests were then used to reduce the attribute list. Additionally, the survey pre-tests and existing research were also used to develop the measures of ski involvement and both destination and ski experience. Factor analysis and Cronbach reliability tests were used to reduce the ski mountain attribute and ski involvement scales.

The final questionnaire asked respondents to describe a specific resort destination choice, starting by listing the resorts which were actively considered (up to four). For each listed resort, respondents were then asked to indicate if they had previously visited the resort and to rate the resort on the selected ski mountain attributes. Following this rating task, the respondents were asked, 'How *confident* are you in your knowledge ratings of this destination?' with a 1 = not at all to 5 = extremely confident response scale. Skiing experience was measured by a series of three questions; years of skiing experience, number of days of skiing last year, and a self-rating of ability level (ranging from first-timer to professional). The ski mountain and ski involvement scales are provided in the appendix.

Data collection

Data collection was by mail survey to a sample of 8000 inquirers. Due to budget and time constraints, only one survey mailing was used. As an incentive to respond, respondents were entered into a draw for a free one-week vacation for four people, including airfare, lodging, and ski lift tickets. The name of the study resort was disguised throughout the study. All mailings and correspondence were conducted through a market research firm located in another state. A sample of 8000 inquirers was selected. Recognizing that telephone inquirers frequently make the inquiry after the destination choice, business reply mail coupon and reader service card inquirers were purposively over-sampled. Specifically, 26.1% of the sample was selected from telephone inquiries versus 39.3% and 34.5%, respectively, for business reply coupon and reader service card inquirers. Of the 8000 addresses in the initial mailing, 460 (5.8%) questionnaires were returned as undeliverable. The final response was 2869 usable questionnaires, a response rate of 38.1%.

Results

As reflected by Table 1, the survey respondents were predominantly male (63.1%), living in households comprised of couples with (36.9%) and without (31.1%) children, with relatively high household incomes (50.1% $\geq$ $100,000). The mean age of the respondents was 38.6 years; the median age was 38.0.

Table 1 Respondent Profile

Respondent Characteristic	Mean	%
Mean Age	38.6	
Gender		
male		63.1
female		36.9
Household Structure		
two parent family with children at home		36.9
single parent family with children at home		5.0
couple with no children at home		31.1
two or more unrelated friends/single		27.0
Household Income		
less than $50,000		26.8
$50,000 to $99,999		23.1
$100,000 to $149,999		16.1
$150,000 to $199,999		1.8
$200,000 to $249,999		22.8
$250,000 to $299,999		6.3
$300,000 or more		3.2

The survey respondents were relatively experienced (mean 15.1, median 13 years of skiing experience) and active skiers (mean 11.9, median 8 skiing days last year) (Table 2). However, both measures of ski experience reflected a wide range. Years of skiing experience ranged from 1 to 65 years. Days of skiing last year ranged from 0 to 200. Of the respondents, 13.3 per cent did not ski last year; 5% skied 40 days or more. On the measure of skiing ability, 60% rated themselves as intermediate skiers; 32.4% rated themselves as expert or professional. The measure of ski involvement ranged from 8 to 56, with a mean of 39.8 and a median of 41.

Of the 2869 survey respondents, 1561 (54.4%) went on a ski vacation during the study season. Of those individuals, 61% had previously visited their chosen destination. Overall, the respondents indicated they had considered visiting 3766 destinations of which 2180 (57.9%) had been previously visited. On a 1 = not at all to 5 = extremely confident scale, the mean confidence rating for the chosen destination was 4.3. Both previous visitation and confidence declined significantly when comparing the chosen destination to the alternative destinations.

The analyses next studied the inter-relationships between ski involvement, ski experience and destination experience (table of results is provided in the appendix). There was very little relationship between ski involvement and destination experience. However, ski experience, particularly years of experience and ability level, were strongly related to destination experience. Similarly, ski experience, particularly days of skiing last season and ability level, were also strongly related to ski involvement.

Regression analysis was conducted to examine the relationships between the confidence in destination attribute rating measure and destination experience, ski involvement, and ski experience (Table 3). These results consistently show that destination experience and ski involvement significantly affect the confidence measure. As shown earlier, the ski experience measures affected destination experience and ski involvement, but had relatively little effect on the consumer's confidence in destination attribute rating measure.

Table 2 Ski Involvement, Destination Experience, Ski Experience and Confidence in Destination Attribute Ratings

Measure	Mean	%
Ski Experience		
mean years of skiing experience	15.1	
mean days of skiing last year	11.9	
highest level of skiing ability		
first time		0.8
novice/beginner		6.8
intermediate		60.0
expert		28.9
professional (instructor, ski patrol, competitor, etc.)		3.5
Ski Involvement (scale alpha = 0.87, range = 8 to 56, std = 12.3)	39.8	
Chose to go on a Ski Vacation during Study Season (n = 2869)		54.4
Destination Experience (%)		
had previously visited chosen destination (n = 1561)		61.0
had previously visited first alternative destination (n=1105)		57.7
had previously visited second alternative destination (n=708)		55.8
had previously visited third alternative destination (n=392)		49.7
Confidence in Destination Attribute Ratings (1 = not at all to 5 = extremely confident scale)		
chosen destination	4.3	
first alternative destination	3.9	
second alternative destination	3.8	
third alternative destination	3.7	

Table 3 Regression Beta Coefficients: Confidence in Destination Attribute Ratings by Ski Experience, Destination Experience, and Ski Involvement

Independent Variable	Chosen Destination	First Alternative Destination	Second Alternative Destination	Third Alternative Destination
Model R^2	.143	.258	.313	.261
Destination Experience	.261**	.466**	.498**	.459**
Ski Involvement	.248**	.161**	.093	.048
Years of Skiing Experience	.049	.074	.121*	.065
Days of Skiing Last Season	.013	-.049	.004	.075
Ski Ability Level	-.039	.017	.038	.073

*significant at alpha ≤ .01
**significant at alpha ≤ .001

    The analysis next focused on the relationship between consumer confidence and destination attribute perceptions. Both ANOVA and regression were conducted. The

ANOVA examined differences in destination attribute ratings by level of confidence. These results are consistently significant, showing increasingly positive destination attribute ratings with increasing levels of consumer confidence (Table 4).

Table 4 Differences in Destination Attribute Ratings by Confidence Level

| | | Mean Ski Mountain Attribute Rating | | |
| | Chosen Destination | First Alternative Destination | Second Alternative Destination | Third Alternative Destination |
Confidence Level				
F Statistic / prob.	50.5 / .000	23.8 / .000	7.84 / .000	3.68 / .012
Level of Confidence				
1/2[1]	21.74[a]	24.63[a]	23.97[a]	24.23[a]
3	25.02[b]	24.61[a]	24.06[a]	23.16[b]
4	26.34[c]	25.48[b]	25.66[b]	24.95[a]
5	27.69[d]	27.29[c]	26.11[b]	25.67[c]

Mean values with different superscripts are significantly different from each other at alpha $\leq$ .05
[1] Confidence levels 1 and 2 were grouped together in this analysis to provide sufficient cell sample sizes.

Table 5 presents the regression results analysing the destination attribute ratings as a function of consumer confidence, destination experience, and ski involvement. Importantly, the low R^2 coefficients were expected. As shown earlier in Figure 1, the primary factor affecting the destination attribute ratings should be the actual attributes of the destination. Consumer confidence, destination experience, and ski involvement are viewed as consumer characteristics that affect or filter the relationship between the actual and perceived destination attributes. Importantly, these results consistently show consumer confidence and ski involvement as significantly influencing the destination attribute ratings. In a stepwise analysis, the order of variable entry was consistently confidence, involvement, and destination experience. The three measures of ski experience were consistently not significant. Thus, the results show consumer confidence and ski involvement as factors which positively affect the perceived attributes of a destination.

Table 5 Regression Beta Coefficients: Ski Mountain Attribute Ratings by Consumer Confidence, Destination Experience, and Ski Involvement

Independent Variable	Chosen Destination	First Alternative Destination	Second Alternative Destination	Third Alternative Destination
Model R^2	.113	.085	.077	.060
Confidence in Attribute Ratings	.285**	.278**	.208**	.184*
Destination Experience	.059	.089	.073	.087
Ski Involvement	.137**	.116**	.190**	.177*

*significant at alpha $\leq$ .01
**significant at alpha $\leq$ .001

Logistic regression was used to examine consumer confidence as a moderator of the relationship between image and destination choice. The data-set was reorganized by resort, including both the chosen and not chosen destinations. Next, the data were sorted by confidence and analysed with the SPSS 9.0 binary logistic regression procedure. The initial logit analysis examined destination choice as a function of image, followed by an analysis of choice as a function of image moderated by confidence (image*confidence). As shown in Table 6, the analysis using image moderated by confidence performed much better than that using only the image measure. The logit analysis of choice as a function of image was then conducted by each level of consumer confidence. As confidence increased, the strength of the relationship between image and choice also increased (Table 6).

Table 6 Logistic Regression: Choice by Image and Confidence

Model	Model X^2	Nagelkerke R^2	Constant	B	R	Wald Stat.
Overall Analysis: (N = 2426):						
Image	86.2***	.047	-0.304	.137	.152	79.2***
Image*Conf.	175.0***	.093	-1.873	.021	.217	159.7***
Analysis by Level of Confidence:						
Confidence = 1 (N = 49):						
Image	0.2	.008	-0.813	-.042	.000	0.2
Confidence = 2 (N = 135)						
Image	0.1	.000	-1.025	-.009	.000	0.1
Confidence = 3 (N = 415)						
Image	2.6	.009	-1.824	.054	.032	2.5
Confidence = 4 (N = 846)						
Image	14.0***	.022	-1.921	.097	.099	13.5***
Confidence = 5 (N = 981)						
Image	35.8	.048	-3.514	.167	.151	32.3***

***significant at alpha $\leq$ .000

Conclusions

The purpose of this paper was to propose consumer confidence as an intervening variable that conditions the effect of experience and involvement on respondent ratings of destination images and moderates the influence of image on destination choice. Prior to discussing the research results, it is important to note three key research limitations. First, the survey respondents were contacted after inquiring for destination information. As such, the data collection occurred, in many cases, after the destination choice. The effect of the destination choice and subsequent trip planning on both the confidence and destination attribute measures is unknown.

Second, the research asked respondents to list the resorts which they had considered during the process of selecting a vacation destination. While this resulted in a set of resorts about which the consumer had some basic knowledge, it also essentially limited the study destinations to the consumers' evoked sets. As such, resorts which the respondents confidently rated as inadequate or unsuited for their vacations were not included in the study. Further, confidence and image may have more influence on evoked set selection as opposed to final destination choice.

Third, the measure of confidence was limited to a single item. Future research needs to develop and test a confidence scale.

Increasing consumer confidence was expected to result in more extreme, both lower and higher, destination ratings. The results did not support this expectation. Specifically, higher levels of confidence were correlated strongly with more positive destination ratings. While this may be a function of the measurement process, I believe it is due to the research design. By limiting people to rating and discussing their evoked destination sets, I may have excluded resorts which the consumer was confident in rating as unacceptable or unsuitable for their vacation choice.

The study findings strongly support confidence as a factor influencing destination image assessments (Figure 2). As confidence increases, the evoked set images are increasingly positive. The primary factors influencing confidence are destination experience and ski involvement. Ski experience affects both destination experience and ski involvement, but has relatively little effect on the confidence measure. Additionally, ski involvement also independently affects the destination ratings. Finally, as consumer confidence increases, the effect of image on destination choice also increases.

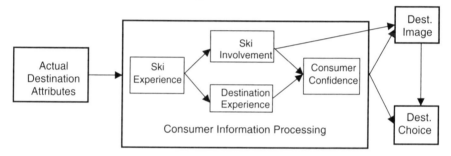

Figure 2 Study Findings: Consumer Confidence, Ski Involvement and Destination Images of Ski Resorts

Further research is needed to extend this research to other settings and address the limitations noted earlier. Specifically, expanding the study beyond a consumer's evoked set for a specific decision may significantly alter the findings, focusing greater attention on confident, but negative destination images. Additionally, further measurement development appears warranted.

References

Alba, J.W. and Hutchinson, J.W. (1987) Dimensions of Consumer Expertise. *Journal of Consumer Research* 13, 411-434.

Anderson, J.R. (1990) *Cognitive Psychology and Its Implications,* 3rd edn. W.H. Freeman and Company, New York.

Antil, J. (1983) Uses of Response Certainty in Attitude Measurement. In: Bagozzi, R. and Tybout, A. (eds.) *Advances in Consumer Research.* Association for Consumer Research, Ann Arbor, MI, pp. 409-415.

Baloglu, S. and Brinberg, D. (1997) Affective Images of Tourism Destinations. *Journal of Travel Research* 35, 11-15.

Berger, I. (1992) The Nature of Attitude Accessibility and Attitude Confidence: A Triangulated Experiment. *Journal of Consumer Psychology* 1, 103-124.

Berger, I. and Mitchell, A. (1989) The Effects of Advertising on Attitude Accessibility, Attitude Confidence, and the Attitude Behavior Relationship. *Journal of Consumer Research* 16, 269-279.

Berger, I., Ratchford, B. and Haines, G. (1994) Subjective Product Knowledge as a Moderator of the Relationship between Attitudes and Purchase Intentions for a Durable Product. *Journal of Economic Psychology* 15, 301-314.

Bloch, P., Sherrell, D. and Ridgway, N. (1986) Consumer Search: An Extended Framework. *Journal of Consumer Research* 13, 119-126.

Corey, R.J. (1996) A Drama Based Model of Traveler Destination Choice. *Journal of Travel and Tourism Marketing* 5, 1-22.

Court, B. and Lupton, R.A. (1997) Customer Portfolio Development: Modeling Destination Adopters, Inactives, and Rejectors. *Journal of Travel Research* 36, 35-43.

Dann, G.M.S. (1996) Tourists' Images of a Destination: An Alternative Analysis. *Journal of Travel and Tourism Marketing* 5, 41-53.

Echtner, C.M. and Ritchie, J.R.B. (1993) The Measurement of Destination Image: An Empirical Assessment. *Journal of Travel Research* 31, 3-13.

Embacher, J. and Buttle, F. (1989) A Repertory Grid Analysis of Austria's Image as a Summer Vacation Destination. *Journal of Travel Research* 27(3), 3-7.

Fakeye, P.C. and Crompton, J.L. (1991) Image Differences between Prospective,First-Time and Repeat Visitors to the Lower Rio Grande Valley. *Journal of Travel Research* 30, 10-16.

Fazio, R. and Zanna, M. (1978a) Attitudinal Qualities Relating to the Strength of the Attitude-Behavior Relationship. *Journal of Experimental Social Psychology* 51, 505-514.

Fazio, R. and Zanna, M. (1978b) On the Predictive Validity of Attitudes: The Roles of Direct Experience and Confidence. *Journal of Personality* 46, 228-243.

Gartner, W.C. (1993) Image Formation Process. *Journal of Travel and Tourism Marketing* 2, 191-215.

Gregan-Paxton, J. and John, D.R. (1997) Consumer Learning by Analogy: A Model of Internal Knowledge Transfer. *Journal of Consumer Research* 24, 266-284.

Havitz, M. and Dimanche, F. (1990) Propositions for Testing the Involvement Construct in Recreation and Tourism Contexts. *Leisure Sciences* 12, 179-197.

Holden, A. (1999) Understanding Skiers' Motivations Using Pearce's 'Travel Career' Construct. *Annals of Tourism Research* 26, 435-438.

Howard, J. and Sheth, J. (1969) *The Theory of Buyer Behavior.* John Wiley, New York.

Hu, Y. and Ritchie, J.R.B. (1993) Measuring DestinationAttractiveness: A Contextual Approach. *Journal of Travel Research* 32, 25-34.

Kim, H. (1998) Perceived Attractiveness of Korean Destinations. *Annals of Tourism Research* 25, 340-361.

Kotler, P., Bowen, J. and Makens, J. (1999) *Marketing for Hospitality and Tourism,* 2nd edn. Prentice Hall, Upper Saddle River, NJ.

Lubbe, B. (1998) Primary Image as a Dimension of Destination Image: An Empirical Assessment. *Journal of Travel and Tourism Marketing* 7, 21-43.

MacKay, K. and Fesenmeier, D. (1997) Pictorial Element of Destination in Image Formation. *Annals of Tourism Research* 24, 537-565.
Milman, A. and Pizam, A. (1995) The Role of Awareness and Familarity with a Destination: The Central Florida Case. *Journal of Travel Research* 33, 21-27.
Murphy, L. (1999) Australia's Image as a Holiday Destination: Perceptions of Backpacker Visitors. *Journal of Travel and Tourism Marketing* 8, 21-45.
Perdue, R.R. (1993) External Information Search in Marine Recreational Fishing. *Leisure Sciences* 15, 169-187.
Reich, A.Z. (1999) *Positioning of Tourist Destinations.* Sagamore Publishing, Champaign, IL.
Ritchie, J.R.B. (1996) Beacons of Light in an Expanding Universe: An Assessment of the State of the Art in Tourism Marketing/Management Research. *Journal of Travel and Tourism Marketing* 5(4), 49-84.
Sample, J. and Warland, R. (1973) Attitude and Prediction of Behavior. *Social Forces* 51, 292-304.
Sieakaya, E., McLellan, R.W. and Uysal, M. (1996) Modeling Vacation Destination Decisions: A Behavioral Approach. *Journal of Travel and Tourism Marketing* 5, 57-75.
Snepenger, D., Meged, K., Snelling, M. and Worrall, K. (1990) Information Search Strategies by Destination Naive Tourists. *Journal of Travel Research* 29, 13-16.
van Raaij, W.F. and Crotts, J.C. (1994) The Economic Psychology of Travel and Tourism. *Journal of Travel and Tourism Marketing,* 3(3), 1-19.
Vogt, C.A., Stewart, S.I. and Fesenmaier, D.A. (1998) Communication Strategies to Reach First-Time Visitors. *Journal of Travel and Tourism Marketing* 7(2), 69-89.
Walmsley, D.J. and Young, M. (1998) Evaluative Images and Tourism: The Use of Personal Constructs to Describe the Structure of Destination Images. *Journal of Travel Research* 36, 65-69.
Woodside, A.G. and Lysonski, S. (1989) A General Model of Traveler Destination Choice. *Journal of Travel Research* 27, 8-14.

Appendix

Ski Involvement Scale
(measured on a 1 = strongly disagree to 7 = strongly agree scale)
Cronbach alpha = .875

- Skiing / Snowboarding is a very important part of my life
- I work very hard to constantly improve my skiing / snowboarding ability
- I keep up with the latest trends in ski / snowboarding equipment
- I work out specifically to get in shape for skiing / snowboarding
- Skiing / snowboarding is my favourite winter recreational activity
- Skiing / snowboarding is kind of a spiritual experience for me
- I take a ski / snowboard vacation every year
- I like to read articles in ski / snowboarding magazines to get excited about different places to go

Ski Mountain Image Scale
(Measured on a 1 = strongly disagree to 5 = strongly agree scale)
Cronbach Alpha = .888

- This destination has excellent overall quality of skiing / snowboarding
- This destination has an excellent variety of terrain for your skills
- This destination has a large ski / snowboard mountain
- This destination has predictably excellent snow conditions
- This destination has a variety of areas to experience
- This destination has excellent slope grooming

Interrelations of Ski Experience, Destination Experience, Ski Involvement and Consumer Confidence

	Chosen Destination	First Alternative Destination	Second Alternative Destination	Third Alternative Destination
Spearman Correlations of Confidence in Destination Attribute Ratings with Ski Involvement	.26**	.15**	.14**	.15**
Differences in Confidence in Destination Attribute Ratings by Destination Experience:				
t-statistic	11.20**	16.30**	15.00**	9.80**
Previous visitor	4.48	4.36	4.28	4.26
Not a previous visitor	4.03	3.41	3.15	3.11
Spearman Correlations of Ski Experience with Confidence in Destination Attribute Ratings:				
Years of Skiing Experience	.120**	.178**	.270**	.175**
Days of Skiing Last Year	.166**	.101*	.166**	.148*
Ski Ability Level	.137**	.108**	.198**	.187**

Differences in Ski Experience by Destination Experience

	Measure of Ski Experience:		
	Years of Experience	Days Last Year	Ability Level
Previous Visitor of Chosen Destination	t = 6.3**	t=2.1	t=3.8**
yes	17.1	13.3	3.4
no	13.6	11.8	3.3
Previous Visitor of First Alternative Destination	t=6.2**	t=0.8	t=3.1*
yes	17.4	13.5	3.4
no	13.5	12.9	3.3
Previous Visitor of Second Alternative Destination	t=6.1**	t=2.1	t=3.6**
yes	17.5	14.8	3.5
no	12.8	12.6	3.3
Previous Visitor of Third Alternative Destination	t=2.6*	t=1.1	t=1.4
yes	16.7	16.1	3.3
no	14.0	14.2	3.4

*significant at alpha $\leq$ .01
**significant at alpha $\leq$ .00

Chapter three
Breaking the Rules: Cognitive Distance, Choice Sets and Long-Haul Destinations

Tracey Harrison-Hill
School of Marketing and Management and CTHMR
Griffith University, Gold Coast, Australia

Abstract

The study investigated the relationship of cognitive distance, actual distance and the allocation of long-haul destinations within US tourists' choice sets. Data was collected on perceptions of Australia and Italy as destinations. Findings suggest that the perceived distance to Australia is significantly different from Italy (even though the destinations are both 14 hours from the test market), is overestimated, and that the error is significant. The findings also indicate that there is inconsistency amongst the factors that influence the accuracy of distance estimates. It was concluded that the inferences drawn from domestic tourism on the relationship between cognitive distance, actual distance and choice set allocation will not necessarily hold true for long-haul destinations and that further research is needed in this area.

Introduction

Within the tourism literature there has been a recent interest in the perception of distance and its relationship to destination decisions by individual tourists (Ankomah and Crompton 1992; Walmsley and Jenkins, 1992; Ankomah *et al.*, 1996). These authors have suggested that subjective or cognitive distance may be a better indicator than actual distance when investigating decision-making processes by tourists. In addition to being an important evaluation criterion used by tourists, cognitive distance is important to destination marketers as its impact may be able to be influenced.

Cognitive distance is a mental representation of actual distance moulded by an individual's social, cultural and general life experiences. A substantial number of researchers have reported findings indicating that cognitive distance estimates significantly differ from actual distance measures (Bratfisch, 1969; Downs and Stea, 1977; Brown and Broadway, 1981; Cadwallader, 1981; Cook and McCleary, 1983; McNamara, 1986).

Error in cognitive distance estimates by tourists will result in false perceptions being used in their decision-making process. Overestimation of distance by tourists can lead to a perception of inflated costs, extended travel time and increased risk, all of which decrease the likelihood of travel. Underestimation of distance by tourists will initially increase the attractiveness of the destination, and increase the likelihood of travel. However, underestimation can be problematic if this leads to unrealistic expectations of a destination. When the tourist's experience does not equate with those expectations, dissatisfaction may result, potentially leading to negative feedback to other tourists who are seeking information about the destination (Ankomah and Crompton, 1992).

Determining the cause of consumers' distortion of distance has been the subject of a significant body of research. However, most of this research has concentrated on the urban environment (Briggs, 1973; Canter and Tagg, 1975; Golledge and Spector, 1978; Brown and Broadway, 1981; Cadwallader, 1981; Lloyd and Heivly, 1987). Ankomah and Crompton (1992) provide a comprehensive list of propositions on the transference of findings from these urban studies to the tourism setting. Yet, transferring findings from these reported studies must be done with caution for two reasons. Firstly, the distance relationships being measured are relatively short when compared to the distances within a tourism context. Secondly, the purpose and frequency of travel within the urban setting can be quite different to that of tourism.

Within the tourism literature the research has been less extensive and noticeably focused upon domestic destinations. One exception was a study conducted by Mayo *et al.* (1988) which examined the relationship between cognitive distance, physical distance and attractiveness. Otherwise, there has been a lack of research into the influence of cognitive distance upon destination decisions for overseas vacations. Moreover, there are very few studies referring to decision making for long-haul[1] travel. This apparent lack of empirical research into the factors influencing long-haul destination choice is curious given the increase in long-haul travel that has accompanied the growth of mass tourism on a global scale, and that distance is a much talked about problem for destinations in attracting long-haul tourists (Burkhart and Medlik, 1981; Mayo and Jarvis, 1981; Smith, 1989; Hall, 1991)

Long-haul overseas travel presents the tourist with a somewhat different set of issues than that of short-haul travel. 'The most obvious of these differences are the increased cost and increased time of travel raising the monetary and psychological barriers to travel' (Crouch, 1994, p.3). Yet within the literature, a contrasting factor has also been reported. Several authors (Baxter, 1979; Mayo *et al.*, 1988; Crouch, 1994) have suggested that distance also acts to facilitate long-haul travel. Despite the general belief that distance acts as an impediment to travel, the attractiveness of destinations has been found to increase with distance (Mayo *et al.*, 1988).

We are therefore confronted with a conundrum. On the one hand, the literature suggests that the attractiveness of a destination increases with distance. On the other hand, the factors that contribute to the 'friction of distance' (Mayo *et al.*, 1988), which operate to deter the act of travelling, also become more salient with distance. The relationship between the distance to the destination and desire to travel to that destination is further distorted by the notion that, as pointed out by Ankomah and Crompton (1992, p. 324), 'subjective distance rather than actual distance may best depict what goes on in individuals' minds when they are making travel decisions'.

Cognitive Distance Literature Review

The literature identifies numerous factors that contribute to the discrepancy between cognitive and actual distances. These will be discussed in three sections: (1) Processing of information about the environment; (2) Source and method of information acquisition; and (3) Emotional involvement.

(1) Processing of information about the environment

Two alternative theoretical perspectives of information processing have been proposed for explaining the distortion of cognitive distance estimates: hierarchical theory and non-hierarchical theory.

Hierarchical theory postulates that different 'regions' of the environment are stored as different branches within memory's network of knowledge (McNamara, 1986). 'Regions' are mostly defined by political boundaries, including state and country borders (Gould and White, 1974), or physical boundaries such as rivers or mountains (Canter and Tagg, 1975). Regions are stored on more dominant branches within memory that are called superordinate units. These branches then have smaller sub-branches that store information about the environment within the region, including cities and attractions. These sub-branches are called subordinate units.

Accordingly, the underlying rationale of the hierarchical theory is that spatial information is processed (encoded) and stored in memory within these strict hierarchies of branches and sub-branches. Hierarchical theorists believe that cognitive distance errors arise when trying to determine the relationship between two points that were not encoded and stored within the same branch (McNamara, 1986).

In contrast, non-hierarchical theory claims that spatial relations among objects within the environment are stored as a simplified cognitive image of that environment (Brown and Broadway, 1981). These representational images have no hierarchical structure; everything is represented on the same level or branch. The image may ordinarily consist of the landmarks on the route and turns to be taken (Byrne in McNamara, 1986). This process has also been referred to as cognitive or mental mapping (Gould and White, 1974).

Non-hierarchical theorists argue that cognitive distance errors occur not in the encoding of information (which is a mirror-image of the environment) but in retrieval of the information. For instance, when an individual retrieves information, the more turns and landmarks remembered on a route, the longer they perceive the route to be (Byrne in McNamara, 1986).

These two information processing theories have traditionally been presented as opposing theories, each with their own advocates. However, as each theory has elements that are intuitively important factors in explaining distortion in distance estimations, it would seem advantageous to consider the two theories jointly. McNamara (1986) called for the two theories to be assimilated, and demonstrated the efficacy of doing so through the use of a partial hierarchical theory. Partial hierarchical theories propose that spatial relations are encoded between locations in different regions of an environment. This view was supported by Ankomah *et al.* (1995) who believe that testing hierarchical theory independently of non-hierarchical theory leads to an incomplete picture of respondents' processing of spatial information.

(2) Source and method of information acquisition

One of the implications of the partial and non-hierarchical conceptualizations is that the source of the information about the environment, and the method of learning that information, will influence the accuracy of retrieval. Individuals learn about their environment over a period of time through both indirect and direct methods.

Indirect methods include education, interaction with others, travel brochures, street maps, mass media and advertising within those media (Downs and Stea, 1977; Cook and McCleary, 1983). The information from these sources may be distorted from the outset causing cognitive distance discrepancies. To illustrate, information processed from conversations with other people will depend on the perceptions of that other individual which may be biased or incorrect. These sources of information also tend to involve fewer sensory experiences and as such are not as critical as direct experience is to environmental learning.

An individual's understanding of the environment results primarily from their spatial interaction or direct experience with the environment (Brown and Broadway, 1981). Factors such as length of residence in an area (Golledge and Spector, 1978) and mode of transportation (Downs and Stea, 1977) are related to an individual's environmental learning.

Generally, the longer an individual is exposed to distance information, the greater the accuracy of cognitive distance estimates. Length of residence in an area is typical of this pattern. Empirical evidence has confirmed the relationship of length of residence to cognitive distance accuracy (Ankomah *et al.*, 1995). Similarly, Golledge and Spector (1978) found length of residence to be inversely related to the amount of error in mental maps of individual's urban surroundings due to more frequent interaction within that environment.

The type of travel experience affects the degree of environmental learning. Active travel experiences, including walking or driving a vehicle, require more attention to the environment than do passive experiences such as being a passenger in a vehicle or aircraft. As such, active travel lends itself more readily to a learning of the environment, which in turn increases the accuracy of perceptions of distance (Downs and Stea, 1977; Ankomah *et al.*, 1995). Additionally, perceptions about distance arising from a travel experience can be distorted due to other factors including stress, boredom, motivation to travel, and speed and duration of a trip (Cook and McCleary, 1983).

(3) Emotional involvement

Emotional involvement has been found to increase the accuracy of cognitive distance estimates. The three factors that have been used to define and measure the level of emotional involvement felt by an individual for a destination include: (1) the importance of the destination to the individual; (2) the level of interest in the destination; and (3) the degree of knowledge about the destination (Bratfisch, 1969). Basic consumer behaviour rationale suggests that high levels of involvement with a product will lead to increased processing of information about the product (Mowen, 1995). As such it seems logical that distance estimates will be more accurate for destinations with which the individual has developed an emotional involvement. It would also seem logical that as a consumer moves toward selecting a destination for a vacation, having collected information and evaluated alternatives, that their distance estimate would also be more accurate.

While emotional involvement increases distance estimate accuracy, the level of involvement with specific locations seems to fall off rapidly with increased distance (Cook and McCleary, 1983). This infers that the accuracy of cognitive distance estimates also diminish with increased distance. The general pattern within the literature to date is that as actual distance increases, corresponding cognitive distance increases, but less than proportionately (Ekman and Bratfisch, 1965; Canter and Tagg, 1975; Mayo *et al.*, 1988; Ankomah *et al.*, 1995). Gould and White (1974) share similar findings, in that accuracy of cognitive distance was discovered to be a function of distance and population.

When applying hierarchical theory, a long-haul destination, when parted from the individual by the physical boundary of an ocean or country border, is likely to be stored in a different superordinate unit to the individual's origin market. As such, correct estimation of distance between the origin and a long-haul destination is unlikely with hierarchical information processing. In addition the same distance between two countries may be estimated differently by individuals from each country due to different perspectives of their surrounding environment. Similarly, with partial hierarchical and non-hierarchical theories the speed of travel and the inactivity in-flight are likely to cause problems with the encoding and decoding of information, leading to a likely distortion of the distance being travelled.

Further, the factor of length of residence in the origin market would not seem to be as important a factor in international tourism as it is in urban studies in influencing the accuracy of cognitive distance estimates. However, the frequency of travel would increase an individual's spatial interaction between the origin and destination. As such, frequency of travel should increase the accuracy of estimations, even though the nature of that travel is inactive. Even so, in many instances the individual may not have travelled to the destination previously, and will be relying upon indirect methods of gathering distance information. This has been shown to distort distance estimates. The exception is when the individual is emotionally involved with a destination, as would be the instance if the destination was within a late evoked choice set.

Destination Choice Literature Review

Throughout the tourism literature there are numerous models of the tourist's vacation destination choice process. Much of this work has grown from the widely accepted models used within the consumer behaviour literature, including the Nicosia model (1966) and the Howard and Sheth model (1969). These authors integrated the major influences on consumer behaviour into frameworks representing the structure of consumers' decision processes. A common feature of these frameworks was the conceptualization of the decision process as a narrowing down of alternatives from all of those brands the consumer is aware of, to a single final choice. This funnelling process was originally modelled by Narayana and Markin (1975) who suggested the existence of a categorization process that led to choice sets in consumer decision making.

The concept of choice sets has since been applied in research on tourist destination choice (Woodside and Sherrell, 1977; Woodside and Lysonski, 1989; Um and

Crompton, 1990; Crompton, 1992; Um and Crompton, 1992; Crompton and Ankomah, 1993). Three specific contributions comprising Woodside and Lysonski (1989), Um and Crompton (1992) and Ankomah *et al.* (1996) provide points of reference of interest to this paper.

(Woodside and Lysonski (1989) proposed a general model of travel decision making based on Narayana and Markin's (1975) conceptualization of three choice sets within the awareness set: the evoked set, the inert set, and the inept set. The evoked set consists of the few brands the consumer is considering for purchase. These brands have been evaluated positively by the consumer, and thus remain potential choices for purchase. The inert set consists of those brands for which the consumer has a neutral evaluation. The consumer is aware of these brands but is not actively considering them for purchase due to a lack of information or the lack of a perceived advantage over the brands being considered in the evoked set. The inept set consists of those brands the consumer is aware of, but is not considering for purchase, either due to an unpleasant experience or negative information. The brand the consumer intends to purchase and the final choice are derived from the evoked set of brands.

Woodside and Lysonski (1989) adapted this framework to the tourism context and proposed an operationalization of the concept that allows travel marketers to determine whether their destination is being considered vis-à-vis other competing destinations, and possible reasons why their destination is not within the evoked or consideration set. Such reasons may include, for instance, lack of information. Knowledge of the categorisation process therefore aids tourism destination marketers in formulating strategies.

Secondly, the study by Um and Crompton (1992) identified a further choice set of use within the tourism context. The late evoked set was identified in a longitudinal study of tourists' attitudes and was later operationalized by Crompton (1992), as those destinations the respondent would most probably visit within a specific time frame.

Thirdly, the study by Ankomah *et al.* (1996) investigated the relationship of cognitive distance to the assignment of domestic vacation destinations into individual's choice sets. It was found that the accuracy of cognitive distance varied significantly with type of choice set, with accuracy increasing for destinations within the late set. It was also hypothesized from the application of cognitive dissonance reasoning that distances to destinations would fall on a continuum ranging from slight underestimates within the late evoked set to substantial overestimates in the inept set. There was some support for this conjecture. Although a trend appeared within the data, it was not statistically significant.

The hypotheses and findings within this study are somewhat in conflict with other findings from the cognitive distance literature in which distance estimates have been found to be a function of actual distance. Additionally, the cognitive distance literature had found that short distances tend to be overestimated and longer distances tend to be underestimated and less accurate. In countenance to this, Ankomah *et al.* (1996, p.146) concluded that the effect of actual distance was 'relatively insignificant' and that the accuracy of cognitive distance varied significantly with type of choice set.

The Case of Australia's US Market

In 1993 Australia ranked number one among all single countries as the most preferred travel destination by the US market (ATC, 1993). Yet the US market at this time was stagnant. Australia's market share was below the pro-rata level and this situation was being exacerbated by a lower than average growth (Faulkner, 1997).

The ATC believes that this phenomenon may have been due to distribution chain blockages and a lack of commitment from retail travel agents to sell Australia. As a result, the ATC implemented the 'Certified Aussie Specialist Program' which was designed to give retail travel agents comprehensive destination training, on-going sales support and up-to-date product information (ATC, 1993). Two other on-going initiatives aimed at removing distribution blockages included the Aussie Helpline and the Travel Agent Manual. These campaigns are on-going but have not yet succeeded in significantly increasing market share.

As the actions by the ATC have not had the desired effect at this time, it appears that other factors are influencing the US market. It is equally plausible that US tourists' perceptions of long-haul travel may have had a bearing on responses to marketing programmes. The conundrum within the literature regarding distant destinations demonstrates that there is confusion with respect to tourists' perceptions of long-haul travel which requires research attention.

This study attempts to address this issue by examining the relationships between cognitive distance, actual distance and choice sets for Australia and Italy. Italy has been selected as a comparison in this study for a number of reasons. Firstly, Italy has been identified as a competitor to Australia for the North American outbound market. Secondly, it is a similar distance from the west coast of the US as Australia. Finally, despite Australia being regarded as a more attractive destination, Italy achieves higher rates of arrivals from the US origin market (ATC, 1996).

Research hypotheses

The first three hypotheses are investigating the three major areas that were identified as influencing the accuracy of cognitive distance; processing of information about the environment, source and method of information acquisition, and emotional involvement. The final hypothesis investigates the finding within the tourism literature that perceived distance is underestimated in most circumstances.

The first hypothesis seeks to confirm propositions from within the hierarchical theory of cognitive distance that suggest that the intervening environment will influence distance estimation. Specifically, from Australia's perspective it is of interest to determine whether competitive destinations a similar distance from the origin market as itself are estimated any more or less accurately than Australia. It is hypothesized that Rome is thought to be psychologically closer to Los Angeles than Sydney. This would most likely be due to the geographical isolation of Australia as an island within the southern hemisphere, whereas much of the travelling time to Italy is spent crossing the North American continent; 'homeland' rather than ocean.

H1: The estimation of the length of time it takes to travel from Los Angeles to Sydney will be significantly different than the estimation of the length of time it takes to travel from Los Angeles to Rome.

The second set of hypotheses seek to confirm propositions from within the partial hierarchical theory of cognitive distance that suggest when acquiring information about the environment directly, such as through travelling that route, the accuracy of distance estimations will increase.

H2a: Individuals from the US who have travelled to Australia previously will estimate the travel time more accurately than individuals who have not travelled to the destination before.
H2b: Individuals from the US who have travelled to Italy previously will estimate the travel time more accurately than individuals who have not travelled to the destination before.

The third set of hypotheses seek to test the relationship between accuracy of estimate and emotional involvement with the destination. This is being examined through choice set allocation (Ankomah *et al.*, 1996) within a long-haul context.

H3a: Estimates of the travel time from Los Angeles to Sydney by individuals who have Australia within their late set will be significantly more accurate than for those individuals who have Australia within their inert and inept sets.
H3b: Estimates of the travel time from Los Angeles to Rome by individuals who have Italy within their late set will be significantly more accurate than for those individuals who have Italy within their inert and inept sets.

The final set of hypotheses seek to confirm the proposition within the literature review conducted by Ankomah and Crompton (1992) which indicated that in past studies cognitive distance estimates have been found to be less than actual distance.

H4a: Estimates of the travel time from Los Angeles to Sydney by individuals from the US will be, on average, less than the actual travel time.
H4b: Estimates of the travel time from Los Angeles to Rome by individuals from the US will be, on average, less than the actual travel time.

Methodology

Cognitive distance has been measured in a number of ways. Within tourism the most widely used method has been to ask respondents for distance estimates in kilometres or miles between their origin and the destination (Walmsley and Jenkins, 1992; Ankomah *et al.*, 1995; Ankomah *et al.*, 1996). This method is specifically suited to driving vacations.
    The other most widely used method is cognitive mapping (Downs and Stea, 1973; Brown and Broadway, 1981) which customarily is used within urban studies. It asks respondents to draw a map from memory of a given area. This method has also been used to estimate cognitive distance between international destinations (Mayo *et al.*, 1988). This method is very time consuming when compared to asking for a distance estimate. It also requires face-to-face contact with the respondents. The advantage is it gives a spatial map showing where destinations are perceived to be in relation to other destinations. This advantage can be duplicated using distance estimates if estimates are gathered for all pairs of destinations and origins, thus allowing for multi-dimensional scaling.

The disadvantage with metric distance estimates for this study is the difficulty of estimating the large distances between overseas origins and destinations. In the tourism studies to this point the actual distance measures have been road distances. For international destinations air distances would be an equivalent. An alternative is to ask respondents to estimate the travel time by air.

Within the cognitive interviews, task complexity was tested for both alternative measures. Respondents were asked to give an estimate of distance and an estimate of travel time between two international cities, then asked to rate the difficulty of the two tasks, to determine which estimate they felt more confident about and to describe how they calculated their responses. It was found that travel time estimates were regarded with more confidence and were less difficult to estimate. Those who felt reasonably comfortable with estimating by distance reported calculating the measure through the air miles received within frequent flier programmes. However, these respondents still felt more confident in estimating the travel time. As such, cognitive distance has been operationalized in this study by asking: *Please estimate the number of hours you think it takes to fly from Los Angeles in the United States direct to Sydney, Australia.*

The actual travel time is the official flight time as recorded by the national airline between the cities. For example, Qantas provided the official flight times from Sydney to Los Angeles and the return leg. This has been compared to the official flight times from Los Angeles to Sydney provided by United Airlines, and reported differences in either direction are less than one hour. Similarly, official flight times from Los Angeles to Rome have been provided by Air Italia. The actual travel time to both destinations for the purposes of this study is 14 hours.

Crompton (1992) created a choice structure taxonomy that outlines the funnelling process resulting in the choice of a final destination from all potential destinations. The choice sets within this taxonomy were outlined within the tourism context and operationally defined. This work is providing a benchmark for tourism researchers as it offers a standardized framework in relation to choice sets permitting consistency within measures and facilitating the development of a cumulative body of knowledge. As such it is appropriate to utilize the operationalization outlined by Crompton (1992) in defining the concepts to be used within this study. The evoked set will be operationalized by asking respondents to: *Please list the names of the countries you would consider visiting for an overseas holiday.* The late evoked set will be operationalized by asking respondents to: *Please list the names of the countries, if any, you are definitely planning to visit for an overseas holiday.* The inept set will be operationalized by asking respondents to: *Please list the names of up to five countries you would definitely not consider visiting for an overseas holiday.* The inert set will be regarded as those destinations not included within the initial consideration set or within the inept set. It will be the remainder set.

The use of choice set structure as an indicator of emotional involvement is confirmed through the analysis of correlation between the three factors proposed by Bratfisch (1969) and choice set allocation. The emotional involvement factors were operationalized using the following questions: *How would you rate your interest in Australia? How important is it to you to visit Australia at some point in time? How would you rate your knowledge of Australia?*

Data collection

A phone survey was employed to collect data on the perceptions of long-haul destinations by individuals who have travelled internationally. The questionnaire was pretested on a convenience sample. Consequently, the questionnaire was modified in wording and scale composition to increase readability and clarity of items. Content validity was established according to the guidelines set forth by Nunnally (1978).

Data for this study was collected from the west coast of the US. There were 250 completed questionnaires, of which 225 were useable for this analysis. The sample was drawn from a database of 5000 names of west coast residents who were self-reported frequent fliers.

Results and discussion

The first hypothesis concerns the effects of the intervening environment on cognitive distance. It was hypothesized that individuals from the US would estimate the length of time it takes to travel from Los Angeles to Sydney differently as compared to the length of time it takes to travel from Los Angeles to Rome, when in reality the flight times are equivalent. A related samples test comparing the means for each estimate was conducted (Table 1). The results show that the means are significantly different, which supports hypothesis 1 and the theories related to the processing of information about the environment. Within exploratory interviews conducted with US tourists a number commented that they often do not feel that they have truly started on their journey until they have left the US. For west-coast residents this may have the effect of lessening the perceived distance when travelling toward Europe.

Table 1 Testing for Equality of Means between the Travel Time Estimates to Australia and Italy

Variable	N	Mean	Standard Devia- tion	Stan- dard Error	Corr.	2-tail Prob.	df	2-tail Prob.
Cog. Esti- mate to Sydney	225	15.81	3.70	0.25				
Cog. Esti- mate to Rome	225	10.78	2.21	0.15				
Paired Difference		5.03	3.88	0.26	0.22	.001	224	.000

The second set of hypotheses referred to the effect of previous travel to a destination on the accuracy of distance estimates to that destination. The error between the cognitive distance estimate and the actual travel time was calculated and the means of the error were compared for those who had not visited the destination, and those who had (Table 2a). For both destinations the non-visitors' estimate errors were found to be significantly different from the visitors' estimate errors (Table 2b). Those who had travelled previously to Australia, estimated the distance more accurately than non-visitors. Surprisingly however, it is found that those who had visited Italy previously underestimated the distance more than those who had not visited. Nevertheless, both groups' estimate errors are significantly different from zero (Table 2c).

The failure of visitors to estimate distance accurately may reflect the influence of passive versus active travel. The literature suggests that active travel, such as walking, leads to more accurate estimates of distance than passive travel, such as a passenger on a flight (Downs and Stea, 1977; Ankomah *et al.*, 1995). Accuracy aside though, for both destinations, visitors estimated the distance to the destinations to be less than the estimates by the non-visitor groups. Intuitively, tourists who have made the effort to collect information, make a decision and travel to a destination are more likely to minimize any negative attributes of the destination such as travel time. This would also be supported by cognitive dissonance theory that suggests when time and effort have been invested in a decision, then consumers may justify that involvement by adapting their perceptions of the negative qualities (Festinger, 1957). The third factor influencing the moderating effect of involvement will be discussed further within the testing and discussion of hypothesis 3.

Table 2a Average Error between Estimated and Actual Travel Time for Those who Have Visited versus Those Who Have not Visited

Destination	Visits	N	Mean Estimate	Mean Error	S.D.	S.E.M.
Australia	1 or more	49	14.65	1.59	1.53	0.22
	no visits	176	16.13	3.06	3.06	0.23
Italy	1 or more	111	10.22	3.80	1.77	0.17
	no visits	114	11.33	2.93	2.09	0.19

The third set of hypotheses referred to the relationship between cognitive distance accuracy and emotional involvement with the destination through choice set allocation. The first step in the testing of the hypotheses is to ensure that choice set allocation is indeed a significant correlate for emotional involvement. Table 3a shows the results of bivariate correlations between the three questions used to operationalize the Bratfisch (1969) factors and choice set allocation. All variables are significantly correlated to the 0.01 level. Table 3b and 3c then test the hypotheses as to whether there is a significant difference in estimates between choice sets.

Unlike the results reported for domestic vacation destinations (Ankomah *et al.*, 1996), the accuracy of estimates was not significantly different for destinations named in the late set as compared to destinations named in the inert and inept sets. As such, hypotheses 3a and 3b were rejected.

Table 2b Testing for Equality of Means between Those who Have Visited versus Those who Have Not Visited

Destination	t	df	Sig. (2 tail)	Mean Difference	S.E.D.
Australia	-3.80	223	.000	-1.72	0.45
Italy	3.38*	219	.001	0.87	0.26

* Equal variances not assumed

Table 2c Testing whether Estimate Errors are Significantly Different from Zero

Destina- tion	Visits	t	df	Sig. (2 tail)	Mean Differ- ence	Confidence Interval
Australia	1 or more	7.30	48	.000	1.59	1.15 ⇔ 2.03
	No visits	14.35	175	.000	3.31	2.86 ⇔ 3.77
Italy	1 or more	22.59	110	.000	3.80	3.47 ⇔ 4.14
	No visits	14.94	113	.000	2.54	2.54 ⇔ 3.32

Table 3a Bivariate Correlations between Emotional Involvement and Choice Set Allocation

	Variables	Impor- tance to Visit	Interest in Destina- tion	Knowledge of Destination	Choice Set Allocation
Australia	Importance to Visit	1.000			
	Interest in Destination	.885 (.000)	1.000		
	Knowledge of Destination	.776 (.000)	.899 (.000)	1.000	
	Choice Set Allocation	.832 (.000)	.786 (.000)	.714 (.000)	1.000
Italy	Importance to Visit	1.000			
	Interest in Destination	.797 (.000)	1.000		
	Knowledge of Destination	.614 (.000)	.840 (.000)	1.000	
	Choice Set Allocation	.723 (.000)	.677 (.000)	.538 (.000)	1.000

The final set of hypotheses referred to the findings of previous studies that cognitive distance was underestimated in most circumstances. In this study, the mean for Australia was higher than, and significantly different from, the actual travel time. This finding rejects hypothesis 4a. The mean for Italy was lower than, and significantly different from, the actual travel time. This finding accepts hypothesis 4b (Tables 4a and 4b).

Long-haul destinations, it would appear, break the rules. In countenance to Ankomah *et al.* (1996, p.146) who concluded that the effect of actual distance was 'relatively insignificant' and that the accuracy of cognitive distance varied significantly with type of choice set, this study has found that cognitive distance does not consistently vary with either distance or choice set. It can be concluded that the travel time to Australia was, on average, overestimated; that direct learning of distance through previous travel did not increase the accuracy of estimates to Italy; that choice set allocation did not improve the accuracy of estimates; and that actual distance is not a good indicator of cognitive distance. It emerges that respondents' perceptions of distance are being influenced by a wider range of factors.

Table 3b Average Cognitive Distance Estimate for Individuals who Placed the Destination in their Late Set versus Those who Placed the Destination in the Inept and Inert Sets

Destination	Choice Set	N	Mean	S.D.	S.E.M.
Australia	late	10	15.50	4.45	0.47
	inert and inept	88	15.50	1.35	0.43
Italy	late	23	10.35	2.25	0.47
	inert and inept	133	10.90	2.23	0.19

Table 3c Testing for Equality of Means between Those who Placed the Destination in their Late Set versus Inept and Inert Sets

Destination	t	df	Sig. (2 tail)	Mean Diff.	S.E.D.
Australia	0.00	96	1.00	0.00	-2.82 ⇔ 2.82
Italy	1.09*	30	0.28	0.55	-4.81 ⇔ 1.59

* Equal variances not assumed

Table 4a Descriptive Statistics of Cognitive Distance Estimates

Destination	N	Mean	S.D.	S.E.M.
Australia	225	15.81	3.70	0.25
Italy	225	10.78	2.21	0.15

Table 4b One Sample Tests to Determine whether Sample Means are Significantly Different from Actual Travel Time of 14 hours

Destination	t	df	Sig. 95%	Mean Diff.	Confidence Interval
Australia	7.320	224	.000	1.81	1.32 ⇔ 2.30
Italy	-21.837	224	.000	-3.22	-3.51 ⇔ -2.93

From the cognitive distance theory, overestimation of distance may be explained by Australia's isolation, causing individual's to encode the physical distance differently. As such, this could assist in the explanation of Australia's performance within the US market, especially if cognitive distance estimates influence the assessment of other destination attributes such as perceived cost and risk. From the cognitive dissonance literature, underestimation of distance by previous visitors may be explained through consumers rationalizing their decisions through perception adjustments. Overall though, it would appear that consumers have difficulty in estimating long-haul distances, and that more active marketing measures need to be adopted to assist tourists in their learning.

Conclusions and Future Research

This study has investigated the accuracy of travel time estimates between origins and long-haul destinations and compared the results across two destinations. It was established from the literature that cognitive distance serves as an important tool in assessing destinations, yet very little research has investigated how it influences long-haul destinations. Findings suggest that the theories developed within urban studies and even domestic vacation studies may not hold true for long-haul destinations. Since distance is an inevitable dimension of long-haul destinations, its role within decision making needs to be better understood.

Results also suggest that first time or prospective visitors may benefit from marketing materials aimed at educating them with respect to distance and travel time expectations. The problem with many materials is that the consumer will not attend to the information unless they have situational involvement which mostly occurs late within the decision-making process. By this point in time, the destination may have already been discarded. As such, future research may benefit from considering whether the accuracy of distance estimates influences other decision factors such as cost, risk and attractiveness.

Endnotes

[1] Long-haul travel for the purposes of this paper is defined as inter-regional travel of at least 6 hours in duration (Archer 1989; ATC 1993).

References

Ankomah, P.K. and Crompton, J.L. (1992) Tourism Cognitive Distance: A Set of Research Propositions. *Annals of Tourism Research* 19, 323-342.

Ankomah, P.K., Crompton, J.L. and Baker, D. (1995) A Study of Pleasure Travelers' Cognitive Distance Assessments. *Journal of Travel Research* (Autumn), 12-18.

Ankomah, P.K., Crompton, J.L. and Baker, D. (1996) Influence of Cognitive Distance in Vacation Choice. *Annals of Tourism Research* 23(1), 138-150.

ATC (Australian Tourist Commission) (1993) *Market Segmentation Studies: Executive Summary for Asia, Europe, Japan.* AGP, Sydney.

ATC (1996) *Market Profile and Strategic Analysis: USA.* AGP, Sydney.

Bratfisch, O. (1969) A Further Study of the Relation Between Subjective Distance and Emotional Involvement. *Acta Psychologica* 29, 244-255.

Briggs, R. (1973) Urban Cognitive Distance. In: Downs, R.M. and Stea, D. (eds.) *Image and Environment: Cognitive Mapping and Spatial Behaviour.* Aldine, Chicago, pp. 361-388.

Brown, M.A. and Broadway, M.J. (1981) The Cognitive Maps of Adolescents: Confusion about Inter-town Distances. *Professional Geographer* 33(3), 315-325.

Burkhart, A.J. and Medlik, S. (1981) *Tourism Past, Present and Future.* Heinemann, London.

Cadwallader, M. (1981) Towards a Cognitive Gravity Model: The Case of Consumer Spatial Behaviour. *Regional Studies* 15(4), 275-284.

Canter, D. and Tagg, S. (1975) Distance Estimation in Cities. *Environment and Behavior* 7, 59-80.

Cook, R.L. and McCleary, K.W. (1983) Redefining Vacation Distances in Consumer Minds. *Journal of Travel Research* (Autumn), 31-34.

Crompton, J.L. (1992) Structure of Vacation Destination Choice Sets. *Annals of Tourism Research* 19, 420-434.

Crompton, J.L. and Ankomah, P.K. (1993) Choice Set Propositions in Destination Decisions. *Annals of Tourism Research* 20, 461-476.

Downs, R.M. and Stea, D. (1973) Cognitive Maps and Spatial Behavior: process and products. In: Downs, R.M. and Stea, D. (eds.) *Image and Environment*. Edward Arnold, Chicago.

Downs, R.M. and Stea, D. (1977). *Maps in Minds: Reflections on Cognitive Mapping*. Harper Row, New York.

Ekman, G. and Bratfisch, O. (1965) Subjective Distance and Emotional Involvement: A Psychological Mechanism. *Acta Psychologica* 24, 446-453.

Faulkner, W. (1997) A Model for the Evaluation of National Tourism Destination Marketing Programs. *Journal of Travel Research* 35(3), 23-32.

Festinger, L. (1957) *A Theory of Cognitive Dissonance*. Stanford University Press, Stanford, California.

Golledge, R.G. and Spector, A.N. (1978) Comprehending the Urban Environment: Theory and Practice. *Geographical Analysis* 10, 403-426.

Gould, P. and White, R. (1974) *Mental Maps*. Penguin, Middlesex.

Hall, C.M. (1991) *Introduction to Tourism in Australia: Impacts on Planning and Development*. Longman Cheshire, Melbourne.

Howard, J. and Sheth, J. (1969) *The Theory of Buyer Behavior*. John Wiley, New York.

Lloyd, R. and Heivly, C. (1987) Systematic Distortions in Urban Cognitive Maps. *Annals of the Association of American Geographers* 77, 191-207.

Mayo, E.J. and Jarvis, L.P. (1981) *The Psychology of Leisure Travel, Effective Marketing and Selling of Travel Services*. CBI Publishing, Boston.

Mayo, E.J., Jarvis, L.P. and Xander, J.A. (1988) Beyond the Gravity Model. *Journal of the Academy of Marketing Science* 16 (Autumn), 23-29.

McNamara, T.P. (1986) Mental Representations of Spatial Relations. *Cognitive Psychology* 18, 87-121.

Mowen, J.C. (1995) *Consumer Behaviour*. Prentice-Hall, Englewood Cliffs, NJ.

Narayana, C.L. and Markin, R.J. (1975) Consumer Behavior and Product Performance: An Alternative Conceptualization. *Journal of Marketing* 39 (October), 1-6.

Nicosia, F.M. (1966) *Consumer Decision Processes: Marketing and Advertising Implications*. Prentice-Hall, Englewood Cliffs, NJ.

Nunally, J.C. (1978) *Psychometric Theory*. McGraw-Hill, New York.

Smith, S.L.J. (1989) *Tourism Analysis: A Handbook*. Longman Scientific and Technical, London.

Um, S. and Crompton, J.L. (1990) Attitude Determinants in Tourism Destination Choice. *Annals of Tourism Research* 17, 432-448.

Um, S. and Crompton, J.L. (1992) The Roles of Perceived Inhibitors and Facilitators in Pleasure Travel Destination Decisions. *Journal of Travel Research* 31 (Winter), 18-25.

Walmsley, D.J. and Jenkins, J.M. (1992) Cognitive Distance: A Neglected Issue in

Travel Behavior. *Journal of Travel Research* 31(1), 24-29.

Woodside, A.G. and Lysonski, S. (1989) A General Model of Traveler Destination Choice. *Journal of Travel Research* 27 (Spring), 8-14.

Woodside, A.G. and Sherrell, D. (1977) Traveler Evoked, Inept, and Inert Sets of Vacation Destinations *Journal of Travel Research* 16 (Winter), 14-18.

Chapter four
The Impact of Seemingly Minor Methodological Changes on Estimates of Travel and Correcting Bias

Jay Beaman and Jeff Beaman
Auctor Consulting Associates, Ltd., Ottawa, Ontario, Canada

Joseph T. O'Leary
Purdue University, West Lafayette, Indiana, USA

Stephen Smith
University of Waterloo, Ontario, Canada

Abstract

In 1998, evidence was provided suggesting that an apparent 15% decline in domestic travel estimated from the Canadian Travel Surveys (CTS) of 1994, 1996, and 1997 was possibly misleading. This decline could actually be the result of methodological changes in the survey rather than a change in travel behaviour. Here, realistic assumptions and a simple computational method are utilized to demonstrate that change in bias may account for the drop in estimated trips. The analysis depends on a trip recall salience scale. Use of this scale allows correction for an under-reporting bias arising from reduced trip recall rates for low-salience trips. When the 1996 and 1997 CTS data are corrected, estimates of change in total trips are near zero. This finding corresponds to perceptions within the tourism industry. The bias correction methodology is applicable to other large surveys involving recall of past behaviour in which multiple events are recalled.

Introduction

It is common to assume that the results of large national surveys conducted under the auspices of official statistical organizations are not seriously biased by methodological problems. However, Kunert (1998) has demonstrated that the German KONTIV surveys (the Continuous Travel Survey of the Ministry of Transport) of 1976, 1982, and 1989, which are based on a well documented design, with samples ranging from 35,000 to 40,000, are nonetheless subject to serious bias problems. Kunert (1998) concludes that 'changes in the survey design which have been considered as minor at the outset . . .

have drastic effects on measured responses' (p. 274).

Statistics Canada made a number of changes to the Canadian Travel Survey (CTS)[1] from 1994 to 1997 (Auctor, 1998). It is reasonable to assume that the changes were made under the belief that the impact on CTS estimates would be minimal. However, the total number of trips estimated with the data obtained from the 1996 and 1997 surveys shows an unexpected drop – a drop that is counter to anecdotal evidence from tourism operators and destination marketing organizations. This discordance between official estimates and the experience of operators raises the question: to what degree do these results stem from a methodological change in the survey rather than a change in travel behaviour? In 1998, Auctor Consulting Associates conducted a review of the CTS (Auctor, 1998) which provided reasons for concluding that the differences between 1994 estimates and those for 1996 and 1997 were partly, possibly even largely, a consequence of change in bias between the surveys. That report prompted university-based research.

Literature review

Research to establish whether or not a change in bias was responsible for changes in CTS estimates began at Purdue University in 1998. Hill *et al.* (1999) employed a paired-comparison method to derive a trip-recall salience (TRS) scale for 288 categories of trips defined by distance, duration, expenditure, mode, and purpose (see Table 1). They treat recall as a long-term memory (LTM) access problem. According to Craik and Lockhart (1972), information is coded for the purpose of storage in LTM. Anderson and Reder (1979), by addressing how memory codes differ, emphasize that people store much more information than they directly observe. For a trip, associations stored could be enjoyment, long duration, long distance, and expense, among others. The encoding principle, as discussed by Tulving and Thomson (1973), implies that memory traces differ in type and durability of information and thus that retrieval depends on encoding. If a recent trip has been distinctively encoded (Schmidt, 1991), e.g. because it is emotionally distinctive, it is considered by some to be a flashbulb memory (Winograd and Neisser, 1992). As a result, the trip being expensive, enjoyable, long in duration, and long in distance may be virtually irrelevant to its recall.

On the other hand, the respondent may search his/her memory for trips based on cues (specific information that the respondent typically uses in storing information about trips). Such a search process defines an order in which trips will be recalled. Similarly, adopting a chronological search strategy dictates a different order in which trips will be recalled.

Woodside and Ronkainen (1993) have addressed the issue of consumer memory and mental categorization. Based on their assessment of the literature, they suggest that preferences for destinations depend on affective associations. In the vernacular, strong affective associations are what make a trip memorable as either good or bad – something we do or do not want to repeat. Woodside and Ronkainen (1993), while showing that we can retrieve information from our LTM based on the types of trips we are and are not interested in, also provide reinforcement for the notion that some trips we take are more memorable than others and that this is based to some degree on trip attributes.

Table 1 Levels Used in Defining Trip Categories Based on Distance, Duration, Expenditure, Mode, and Purpose

Variable	Category Definition
Distance	1 is distance under 150 km one-way; 2 is from 150 to 349 km; and 3 is 350 km and over
Duration	1 is day trips; 2 is 1 night; 3 is 2 or 3 nights; 4 is 4 or more nights
Total Trip Expenditure	1 is under $100; 2 is $101 to $275; 3 is $276 or more
Mode	1 is personal vehicle and 2 is all other modes
Purpose	1 is visiting friends or relations; 2 is personal; 3 is pleasure; 4 is all other (dominantly business)

In the marketing literature, Menon (1997), in research on respondents reporting on the frequency of events, also provides evidence of the importance of categories in recall. If you ask people about a general category (trips) and about more specific categories (day trips and overnight trips), one may expect to get a different number of trips per month for the general category than was obtained for the sum of the two mutually exclusive categories. In addition, the fact that asking people general questions about the frequency of events produces less reliable, and in many cases quite different estimates, shows that context influences recall. In other words, when the conditions for recall are altered, e.g. chronological recall, the recalled information can be expected to differ from what would be recalled using a different memory search.

An exploration of the literature regarding the conditions for recall might start from concepts of episodic and semantic memory (Schacter, 1987). If a search tends to be of semantic memory, a successful search may in fact allow a respondent to switch to episodic memory to provide details on a trip. In particular, one can expect some general tendency to recall long duration, long distance, and expensive trips more readily than short, cheap ones.

CTS procedures

The CTS is conducted as an add-on to Statistics Canada's monthly Labour Force Survey (LFS) (for details see Beaman *et al.*, 1999). Households included in the LFS are selected through the use of a sophisticated cluster sample. Once selected, the household is contacted once a month for 6 months to obtain labour force information. They are generally contacted in about the third week of the month following the month for which travel information is requested. The first LFS interview is conducted in person and, if possible, all subsequent LFS-related interviewing is conducted over the telephone. CTS interviews and other surveys that are add-ons to the LFS are not conducted during the first month that a household is in the LFS. When the CTS is to be administered, the individual to respond to the CTS is selected randomly from household members 15 years of age or older. When the same household must provide a respondent for the CTS more than once, the same person can be asked to complete the CTS and/or other add-ons in months two through six of a household's LFS participation. When a respondent from a household answers CTS and another add-on is also administered, there is no way of knowing if the CTS respondent answered both when there are two or more potential respondents. If one person responded to two or more surveys one does not know which questionnaire was administered first. In Auctor's (1998) review, such variables were identified as important and easily kept with automated collection software in use after 1994. Such data was not being kept as of July 2000.

When a respondent is selected for the CTS, he/she is asked how many day trips and how many overnight trips they took in the previous month that met CTS criteria for a trip for their province. If trips were taken, he/she is asked a series of questions about each trip. After a person reports on his/her first trip, the individual is asked if he/she took any similar trips during the reporting month. If he/she has, the number of such trips is recorded in a 'similar trip' variable; no data on any of these similar trips are collected. Data on the first trip and the number of trips similar to it are kept in a trip-report record. By asking about other trips, trip-report records are accumulated for a respondent with the sequence of reporting as a variable in the data.

Table 2 provides general information showing the magnitude of the CTS data collection. For example, based on the data files used in this analysis (which are not exactly the same as the ones on the published CTS compact disks), in 1994, 117,818 interviews were completed. On a monthly basis, the number of interviews completed ranged from 8251 to 12,211. In 1994, a total of 59,242 trip-report records were collected; monthly totals ranged from 3299 to 8219. These trip-report records cover 80,725 trips because some records were for one or more 'similar trips'. Data on 'pairs' refer to the number of records in which a respondent provided data on two or more trips. About 67,000 pairs were generated (for the method, see Appendix 2 of Beaman *et al.*, 2000) in 1994. Only 12,989 pairs were recorded for 1997 and 30,795 for 1996. This variability in numbers of pairs is largely a result of Statistics Canada conducting different numbers of interviews in different years. For example, the figures reflect that only half as many interviews were conducted in 1997, using the standard CTS approach, as in 1996. The number of interviews was also influenced by an adjustment to the LFS sampling design that placed a somewhat greater proportion of interviews in urban areas in years subsequent to 1994.

Table 2 Summary of Unweighted Information about the CTS Data Used in this Study

Summary for Variable	Year			Grand Total
	1994	1996	1997	
Number of Interviews	117,818	185,690	91,248	394,756
Max Interviews per Month	12,211	16,029	8,022	
Min Interviews per Month	8,251	14,907	7,134	
Number of Pairs for Analysis	23,217	30,795	12,989	67,001
Max Pairs for Analysis per Month	3,930	4,859	1,771	
Min Pairs for Analysis per Month	1,114	1,885	795	
Total Trip Report Records	59,242	79,873	35,657	174,772
Max Pairs for Analysis per Month	8,219	9,899	4,308	
Min Pairs for Analysis per Month	3,299	5,296	2,289	
Total Trips Reported	80,752	108,355	48,467	237,574
Max Trips Reported per Month	10,938	13,150	5,701	
Min Trips Reported per Month	4,484	7,195	3,076	

In the CTS, each trip-report record includes information on distance, duration, expenditure, mode, and purpose. Table 1, as will be recalled, identified a number of trip characteristics grouped into nominal or ordinal classes used by Hill *et al.* (1999). The combinations of these characteristics result in a total of 288 trip types (288 = 3 × 4 × 3 × 2 × 4), so every trip reported in the CTS can be classified into one of 288 categories (Beaman *et al.*, 1999).

CTS changes and considerations in bias estimation

A number of changes were implemented in the administration of the CTS between 1994 and 1997 (for details and references, see Beaman *et al.*, 1999). These include the following:

1. The structure of the LFS cluster sample was changed to place more emphasis on urban areas.
2. In 1994, interviewers were told that they could suggest to respondents that they report their trips chronologically; in 1996 and 1997, this practice was formally forbidden.
3. Though respondents usually did not see the interviewer record their responses on a computer, use of computer assisted telephone interviewing (CATI) was introduced in 1996, causing the order, and to a degree the timing of questions to be dictated by a computer.
4. While in 1994 interviewers were instructed to ignore certain inconsistencies, in 1996 and 1997 the CATI software recognized inconsistent answers and prompted the interviewer to resolve specific inconsistencies.
5. The 1996 and 1997 CTS questionnaires required the interviewer to request more trip details than those requested in 1994, causing the largest increase in burden on those who should provide the most information.
6. Respondents had a higher probability of being asked to complete the CTS a second time in 1996 and 1997 than 1994, thus increasing burden for some respondents.
7. After 1994, some respondents were asked to complete add-ons to the LFS in addition to the CTS, thus increasing respondent burden.

Each of these seven changes, except possibly 1, has the potential to affect recall of trips. For example, given that in 1996 and 1997 Statistics Canada interviewers were instructed not to suggest to respondents that they report chronologically, it is reasonable to expect that far fewer respondents reported chronologically. As a result, the role of salience in reporting would increase. Such changes could, on a year-over-year basis, result in changes in trip-reporting that could erroneously be interpreted as a shift in behaviour.

One could argue in relation to change 1 that a difference exists between rural and urban trip salience scales and that this actually caused some or all of the bias change reported by Hill *et al.* (1999). The authors do not consider that it is plausible that the shift in LFS sampling to a greater urban weighting had very much to do with change in bias. Unfortunately, proving this in quantitative terms is a task which may not even be possible. The development of the regression method of estimating salience scales and features in the estimation software (Beaman *et al.*, 2000) only provide some of the necessary capabilities to deal with this matter. Therefore, proof that there is or is not a problem is left to critics of this research.

Given changes, the operational question became, 'What consequences resulted?' One consequence was that trips were reported in a different order. Beaman *et al.* (2000) and Hill *et al.* (1999) conclude that this is proof of the existence of a change in bias. The argument made is that the change in bias documented by the order change suggests that there will be differences between estimates of trips taken in 1994 and the other survey years. However, Hill *et al.* (1999) acknowledge that the difference in reporting order could occur without a change in trip estimates being a consequence. With perfect recall, recalling chronologically, or based on any other trip attribute search strategy, the same trips would be reported, but in a different order.

Work here is predicated on acceptance that a trip recall salience scale has been estimated which explains changes in the order of trips reported (Beaman *et al.,* 2000; Hill *et al.,* 2000). This paper demonstrates how the scale can be employed to estimate bias and shows how to make corrections for that bias based on modest assumptions, such as:

1. The most salient trips are reported reliably.
2. The way respondents implicitly define trip salience of categories of trips did not change or, at most, changed slowly over time from 1994 to 1997.
3. Short-term demographic and socio-economic changes (e.g. from 1994 to 1997) have little influence on the relative frequency with which trips of different salience are taken.

Change in salience scales and change in Canadian society during the period of analysis

Surrounding the 1994 to 1997 period of concern in this analysis, there were no significant economic or social shocks to Canadian society, so the following is offered in support of the propositions just introduced:

1. The way respondents define salience did not change significantly because nothing happened (e.g. a gas crisis) that would cause any relatively rapid change in something subconscious such as the way they recalled trips.
2. The characteristics of the population did not change enough to cause shifts in the ways that respondents recall trips (e.g. some new and different ethnic/refugee group becoming an important element of the population).
3. Change in total trips taken did not significantly alter the relative frequency with which trips of differing salience are generated because such shifts would have been driven by social or economic changes.

To elaborate further, consider the following. For the first assumption, if the CTS methodology did not change from 1994 to 1997, then all one is asked to accept is that the mental process used by respondents in developing their responses when they responded based on trip salience did not change significantly. The fact that in 1994, a prompt to report chronologically is expected to have caused some respondents to, at least initially, ignore salience in reporting trips just means that in 1994 salience-specific rates of trip-taking may show an excessive influence of chronological reporting.

The second assumption simply registers the fact that, both nationally and locally, there were not significant changes in the characteristics of the population that impacted on travel and the perception of trip salience. Over the three survey years, Canada did not gain some group into the population that perceived salience of trips differently than the average perception of the rest of the population and that was large enough to have any influences on a national average. In a similar way, the ageing of the population by three years cannot be expected to have a big impact on the kinds of trips that people take, their frequency of trips taken, or the way they define the salience of those trips.

Finally, the third assumption implies that from 1994 to 1997, growth in travel in Canada did not focus on, for example, high-salience trips. In this regard, there are several matters to consider. If travel really did not change much in gross terms, was there actually a significant shift going on in trip taking that is reflected in taking a relatively greater or lesser number of high-salience trips? The assumption asserts that no such shift was occurring. If there were a decline in travel for economic reasons it would be expected that the high-salience trips would be impacted. Does one really expect that short weekend trips for fun or visiting friends and relatives are going to be dropped to maintain long expensive holidays? To explain certain patterns of change in salience-specific trip rates, one must argue for such behaviour rather than accepting the third assumption.

The Formulation of A Recall Salience Model

The methods used to formulate the recall salience model were suggested by experience in demography working with stable population theory and standardization of estimates such as fertility rates. By treating trip recall salience in relation to travel similarly to the treatment of age in stable population analysis and by using the idea that certain values provide standards, one may arrive at a model for the estimation and correction of bias. The way CTS respondents 'assign' a salience value to a given category of trip is not a conscious process and thus, as indicated above, it is not typically going to change significantly from year to year.

Based on trip recall salience scores derived by Hill *et al.* (1999), one may assign salience scores to trips. Once salience scores are assigned, one may then classify trips into high (h), medium high (mh), moderately low (ml), and low (l) salience. If a trip's salience was less than 0.35, the trip was classed as having low-salience. Trip types with recall salience scores from 0.35 to 0.44 were classed as medium-low-salience. Values from 0.45 to 0.54 were classed as medium-high-salience. A value of 0.55 or greater was classed as high-salience.

Methodological changes to the CTS appear to be 'salience scale neutral' in that, with one exception, from 1994 to 1997 Statistics Canada continued to ask people about travel in such a way as to cause people to recall trips based on salience if they do not recall them chronologically. The exception is about two-thirds of the data collected in 1997, which are two out of three rotations per month in the LFS rotating panel (Beaman *et al.*, 1999). These 'special' data, which are not used in this analysis, do not include information on intraprovincial trips and thus recall is evoked in a way that does not even allow certain types of trips to be reported even if recalled. Huan *et al.* (2000) report on the bias change between the 'special' data and the one rotation of the 1997 CTS 'standard' data used here. Again, references here to CTS data are only to the 'standard' CTS data.

The development of a trip recall salience scale

The existence of a trip recall salience (TRS) scale is founded on the notion that if in a given context some categories of trips are more readily recalled than others, then a scale, $s(C(x))$, can be defined for trips, x and y, in two categories, $C(x)$ and $C(y)$, that gives their relative ease of recall based on the relation that if $s(C(x)) > s(C(y))$ then x is more readily recalled than y. If all respondents who report two or more trips during a one month time period only report one trip in any given category; if trips reported have no expected temporal relation (one does not tend to precede the other in time); and if a single perfectly accurate scale is applied to all respondents, then, for the trip categories for which there are trips, the responses will establish: a category of trips that is most salient, a second most salient category, etc. Ties (equal scale values) would be indicated by, for example, a trip y being reported both before and after a trip x.

The condition that for information to be useful in estimating a scale, only one trip in a category can be reported in a month, is required to avoid false inferences. If two trips are reported for one category, C_1, and one for another, C_2, a trip in category C_1 will, on average and based on random occurrence in time, be reported first twice as frequently as a trip in C_2. The false impression of C_1 being more salient skews the salience score for C_1 (see Beaman *et al.*, 2000).

Based on the theoretical considerations given above, Hill *et al.* (1999) assume that respondents implicitly define trip salience as:

$$\theta(t_x) = F(duration,\ distance,\ expenditure,\ trip\ type,\ and\ mode) + \varepsilon \qquad \text{Equation 1}$$

where θ is trip salience, t_x is a trip in category x, and ε is random error (factors not measured in the CTS and socio-economic factors available in the CTS but not studied). Since $\theta(t_x)$ is not directly observable, one determines a function $\Omega(t_x)$ such that if a and b are trips in different categories and if $\theta(t_a) > \theta(t_b)$, then within the limits of estimation accuracy $\Omega(t_a) > \Omega(t_b)$. Using Saaty's (1977) model, salience weight can be estimated using:

$$P(c_x, c_y) = (W_x/W_y)E \qquad \text{Equation 2}$$

where $P(c_x, c_y)$ is the proportion of times trip category x is mentioned ahead of y, W_x and W_y are TRS scale values, and E is an error term.

By taking logarithms of both sides of Equation 2, one obtains Equation 3. The logarithms of the weights are estimated using weighted-least-squares regression (Beaman *et al.*, 2000):

$$log(P(c_x, c_y)) = log(W_x) - log(W_y) + log(E) \qquad \text{Equation 3}$$

With this estimation method salience scale values have been estimated for all trip categories such that trips in the category are reported by somebody and are reported along with a trip in a different category. Salience scale values can be estimated for 285 of the 288 trip categories with this estimation method. Scores derived by Hill *et al.* (1999) are used in this work because as of the date of preparation of this paper, scores computed by regression are not being released for use for CTS bias estimation. Use of the new salience estimates in bias estimation is part of a research proposal awaiting review for funding. Salience scale values used here were estimated for trip categories with sufficient data to allow the ratios computed to have well over a 50% chance of correctly reflecting the salience relation of a trip with other trips. Over 90% of CTS trips could be assigned a TRS scale value using this method.

Bias and salience-specific trip rates

To determine what salience-specific trip rates show about bias in the CTS, the earlier assumption must be reformulated as follows:

1. The trips of highest salience have the greatest average probability of being reported in a survey when recalled based on salience.
2. When trips are recalled based on the salience of a trip and when controlling on context, the lower the salience of the trip, the lower the probability that the trip will be recalled in a survey.

These reformulated assumptions hardly merit discussion given their logical link to the definition of salience. Clearly, the way that a trip attains high-salience is to be reported ahead of other trips. However, if a lower salience trip is not reported part of the time, all that matters is that it is reported enough of the time to 'establish' its legitimate position/salience score in relation to trips in other categories. A salience score clearly must reflect reporting position and thus recall sequence. Imagine that burden on a respondent changes. A trip in a given category being later, on average, in a reporting sequence then means that the trip is even less likely to be reported after a trip, that on average is reported ahead of it, than it was prior to the change.

Table 3 Canadian Travel Survey (CTS) Estimates for Total Trips (millions of trips) and Percentage Change from 1994*)

	Total Estimated Trips (k) from CTS			Percentage Change	
Total Trips	1994	1996	1997	94 to 96	94 to 97
January	10.4	10.2	6.8	-1.9%	-34.6%
February	10.9	9.9	7.8	-9.2%	-28.4%
March	10.4	8.7	6.5	-16.3%	-37.5%
April	9.9	9.0	7.3	-9.1%	-26.3%
May	10.7	8.9	8.4	-16.8%	-21.5%
June	10.8	9.3	8.7	-13.9%	-19.4%
July	13.9	11.7	10.7	-15.8%	-23.0%
August	14.9	13.1	11.2	-12.1%	-24.8%
September	11.0	9.8	9.8	-10.9%	-10.9%
October	9.2	8.6	8.9	-6.5%	-3.3%
November	8.2	7.1	7.8	-13.4%	-4.9%
December	10.1	8.1	8.8	-19.8%	-12.9%
Year Total	130.5	114.4	102.7	-12.8%	-21.3%

* estimates are based on 'complete' data files provided for the 1998 Auctor review of the CTS and thus should not and do not give exactly the same results as obtained using 1996 and 1997 data files available from Statistics Canada on compact disc.

Trip salience and the search for bias in CTS

Table 3 gives estimates of the total number of trips taken in 1994, 1996, and 1997, and the percentage change from 1994 levels. The first three data columns in Table 3 are estimates of total trips made by Canadian residents for 1994, 1996, and 1997 by month. These are weighted estimates. In other words, Statistics Canada has supplied numbers such that, for example, each trip reported by a respondent can be treated as the number of trips specified in the weight to impute total trips taken by the entire population. Statistics Canada provides information on the theory behind their weights, the different weights provided, and their use in analysis of data (Statistics Canada, 2000). In 1994, it is estimated that about 131 million trips were made. The last two data columns of Table 3 indicate percentage changes from 1994. There were substantial declines in total trips between 1994 and both 1996 and 1997. For example, there was a 21.3% drop for annual totals from 1994 to 1997.

A review of the monthly figures in Table 3 confirms that changes between years are consistent with annual variations. The few cases where there is departure from the downward trend, such as a rise from 8.1 million trips in December of 1996 to 8.8 million for December 1997, could well result from small sample sizes for those segments. In general, monthly estimates for 1994 are substantially larger than those for the other years.

Can the pattern of declining number of trips shown in Table 3 be taken at face value? An alternative is that the drop observed, to some degree, reflects a change in bias in estimates resulting from changes in CTS methodology. This is the position presented in Auctor's (1998) report cited earlier. To appreciate that position, consider the differences in the way in which 1994 respondents were asked to recall trips versus recall in 1996 and 1997. In 1994, because of instructions to interviewers, one must assume that many respondents were encouraged to report trips chronologically. In 1996 and 1997, it must be assumed that respondents were simply invited to report the details of any trip taken. The likely result is that relatively more respondents recalled the most memorable or 'salient' trip first in 1996 and 1997 than in 1994. The most salient trip might be the most expensive, longest distance, or longest duration trip taken that month. Although for 'off the top' recall, recalling one trip might prompt recall of another, one still expects a tendency to report additional trips in decreasing order of salience. One can argue that this 'off the top' approach is not systematic; it does not draw on the respondent's ability to relate specific events in a sequence or to a particular week or weekend. Nor does it encourage the respondent to probe semantic memory effectively. Less memorable events could easily be missed. Also, increased response burden from 1994 to 1996 and 1997 was identified above.

If a respondent feels some form of response burden then they might terminate the CTS interview by, e.g., stating, 'That's all I remember'. If the respondent was not reporting trips chronologically, higher salience trips tend to get reported (by definition), but some, or possibly all, low-salience trips may not be reported. It is to be expected that an increasing number of trips of low-salience will go unreported when situational change from 1994 to later surveys involves: (a) moving to more 'off the top' (and thus inefficient) recall, (b) the questionnaire on average takes longer, (c) odds are higher that the respondent is being interviewed for the CTS a second time, and (d) the probability is greater that he/she has also been interviewed for another LFS add-on. To be fair, if chronological reporting results in more trips being reported, one may argue that the greater number of trip reports was a 'compensating' burden in 1994. One may also argue that the greater tendency to report less-salient trips first in 1994 meant that burden often did not become an issue, because little information needs to be provided for less salient trips compared to longer and more complicated trips. The fact is that some things about what respondents were thinking will never be known for sure. Nevertheless, it is worth noting that chronological reporting could be carried out by the interviewer obtaining summary information on trips quickly and then attempting to obtain all details that are needed about trips. Such an approach could result in better recall than achieved in 1994 and if burden became an issue resulting in an interview being terminated, one would still have data on trips for which details were not obtained.

Now consider what behaviour is observed if one only looks at the reporting of the most salient trips. The first two data rows of Table 4 contain what may be described as a 'Baseline Correction' factor (BLC) for 1996 and 1997. The BLC is simply the ratio of the number of high-salience trips reported in 1996 or 1997 to the number of high-salience trips reported in 1994. The annual total value of 1.03 for 1996 indicates that it is estimated that there were 3% more high-salience trips in 1996 than there were in 1994. The 3% increase in total high-salience trips is probably not significant, given the limited sample size for high-salience trips. The value of 0.98 for 1997 shows that, within two percentage points, the same number of high-salience trips was estimated for 1997 as for 1994. Again, this is not likely a significant difference. Relatively similar values are seen month after month. In other words, rather than observing the large decline in estimated trips that is recorded in Table 3, one sees that total numbers of high-salience trips remain relatively constant from 1994 to 1997. The fact that the estimated number of high-salience trips does not decline is important. One reason for its importance is that it is so different from the official estimates for all trips. Another is because there are a large number of factors that could potentially influence the number of high-salience trips taken more than they would influence trips of lower salience. For example, taking high-salience trips should, in theory, be more responsive to socio-economic change than taking low-salience trips. It is reasonable that a once-a-month, one-day car trip to visit relatives is less likely to stop happening or decrease in frequency because of a gas price increase than taking a family summer vacation trip that can involve driving long distances. In other words, it would not be surprising to see a variation in the number of high-salience trips taken from year to year, accompanied by a lesser variation in less salient trips. Instead, the number is quite stable over the study period, with a very large variation in the numbers of less salient trips.

Sections A, B, and C of Table 4 help one see a pattern related to differences in CTS responses from year to year. Section A of Table 4 presents the proportion of all trips in a year or month that were of high-salience. This proportion was only 0.26 in 1994 but 0.31 in 1996 and 0.33 in 1997. These figures show an increase in the relative proportion of all reported trips that are of high-salience from 1994 to 1997. Section B provides the proportion of trips with low-salience. Here one may observe that the proportion of trips of low-salience was about 0.40 in 1994 and that it drops to 0.37 in 1996 and 0.36 in 1997. Section C shows the ratio between Section B (low-salience trips) and Section A (high-salience trips). The value of 1.54 indicates that it is necessary to multiply the number of high-salience trips in 1994 by this factor to obtain the number of low-salience trips for that year. The comparable multiplier for 1996 is 1.22 and just 1.08 for 1997. In other words, the ratio of low-salience trips to high-salience trips drops from 1994 to 1997. This suggests that there may be an under-reporting of low-salience trips

Table 4 Information to Use in Understanding the Estimation of Recall Salience Bias and its Correction in 1994, 1996, and 1997 Canadian Travel Survey (CTS) data

Information	Year	\multicolumn{13}{c}{Months}

Information	Year	1	2	3	4	5	6	7	8	9	10	11	12	Total
(BLC) Baseline	1996	1.09	1.12	0.95	0.97	1.05	1.16	0.97	1.08	1.09	1.06	1.01	0.81	1.03
Correction	1997	0.86	1.03	0.88	0.97	0.83	1.04	0.92	1.07	1.13	1.06	1.16	0.92	0.98
(A) Proportion	1994	0.24	0.22	0.27	0.26	0.25	0.23	0.33	0.31	0.24	0.25	0.23	0.29	0.26
of Trips of	1996	0.26	0.26	0.30	0.27	0.33	0.31	0.38	0.37	0.30	0.29	0.28	0.29	0.31
High-salience	1997	0.30	0.31	0.38	0.34	0.28	0.30	0.39	0.44	0.31	0.28	0.29	0.30	0.33
(B) Proportion	1994	0.45	0.49	0.49	0.43	0.41	0.42	0.34	0.35	0.39	0.41	0.42	0.35	0.40
of Trips of	1996	0.41	0.44	0.42	0.42	0.37	0.36	0.31	0.31	0.36	0.41	0.39	0.34	0.37
Low-salience	1997	0.12	0.12	0.32	0.34	0.40	0.38	0.31	0.29	0.35	0.39	0.39	0.33	0.36
(C) Example of	1994	1.91	2.26	1.66	1.68	1.60	1.81	1.01	1.17	1.61	1.61	1.85	1.24	1.54
Normalization	1996	1.58	1.69	1.43	1.54	1.12	1.15	0.83	0.84	1.22	1.38	1.43	1.18	1.22
of (B) to (A)	1997	1.37	1.37	0.85	1.02	1.44	1.25	0.79	0.68	1.15	1.40	1.34	1.07	1.08
(D1) Adjustment	1996	1.23	1.34	1.16	1.09	1.48	1.58	1.21	1.39	1.32	1.17	1.30	1.05	1.26
Factor for s <= .35	1997	1.39	1.65	1.94	1.64	1.11	1.45	1.27	1.73	1.40	1.15	1.38	1.16	1.42
(D2) Adjustment Factor	1996	1.05	0.96	1.10	0.87	1.53	1.09	1.17	1.32	1.20	1.32	1.15	0.97	1.14
for .35 < s <= .45	1997	1.32	1.04	1.40	0.92	0.86	0.89	1.12	1.70	0.97	1.03	1.00	0.99	1.08
(D3) Adjustment Factor	1996	1.09	1.25	1.22	1.15	1.46	1.52	1.22	1.30	1.37	1.29	1.32	1.03	1.26
for .45 < s <= .55	1997	1.51	1.89	1.44	1.47	1.23	1.71	1.34	1.81	1.57	1.12	1.69	1.04	1.45
Total Estimated	1994	10.40	10.90	10.40	9.90	10.70	10.80	13.90	14.90	11.00	9.20	8.20	10.10	130.50
Trips (k) from CTS	1996	10.20	9.90	8.70	9.00	8.90	9.30	11.70	13.10	19.80	8.60	7.10	8.10	114.40
	1997	6.80	7.80	6.50	7.30	8.40	8.70	10.70	11.20	9.80	8.90	7.80	8.80	102.70
Salience Corrected	1994	10.40	10.90	10.40	9.90	10.70	10.80	13.90	14.90	11.00	9.20	8.20	10.10	130.50
Estimated Trips (k)	1996	11.40	11.9	9.70	9.50	11.60	12.60	13.20	16.00	12.10	10.00	8.50	8.30	134.00
	1997	8.70	11.1	9.30	9.60	9.10	11.50	12.60	16.00	12.50	9.70	9.90	9.30	128.90
Per cent Change CTS	1996	11.80	19.9	11.70	6.00	30.10	34.50	13.40	21.90	22.90	15.80	20.40	2.20	17.20
Estimate to Corrected	1997	29.30	42.5	43.30	31.80	9.50	31.70	17.20	42.50	27.30	9.10	26.80	6.00	25.50

Note. s = salience value

in 1996 and 1997.

An under-reporting of low-salience trips is consistent with the methodological changes cited earlier in this paper, such as an increase in the length of the survey and the trend toward interviewing LFS respondents more frequently. A corollary of accepting that 1996 and 1997 CTS estimates are low as a consequence of under-reporting of low-salience trips is that 1994 data are better than those for 1996 and 1997. If one accepts the 'better than' characterization, it follows that it would be appropriate to somehow correct 1996 and 1997 estimates. Specifically, a weight could be developed to adjust for under-reporting of low-salience trips in the 1996 and 1997 CTS. Section D1 summarizes this type of correction for low-salience trips. In Section D1, one can see a value of 1.26 for 1996. This is obtained by dividing the 1994 ratio of low-salience trips to high-salience trips (from Section C) by the 1996 ratio: 1.54 / 1.22 = 1.26. Section D2 and Section D3 provide adjustment weights for trips of medium-low and of medium-high-salience.

Application of the corrections to estimated trip totals by level of salience for 1996 and 1997 yields the new estimates shown in Table 4. Table 4 also presents the magnitude of the adjustment. In other words, the magnitude of the under-reported trip bias for 1996 was 17.2% and it was 25.5% for 1997.

General Findings and Their Implications

It may be worth noting that the overall magnitude of trip-salience bias could actually be inferred from the baseline (BLC) in Table 4. Even if the overall magnitude of bias can be inferred, the weighting and calculations described in the previous paragraphs are important because the magnitude of the bias varies by level of trip salience. Bias in a national estimate can be 17%, while it can be quite different for estimates of intraprovincial travel. The observation that bias differs radically for different types of trips can be expected to lead to some very interesting consequences. Estimates of intraprovincial travel, and especially intraprovincial same-day trips, will generally have average correction factors for under-reporting that are well above the overall factors, because most of these trips have low-salience. A correction of 50% would not be unexpected. On the other hand, an estimate of such trips being much larger may have relatively little impact on national expenditure estimates, because low-salience trips do not contribute much to expenditure totals. Still, since travel within a province includes a large number of low-salience trips and may not include many high-salience trips, some provincial expenditure estimates could be substantially altered by correction.

As with any scientific endeavour, the results presented are open to alternative interpretations. It is conceivable that at least some of the bias observed may simply be random error. Then there may be external factors that have not been recognized that relate both to change in taking trips and to the salience of trips taken. The results from Beaman *et al.* (1999) identifying external factors as a basis for challenging the ideas presented in this paper were presented to the research committee for the CTS including the Canadian Tourism Commission (CTC), provincial tourism department representatives, and Statistics Canada, in 1999. Subsequently, a specific request for critical comment was made to CTC. Within the roughly one year between the bias explanation procedure presented here being made available and submission of this paper for publication, no evidence of external factors explaining anything has been offered. In fact, as of July 2000, no communication has been received by the authors either supporting alternative explanations for their findings or citing technical flaws with their analysis.

Though this paper is not intended for CTS clients, some findings presented in a paper for these clients (Beaman *et al.,* 1999) should interest readers of this paper. Prior to this research, Statistics Canada was proposing that: (a) the 1994 CTS survey should not be compared to 1996 and 1997 surveys to define trends; (b) the 1996 and 1997 surveys can be compared to establish trends; and (c) it is not possible to declare one survey as better or less biased than the others. In contrast, the results of this study lead to the conclusions: (a) that 1994, 1996, and 1997 can be compared after correction; (b) incorrect results will be obtained if 1996 and 1997 are compared without correction; and (c) 1994 is the least biased of the three surveys.

Some important practical matters related to data collection arise from this research. First, if chronological reporting produces better results than current CTS methodology, should a switch be made? The problem is that it is important to take measures to ensure consistency of CTS estimates over time. Switching to chronological reporting without a viable plan to preserve continuity over time can be expected to invalidate the CTS time series, much as this paper implies that the consistency of the CTS series was destroyed by the post-1994 changes in CTS methodology. Furthermore, increasing accuracy by utilizing chronological reporting is not the only option that should be considered. The research by Menon (1997) introduced earlier suggests that one strategy that could be incorporated into many options is to be more explicit in requesting types of trips (e.g. one could ask for chronological reporting of several categories of trips with the order of the categories being systematically changed so bias caused by 'order of asking' could be estimated and eliminated). A second option is to use the method presented here to produce corrected CTS estimates so that one has comparable estimates starting from 1994. This line of consideration has at least three elements: (a) Is the correction well enough developed that it should currently be applied for other than research purposes? (b) Would the clients for the data use the corrected data if produced? and (c) Who would do the correction and who would update TRS salience scales? The authors support the position that more research is necessary. Whether that research will be supported or a correction will be tested or implemented presumably depends on the clients for the CTS data.

From the perspective of theory development and hypothesis testing, ideas and approaches in this paper also suggest lines of research. For example, the problems raised by the TRS scale being estimated in a simplistic way have already been addressed (Beaman *et al.,* 2000) by developing the regression estimation approach introduced earlier. From a different perspective, a number of bias factors may be operative in the CTS. It will be fascinating to see estimates of impacts on CTS results when Statistics Canada collects certain control data (e.g. data on other surveys responded to by a CTS respondent in an LFS interview, order of responding to various surveys, and number of times the CTS respondent has already responded to CTS in earlier LFS interviews). It could be very interesting if Statistics Canada, as they can using CATI, applied treatments such as add-on surveys in a designed way so as to allow their impact to be estimated. Hopefully, future designs of the CTS will also address the possibility that there is a CTS bias occurring that the correction procedure introduced here cannot detect. Specifically, given the 1992 attempt to collect CTS data from the same respondent several times (one can obtain information on this matter from Statistics Canada at the addresses given in Appendix 1), it is reasonable to believe that some respondents who are approached for a second time for the CTS will simply report 'no trips'. The bias correction method introduced can adjust for under-reporting of low-salience trips but it does not adjust for complete non-reporting. It is only when one has data on number of times that a respondent has been asked to reply to the CTS, and can obtain data on respondents in a given month who have been in the LFS for the same number of months, but differ in number of times responding to the CTS, that one can make estimates to determine what proportion of respondents report no travel to avoid answering the CTS a second or third time.

Finally, there is no question that the bias estimation and correction method introduced depends on the validity of the assumptions upon which it is based. The other side of the coin is that the only simple explanation for the radical change in the distribution of trips according to their TRS scale values is that the methodological change in the CTS is the cause. In this context, constructive critique of this research can follow two lines. One is to offer an alternative rationale for the large change in the salience distribution of trips. The other is to pursue the research avenues opened to show their viability or where they fail. Proposals for pursuing salience-based research that have been presented or are being acted upon are:

1. More accurate measurement of salience.
2. The structure behind the salience measure and change in the salience distribution between years.
3. Studying the influence of multiple administrations of the CTS to the same respondents and the influence of add-ons on bias by examining the relationship between salience distributions and the add-on surveys administered to different LFS rotations (although data are not available on individuals on the number of times the CTS was responded to and the add-ons responded to, data are available on the LFS rotation of respondents and thus aggregate information on the add-on treatment administered to respondents by Statistics Canada).
4. Using new estimates of salience and new analysis methods that do not depend on putting salience estimates into categories to develop more accurate computation of bias correction factors.
5. Research on the influence of asking more specific questions about types of trips and the influence of having to report on fewer trips is possible because of a special strategy pursued in 1997 in which two-thirds of CTS respondents only reported on interprovincial trips. Huan *et al.* (2000) show a significant impact on estimates of change in travel as a consequence of the altered interview strategy, while the estimation approach adopted by Statistics Canada for 1997 assumes no impact. Such research may, in fact, show that 1997 estimates are biased differently from 1994 and 1996 for a reason that has not yet been recognized.

Conclusions

This paper has introduced a methodology that has high potential value. One consequence should be to encourage research that will result in better CTS estimates and thus better analyses of these important Canadian data. Obviously, 'better' must be taken in context and further research, such as that identified above, should serve to clarify the benefits of and the problems with the bias correction methodology. Certainly, when large amounts of money are spent on data, and significant expenditures on the tourism plant and marketing may be partially predicated on those estimates, then taking appropriate actions to see that the estimates are not misleading (such as examining estimates corrected for bias based on the method suggested) is a low cost way to guard against costly mistakes. It is worth noting that prior to this research, the vehicle did not exist to make corrections for the bias in the CTS identified by this research. Naturally, there may be legitimate worries that the methodology introduced is experimental. The fortunate matter is that by providing corrected estimates to clients for the CTS, or clients for other data to which the method is applied, an opportunity is created. When clients have alternative estimates, let us say corrected estimates, they can see if the correction makes a difference and if it does they have a chance to consider how proposed planning or spending strategies may fare if the future resembles the situation implied by the corrected estimates more than that suggested by the original ones.

Endnotes

[1] Contact Information: General information on the Canadian Travel Survey can be obtained from the Culture and Tourism Program of the Culture, Tourism, and Centre for Education Statistics Division; R.H. Coats Building, Statistics Canada, Ottawa, Ontario, K1A 0T6. Information on methodology can be obtained from the Special Surveys Division, Statistics Canada, Jean Talon Building.

References

Anderson, J.R. and Reder, L.M. (1979) An elaborative processing explanation of depth of processing. In: Cermak, L.S. and Craik, F.I.M. (eds.) *Levels of Processing in Human Memory.* Erlbaum, Hillsdale, NJ, pp. 385-403.

Auctor Consulting Associates, Ltd. (1998, July) *The Canadian Travel Survey - An External Review: Presentations of Findings.* Study presented to the Canadian Tourism Commission. Ottawa, Canada. (Available from auctor@igs.net upon request.)

Beaman, J.G., Beaman, J.P., O'Leary, J.T. and Smith, S. (1999*) Implications of methodological differences among the 1994, 1996, and 1997 Canadian Travel Surveys.* Manuscript submitted for publication.

Beaman, J.G., Hill, A. and O'Leary, J.T. (2000) *Recall salience: Concept, use, and estimation.* Manuscript submitted for publication. (Available from auctor@igs.net upon request.)

Craik, F.I.M. and Lockhart, R.S. (1972) Levels of processing: A framework for memory research. *Journal of Verbal Learning and Verbal Behavior* 11(6), 671-684.

Hill, A., Beaman, J.G. and O'Leary, J. (1999) Does the suggestion that respondents recall events chronologically significantly influence the data collected? Forthcoming in: *Proceedings of the 2000 Northeastern Research Symposium, USFS, Northeastern Forest Experiment Station.* (Available from auctor@igs.net upon request.)

Hill, A., Beaman, J.G. and O'Leary, J. (2000) Does the Suggestion that Respondents Recall Events Chronologically Significantly Influence the Data Collected? Presented to NERR in April 1999. In: U.S. Department of Agriculture, Forest Service (ed.) *Proceedings of the 2000 Northeastern Recreation Research Symposium.* Northeastern Forest Experiment Station.

Huan, T.C., Beaman, J.G. and Grenier, M. (2000) The impact of an apparently insignificant question change on estimates of travel. Unpublished manuscript.

Kunert, U. (1998) Detecting long-term trends in travel behaviour: Problems associated with repeated national personal travel surveys. In: Ortúzar, J., Hensher, D. and Jara-Díaz, S. (eds.) *Travel Behaviour Research: Updating the State of Play.* Elsevier Science Ltd., Oxford, pp. 263-277.

Menon, G. (1997) Are the parts better than the whole? The effects of decompositional questions on judgments of frequent behaviors. *Journal of Marketing Research* 34(3), 335-346.

Saaty, T.L. (1977) A scaling method for priorities in hierarchical structures. *Journal of Mathematical Psychology* 15(3), 234-281.

Schacter, D.L. (1987) Implicit memory: History and current status. *Journal of Experimental Psychology: Learning, Memory, and Cognition* 13(3), 501-518.

Schmidt, S.R. (1991) Can we have a distinctive theory of memory? *Memory and Cognition* 19(6), 523-542.

Statistics Canada (2000, March) Canadian travel survey microdata user's guide (Catalogue Nr.87M0006GPE). Available via:
www.statcan.ca/english/IPS/Data/87M0006GPE.htm

Tulving, E. and Thomson, D.M. (1973) Encoding specificity and retrieval processes in episodic memory. *Psychological Review* 80(5), 359-380.

Winograd, E. and Neisser, U. (eds.) (1992) *Affect and Accuracy in Recall: Studies of 'Flashbulb' Memories.* Cambridge University Press, Cambridge, NY

Woodside, A.G. and Ronkainen, I.A. (1993) Consumer memory and mental categorization in international travel destination decision making. *Journal of International Consumer Marketing* 5(3), 89-104.

Chapter five
A Review of Choice Modelling Research in Tourism, Hospitality and Leisure

Geoffrey I. Crouch
School of Tourism and Hospitality, Faculty of Law and Management,
La Trobe University, Bundoora, Melbourne, Victoria, Australia

Jordan J. Louviere
University of Sydney, Australia

Abstract

An understanding of how consumers make choices in the field of tourism, hospitality and leisure (THL) is of great interest to enterprises, organizations and destinations operating in this sector of the economy. Choice Modelling (CM) offers powerful methodologies for the analysis of consumer choice, and the growing application of this approach in THL holds the promise of major advances in knowledge if such studies are well designed and executed. This paper reviews methodological developments in CM and the state of CM research in THL through a review of 43 CM studies. The paper emphasizes the theoretical and methodological advantages of Discrete Choice Analysis based on Random Utility Theory combined with state-of-the-art experimental design procedures for the gathering of Stated Preference data.

Introduction

Consumer behaviour and choice in the tourism, hospitality and leisure (THL) industries, while sharing many things in common with other industry or product contexts, possesses a number of distinguishing characteristics (Johnson and Thomas 1992, pp. 4-5). For example, the buying process typically is more highly involved when consumers purchase THL products. Although some choices are relatively simple and well-defined (e.g. choosing a fast-food restaurant for a meal), many choices are extremely complex and multifaceted (Dellaert *et al.*, 1998a, p. 313) (e.g. the array of choices involved when a family undertakes a vacation). Compared, say, to purchasing a package of breakfast cereal from among a discrete, readily identified range of options, the choices involved in assembling the elements of a vacation, including its quantity and quality, makes the modelling of choice much more challenging in THL.

Several other issues complicate THL choice-modelling: (1) THL services often are extended in time; (2) THL choices occur in both pre-consumption and consumption stages; (3) THL choices often have considerable emotional or affective content, and choice models must take into account effect and cognition (Neelameghan and Jain, 1999; Shiv and Fedorikhin, 1999) (4) many THL choices may involve variety-seeking for particular individuals; and (5) many THL products (e.g. tourist destinations) have attributes that are inherently fixed to the brand, insofar as brand attributes cannot be readily varied to study choice behaviour.

Models of consumer choice are of widespread interest because they help us to understand demand and its economic impacts. Choice models can vary from very general conceptual models such as the Howard-Sheth model of buyer behaviour (Howard and Sheth, 1969), or Bettman's information-processing model of consumer choice (Bettman, 1979), to more specific numerical models addressing particular products and consumption situations. In this article, we focus on the theory, research and development of the latter type of choice model. In particular, we are concerned with decompositional choice models (June and Smith, 1987; Ding *et al.*, 1991, p. 21) that is, models that decompose the total utility of each choice alternative by estimating the partial utilities associated with each attribute that defines alternatives.

Decompositional models of choice processes have been derived in previous research using a variety of approaches known variously as conjoint analysis, discrete choice analysis, or tradeoff analysis. Although, in our view, only methods consistent with random utility theory are appropriate for choice models, for the purpose of this paper we consider other decompositional models of choice as well.

Choice modelling studies in THL have begun to grow in numbers, as we shall see shortly. In leisure and recreation research, 'conjoint preference and choice models have been used ... for a considerable time now' (Stemerding *et al.*, 1999, p. 155). In tourism and hospitality, most studies have focused on destination choice (Dellaert *et al.*, 1998a, p. 314; Jeng and Fesenmaier, 1998), hotel design, and restaurant selection.

The next section briefly compares these approaches. Then we review a number of THL choice-modelling studies, and briefly describe methodological issues and challenges. We conclude with some thoughts on future directions for choice modelling in THL.

Approaches to Choice Modelling

The purpose of this section is to focus on some issues that are particularly germane to applications of the theory and methods of choice modelling to THL research.

The literature on choice modelling is sometimes inconsistent and confusing. Different techniques, analytical methods, and theories can be used decompositionally to model consumer choice, and the literature often has not been consistent in the labels assigned to these various approaches. Marketing researchers typically use the term *conjoint analysis* and focus on the deterministic character of choice. Econometricians study the probabilistic nature of choice using *discrete choice analysis* derived from random utility theory (RUT). In marketing, the term 'conjoint analysis' (CA) has been used to refer to all forms of choice modelling as well as methods not explicitly based on random utility theory. However, CA does not include all forms of choice modelling; hence, is inherently a more limiting term, despite widespread attempts in marketing to try to generalize it (see, for example, Louviere *et al.*, 1999a). Indeed, strictly speaking, any given application of CA may or may not be consistent with RUT, and many sources of choice data need not resemble CA. Thus, we will use the term 'discrete choice analysis' (DCA) to refer to methods that are consistent with RUT. The focus of this paper is on DCA methods.

More importantly, the vast majority of CA applications are based on statistical theory rather than behavioural theory (Verma *et al.*, 1999, p. 263, 265). In contrast, DCA is based on RUT, which is a behavioural theory that recognizes that preferences have both deterministic and stochastic (random) components. Probabilistic DCA models 'permit the researcher to make inferences about the parameters of utility models, and in so doing reject incorrect models' (Louviere, 1984, p. 86).

Random utility-based choice models

Random utility theory is not new. Thurstone (1927) first proposed it as a way to study and model comparisons of and choices between pairs of options. RUT posits that the utility of a choice option, such as a particular convention site option, is an unobservable or *latent* quantity that exists in the mind of a decision-maker (DM). Although researchers cannot peer into DMs' minds, they can observe the choices that DM's make, and with appropriate study design, they can make inferences about factors that drive choices.

In particular, RUT posits that the latent utility can be decomposed into an explainable or *systematic* component and an unexplainable or *random* component:

$$U_{in} = V_{in} + \varepsilon_{in}$$

where U_{in} is the unobservable, latent utility that consumer n associates with choice option i; V_{in} is the observable, systematic component of utility for consumer n and choice option i; and ε_{in} is the random component associated with option i and consumer n. The random component implies that individual consumer choices are inherently stochastic when viewed from a researcher's perspective. Thus, one can predict the probability that a randomly selected consumer will choose each of several options offered, but not the exact choice itself. That is,

$$P(i|C_n) = P[(V_{in} + \varepsilon_{in}) > (V_{jn} + \varepsilon_{jn})]$$

for all j options in choice set C_n faced by consumer n.

In other words, the probability of choosing option i is equal to the probability that the sum of the systematic and random components for option i (i.e., the 'total utility' of i) is larger than the corresponding sums (or total utilities) of all $j = 1, 2, \ldots, J$ options in choice set C faced by consumer n. All RUT-based choice models are derived by making assumptions about the distribution and statistical properties of the random components of utility. Once an assumption is made, then it is possible to estimate the derived model form using various estimation methods, such as maximum likelihood or more recently, various forms of Bayesian estimation. To do this, one has to impose additional structure on the $V_{\bullet}$'s, and this usually is achieved by assuming a linear in the parameters, regression-like form, such as:

$$V_i = \beta_{0i} + \sum_k \beta_k X_{ki} + \sum_m \gamma_m Z_{mi}$$

where β_k and γ_m are parameters that capture effects due to variables that describe the choice options (X_{ki}) or the DMs (Z_{mi}). This specification is not limiting, but rather can be generalized to include a wide array of possible non-linear and non-additive effects, such as interactions of $Z_.$'s with model intercepts or $X_.$'s.

By 'statistical properties' of distributions we mean whether (a) errors are independent, serially or otherwise correlated, (b) model intercepts and parameters are fixed for all consumers, or follow some type of joint multivariate distribution and/or are fixed for discrete groups (segments) or consumers, or (c) others. McFadden (1974) significantly advanced Thurstone's (1927) contribution by extending RUT to multiple choices by considering distributions other than the Normal. That is, Thurstone assumed the random components to be Normally distributed with a general variance–covariance structure. Unfortunately, the Normal does not permit one to derive choice models that have a simple closed form for the probabilities, and computation of the multiple integrals beyond the case of three choice options proved to be a formidable barrier to progress until the last decade or so (e.g. see Revelt and Train, 1998).

McFadden (1974) assumed that the random components were independently and identically distributed (IID) Gumbel (Weibul, Extreme Value Type I) random variates, which leads to a simple closed form specification for the choice probabilities known as the multinomial logit (MNL) model. Over the past 25 years there has been steady progress in relaxing various aspects of the IID assumption that results in MNL. Thus, MNL is a very popular, computationally tractable model, and software for the estimation of MNL models is now widely available in many popular statistical software packages, but it also is fair to say that MNL rarely has been shown to be a good approximation to the choice process of consumers despite many tests of its adequacy. Thus, the choice modelling community, or more correctly the practitioner community, must tradeoff computationally simple, easy-to-estimate and apply MNL models that almost always are incorrect for more accurate, computationally demanding and much less easily applied choice model forms, such as multinomial probit (MNP), random parameter-mixed logit (RPML) or various other forms that relax the IID assumptions (see for example Hensher et al., 1999; Revelt and Train, 1999; Louviere et al., 2000).

Review of choice modelling studies in THL

An effort was made to identify, obtain and review as many published research studies that have attempted to model consumer THL preferences as possible. Table 1 summarizes 42 such studies, briefly describing their aim, design, and analytical method. Nineteen of the studies employed discrete choice analysis (DCA) on stated preference data (SP) based on random utility theory (RUT). Another 16 studies applied conjoint analysis (CA). Of the other eight studies, the analytical method was unclear in four cases; four studies used MNL DCA models to analyse revealed-preference (RP) data. The majority of studies modelled the choice process related to tourism destinations (9), restaurants (8), recreational activities (6), and hotels (5). Others included transportation (5), travel packages (3), events (2), other hospitality (2), incentive travel (1), amusement parks (1), and tourism developments (1). The majority of studies undertook an experiment of some sort to gather stated-preference data.

The studies vary a great deal in terms of complexity and sophistication. For example, the study by Goldberg *et al.* (1984) included 43 hotel attributes (at 2 to 5 levels each) grouped into 6 facets each represented at 5 levels. Louviere and Hensher (1983) used two, interlocking choice experiments to combine 5 World Expo types at 2 levels each, with price at 2 levels and 6 Expo attributes in a $4^3 \times 2^3$ factorial design. The four THL studies reported by Louviere and Woodworth (1983) illustrate the power and flexibility that careful and thoughtful experimental design offers the choice modeller. The complex study by Wind *et al.* (1989) resulted in the design of 50 attributes for a new hotel concept. Their choice experiment represented these 50 attributes with 2 to 8 levels. The attributes were grouped into 7 facets each represented at 5 levels. In contrast, the studies by Morey *et al.* (1991) and Morley (1994) employed as few as 6 and 3 attributes respectively in relatively more simple experimental designs.

The more simplistic studies produced results of limited value. For example, in a number of cases it was clear that the studies were undertaken for illustrative purposes with small convenience samples of respondents. Studies that focused on producing results for real managerial decisions seemed to be more complex and sophisticated.

It is clear that successful and useful choice modelling studies that produce reliable and valid results require an in-depth knowledge of choice modelling theory, experimental design procedures, analytical methods, and the substantive area of application in THL. Particularly in a THL context, where products and choice alternatives tend to be more complex, choice attributes are usually more numerous and are harder to define and measure or represent, and sizes of choice experiments may be very large if all important factors are included in experiments and subsequent model(s). The latter considerations strongly suggest that considerable knowledge, expertise, skill and great care are required to be successful.

Finally, it is fair to say about the THL studies we reviewed that, collectively their results probably do more for advancing choice modelling theory and design than they do with respect to advancing our understanding of choice theory in a THL context.

Methodological Issues and Challenges

Preference elicitation procedures consistent with RUT

The earlier discussion provided a framework for understanding the basics of RUT, and how one derives a choice model by making various assumptions about the random utility components of choice options. That naturally leads to a discussion about types of data that can be used to implement the models by estimating the parameters of the various models derived from RUT. This discussion is particularly germane to THL applications of choice models because many such applications pose special challenges that we will discuss later.

We begin by noting that any source of preference information or data that contains ordinal (or rank order) information about preferences or choices is consistent with RUT (see Louviere *et al.*, 1999b, 2000). Economists traditionally have relied on so-called 'revealed preference' (RP) data that consists of observations of the actual choices made by samples of consumers. Some RP data sources provide accurate information about other choice options that were available for choice, but were rejected, but analysts who use RP data often do not really know what was considered and rejected. Unfortunately, as Swait (1984) demonstrated, incorrect specification of choice sets (i.e. the set of both chosen and rejected choice options) for individual consumers can lead to considerable estimation bias. Thus, despite the fact that RP data continues to be held up by many as the 'gold standard' the reality is that very often one trades-off apparent external validity for unknown levels of bias due to incorrect choice set specification.

The latter problem is very difficult to remedy unless one can observe each DM's choice set accurately at the time of choice. For example, scanner panel data appear to provide highly relevant and externally valid observations of consumer choices of fast moving consumer goods. However, in reality analysts have little to no knowledge of the actual choice sets faced by individual DMs, nor can they accurately detect and define the nature of a non-choice decision. For example, suppose a DM goes to a store but does not buy Munchy-Crunchies (MC). Did the DM go to the MC shelf, consider MCs and competing brands and decide not to buy any? Or, did the DM not go near the MC shelf, and subsequently checkout without ever having considered MCs on that visit? Differences in these types of behaviour have profound implications for choice models because they bear on whether models accurately reflect demand.

More importantly, perhaps, is the simple fact that RP data only contain information about preferences for existing options. Often existing markets exhibit very high correlations among key variables that describe choice options due to market forces (e.g. competitors tend to copy and/or match successful product features and prices) and technological limitations (e.g. physics dictates that heavy autos cannot have fast acceleration and low fuel consumption). These characteristics of markets and the RP data observations taken in them unfortunately suggest that very rarely will RP data be of much use for modelling purposes. The reasons are simple, obvious, logical and compelling: much RP data exhibits very high or even extreme levels of collinearity, there is a lack of identification of some options due to perfect correlations with other options (Morley, 1994, p. 8), and there is no information about how preferences and choices will change if new features or choice options are added or environmental or related circumstances depart much from recent past conditions (Haider and Ewing, 1990, p. 34).

For the aforementioned reasons, many researchers have turned to stated preference (SP) data in the past two decades (Lieber and Fesenmaier, 1984, p. 32; Ewing and Haider, 1999; and Stemerding *et al.*, 1999, p. 135). SP data consist of observations about what consumers say that they will do, instead of what they actually did. Many forms of such data exist and are consistent with RUT: consumers (a) report on their most recent choice; (b) report on which options in a list they would actually choose; (c) report on how they would rank options in preference order (including indicating all the options that they would not choose no matter what); (d) report on preferences for options by rating each on a scale; or (e) many more. Because such SP reports are consistent with RUT, these sources of preference information can be compared on a level playing field and, perhaps more importantly, they also can be compared with RP data from the same or independent samples of consumers.

The latter ability may surprise many researchers, but in fact the theory to compare preference data sources has been available for some time. For example, Ben-Akiva and Morikawa (1989) demonstrated that one could combine SP and RP data to test whether the underlying preferences revealed by each source were the same using RUT (they were). Since the path-breaking work of Ben-Akiva and Morikawa, quite a few additional tests have compared RP and SP data; and it is fair to say that most suggest that preferences in both decision environments are very similar. Some recent reviews of this research include Hensher *et al.* (1999) and Louviere *et al.* (1999a,b, 2000).

Finally, we note that theory to design choice experiments consistent with RUT has been available for more than 15 years. Choice experiments represent ways to design choice options and choice sets presented to samples of consumers in surveys to observe their choices under controlled conditions. Since the pioneering work on choice experiment design by Louviere and Woodworth (1983), there have been many advances in our understanding of the consequences of various ways to design such experiments. However, despite the passage of time, much remains unknown and unresolved about design. Specifically, we understand how to design choice experiments that are consistent with very general forms of choice models, such that identification of these models can be achieved. However, the quality (efficiency) of the parameters estimated from such experiments and the power of the resulting tests remains largely unexplored, although there has been progress in understanding efficiency in the binary choice case (e.g. Street *et al.*, 1999).

Choice experiments are attractive to academics and practitioners because they avoid many, if not most, of the problems associated with RP data. As well, choice experiments can be designed to simulate actual choices and choice conditions faced by real consumers as closely as possible, the barriers being time and resources. Thus, it should be noted that one can design a choice experiment to resemble a real market as closely as one wants, including, at the limit, designing the real choice environment itself. Thus, the key issue is the external and predictive validity of choice experiments, and this has been the subject of considerable research attention since the mid-1980s. As previously noted, there have been a number of tests of the comparability of RP and choice experiment SP data, and again it is fair to say that the research record supports the conclusion that very often preferences in both markets are quite similar (see previous sources cited).

Designing the choice experiment in complex cases to match the real choice environment can present some methodological challenges. As the choice environment in THL is often complex in terms of the number of potentially significant choice attributes, full factorial experiments are normally not possible for resource reasons. Nor are they feasible in terms of the quantity and quality of data required from each subject of the experiment. Many of these problems can be addressed, however, through careful experimental design using fractional factorial designs, hybrid methods of data collection (Goldberg *et al.,* 1984, p. S115), or hierarchical choice models (Oppewal *et al.*, 1994).

Illustration: convention site choice

To illustrate methodological issues and challenges in THL further, we consider the case of convention site choice. The authors are presently designing a choice modelling study to understand how association meeting planners and the Executive Boards of such associations choose from among potential convention host cities that compete nationally or internationally. The following considerations are germane:

- There are very large numbers of convention sites from which to choose regionally and globally, and often within a particular large city such as New York, London or Sydney, there can be many options.
- Many sites possess unique features in the sense that one cannot separate the Sydney harbour from Sydney, nor can one manipulate or change things like climate, geography and the like.

The problem posed by large numbers of choices is that, in the absence of accurate information about the actual sites that were/are/will be considered by one or more persons responsible for the ultimate choice, one risks serious bias by mis-specifying choice sets. That is, one needs highly accurate information about the actual candidate convention sites that were considered and rejected as well as what was chosen. Without that, one must make assumptions that are likely to be untenable, such as assuming that all possible convention sites were considered. The problem posed by unique site features is that one cannot use the actual names of sites as choice options because the random components will be correlated with these unique features, leading to a variety of nasty bias problems.

Choice experiments can successfully overcome both problems, but choice experiments require the following issues to be resolved to be successful:

1. Identification of the key drivers (attributes) of site choice;
2. Assignment of appropriate levels, and ranges of levels, to the drivers;
3. Identification and development of appropriate choice options from which site selection DMs choose;
4. Development of appropriate ways to design choice experiments that will simulate the DM's choice process accurately and permit us to understand and predict their choices.

Much progress has been made in identifying a comprehensive, mutually exclusive and exhaustive enumeration of convention site selection factors or attributes by Crouch and Ritchie (1998). This represents a useful first step, but we require considerable research and pilot testing to resolve issues 2 to 4 above.

Choice experiments come in two basic flavours – generic and alternative-specific. The former refers to experiments in which the choice options do not have names or labels that convey meaningful information to DMs about unobserved or missing information; and the latter refers to experiments in which choice options are named or labelled, and the moniker itself may convey information about unobserved or missing information. For example, 'Option A' conveys no information useful to a DM, but the name 'Sydney' may (e.g. beautiful harbour, mild climate, excellent restaurants, etc.). To the extent that certain attributes that are uniquely associated with a particular site cannot be varied, one risks bias induced by using site-specific names or labels that convey this information. For example, one cannot realistically vary the nature of Sydney's harbour or climate in an experiment, except in a limited way, such as providing possible weather scenarios for the time of the convention. However, one can vary things like restaurant quality and numbers, cultural attractions, etc. In general, physical features that cannot be changed readily, if at all, cannot be varied, but human features can be varied if one provides consumers with plausible and believable reasons why they might vary.

Due to time and resource constraints, it is unlikely that convention planners realistically consider very many sites for any particular convention. What we need to understand is the distribution of numbers and types of sites that are considered by various types of convention planners and site selectors. In that way, we can make appropriate tradeoffs between numbers of choice options and numbers of attributes and features about which to provide information. Unfortunately, to characterize the decisions accurately, we also need to know how DMs process the information to make choices; that is, we need to know what types of choice models best approximate the underlying choice processes. For example, it is likely to be the case that DMs first consider general locations, such as Florida, Southern California or Arizona for a winter convention in North America. Within each of these choices are additional, more specific locations, such as Los Angeles, San Diego, Palm Springs or Santa Barbara for California. And within each of these cities, there are likely to be multiple hotel or related convention venue choices. Such a progress is hierarchical or tree-like in nature, which can be represented by various sequential choice process models like nested logit. However, before one designs and implements a choice experiment, one needs to have a reasonable idea of which process(es) is(are) likely to be most appropriate so that one can develop the best possible ways to design the experiment to estimate these classes of models.

Fortunately, choice experiments are very flexible and powerful ways to obtain preference or choice information. Thus, if the above issues can be satisfactorily resolved, it is possible to design experiments that will maximize one's ability to estimate valid and accurate models of the choice process. Hopefully, this discussion has made it obvious that successful choice modelling is not simple, and success is not insured by acquiring and using off-the-shelf commercial software in the absence of very significant investments of research and understanding in advance of the primary research effort itself.

Conclusions and Future Directions

Over the past couple of decades, CM theory and practice has progressed significantly. A substantial number of studies have accumulated, yielding important advances in a number of areas including: (1) the application of random utility theory to CM applications; (2) understanding the statistical properties of the multinomial logit model; (3) combining the principles of experimental design with discrete choice analysis to develop innovative, powerful and flexible approaches to CM limitations and challenges; and (4) improving efficient approaches to handling large factorial problems, among others.

In the field of THL, although a range of simplistic to quite sophisticated CM studies have been identified, THL remains a fertile field for further research in this area. Several researchers have pointed to specific needs. Haider and Ewing (1990, p. 45) note the suitability of choice modelling for destination planning purposes, and observe that 'there is considerable scope for the application of this form of preference analysis in a wide range of situations in tourism research.' Dellaert *et al.* (1997, p. 32) emphasize the need for modelling destination choice as a 'portfolio or interrelated choice behaviour' rather than as a problem of single choices. This point, and the need to consider socioeconomic constraints and social structures in choice models was reiterated by Dellaert *et al.* (1998a, p. 319). The importance of modelling multidestination travel choice was acknowledged by Jeng and Fesenmaier (1998) who suggested 'that there is a gap between the conventional choice models and "real" destination choice behaviour' (p. 85). The THL sector of the economy, although already very large, continues to grow strongly. Accordingly, the need to understand both consumer and organizational choice in a THL context will attract increasing attention. 'It is suggested that consumer perception and behaviour studies, as well as being conceptually challenging, are vitally needed areas of tourism research' (Carmichael, 1992, p. 104).

The challenging nature of the choice process in THL, as outlined in this paper, will stretch the skills of CM researchers. In the process, it is reasonable to expect and hope that future work in this area will produce both advances in CM methodology as well as advances in choice theory in THL. While many CM studies will, no doubt, be designed to address specific management decisions and situations, there is a clear need for CM research in THL to contribute more to general THL choice theory.

In this paper we have briefly outlined some of the features of THL that present a challenge to CM researchers. We have argued that random-utility based discrete choice analysis provides the most sound foundation for addressing these challenges. We have also suggested that stated preference data elicitation procedures supported by careful experimental design and analysis can be used to tackle many of the questions confronting managers and researchers who desire to understand THL choice processes with greater insight.

Appendix

Table 1 Summary of Choice Modelling Studies in THL

Reference	Project Aim	Design	Analytical Method
Anderson, Williams, Haider and Louviere (1995) (See also Orland, Daniel and Haider 1995; and Ewing and Haider 1999)	To assess effect of timber industry management on remote tourism/fishing location choice.	- 20 attributes with 2 to 8 levels - orthogonal resolution III fractional factorial design - 256 choice profiles locked into 8 sets of 16 pairs - visual depiction of certain attributes 800 respondents	- DCA - MNL using maximum likelihood
Bull and Alcock (1993)	Analyse the preferences of patrons for features of licensed clubs in Australia.	- 6 attributes at 3 or 4 levels (3^7x4^1) - 206 respondents rated either 16 or 26 full profiles from an orthogonal design	- CA - used Conjoint Analyzer and SPSS
Carmichael (1992)	Analysis of destination choice by downhill skiers in Victoria, British Columbia.	- 6 attributes each at 4 levels - orthogonal fractional factorial design - ranking of full profiles - 29 profiles (4 holdouts) - 100 respondents	- CA - OLS regression
Claxton (1994)	1. To develop a measure of quality of air service as perceived by business and pleasure travellers. 2. To determine importance of air trip components for Air Canada. 3. To assess consumers' perceptions of transatlantic airfare packages for non-business travel.	- 13 attributes at 3 to 5 levels - 60 tradeoff 'matrices' - 27 attributes at 2 to 5 levels - pictures used to depict some attributes - 12 attributes at 2 to 8 levels	- not reported - not reported - not reported
Cosper and Kinsley (1984)	Develop a choice model of preferences for cultural and leisure events in Canada.	- used a 4^4 deign - produced 8 profiles with the aid of 2 superimposed orthogonal Latin Squares - profiles were rank ordered	- CA - MONANOVA
Dellaert, Borgers and Timmermans (1997)	To assess interaction between destination choice and transportation choice as an example of a multi-choice problem.	- 8 destination attributes each at 3 levels - 2 transportation mode attributes at 3 levels - used 209 portfolio choice sets - orthogonal fractional factorial design	- DCA - 4 models tested: joint logit, nested logit, probit, and component-based logit - maximum likelihood estimation

Study	Purpose	Design	Method
Dellaert, Prodigalidad and Louviere (1998b)	Investigate the influence of family members on family travel preferences.	- Contrasts day trips with 1-week holidays - 4 attributes at 2 to 4 levels - 70 families of respondents - ½ fractional factorial	DCA - uses a hierarchical approach to link individual preferences with family preferences
Ding, Geschke and Lewis (1991)	Model the choice of weekend hotel packages.	- 6 attributes with 2 to 4 levels - orthogonal fractional factorial design - 102 respondents - 16 profiles rated	CA - used Bretton Clark's Conjoint Designer and Conjoint Analyzer - OLS regression
Feather, Hellerstein and Tomasi (1995)	Analyse choice behaviour of Minnesota anglers.	- uses RP data - 1488 anglers	DCA - nested MNL - full information maximum likelihood estimation
Filiatrault and Ritchie (1988)	Investigate the effect of situational factors on the evaluation of a restaurant service.	- Experiment covers 3 dining situations - 5 attributes at 2 to 4 levels - rank ordering of 16 choice profiles in a fractional factorial design - 192 respondents	CA - used MONANOVA
Goldberg, Green and Wind (1984)	Investigate the determinants of hotel choice focusing on the role of price premiums.	- 43 attributes (at 2 to 5 levels) grouped into 6 hotel facets - 180 respondents - visual aids used to portray some attributes - 6 facets represented at 5 levels - 5 full profiles rated by each respondent	CA - hybrid approach used incorporating self-explicated utilities - dummy variable canonical correlation
Haider and Ewing (1990) (See also Ewing and Haider, 1999)	Analyse choice preferences of winter beach vacationers to Caribbean destinations.	- 10 attributes each at 3 levels - 27 profiles from a fractional factorial (310) design - 11th attribute used 5 island destinations - profiles manipulated in a 10x10 Latin Square design yielding 54 choice sets - 159 respondents evaluated 9 choice sets each	DCA - used MNL
Hu and Hiemstra (1996)	Examine hotel choice by meeting planners.	- 6 attributes at 2 or 4 levels - 1/64 fractional factorial $(4^5 x 2^1)$ design - 32 profiles in 4 blocks of 8 plus 2 holdout profiles	CA - used Bretton Clark's Conjoint Designer - used OLS regression

Author (year)	Objective	Details	Method
Jeng and Fesenmaier (1998)	Investigate interdependencies between choice of travel destinations by studying sign and significance of interaction terms in a choice model.	- 96 respondents - incomplete random block design of destination pairs - 78 scenarios were divided into 3 blocks of 26 - 1st model studied main and interaction effects - 2nd model entered perceived destination similarities as a covariate	- not clearly reported
Johnson and Nelson (1991)	Develop a choice model to predict market response to a range of service alternatives that could be offered by a long-distance passenger rail service known as the Indian Pacific in Australia.	- 6 attributes at 2 levels (2^5) - 1/4 fractional factorial of 16 profiles - rating and binary choice for each profile - 413 non-business respondents	- DCA - MNL - Weighted least squares estimation
June and Smith (1987)	Study choice of a restaurant meal in terms of service attributes and situational factors.	- 5 service attributes at 2 or 3 levels ($3^4 \times 2^1$) - 3 meal contexts (situations) - 18 profiles used for each context profiles were rank ordered - 50 respondents	- CA - dummy variable regression analysis
Lieber and Fesenmaier (1984)	Analyse choice of recreation trails.	- 5 attributes at 3 levels each (3^5) - 27 profiles based on 1/9 fractional factorial design - 173 respondents - each profile was rated	- CA - Regression analysis - 3 model functions: (a) linear additive model, (b) main effects and two-way interaction model, (c) log-linear model
Lindberg, Dellaert and Rassing (1999)	Study the tradeoffs residents are willing to make with respect to the impacts of tourism development.	- 4 attributes at 4 levels each - 16 profiles split into 2 halves - 391 respondents each assessed 8 profiles	- DCA - used MNL
Louviere and Hensher (1982)	Report results of a choice model for the selection of fast-food restaurants.	- 5 restaurants each at 2 levels (available/unavailable) (2^5) - 1/4 fractional factorial design - 99 respondents	- DCA - weighted least squares regression
Louviere and Hensher (1983)	To predict levels of attendance at a World Expo.	- 2 interlocking choice experiments - 1st had 5 attributes at 2 levels (2^5) - 1/4 fractional factorial design produced a 8 expo types - adding price at 2 levels produced a 2^8 factorial reduced to 16 treatments - 2nd experiment used 6 attributes at 2 and 4 levels - 698 respondents for 16 treatments	- DCA - used MNL

Study	Objective	Design details	Method
Louviere and Woodworth (1983)	1. Estimate the utilities of 11 alternative overseas holiday destinations by Australians.	- each of the 11 alternatives were modelled as a factor at 2 levels (2^{11}); chosen or not chosen - 2^4 fractional factorial design - 17 choice sets (2 for practice) - 75 respondents	- DCA - MNL - weighted least-squares regression
	2. Model vacation destination choice as a function of destination and air travel costs.	- models 5 destinations each at 3 levels of air fare (3^5) - orthogonal fractional factorial produced 18 choice sets - 40 respondents	- DCA - MNL - estimated generic linear cost, alternative-specific linear cost, and quadratic cost models
	3. Model choices among fast-food menus at various prices.	- 3 food attribute at 3 levels (3^3) - 1/3 fractional factorial (9 alternatives) - each alternative at 2 price levels (2^9) - 12 choice sets from orthogonal main effects plan - 99 respondents	- DCA - MNL - linear and quadratic models
	4. Model choice among alternative reduced airfare tickets from Sydney to the US west coast.	- 4 attributes of reduced fare tickets each at 2 levels (2^4) - 12 ticket combinations developed; each ticket treated at 2 levels (2^{12}) (i.e. selected or not selected) - 16 treatment-combinations selected - 35 respondents	- DCA - MNL - weighted least-squares regression
Louviere (1984)	Study a choice model for fast-food restaurants.	- 3 retail outlets - 2^5 design of 5 strategies at 2 levels - 1/2 fractional factorial of main effects and 2-way interactions - 116 respondents	- DCA - used MNL - generalized, weighted least squares
Mattila (1999)	Study tradeoffs that luxury hotels' business travellers are willing to accept between functional physical environments and personalized services.	- 6 attributes at 2 levels - fractional factorial design produced 10 scenarios - scenarios rated on value for money - 139 respondents	- CA - few details reported
Morey, Shaw and Rowe (1991)	Study demand for and benefits from marine recreational fishing along the Oregon coast as a function of species availability.	- uses RP date from 5855 anglers	- DCA - MNL - maximum likelihood estimation
Morley (1994)	Study the effect of tourism price components on the choice of international travel destination.	- 3 price attributes at 2 or 3 levels for the destination of interest (Sydney) - 12 choice sets - choice sets included 7 other destinations with fixed attribute levels - 193 respondents	- DCA - MNL - weighted least squares
Mouthino and Trimble (1991)	Develop a choice model of repeat visitation to the Grand Canyon.	- 9 attributes covering the individual and the trip - data from 404 personal interviews	- DCA - binary logit - maximum likelihood

Study	Objective	Design	Method/Analysis
Muhtbacher and Botschen (1988)	Examine the preferences for holiday package features.	- 5 attributes at 3 levels each (3^5) fractional factorial design of 16 profiles - profiles were rank ordered using the full-profile approach	- CA - ad hoc analytical method used
Neelameghan and Jain (1999)	Develop a choice model for the selection of new movies emphasizing the integration of psychological variables and processes within discrete choice model formulations.	- experiment used fixed advertising and manipulated critic reviews and word-of-mouth in a 2x2 design - 202 respondents	- DCA - confirmatory factor analysis - probit measurement error model - maximum likelihood
Renaghan and Kay (1987)	Model meeting planners' choice of meeting facilities.	- 5 attributes at 2 or 3 levels (2^2x3^3) ¼ fractional factorial design of 16 profiles - orthogonal design based on Latin Square - 113 respondents rated each profile	- CA - few details reported
Sheldon and Mak (1987)	Study the choice of vacation modes: independent travel, inclusive tour package, and basic tour package.	- uses RP data from 1292 respondents - choice modelled as a function of 8 variables	- binary logit model - maximum likelihood estimation
Sheldon (1995)	Model the choice by Fortune 1000 companies to use incentive travel to reward employees.	- uses RP data from 127 companies - choice modelled as a function of 7 variables	- binary logit model - maximum likelihood estimation
Siderelis and Moore (1998)	Analyse the choice by boat owners from among 17 alternative lakes in the North Carolina/Virginia region.	- used RP data from surveyed boat owners - 1336 cases covering 17 lakes plus no-lake alternative - model nested 17 lakes into 5 regions	- conditional logit - LIMDEP software for analysis
Stemerding, Oppewal and Timmermans (1999)	Develop a model of consumer choice of amusement parks in The Netherlands paying particular attention to leisure constraints.	- 4 amusement parks studied - 3 constraints at 2 levels (2^3) design - 8 car and 8 train modes nested within the constraints conditions - 256 single-profile and 1024 two-profile choice sets - 'no go' base alternative - 585 respondents received 8 single and 24 two-profile choice sets	- DCA - MNL - maximum likelihood
Sweeney, Johnson and Armstrong (1992)	Model the tradeoff choice of restaurant for two dining situations.	- 9 attributes at 2 or 3 levels (2^8x3^1) 1/48 fractional factorial design - 16 profiles plus 4 holdout profiles - 56 respondents	- CA - few details reported
Tucci and Talaga (1997)	Examine the influence of a service guarantee on the choice of a restaurant.	- 5 attributes at 3 levels (3^5) main effects only design - 32 restaurant profiles - 161 respondents	- CA - few details provided
van Limburg (1998)	Model the selection of tourist cities in a European context.	- 4 attributes at 2 or 3 levels (3^3x2^1) 9 city profiles were ranked by 45 respondents	- CA - OLS regression

Verma, Thompson and Louviere (1999) (See also Verma and Thompson, 1996)	Develop a choice model for the selection of a pizza delivery service.	- 7 attributes at 2 levels each (7^2) - 1/8 fractional factorial design producing 16 profiles - each profile was paired with its 'fold over' and a 'no choice' option - 128 respondents	- DCA - MNL using LIMDEP
Wind, Green, Shifflet and Scarbrough (1989)	A very detailed study for the purpose of designing the attributes of a new hotel concept – Courtyard by Marriott.	- used 7 facets of attributes each at 5 levels (5^7) - 50 attributes in total using 2 to 8 levels - used orthogonal fraction of 50 profiles - 601 respondents each rated 5 profiles	- CA - hybrid model using self-explicated utilities

References

Anderson, D.A., Williams, M.J., Haider, W. and Louviere, J.J. (1995) Efficient Experimental Designs for the Study of Remote Tourists' Destination Choice. In: Power, M.J., Strome, M. and Daniel, T.C. (eds.) *American Society for Photogrammetric and Remote Sensing.* Bethesda, Maryland, pp. 909-918.

Ben-Akiva, M.E. and Morikawa, T. (1989) Estimation of Switching Models from Revealed Preferences and Stated Intentions. *Transportation Research* 24A, 485-495.

Bettman, J.R. (1979) *An Information Processing Theory of Consumer Choice.* Addison Wesley, Reading, MA.

Bull, A.O. and Alcock, K.M. (1993) Patron Preferences for Features Offered by Licensed Clubs. *International Journal of Contemporary Hospitality Management* 5(1), 28-32.

Carmichael, B. (1992) Using Conjoint Modelling to Measure Tourist Image and Analyse Ski Resort Choice. In: Johnson, P. and Thomas, B. (eds.) *Choice and Demand in Tourism.* Mansell Publishing Limited, London, pp. 93-106.

Claxton, J.D. (1994) Conjoint Analysis in Travel Research: A Manager's Guide. In: Ritchie, J.R.B. and Goeldner, R. (eds.) *Travel, Tourism and Hospitality Research: A Handbook for Managers and Researchers,* 2nd edn. John Wiley and Sons, New York, pp. 513-522.

Cosper, R. and Kinsley, B.L. (1984) An Application of Conjoint Analysis to Leisure Research: Cultural Preferences in Canada. *Journal of Leisure Research* 16(3), 224-233.

Crouch, G.I. and Ritchie, J.R.B. (1998) Convention Site Selection Research: A Review, Conceptual Model, and Propositional Framework. *Journal of Convention and Exhibition Management* 1(1), 49-69.

Dellaert, B.G.C., Borgers, A.W.J. and Timmermans, H.J.P. (1997) Conjoint Models of Tourist Portfolio Choice: Theory and Illustration. *Leisure Sciences* 19, 31-58.

Dellaert, B.G.C., Ettema, D.F. and Lindh, C. (1998a) Multi-faceted Tourist Travel Decisions: A Constraint-based Conceptual Framework to Describe Tourists' Sequential Choices of Travel Components. *Tourism Management* 19(4), 313-320.

Dellaert, B.G.C., Prodigalidad, M. and Louviere, J.J. (1998b) Using Conjoint Analysis to Study Family Travel Preference Structures: A Comparison of Day Trips and 1-Week Holidays. *Tourism Analysis* 2, 67-75.

Ding, S., Geschke, U. and Lewis, R. (1991) Conjoint Analysis and Its Application in the Hospitality Industry. *Journal of the International Academy of Hospitality Research,* electronic issue no. 2, 1-31.

Ewing, G. and Haider, W. (1999) Estimating What Affects Tourist Destination Choice. In: Pizam, A. and Mansfield, Y. (eds.) *Consumer Behavior in Travel and Tourism.* The Haworth Hospitality Press, Binghamton, New York, pp. 35-58.

Feather, P., Hellerstein, D. and Tomasi, T. (1995) A Discrete-Count Model of Recreation Demand. *Journal of Environmental Economics and Management* 29, 214-227.

Filiatrault, P. and Ritchie, J.R.B. (1988) The Impact of Situational Factors on the Evaluation of Hospitality Services. *Journal of Travel Research* (Spring), 29-37.

Goldberg, S.M., Green, P.E. and Wind, Y. (1984) Conjoint Analysis of Price Premiums for Hotel Amenities. *Journal of Business* 57(1), 111-132.

Haider, W. and Ewing, G.O. (1990) A Model of Tourist Choices of Hypothetical Caribbean Destinations. *Leisure Sciences* 12, 33-47.

Hensher, D.A., Louviere, J.J. and Swait, J. (1999) Combining Sources of Preference Data. *Journal of Econometrics* 89, 197-221.

Howard, J.A. and Sheth, L.N. (1969) *The Theory of Buyer Behavior.* John Wiley and Sons, New York.

Hu, C. and Hiemstra, S.J. (1996) Hybrid Conjoint Analysis as a Research Technique to Measure Meeting Planners' Preferences in Hotel Selection. *Journal of Travel Research* 35, 62-69.

Jeng, J.M. and Fesenmaier, D.R. (1998) Destination Compatibility in Multidestination Pleasure Travel. *Tourism Analysis* 3, 77-87.

Johnson, L.W. and Nelson, C.J. (1991) Market Response to Changes in Attributes of a Long-Distance Passenger Rail Service. *Managerial and Decision Economics* 12, 43-55.

Johnson, P. and Thomas, B. (1992) The Analysis of Choice and Demand in Tourism. In: Johnson, P. and Thomas, B. (eds.) *Choice and Demand in Tourism.* Mansell Publishing Limited, London, pp. 1-12.

June, L.P. and Smith, S.L.J. (1987) Service Attributes and Situational Effects on Customer Preferences for Restaurant Dining. *Journal of Travel Research* (Fall), 20-27.

Lieber, S.R. and Fesenmaier, D.R. (1984) Modelling Recreation Choice: A Case Study of Management Alternatives in Chicago. *Regional Studies* 18(1), 31-43.

Lindberg, K., Dellaert, B.G.C. and Rassing, C.R. (1999) Resident Tradeoffs – A Choice Modeling Approach. *Annals of Tourism Research* 26(3), 554-569.

Louviere, J.J. (1984) Using Discrete Choice Experiments and Multinomial Logit Choice Models to Forecast Trial in a Competitive Retail Environment: A Fast Food Restaurant Illustration. *Journal of Retailing* 60(4), 81-107.

Louviere, J.J. and Hensher, D.A. (1982) Design and Analysis of Simulated Choice or Allocation Experiments in Travel Choice Modeling. *Transportation Research Record* 890, 11-17.

Louviere, J.J. and Hensher, D.A. (1983) Using Discrete Choice Models with Experimental Design Data to Forecast Consumer Demand for a Unique Cultural Event. *Journal of Consumer Research* 10(December), 348-361.

Louviere, J.J. and Woodworth, G. (1983) Design and Analysis of Simulated Consumer Choice or Allocation Experiments: An Approach Based on Aggregate Data. *Journal of Marketing Research* 20, 350-367.

Louviere, J.J., Hensher, D.A. and Swait, J. (1999a) Conjoint Analysis Methods in the Broader Context of Preference Ellicitation Methods. In: Gustafsen, A., Hermann, A. and Huber, F. (eds.) *'Conjoint Measurement: Methods and Applications'.* Springer-Verlag, Berlin.

Louviere, J.J., Meyer, R.J., Bunch, D.S., Carson, R., Dellaert, B.G.C., Hanemann, W.M., Hensher, D.A. and Irwin, J. (1999b) Combining Sources of Preference Data for Modelling Complex Decision Processes. *Marketing Letters* 10, 187-204.

Louviere, J.J., Hensher, D.A. and Swait, J. (2000) *Stated Choice Methods: Analysis and Applications in Marketing, Transportation and Environmental Valuation.* Cambridge University Press, Cambridge (forthcoming).

Mattila, A. (1999) Consumers' Value Judgments: How Business Travelers Evaluate Luxury-Hotel Services. *Cornell Hotel and Restaurant Administration Quarterly* (February), 40-46.

McFadden, D. (1974) Conditional Logit Analysis of Qualitative Choice Behaviour. In: Zarambka, P. (ed.) *Frontiers in Econometrics.* Academic Press, New York, pp. 105-142.

Morey, E.R., Shaw, W.D. and Rowe, R.D. (1991) A Discrete-Choice Model of Recreational Participation, Site Choice, and Activity Valuation When Complete Trip Data Are Not Available. *Journal Of Environmental Economics* 20, 181-201.

Morley, C.L. (1994) Discrete Choice Analysis of the Impact of Tourism Prices. *Journal of Travel Research* 33 (Autumn), 8-14.

Mouthino, L. and Trimble, J. (1991) A Probability of Revisitation Model: The Case of Winter Visits to the Grand Canyon. *The Service Industries Journal* 11(4), 439-457.

Mühlbacher, H. and Botschen, G. (1988) The Use of Trade-Off Analysis for the Design of Holiday Travel Packages. *Journal of Business Research* 17, 117-131.

Neelameghan, R. and Jain, D. (1999) Consumer Choice Process for Experience Goods: An Econometric Model and Analysis. *Journal of Marketing Research* 36(3), 373-386.

Oppewal, H., Louviere, J.J. and Timmermans, H.J.P. (1994) Modeling Hierarchical Conjoint Processes With Integrated Choice Experiments. *Journal of Marketing Research* 31(1), 92-105.

Orland, B., Daniel, T.C. and Haider, W. (1995) Calibrated Images: Landscape Visualizations to Meet Rigorous Experimental Design Specifications. In: Power, M.J., Strome, M. and Daniel, T.C. (eds.) *American Society for Photogrammetric and Remote Sensing.* Bethesda, Maryland, pp. 919-926.

Renaghan, L.M. and Kay, M.Z. (1987) What Meeting Planners Want: The Conjoint Analysis Approach. *The Cornell Hotel and Restaurant Administration Quarterly* 28(May), 67-76.

Revelt, D. and Train, K. (1998) Incentives for Appliance Efficiency in a Competitive Energy Environment: Random-Parameters Logit Models of Households' Choice. *Review of Economics and Statistics* 80, 647-657.

Revelt, D. and Train, K. (1999) Customer-Specific Taste Parameters and Mixed Logit. Unpublished Working Paper, Department of Economics, University of California, Berkeley, November 23.

Sheldon, P.J. (1995) The Demand for Incentive Travel: An Empirical Study. *Journal of Travel Research* (Spring), 23-28.

Sheldon, P.J. and Mak, J. (1987) The Demand for Package Tours: A Mode Choice Model. *Journal of Travel Research* (Winter), 13-17.

Shiv, B. and Fedorikhin, A. (1999) Heart and Mind in Conflict: The Interplay of Affect and Cognition in Consumer Decision Making. *Journal of Consumer Research* 26(3), 278-292.

Siderelis, C. and Moore, R.L. (1998) Recreation Demand and the Influence of Site Preference Variables. *Journal of Leisure Research* 30(3), 301-318.

Stemerding, M., Oppewal, H. and Timmermans, H. (1999) A Constraints-Induced Model of Park Choice. *Leisure Sciences* 21(2), 145-158.

Street, D.J., Bunch, D.S. and Moore, B. (1999) Optimal Designs for 2^k Paired Comparison Experiments. Unpublished Working Paper, School of Mathematical Sciences, University of Technology, Sydney.

Swait, J. (1984) *Probabilistic Choice Set Formation in Transportation Demand Models.* PhD dissertation, Department of Civil Engineering, MIT, Cambridge, MA.

Sweeney, J.C., Johnson, L.W. and Armstrong, R.W. (1992) The Effect of Cues on Service Quality Expectations and Service Selection in a Restaurant Setting. *The Journal of Services Marketing* 6(4), 15-22.

Thurstone, L.L. (1927) A Law of Comparative Judgment. *Psychological Review* 34, 273-286.

Tucci, L.A. and Talaga, J. (1997) Services guarantees and consumers' evaluation of services. *The Journal of Services Marketing* 11(1), 10-18.

van Limburg, B. (1998) City Marketing: A Multi-Attribute Approach. *Tourism Management* 19(5), 475-477.

Verma, R. and Thompson, G.M. (1996) Basing Service Management on Customer Determinants. *Cornell Hotel and Restaurant Administration Quarterly* (June), 18-23.

Verma, R., Thompson, G.M. and Louviere, J.J. (1999) Configuring Service Operations in Accordance With Customer Needs and Preferences. *Journal of Service Research* 1(3), 262-274.

Wind, J., Green, P.E., Shifflet, D. and Scarbrough, M. (1989) Courtyard by Marriott: Designing a Hotel Facility with Consumer-Based Marketing Models. *Interfaces* 19(1), 25-47.

Chapter six
Qualitative Comparative Analysis of Travel and Tourism Purchase-Consumption Systems

Robert L. King
University of Hawaii at Hilo, Hawaii

Arch G. Woodside
Carroll School of Management, Boston College, Massachusetts, USA

Abstract

A purchase-consumption system (PCS) is the sequence of mental and observable steps a consumer undertakes to buy and use several products for which some of the products purchased lead to a purchase sequence involving other products. Becker (1998) and others (e.g. Ragin, 1987) recommend the use of qualitative comparative analysis (i.e. the use of Boolean algebra) to create possible typologies and then to compare these typologies to empirical realities. Possible types of streams of trip decisions from combinations of 5 destination options with 6 travel mode options and 4 accommodation categories, 3 accommodation brands, 5 within-area route options, and 4 in-destination area visit options result in 7200 possible decision paths. The central PCS proposition is that several decisions within a customer's PCS are dependent on prior purchases of products that trigger these later purchases. In the article, four additional propositions are presented for examination in future research. To examine the propositions and the usefulness of the PCS framework for tourism research, qualitative, long interviews of visitors to an island tourism destination (the Big Island of Hawaii) were conducted. The results include strong empirical support for the five propositions. Several suggestions for future research are offered.

Introduction

Solomon (1983) and Solomon and Assael (1988) proposed the concept 'consumption constellations' to describe individual consumption behaviours that express a specific lifestyle. A consumer purchases a given consumption constellation to define, communicate, and perform social roles. 'For example, the American "Yuppie" of the 1980s was defined by such products as a Rolex watch, BMW automobile, Gucci briefcase, a squash racket, fresh pesto, white wine, and brie' (Solomon, 1994, p. 441).

A purchase-consumption system (PCS) is a related but distinct concept. PCS is the sequence of mental and observable steps a consumer undertakes to buy and use several related products for which some of the products purchased lead to a purchase sequence involving other products. ('Product' is used broadly to refer to goods and services.) This PCS conceptualization is similar but extends beyond the proposal by Mittal *et al.* (1999). Mittal *et al.* (1999, p. 89) define a 'consumption system' as consisting of 'a bundle of goods and services that are consumed over time in multiple consumption episodes,' for example, the relationships involved in buying both a private automobile and the maintenance service for the vehicle.

Leisure Travel Purchase-Consumption System

The study of PCSs in travel and tourism seeks to increase understanding of the relationships among travelling to one versus several destinations during a trip; travelling by plane, bus, or train with renting a car or using public transportation; staying in a hotel or with friends overnight; dining in restaurants; buying gifts; and travelling extensively versus little within destination areas. Figure 1 shows a total of 19 variables in three principal boxes that may be involved in travel and tourism related PCSs. The eight variables in Box 1 influence thinking and planning actions prior and during travel. The eight variables in Box 2 are specific decisions/actions that comprise a trip. The three variables in Box 3 are trip event-specific and trip-global evaluations and conations that occur following trip-specific experiences, near the end of the trip, and after the trip is completed. Note the feedback loop at the bottom of Figure 1 that connects Box 3 to Box 1; this feedback arrow indicates the proposition that post-trip evaluations and conations influence most of the variables in Box 1.

Leisure travel decision streams

The study of PCS in travel and tourism seeks to learn how different streams of behaviour influence the traveller's satisfaction with the destination and trip, as well as the traveller's intentions to return to the destination. From a theoretical perspective, the study of PCSs seeks to 'maximize the possibility of finding what you hadn't even thought to look for' (Becker, 1998, p. 164).

Becker (1998) and others (e.g. Ragin, 1987) recommend the use of qualitative comparative analysis (i.e. the use of Boolean algebra) to create possible typologies and then to compare these typologies to empirical realities. Exhibit 1 presents possible types of streams of trip decisions from combinations of 5 destination options with 6 travel mode options and 4 accommodation categories and 3 accommodation brands and 5 within-area route options and 4 in-destination area visit options. The result is 7200 possible decision paths.

Exhibit 1 is a limited example: decisions and behaviours involving destination activities, dining-out decisions, and gift-buying decisions are not included. Of course, not all possible paths are considered by a traveller in planning a trip; some paths taken without conscious thought (see Uleman and Bargh, 1989) and only a few of many possible alternatives are likely to be compared for each variable in Box 2 in Figure 1.

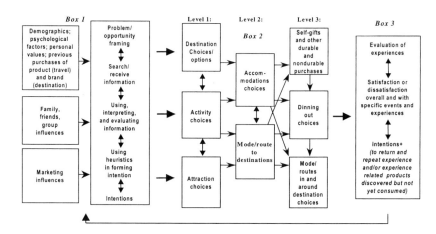

Figure 1 Framework of purchase-consumption system applied to leisure travel

Exhibit 1 Identifying pattern diversity related to leisure travel

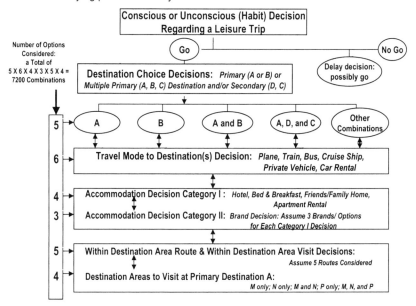

While several categories of PCSs can be identified, the focus here is on consumer purchase systems of leisure-travel related products. Other PCSs include new house buying leading to purchases of moving services, new banking services, furniture, and garden products. Acquiring a cat often leads to buying cat food, cat toys, veterinarian care, rug cleaners, a pet carrier, and medicinal pet drugs.

PCS propositions for evaluation and research

Five propositions, based upon the results of past studies, are presented to develop and validate the PCS framework. The central proposition and three additional propositions are developed in this section. The fifth proposition is introduced in the next section.

Product trigger proposition (P₁)

The central proposition (P₁) in this article is that several decisions, within a customer's leisure travel PCS, are dependent on prior purchases of products that trigger these later purchases. For example, the buying problem of hotel choice often comes after a traveller's primary destination choice decision. Gift purchases while at a primary or secondary destination may often be dependent on the leisure-travellers' accommodation location and local-area travel behaviour around their primary destination. For many firms in different travel-related industries, learning travellers' specific sequences of decisions and the triggers leading to selection/rejection of these firms' services may provide information important for increasing the effectiveness of their marketing strategies. For example, a manager of a retail store or shopping mall may need to work closely with other tourism-marketing planners on how to influence travellers' destination choice decisions along with developing an effective retailing strategy to influence visitors to shop in her or his store(s).

While the central proposition may appear obvious to the point of being unworthy of study, developing and testing a detailed theory of such mundane realism may be useful for improving our understanding of PCSs. Also, the study of leisure-travel PCSs is likely to be helpful in designing products travellers prefer to buy. Several unexpected insights may result from mapping the seemingly mundane thoughts, choices, and events occurring during travellers' leisure trips.

At the micro-level, behavioural tourism models provide insight into travellers' thoughts to help to explain their behaviours and decision processes. However, the findings from this literature do not provide a complete framework for understanding their multiple-product choice processes nor the triggers activating these choices and subsequent product choices. Researchers need to understand the complexity of these triggers and how the activating events may lead to seemingly distinct, but related travel decision processes.

Specific tourism services, for example, Delta Airlines, compete not only with other service providers in the same service industry, but with other ways people can spend their time. ' "Our competition is Las Vegas, Disney World, cars, jewellery ..." says Bob Dickinson, president of Carnival Cruise Lines. ... Like the entertainment industry, tourism sells an experience, a way for people to enjoy their free time. The difference is that the entertainment industry delivers an experience to its customers, whereas the travel industry delivers its customers to an experience' (Roberts, 1998). Thus, tourism-related strategists may benefit by developing a deep understanding of the

PCS relevant to several segments of consumers.

A relevant point here is that a traveller's choices and rejections of destinations are preceded, even if only implicitly, by the decision to travel versus the decision to purchase other time- and or money-consuming products. What do we know about how households frame a purchasing problem/opportunity to buy leisure travel versus alternative products-experiences and/or buy nothing at all? Developing a general theory of leisure travel behaviour needs to include in-depth description and explanation of this framing issue, as well as how the traveller goes about solving the problem/opportunity once it is framed.

A review of tourism literature reveals extensive consideration of travellers' decision-making processes focused on destination choices. For example, van Raaij (1986) proposes that tourism planning be based on consumers' perceptions and preferences. Other studies of leisure travellers' choice behaviour offer cause-and-effect linear relationships among marketing variables (e.g. advertising, see Woodside *et al.*, 1997), mental constructs (e.g. destination choices, and satisfaction levels see Pearce, 1992). The methodologies employed primarily examine travellers' choices through quantitative techniques. For example, Woodside and Lysonski (1989) propose a path model of direct and indirect relationships for destination choices. Davidson (1985) and Bonner and de Hoog (1985) indicate the value of micro-segmentation for travellers' destination decisions. Woodside and Sherrell (1977) and Bonner and de Hoog (1985) suggest that travellers making destination choices for holidays consider several alternatives and use heuristics, or choice rules, to set priorities for their choice decisions.

Unplanned purchases proposition (P₂)

A second proposition (P₂) in the PCS framework is that some product purchases made subsequent to the destination choice are not planned before the start of the trip. These purchases often include destination-area restaurant decisions, gift purchases, and activity purchases (e.g. the activity of deep-sea fishing and the choice of a specific deep-sea charter boat). Because such purchases may depend on a loose coupling of a sequence of prior events, a deeper understanding of the impact of antecedent and situation influences should be examined (see Lewin, 1936, 1951). Other situation-related research findings by Belk (1975) and Woodside and Bearden (1978) imply that it may be appropriate, even necessary, to study the interactions of travellers' decisions for destination choices, while-on-the-trip purchases, and trip outcomes. This view is expressed for two reasons: (1) a large share of monetary expenditures by travellers may be unplanned prior to the start of their trips, and (2) the travellers' overall satisfactions with their trips are likely to depend on these highly situation-influenced decisions.

Generic or brand decisions proposition (P₃)

The third proposition (P₃) indicates that two categories of choice decisions occur for many travellers within a leisure-travel PCS: (1) the generic product decision (e.g. should I plan a trip?); and (2) the brand choice decision (e.g. which destination alternative should I select?). These two choice decisions are labelled: (1) single-option accept/reject decisions and (2) competing-option decisions, respectively. While all competing alternative decisions may be viewed as an extension of a single option accept/reject decision, in most cases travellers are likely to use more complex heuristics when making the multiple-option decision compared to single-option decisions.

Information usage (P₄)

Information usage (P_4)

The fourth proposition (P_4) is that destination visitors who are high information users tend to participate more in activities, spend more money per day in an area, are more positive about their experiences, and indicate higher intentions to return compared to low information users and nonusers (see Woodside *et al.*, 1997).

This article provides an examination of these four propositions. It also provides a description of how to frame and examine the interaction of variables that may trigger decisions made by leisure-travellers before, during, and after a leisure trip. The specific objective of the study is to describe a general framework useful for mapping travellers' choice decisions before and during a trip, and for evaluating the actual trip experiences that may influence their future trip choices.

The results indicate that while some idiosyncratic decisions and events can be identified for each travel party, distinct segments of leisure-travellers can be identified by sequences of thought processes and purchases occurring in their PCSs. For example, a 'day-tripper' may include the following sequence of purchases in a secondary leisure trip: a flight to a destination for a 12-hour visit, travel to one primary local attraction in the destination area by tour bus, purchase of one or both of two local products as gifts, lunch at a planned stop made by a tour bus operator, and visits to one of three specific secondary attractions during the visit.

A secondary leisure destination/trip is defined here as one made before, during, or at the end of a visit to one or more destinations defined by travellers as their primary destinations. A secondary leisure trip destination is usually, but not always, shorter in length-of-stay than a primary destination.

PCS framework details and Proposition Five

As proposed here, the micro-decision processes of tourists' behaviours deal with multiple causes and interacting variables that affect the choices facing tourists. Figure 1 summarizes a process framework that shows the complexity and the dynamics of travellers' choice decisions.

The arrows in Figure 1 indicate, directly and indirectly, the potential predictors of travellers' choices, and they identify potential hypotheses or propositions for examination. Figure 1 shows three stages of pre-trip, during-trip, and after-trip information exposure, comprehension-acceptance, and decision to buy or reject. In Figure 1, single and double-headed arrows linking specific constructs indicate direct influences. Indirect influences are indicated by multiple-step linkages between constructs, for example, the influence of the constructs in the pre-trip phase on the constructs in the post-trip phase via the during-trip phase of the PCS. Within the three phases, the variables themselves are interactive, and any one of them may impact upon another one. Pre-trip and during-trip phases may involve destination consideration sets and activity sets (i.e. activity sets are the competing and complementary things-to-do while visiting destination areas). Choice sets are the decisions to be made, and decision sets are the influences, information search and usage, heuristics, and intentions.

The after-trip stage involves outcomes and evaluations that are predicted to impact future travels. Figure 1, therefore, provides a process behavioural model that may be employed to operationalize an understanding of travellers' behaviours before, during, and after a leisure trip.

The decision-making processes for leisure-travellers' choices may be classified as extensive problem solving to limited or routine problem-solving (see Howard and Sheth, 1969) and occasionally as impulse problem-solving (e.g. 'what shall we do today' and some restaurant choices). These four problem-solving situations for tourists are influenced by multiple variables as illustrated in Figure 1. Box 1 presents context variables of the traveller's environmental influences including demographic, psychological, and personal variables such as income, education, and value system (see Pitts and Woodside, 1986) of household members. Note that an important personal context variable included in the personal variables in Box 1 is whether or not the traveller has completed the travel activity previously, for example, made prior visits to a destination being considered. Such prior-direct experiences are likely to have major impacts on whether the traveller uses extensive, limited or routine problem-solving processes.

Box 1 includes the influence of family, friends, peers, and groups on a traveller's trip choices as well as the influence of marketing activities on the activation and the selection of options in travellers' choice sets. Some of these are examined in the literature and others are observed in this study; for example, discretionary travel is usually an activity of upscale households with a print media orientation (Woodside *et al.*, 1987).

Other marketing activities such as travel agent recommendations, media advertising, direct mail, and travel shows are often catalysts to activate travellers' choice sets and to influence their selection decisions. These marketing programmes affect the choices to be made for the trip during the decision steps: collecting information, evaluating it according to a set of rules, and developing intentions for deciding on the offerings. Box 1 variables, therefore, are predicted to influence leisure travel choices, and they suggest the complex, dynamic environment influencing tourists' decisions.

For most travellers, primary destination-choice decisions for a trip are often high-involvement situations. The eight choice-sets or subsystems in Box 2 of travellers' choices may occur prior and/or during the trip. These include selecting specific destinations, accommodations, activities, attractions visited, travel modes and routes, eating choices, and destination area-choices, plus take-home self-gifts, gifts for others not on the trip, and other durable purchases. For during-trip decision-making, these eight choice variables may influence and activate decisions about each other. For example, some of the traveller's pre-trip planning affects the destination and route choices, while other during-trip choices are triggered by the routes and destinations already chosen. The mode and route choices of travel to one's destination, for example, may trigger a travel party to visit a destination because it is in close proximity to an original destination choice. Within a chosen destination, the local areas visited and the travel routes chosen are also likely to influence some of the traveller's choices of activities, eating places, purchases, attractions, and accommodations. Therefore, examining the destination area and the route choices in relation to the other travel choices may increase our understanding of travellers' decision processes. The choices of accommodation, attractions, and activities may also affect and trigger behaviour.

In these pre-trip and during-trip stages, several theoretical constructs are relevant: images, attitudes, and perceived risk. Images of a tourist product, for example, are associated with both cognitive and emotional interpretations. These interpretations are based on reality or lack of it and are important, especially in the early stages of a tourist's product evaluation. Attitudes, combined sometimes with perceived risk, also influence travellers' choices. The information search step (Box 1) is when the traveller gains personal knowledge and facts for a trip and is able to set choice criteria and to generate an attitude toward a product. Such information search-comprehension is important because prior research findings strongly support the fourth proposition: degree of information use affects positively the tourist's participation in activities, expenditures per day in an area, positive feelings about experiences, and intentions to return (Woodside *et al.*, 1997).

Travellers' evaluations proposition (P$_5$)
The post-trip stage provides the outcomes of the trip experiences. *Proposition five (P$_5$) predicts that the eight travel choices (Box 2) affect the travellers' evaluations of their experiences, the satisfaction and dissatisfaction of these experiences, and the intention to repeat the visit to the same destinations.*

In Box 3, intentions+ refer to post-behaviour intentions versus the intentions of first-time visitors shown in Box 1 (see Howard and Sheth, 1969). The evaluation of leisure travellers' choices in Box 3 may use the multiple-step model proposed by Woodside *et al.* (1989): customers form summary beliefs about the quality of their experiences; these summary beliefs affect their overall satisfaction (with visiting the destination); their overall satisfaction affects their intentions+. The outcomes, evaluations, and feedback of the choice results imply the cyclical nature of travellers' choices on their own future travel choices and the influence on other travellers to a destination. In this post-trip stage, travellers may also experience cognitive dissonance about their decisions. These negative feelings may create post-choice conflict, but travellers may also have positive performance-expectations from their travel choices. Both of these types of post-trip experiences will impact future travel choices. Figure 1, therefore, outlines how traveller's behaviour evolves through decision sets, choice sets, and outcomes to affect future decisions.

Qualitative Research Method

A better understanding of theory and data collection is needed to portray the real-life mapping of travellers' choice processes. The complexity of travellers' decision-making is examined in this study by employing qualitative research to study the temporal effects of the categories of travellers' choices. Qualitative research provides insights from 'thick descriptions' (Geertz, 1973) in the travellers' own words about their decision processes and about their interactive decision-making for trip choices. Thick descriptions include detailed information about the process being examined from the viewpoints of the participants in the process (see Geertz, 1973; Sanday, 1979). Use of qualitative research methods, since the 1950s and 1960s, has been increasing in sociology, psychology, anthropology, and the administrative sciences (see Goetz and LeCompte, 1984; Bartos, 1986; and Belk, 1987 as examples). For this present paper, to examine the propositions and the usefulness of the general framework in Figure 1, we collected data using the long interview method as described by McCracken (1988) and Woodside and Wilson (1995). The value of the long interview is to learn the triggering variables that activate travel choices, for the present and for the future. By examining the thick descriptions provided by this technique, a better understanding of the activations of choice processes is gained. Such knowledge is useful in theory building and in industry planning. Generalizations may be reached by categorizing travel decisions and processes of the various segments.

Data collection

The fieldwork was done in a destination where tourism is the principal industry, the Big Island of Hawaii. (The expression 'Big Island,' rather than 'Hawaii' is used here to make clear that we are referring to one of four principal island destinations in the State of Hawaii.) As an island destination without connecting bridges elsewhere, the Big Island has two highly geographically restricted entry and exit points.

An advantage for the study is that a great deal of information was known already about the seasonal behaviour of visits to both entry/exit points for this destination. For example, for the Big Island close to 97% of visitors arrive via air flights; 3% arrive by cruise ships. For the Big Island, all interviews were conducted at the two airports with scheduled flights to Honolulu. For the purposes of conducting an exploratory empirical study, the interviews were conducted in September in the waiting areas of the airports with visitors about to leave the island.

A ten-page questionnaire was developed for use in face-to-face interviews. To cover the 20 variables in Figure 1, the questionnaire includes 48 topic areas. (A copy of the questionnaire is available by request to either author.) Trained interviewers collected the data. The training included three stages of instruction: (1) lectures and reviews of written guidelines on each question in the instrument, (2) guided individual practice sessions, and (3) direct observation of an actual interview completed in a classroom setting.

Each interviewer wore an identity button as a member of the University Hawaii at Hilo Visitor Research Program. Each respondent was given a coffee/tea mug as a gift for participating in the interview.

A total of 68 exit interviews was completed. The average time needed for the interviews was 30 minutes. The average waiting time in the airports on the Big Island before flights was 45 minutes; nearly all passengers arrive more than 30 minutes before their scheduled flights.

Data analyses

Analysis began by writing thick descriptions of the prior-trip planning, during-trip planning and experiences, and as many of the fine details of the visits as possible. In most of the cases the interviews were summarized in 12 to 15 pages for each respondent. To examine all the traveller's choice experiences, a map-shell (e.g. see Exhibit 3) was developed and examined with respect to the framework of Figure 1. The data were also placed into a data file (using the SPSS software statistical package).

Our analysis focuses on describing and understanding configurations (i.e. 'combinatorics,' see Becker, 1998, p. 165) of travel-related phenomena rather than the individual 'contributions' of changes in independent variables to explain variance in one or more dependent variables. Thus, the analysis relies on the qualitative comparative paradigm (see Becker, 1998; Ragin, 1987) rather than on the more dominant analysis-of-variance paradigm.

Research limitations

Applications of the long interview technique do not result in quantitative modelling of satisfaction and intentions. Rather, the field study offers an empirical typology of what occurs in various thinking and doing streams for the subject of visitor behaviour. The aim is to comprehend the diversity that exists within and across the empirical streams of traveller thinking-doing streams. Control over sequencing questions for qualitative research is not as precise as for all-closed-end surveys.

Questions arise because qualitative research is often judged in the social sciences by quantitative standards. The humanities, however, have used qualitative research methodologies the longest, and their standards of interpretation and control may be considered. For example, McCracken (1988) proposes the use of a scheme by Bunge (1961) that assessment of scientific theory be applied to the long interview technique. This assessment suggests the following criteria: ensuring no unneeded ambiguity; minimizing assumptions and yet explaining the data; being mutually consistent and unified; explaining the data with accuracy; and suggesting new ideas and opportunities for study.

Other researchers such as Kirk and Miller (1986) use a paper trail to indicate reliability in qualitative inquiry. This may include verbatim quotes from interviews, audio transcript, and the records of analysis stages. In this study, a paper trail exists of the interviewers' observations, questionnaires, and written reports to ensure quality findings. A triangulation method (Miles and Huberman, 1984) also increases verification through collecting from multiple sources of data, thus controlling for possible researcher bias.

Overall, several of these steps were taken to ensure reliability and validity in this study. For example: the respondents were asked to show copies of brochures, travel books, and maps they reported using during their visits. They were asked to describe specific locations visited to confirm the sights/events they claimed to have witnessed; in many cases, multiple persons were included in the interview who could elaborate on reported itineraries/activities and correct false responses to questions; seemingly paradoxical responses were identified and clarifications were requested.

Research Findings

The findings support the view that travellers' decision-making behaviours have many variables in relationships that are interactive rather than linear, as often discussed in the travel research literature. The framework shown in Figure 1 may be operationalized using cognitive mapping to obtain a better understanding of the interactions of travellers' choices, their decisions for a complete trip, and the potential impact on future trips. The findings, therefore, help to portray the full complexity of travellers' behaviours and the real-life mapping of travellers' choice processes.

Exhibit 2 Decision frames, decisions, and behaviour streams among respondents

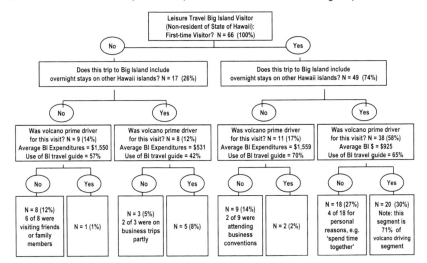

Decision streams

Exhibit 2 shows eight traveller segments resulting from cross-classifying respondents by three categories: first-time versus repeat visitors; overnight stays on other islands in the State of Hawaii; and the Big Island volcano being a prime driver for the visit.

Even though the focus here is on examining possible streams of decisions and behaviour rather than hypotheses testing of the behaviours of different traveller segments, Exhibit 2 provides details of the principal and secondary visitor segments classified by decision-behaviour streams. For example, the majority of the respondents were first-time visitors to the Big Island (74%); the majority of the respondents was also staying overnight on two or more islands in the State of Hawaii and were first-time visitors to the Big Island. Note after examining all possible combinations of just three issues (first-time visitor? overnight stay on other Hawaii islands? and the volcano being a prime driver for the visit?), no one stream includes more than 50% of the total respondents. (Due to non-responses to some questions, the percentages in the bottom row of boxes total to less than 100%.)

The volcano on the Big Island has lava flows several times each year. Fissures are present in several locations in the Hawaii Volcano National Park (HVNP). Visiting the HVNP, and experiencing a unique natural wonder first-hand, is the most often reported reason for visiting the Big Island among actual visitors.

Note in the third row of boxes in Exhibit 2 that expenditures are higher among respondents reporting not staying overnight at other Hawaiian Island destinations besides the Big Island; this finding holds for both repeat and first-time visitors.

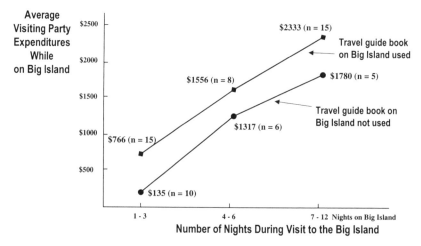

*Note. Parsimonious results of multiple regression analysis: adjusted R² = .39 (p < .000); d.f. = 2, 51;
beta for nights = .443 (p < .001); beta for interaction of nights by use of guide = .287 (p < .028)
beta for use of guide did not enter this stepwise model. The simple correlation of use of guide and
visitor expenditures on the Big Island was r = .24, p < .04, one-tailed test.*

Figure 2 Influence of using travel guide books and number of nights on expenditures

Visitors' expenditures on the Big Island increase dramatically as the number of nights spent on the Big Island increases. Visitors' expenditures on the Big Island also increase when they use (versus not use) travel guide books in planning and during their visits; see Figure 2 for detailed findings.

Figure 2 illustrates the central point of this article: the interactions (i.e. the combinatorics) of travellers' decisions and behaviours dramatically influence additional decisions-behaviours, as well as trip outcomes. Outcomes include evaluations of experiences and destinations, global satisfactions related to the trip and destination, and willingness to recommend visiting the destination to friends and family.

Proposition support

Analysis of the interview and mapping data collected provides support, in most cases strong support, for each of the propositions developed earlier. The finding for each proposition follows:

P₁ supported: Many discretionary travel decisions trigger additional purchases
Extensive confirmations were found in the majority of the case interview studies (detailed data analysis not reported here) in support of P₁: several decisions within a customer's leisure travel PCS are dependent on prior purchases of products that trigger these later purchases. For the Big Island study, the majority of the travel parties interviewed reported that destination choices and activity/attraction choices interacted with each other and dominated early in the trip planning process. These two decision

areas are categorized as Level 1 decisions in Box 2 in Figure 1.

These two Level 1 decisions were then followed most often by accommodation and mode/route decisions to the destination area. Thus, we suggest accommodations and mode/route decisions be labelled as Level 2 decisions. No clear picture emerges as to the occurrence of mode/route decisions being done prior to or following accommodation decisions. Both mode/route and accommodation decisions appear to have been made most often independently of the other decision, and both were completed prior to visiting the Big Island.

Level 3 decisions-behaviours shown in Figure 2 occurred among all respondents after arriving on the Big Island, except car rental decisions. Most (72%) of the respondents reported renting a private vehicle during the visit. Contrary to our prior expectations, renting vehicles was not associated with first-time visits, visiting other Hawaiian Island, or with the Volcano being the prime driver for visiting the Big Island. Consequently, the car rental industry is very successful on the Big Island. Car rental industry sales are not dependent on the alternative streams of visitors' decisions-behaviours examined here. Given the large size, scenic splendour, and the large number of natural and historical attractions of the Big Island, the decision to rent a private vehicle may depend mainly on demographic variables (income and credit card availability). The desire to rent a private vehicle for touring the Big Island is very high among most overnight visitors.

P_2 supported: A substantial number of purchases of travel-related products are not pre-planned before the start of the trip

The analysis of all the case studies provided strong support for P_2: some of the important product purchases made subsequent to the destination choice are not planned before the start of the trip. More than 85% of the leisure parties reported gift-purchases of products they planned to return home with but had no plans for buying on their arrivals. Surprising to us was the substantial share of non-durable gift buying among visitors – examples include coffee purchases on the Big Island. Just as important were the widespread purchases of unplanned attraction experiences – fishing excursions, for example.

Level 3 decisions most often include local area route decisions, local transportation decisions, and dining-out decisions – in more than half of the cases for the Big Island. Many level 3 decisions, especially self-gift buying and other durable purchases, were not pre-planned decisions – visitors rarely reported planning on durable and non-durable purchases before their visit.

P_3 supported: Both single-option and multiple-option destinations occur in travellers' PCSs

With respect to P_3 the following general observations are supported by the data from visitors to the Big Island. Destination choices are multiple-option decisions for most travel parties; travellers make use of single-option choices for the greatest number of their purchases while in a destination area. A very limited number of attributes/benefits are thought about when deciding (i.e. 2 to 4) across a wide spectrum of purchase decisions. Thus, strong support is found for the limited capacity propositions expressed by Peter and Olson (1999, p. 48): 'People can consciously consider only a small amount of knowledge at one time. ... For instance, it is unlikely that consumers can consider more than a few characteristics of a brand in forming an attitude or intention to buy the brand.'

The majority (60%) of respondents reported that they did not consider and reject alternative destinations when deciding on visiting the Big Island. Almost all respondents reporting the volcano to be the prime driver for their visit also reported not considering and rejecting other destinations. Thus, these findings are additional evidence of the strong magnetic power of the volcano in attracting visitors to the Big Island.

P_4 supported: High information users differ in their decisions and behaviours compared to light information users

Substantial support was found among respondents in support of P_4: destination visitors who are high information users tend to participate more in activities, spend more money per day in an area, are more positive about their experiences, and indicate more intentions to return compared to low information users and nonusers. Surprisingly, given the expenditures of several hundred to several thousands of dollars, close to one-third of the visitors to the Big Island arrived without prior search for information from travel guides, province or state governments, or travel magazines. Substantial differences in average numbers of activities visited, money spent, reported quality of the visit, and intentions-to-return were found between low-search and high-search segments for visitors to both islands. The evidence leads us to conclude that some leisure travellers may need training on the usefulness of information to increase the quality and enjoyment of their trips.

P_5 supported: The eight decision areas in the PCS framework influence traveller judgements of destination quality and overall satisfaction

While intuitive, there is substantial support to verify the large impact of the eight decision areas on post-trip evaluations, satisfactions, and intentions-to-return. Thus, P_5 was supported by the results: the eight travel choices, and resulting outcomes, affect the travellers' evaluations of their experiences, the satisfaction and dissatisfaction of these experiences, and the intention to repeat the visit to the same destinations. Almost all visitors could recall vividly two to four experiences that resulted in positive impacts on their trip summary evaluations. When pressed, nearly all could also identify at least one negative experience.

We did press to learn negative experiences. For example, we asked toward the end of the Big Island visitor interview, 'What negative experience, turn-off, occurred for you during your current visit to the Big Island, if any? No matter how minor, small the incident, please be blunt!' Nearly all travel parties displayed substantially greater emotion in reporting their positive experiences than negative experiences; about one-fourth of the respondents reported being unable to describe negative experiences of any type; all respondents were able to report positive experiences.

'Too much rain in Hilo' was mentioned most often as a turn-off (nine mentions); four respondents mentioned not actually seeing lava flowing into the Pacific Ocean as a turn-off. Both of these issues illustrate the need to train visitors about what to expect and not to expect when visiting natural attractions.

Long interview and cognitive mapping examples

As stated, the objective for this present study was to develop a dynamic and complete model for an in-depth understanding of travellers' PCSs before and during the trip. An evolutionary and dynamic framework was developed and presented in Figure 1 to make explicit the complexity of travellers' choice decisions. The findings from the field surveys using the long interview technique helped to test and to refine this proposed framework. Travellers' choices and triggers of later purchases were considered as well as outcomes of the trip experiences that may affect future travel choices. To examine all the travellers' choice experiences, maps showing the dimensions of categories and hierarchies among the concepts were created. Cognitive mapping was used to construct the category maps for each respondent's interview findings.

Newlyweds case example

Evidence in support of a single-option, as well as multiple-option decisions (i.e. the third proposition) is found in several case study interviews involving visitors to the Big Island. The following summary is one example: this case includes a honeymoon couple travelling from Pueblo, Colorado. The couple considered three destination options in Hawaii – all three had beautiful sunny beaches. A lexicographic choice rule was used in making the final selection of the Big Island: only the Big Island offers the sights of an active volcano to visitors – a key driver for their visit. They did not want to visit Oahu and Honolulu (to avoid city life), but they did want to visit local areas where they would experience peace and quiet. They used the *Guide to the Big Island* (a 32-page newspaper publication) prior to their visit to confirm what activities they wanted to experience and to confirm the decision to visit only the Big Island.

The couple did extensive information gathering and reading as part of their pre-trip planning process. They visited a travel agent, used the Internet, requested information about visiting several islands from the State of Hawaii prior to the visit, and requested brochures from three hotels. They reported that pictures and details of features were helpful. The *Big Island Visitor Guide Book* gave detailed information about the attractions and activities. While such a statement may appear to be mundane and lacking useful information, many states and countries do not provide potential visitors with detailed information about what to do and how to go about doing it regarding their destinations. In total, the couple spent over 4 months gathering information and planning the details of their visit.

The couple arrived on the Big Island at the Kailua-Kona International Airport. This airport receives the majority of visitor arrival traffic; many marketers in several travel-related industries on the eastern side of the Big Island (i.e. 'the Hilo side') look with envy at share visitors held by the western, Kona-side of the Big Island. (While the Big Island has 11 of the 13 Earth's weather zones, the two weather zones dominating the island include the very dry Kona-side and the tropical rain forest Hilo side.) Lush vegetation with lots of rain, including large orchid farms, are located on the Hilo side; deserts and several white sandy beaches are located mostly on the Kona side. The main city on the Kona side is Kailua-Kona; the main city on the Hiloside is the County of Hawaii capital: the City of Hilo. The Big Island is big: over 6 hours is required to drive around the island on its main highways.

Related to their choice of Hapuna Prince Hotel, the couple considered two other serious contenders for their accommodation decision. The famous white sandy beach of Hapuna State Park Beach was the dominant factor in their choice of hotels. Thus, if this finding is replicated extensively, Hapuna Prince Hotel is provided with supporting evidence that the positioning of the hotel next to this famous beach is a key driver for gaining hotel guests. The couple's five-night stay at the Hapuna Prince Hotel resulted in a hotel expense of $600.

Case evidence supporting P_1 was found in this couple's report. The choice of car rental firm (4-wheel-drive vehicle from Avis) and including golfing as an activity were made after the couple's decision to visit the Big Island and to select the Hapuna Prince Hotel. The car rental firm decision was made before their arrival on the Big Island; golfing as an activity was decided after reaching the hotel based on the easy access to a world-class golf course. The purchases of $250 in Kona coffee and Macadamia nuts were made only after the couple had tasted both products; they did not report that knowledge about either product was involved in the planning of their visit. These purchases were the largest gift expenditures they made during their visit.

Activities that the couple did engage in included the following: a luau (an evening show and dinner of Hawaiian music, dance, and food); sport fishing; touring the Hawaii Volcanoes National Park; touring Waipio Valley (a tropical rainforest valley leading out to the Pacific Ocean on one side and high cliffs on two other sides), snorkelling and a day of ocean sightseeing down the west coast to see Captain Cook Monument; touring Waimea town and Parker Ranch; fine dining at the Chart House restaurant on the Kona (western and very dry side) of the Big Island. The couple spent only 3 hours at the Hawaii Volcanoes National Park; they did some hiking in the park and view their park visit as a highlight of their stay; they visited Mauna Kea ('White Mountain') astronomical observatory; they visited the coffee estates.

The couple did not visit the Hilo side or the Puna area (south-eastern side of the Big Island). In total, the couple physically visited about half of the Big Island during their 5-night, 6-day visit. This case example is a reflection of the relatively more successful tourism industry on the Kona side versus Hilo side of the Big Island. However, for both sides of the island, tourism is the number-one industry – for the most part, the only viable business-related industry on the island.

Choices mapping example

A summary, decision-category map for the Big Island honeymoon couple is provided in Exhibit 3. Examining all their answers to the planning questions and their actual time spent at the Volcano National Park, the conclusion may be accurate that the Volcano area of the Big Island alone was not a sufficient trigger to cause their visit, but it was a necessary scenic feature. Substantial use of open-ended questions and their responses leads to the conclusion that this couple wanted and got a unique honeymoon countryside and mountain scenic beauty, outdoor hiking and beach area/resort trip that included a brief visit to an active volcano area. They actively decided to avoid visiting a large city area located nearby to their primary destination. The last page of the survey form included a listing of 13 categories of trip reasons; respondents are asked to check all that applied for their immediate visit to the Big Island. Reflecting their prior answers, the honeymoon couple checked five reasons: a touring trip; an outdoors trip; a beach area/resort trip; a country or mountain area/resort trip; and own category (honeymoon) trip. Responding to the final question of identifying the one category that applies most, they selected beach area/resort trip.

Exhibit 3 Honeymoon couple from Colorado visiting Big Island

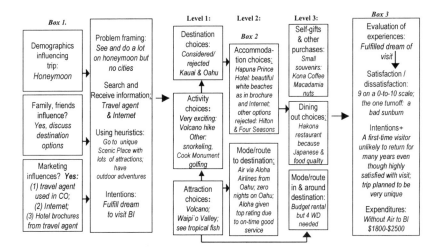

Thus, the reliance on only the couple's initial answers as to the 'main attraction' for their visit was modified by their visit experiences. This conclusion is not meant to negate their reported prior-to-visit belief that the volcano area was the main attraction.

Note that the total expenditures in the destination area (i.e. the amount does not include airfare to and from the Big Island) are reported in Exhibit 3 (about $2,000). For a five-night stay involving hotel accommodations, a car rental, and fine dining, this total expenditure level may be underestimated.

Recommendations for Additional Research

Employing qualitative research techniques has several advantages for examining PCSs in future leisure travel research. The long interview method employed in the study reveals the value of gaining deep knowledge of travellers in their own words and interpretation. By examining the thick descriptions provided in the long interview technique, for example, a better understanding of the activations of choice processes is obtained and this may be applied to any type of future tourism research. Generalizations are then reached by categorizing travel decisions and processes for the various segments.

Gaining a deep understanding of travellers' decision-making better enables the tourism industry and the various levels of governments to improve industry planning at both a macro and a micro level. These various tourism-related services may work together to develop a macro plan in order to market more effectively to many segments. A deep understanding also enhances the development of more predictive tourism models. Such results may be especially useful for international tourism marketers and for small and medium-sized firms, which do not have the individual resources to study each particular traveller segment. With world tourism predicted to continue growing at a rapid rate over the next decade, this type of in-depth research will provide the knowledge for effective and socially responsible tourism marketing.

References

Bartos, R. (1986) Qualitative Research: What It Is and Where It Came From. *Journal of Advertising Research* 26(3), 13-53.

Becker, H.S. (1998) *Tricks of the Trade*. University of Chicago Press, Chicago.

Belk, R.W. (1975) Situational Variables and Consumer Behavior. *Journal of Consumer Research* 2(3), 157-164.

Belk, R.W. (1987) The Role of the Odyssey in Consumer Behavior and in Consumer Research. *Advances in Consumer Research* 14, 357-361.

Bonner, F. and deHoog, R. (1985) A Recipe for Mixing Decision Ingredients. *European Research* 13, 109-115.

Bunge, M. (1961) The Weight of Simplicity in the Construction and Assaying of Scientific Theories. *Philosophy of Science* 28(2), 120-149.

Davidson, T.L. (1985) Strategic Planning: A Competitive Necessity. *Travel and Tourism Research Association* University of Utah, 103-108.

Geertz, C. (1973) *The Interpretation of Cultures*. Basic Books, New York.

Goetz, J.P. and LeCompte, M.D. (1984) *Ethnography and Qualitative Design in Educational Research*. Academic Press, Orlando, FL.

Howard, J.A. and Sheth, J.N. (1969) *The Theory of Buyer Behavior*.Wiley, New York.

Kirk, J. and Miller, M.L. (1986) *Reliability and Validity in Qualitative Research*. Sage, Newbury Park, CA.

Lewin, K. (1936) *Principles of Topological Psychology*. McGraw-Hill, New York.

Lewin, K. (1951) *Field Theory in Social Science*. Harper & Row, New York.

McCracken, G. (1988) *The Long Interview*. Sage, Newbury Park, CA.

Miles, M.B. and Huberman, A.M. (1984) *Qualitative Data Analysis: A Sourcebook of New Methods*. Sage, Newbury Park, CA.

Mittal, V., Kumar, P. and Tsiros, M. (1999) Attribute-Level Performance, Satisfaction, and Behavioral Intentions over Time: A Consumption-System Approach. *Journal of Marketing* 63(April), 88-101.

Pearce, D.G. (1992) *Tourist Organizations*. Longman Group UK Ltd., UK.

Peter, J.P. and Olson, J.C. (1999) *Consumer Behavior and Marketing Strategy*. McGraw-Hill, Boston.

Pitts, R.E. and Woodside, A.G. (1986) Personal Values Influence on Destination Choice. *Journal of Travel Research* 25, 20-25.

Ragin, Ch.C. (1987) *The Comparative Method: Moving Beyond Qualitative and Quantitative Strategies*. University of California Press, Berkeley.

Roberts, M. (1998) Travel and Tourism. *The Economist* 346 (8050), January 10, 47 ff.

Sanday, P.R. (1979) The Ethnographic Paradigm(s). *Administrative Science Quarterly*

24(December), 527-538.

Solomon, M.R. (1983) The Role of Products as Social Stimuli: A Symbolic Interactionism Perspective. *Journal of Consumer Research* 10(December), 319-329.

Solomon, M.R. (1994) *Consumer Behavior*, 2nd edn. Allyn and Bacon, Boston.

Solomon, M.R. and Assael, H. (1988) The Forest or the Trees?: A Gestalt Approach to Symbolic Consumption. In: Umiker-Sebeok, J. (ed.) *Marketing and Semiotics: New Directions in the Study of Signs for Sale*. Mouton de Gruyter, Berlin, pp. 189-218.

Uleman, J.S. and Bargh, J.A. (eds.) (1989) *Unintended Thought*. Guildford Press, New York.

van Raaij, W.F. (1986) Consumer Research on Tourism: Mental and Behavioral Constructs. *Annals of Tourism Research* 13, 1-9.

Woodside, A.G. and Bearden, W.O. (1978) Field Theory Applied to Consumer Behavior. In: Sheth, J.N. (ed.) *Research in Marketing*, vol.1. JAI Press, Stamford, CT, pp. 303-330.

Woodside, A.G. and Lysonski, S. (1989) A General Model of Traveler Destination Choice. *Journal of Travel Research* 27(Spring), 8-14.

Woodside, A.G. and Sherrell, D. (1977) Traveler Evoked, Inept, and Inert Sets of Vacation Destinations. *Journal of Travel Research* 16, 14-18.

Woodside, A.G. and Wilson, E.J. (1995) Applying the Long Interview in Direct Marketing Research. *Journal of Direct Marketing* 9(1), 37-55.

Woodside, A.G., Cook Jr., V.J. and Mindak, W.A. (1987) Profiling the Heavy Traveler Segment. *Journal of Travel Research* 26(Spring), 9-14.

Woodside, A.G., Frey, L.L. and Daly, R.T. (1989) Linking Service Quality, Customer Satisfaction, and Behavioral Intention. *Journal of Health Care Marketing* 9, 5-17.

Woodside, A.G., MacDonald, R.M. and Trappey, R.J. (1997) Measuring Linkage-Advertising Effects on Customer Behavior and Net Revenue. *Canadian Journal of Administrative Sciences* 14(2), 214-228.

Chapter seven
Representing and Predicting Tourist Choice Behaviour: Rule-Based vs. Utility-Based Approach

Manon van Middelkoop, Aloys W.J. Borgers,
Theo A. Arentze and Harry J.P. Timmermans
Urban Planning Group, Eindhoven University of Technology,
5600 MB Eindhoven, The Netherlands

Introduction

To understand tourist behaviour we need information about which activities they pursue, when, where and with whom these activities are pursued, and how these activities are scheduled. More importantly, we need to understand how these decisions are made (Mansfeld, 1992) and how personal and institutional influences affect these decisions (Dellaert *et al.*, 1998b; Richards, 1998). In tourism research these choices are typically analysed using quantitative models that assume an a-priori functional form (e.g. additive or multiplicative) and that require variables to follow a particular distribution (e.g. normality). Although in principle (approximations to) non-compensatory decision processes can be formulated, virtually all models of tourist choice behaviour assume that tourists will balance positive evaluations on one aspect of the decision situation against negative evaluations of other aspects.

Qualitative models offer more flexibility in modelling tourist choice behaviour. These rule-based or computational process models assume individuals to use heuristic decision-making rules that represent decisions that have worked out satisfactorily under similar conditions in the past. These heuristics may include both compensatory and non-compensatory decision rules.

The potential higher flexibility in representing alternative decision processes of qualitative rule-based models does not necessarily imply that they are better predictors of observed choice behaviour than conventional quantitative models. Several studies in spatial choice behaviour (e.g. shopping location choices (Thill and Wheeler, 2000) and daily activity scheduling and transportation (Arentze *et al.*, 2000; Wets *et al.*, 2000) indicate that decision tree induction systems at least equal the results of more conventional discrete choice models. The purpose of this paper is therefore to compare the predictive performance of rule-based systems to the more traditional qualitative modelling approaches in the context of tourist decision making. More specifically, the performance of four models estimated and tested on the same data-set will be compared: (1) a Chi-squared Automatic Interaction Detection (CHAID)-based model of decision rules; (2) a traditional logit model that uses the same condition variables and states as the CHAID-based model (i.e. without adaptations); (3) a traditional logit model that uses the condition states that appear in the CHAID-based model (i.e. the condition variables are globally merged into optimal condition states); and (4) a traditional logit model that uses condition states that are individually merged (i.e. the condition variables are merged into optimal condition states by entering each condition variable separately into a CHAID-based algorithm). The choice of season for holidays is selected to provide the context for this study.

In order to compare the rule-based system to the more traditional quantitative modelling approaches to tourist choice behaviour, this chapter is organized as follows. First, a CHAID-based approach to inducing tourist decision rules is discussed. Next, the data that are used to estimate the four models will be presented. Subsequently, the decision tree induced by the CHAID-based algorithm will be discussed. This section will show how the induced tree can be interpreted in terms of the tourist decision making process and how decision rules and interactions between condition variables are represented. The subsequent section will compare the performance of the CHAID-based algorithm to that of the three logit models applied to the same data-set. Finally, this paper will summarize the conclusions that can be drawn from this study and identify avenues of future research.

Inducing Decision Rules Using the CHAID Tree Induction Algorithm

Qualitative rule-based models use decision rules to describe observed behaviour. Traditionally, rule-bases were obtained from qualitative techniques such as expert interviews and think-aloud protocols (Arentze *et al.*, 1997, Thill and Wheeler, 2000). However, these techniques lacked the ability to test the validity and the predictive power of the derived rule-base. Only recently, algorithms originating from *artificial intelligence* and *machine learning* (such as C4.5 developed by Quinlan (1993) or genetic algorithms (Goldberg, 1989) applied to rule-based approaches by Oliver (1994) and Greene and Smith (1987)) and *statistics* (e.g. CART (Breiman *et al.*, 1984) and CHAID (Kass, 1980)) have been developed to induce tree-structures from empirical data. Originally, these tree-induction techniques were developed as exploratory techniques for investigating data. That is, they were used in the pre-analysis stages of more quantitative techniques. However, as Kass (1980) noted, they can also be used as a model in itself (Kass, 1980; Strambi and Van de Bilt, 1998). In the context of tourist decision making, these tree induction systems use condition variables to repeatedly partition the sample of observed tourist choices in mutually exclusive and exhaustive sub-groups that are more homogeneous with regard to the tourists' decisions (or actions). The sub-groups are thus defined by combinations of (i.e. interactions between) condition states (Magidson, 1995; Strambi and Van de Bilt, 1998). By linking the distribution (in %) of a sub-group defined by a particular set of condition states over the actions, a decision rule is obtained. By considering splits and merges as the only permissible operations, these techniques make sure that the sets of tourist decision rules are complete, exhaustive and consistent.

The CHAID algorithm partitions the observed choices into mutually exclusive and exhaustive sub-groups by maximizing the significance of the chi-squared statistic at each partition (Kass, 1980). The first step in CHAID is merging. Based on a decision table[1], the chi-square statistics and corresponding 'pairwise' p-values are computed for each pair of the condition states that is eligible to be merged. In this process, missing values are viewed as a separate condition state. If the largest of all pairwise p-values is greater than the specified α-level, this pair of states is merged into a single compound condition state, and the whole process is repeated (with this new state) until the largest pairwise p-value at a certain stage is smaller than the specified α-level. Finally, for each compound condition state consisting of three or more of the original states, the algorithm finds the most significant binary split. If the significance is beyond a critical value, this split is implemented and the algorithm returns to the merging stage. The merging process is repeated for each condition variable and its states in turn.

The second step in CHAID is splitting. For each optimally merged condition variable, the adjusted p-value is computed by using a proper Bonferonni adjustment. Basically, the Bonferonni adjusted p-value is corrected for the number of possible merges given the type and the number of states of the condition variable. Next, the most significant condition variable (i.e. lowest p-value) is isolated, and if the p-value of this condition is less than or equal to the specified α-level, the group of observations is split according to the (merged) states of this condition variable. If no condition variable has a significant p-value, the group is not split, and the process is terminated. For each partition of the data that has not been analysed, the algorithm returns to the first step. The tree-growing process continues until all sub-groups have either been analysed or contain too few observations.

The CHAID algorithm may not find the optimal split for a condition variable because the merging process is terminated when all remaining states are found to be statistically different. 'Exhaustive CHAID' is a modification of CHAID (Biggs *et al.*, 1991, in: SPSS, 1998, pp. 188-192) that counteracts this bias by continuing to merge the states of the condition variables until only two states remain. The p-values and the corresponding sets of (compound) states at each successive stage are stored. Next, the successive merges for each condition are considered, and the set of (compound) states that gives the strongest association with the actions is selected as the optimal merge for each condition variable. Exhaustive CHAID than proceeds with computing the adjusted p-values and selecting the most significant condition.

In this study, the decision-rules for the tourists' choice of season will be induced using the Exhaustive CHAID-algorithm available as part of SPSS's AnswerTree® version 2.1 (SPSS, 1998). For continuous condition variables, the 'equal-frequency method' is applied to create categorical states. This method divides the quantitative scale into ranges of values so as to assure that each interval contains approximately the same number of observations; these ranges are than treated as 'normal' condition states.

The stopping criteria will be a minimum of 25 observed trips in each group before splitting or 10 trips after splitting. These criteria are set rather low in comparison to the number of condition variables in order to also identify decision rules at lower levels of aggregation. The significance level for condition state splitting and condition variable eligibility will be 5% ($\alpha_{split} = 0.05$). The algorithm will be set to allow for the splitting of merged states.

Data

A large panel-based survey was used for the analyses. The 'CVO-survey' (i.e. Continuous Vacation Research) is an extensive consumer panel managed by the Dutch Research Institute for Recreation and Tourism (NRIT) and the Dutch Bureau for Tourism (NBT) (Van der Most, 1996). Based on four quarterly measurements, it records the vacation behaviour, the socio-demographics and vacation-related variables of a panel that is representative of the Dutch population[2]. Every year, the March-survey takes off with over 5500 respondents. On a yearly basis, the attrition rate of the panel is 30 to 40%, resulting in a sample of approximately 3500 respondents at the end of the year. Finally, the panel is replenished to 5500 members, and the cycle is repeated.

Data on the vacations of 3562 respondents aged 0 and over were obtained by acquiring the 1998 CVO-data-set (a 'CVO-year' runs from December to November of the following year inclusive). In total, 7121 vacations (2 days or more) were made by 2791 respondents, resulting in a participation rate of 78.4% and an average of 2.55 trips per participant (2.00 trips for the entire sample). The maximum number of trips made by one respondent in 1998 amounted to 47 (see Table 1).

Table 1 Characteristics of the 1998 CVO-panel

1998 CVO-panel		1998 CVO-panel		
$N_{respondents}$	3562	Regional	- North	1262 (35.4 %)
- making holidays	2791 (78.4%)	spread of	- Mid	1016 (28.5 %)
- non-participants	771 (21.6%)	holidays	- South	1284 (36.0 %)
N_{trips}	7121	Age (sd)		37.9 years (21.4)
Average no. of trips	2.00	Education	- mode	2nd ed. - vocational
- per participant	2.55	level	- median	higher ed. – voc.
Max. no. of trips	47 per year	Av. Household size		3.01 people
Duration of holidays	9.13 days	Household	- mode	NLG 45-55,000
(sd)	(7.57)	income	- median	NLG 40-45,000
No. of day-trips 98'	14.0 (21.9)			
(sd)*	(based on 1701 resp.)			

* Data on the respondents' day-tripping behaviour was collected by participating in the fourth quarterly CVO-measurement in December 1998. The questions on day-trips were presented to those aged 16 years and over, reducing the sample to 2836 respondents. The information on day-trips is included at the level of the Activity Programme only. The timing of day-trips will therefore not be addressed.

In our example, the choice of season for each tourist trip constitutes the action variable, including the 'actions' winter, spring, summer and autumn. 'Winter' is defined as the period from December 1, 1997 to February 28, 1998 inclusive. 'Spring' is set from March 1 to July 2, 1998. 'Summer' is defined as the 9-week period during which (primary and secondary) schools throughout the country are closed for the summer holiday starting at July 3 and ending at September 5, 1998. 'Autumn' constitutes the remaining period running from September 6 to November 30, 1998 inclusive.   The distribution of the 7121 trips across these actions is displayed in Table 2.

The choice of season is considered to be part of a hierarchical scheduling process in which the facets of a number of interrelated trips are scheduled sequentially and in which decisions made in an early stage of the process frame the decisions yet to come (Woodside and MacDonald, 1994; Lindh *et al.*, 1995; Jeng and Fesenmaier, 1997; Dellaert *et al.*, 1998a). The final outcome of this scheduling process is referred to as a 'tourist activity pattern' and includes information on which tourist activities (e.g. day-trips, short breaks and holidays) people pursue during a particular period (e.g. a year), where and with whom these activities are pursued, and how these activities are scheduled in time (including the choice of season). As a consequence of the sequential scheduling process, not all the information about the tourists' activity pattern may be included as conditions at each stage.

Given our assumptions regarding the tourist decision-making process, the following type of conditions are available for inducing decision rules that explain tourists' choices of season (see Table 3): (1) the tourists' annual Activity Programme, that is the set of trips the tourist will pursue during a year, including both day-trips and overnight holidays; (2) subdecisions regarding the trip under consideration that have been taken previously, including the importance of the trip within the activity programme[3], the duration and the travel party; (3) personal and household characteristics, including the possession of various tourist-recreation accessories; and (4) conditions that represent the influence the various tourist trips in the tourist's annual Activity Programme have on each other – these condition variables summarize the choices of season of the trips that are more important than the trip under consideration.[3]

Table 2 Distribution of the Tourist Trips over the Four Seasons

	Training	Set Validation	Total
Winter	628	218	846 (11.9%)
Spring	1911	640	2551 (35.8%)
Summer	1968	644	2612 (36.7%)
Autumn	840	272	1112 (15.6%)
Total	5347	1774	7121
	(75.1%)	(24.9%)	

Table 3 Condition Variables Entered into the CHAID-based Algorithm

Condition	Type[a]	States
Characteristics of the Activity Programme		
NDAY-TRIPS	O	Annual no of day-trips: 0 day-trips; 1-5 day-trips … to … 51 or more day-trips; younger than 16 years; unknown (=missing)
NHOLIDAY	C	Annual no. of vacations: 1-47 vacations
Characteristics of the trip (subdecisions that have been taken previously)		
PRIORITY	O	Importance of the trip[b]: most important; first but one; first but two; not in top-3
DURATION	O	Duration of the trip: short break (2-4 days); extended holiday (5-8 days); medium long holiday (9-15 days); long holiday (16-28 days); extra long holiday (29+ days)
PARTY	N	Travel party: not alone − with schoolchildren (aged 6-14 years); not alone − with other children (0-5/15-19 years); not alone − travel parties of at least nine people; not alone − without children (all aged >=20 years); alone; unknown
Personal and Household Characteristics		
AGE	C	0-98 *years*
INCOME	O	Net annual household income in 8 categories: less than € 10,227 (NLG 22,500) to > € 29,545 (NLG 65,000)
EDUCAT	O	Education in 9 levels: 'no school yet' to 'highest level'
GENDER	N	female; male
CIVILST	N	Civil Status: married; cohabiting; divorced; widow(er); single; other
CHILD	N	Children in household: children aged 0-5 only; (some) children aged 6-17; no children under 18
HHSIZE	O	no. of people in household: 'single' to '10 or more'
WORK	N	job 0-30 hrs/week; job 30+ hrs; no job; unknown
WORKHRS	C	no. of working hours: 0-99 hrs
WORK-WEEK	O	Work during weekend: never; sometimes (1-5 times per year); regularly (6-12 x); often (13 +); younger than 16 years; unknown
FREEDAYS	C	no. of free days in 1998; unknown
URBAN	O	Urbanization in 5 levels
REGION	C	Holiday region: North; Mid; South
CLASS	O	Social class in 5 levels
CAR	N	Car(s) household; no car in household
SKIS	N	Has skis; has no skis
FREEACC	N	Boat/tent/caravan without fixed place; other
FIXEDACC	N	Tourist accommodation with fixed place; other
Summary Variables Regarding Previous Timing Decision		
#Dtotal	C	TOTAL No. of DAYS already scheduled
#Tremain	C	No. of REMAINING TRIPS to be scheduled
#Dwinter	C	No. of DAYS already scheduled in WINTER
analogous	C	Idem SPRING, SUMMER and AUTUMN
#Twinter	C	No. of TRIPS already scheduled in WINTER
analogous	C	Idem SPRING, SUMMER and AUTUMN

[a] (N) Categorical/Nominal; (O) Ordinal; (C) Continuous
[b] Based on the duration of the trip (longer = higher) and the travel party

Results

The set of decision rules for the tourists' choice of season was induced using approximately 75% of the data-set (training set = 5347 trips); the remaining 1774 trips were used for validation purposes only (see also Table 2). The first three levels of the decision-tree induced by the CHAID-based algorithm are presented in Figure 1. The generated tree consists of 10 levels and 176 nodes, 100 of which are terminal nodes or leaves. These leaves represent decision rules, and the CHAID-based model thus comprises a set of 100 exclusive and exhaustive decision rules to describe tourists' choice of season. This section will first show an example of one of these decision rules. Next, it will discuss the first three levels of the decision that include the splits and conditions that lead to this particular rule.

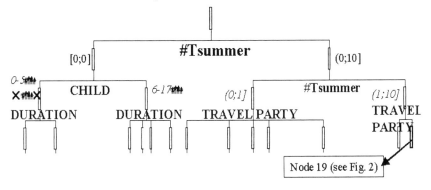

Figure 1 Decision tree for tourists' choices of season induced using a CHAID-based algorithm (first tree levels)

The exemplar rule can be found in Node 19 of the CHAID-based decision tree (see Figures 1 and 2). Following the branch on the utmost right side of the tree, and using the 'all-or-nothing' decision principle, the following rule is obtained:

```
IF      '#Tsummer = (0;10] '
AND     '#Tsummer = (1;10]'
AND     'TRAVEL PARTY = People9+ or nokids or kidother
        or schoolkid'
THEN    'seasonal choice = spring'
```

because 'spring' is the dominant season in this leaf (including 43.51% of the cases; see Figure 2). Since this decision rule will correctly classify 43.5% of the trips that comply with the prevailing set of condition states (for the training set), it can be stated that the confidence value of this decision rule is 0.435.

SEASON (Training) : Node 19		
Cat.	%	n
winter	18,32	24
spring	**43,51**	**57**
summer	5,34	7
autumn	32,82	43
Total	(2,45)	131

Figure 2 Example of a node (node 19, a terminal leaf)

In terms of the decision tree, the first split is made on the condition 'the number of trips already scheduled in the summer', indicating that in the tourist scheduling process holidays indeed influence each other. When no trips have been scheduled in the summer yet, summer is the dominant season (51.95%), whereas spring is the dominant season when one or more trips have already been scheduled during the summer (49.32%).

In the sub-group of observations where no trips have been scheduled in the summer yet, the second split is based on the presence of children in the household. When schoolchildren (6-17♦) and very young (0-5♦) or no (✗♦✗) children are present in the household, summer is still the dominant action, but for the first sub-group summer represents 80.49% of all trips, whereas for the latter groups this share is only 39.89%. For both sub-groups, the third split is made based on the duration of the trip. For the sub-group of households with very young or no children, spring is the selected season for shorter trips (2-8 days) with 33.63% of trips belonging to this action, whereas summer is dominant with 48.66% for longer trips (9 or more days). For households with schoolchildren, short breaks (2-4 days) are predominantly scheduled in the spring (40.00%), whereas summer is the dominant season for extended holidays (5-8 days), middle long holidays (9-15) and long and extra long (16 days or more) holidays, with the share of summer vacations increasing with the length of the trip (respectively 66.51%, 85.41% and 96.26%).

Moving to the right-hand branch of the decision tree where the exemplar decision rule is located, the number of trips in the summer is again used to split the group of observations. When only one trip has been scheduled in the summer, spring is still the dominant season, but now with 51.81%. In contrast, when two or more trips have already been scheduled in the summer, the dominant position of the spring season decreases to 40.65%. For both these sub-groups, the travel party is used to further split the observations at the third level. While spring is still the dominant action for all travel party sub-groups, again the share of this season relative to the other actions varies. When only one trip has been scheduled in the summer already, independent travellers (travel party = alone) select spring in 44.07% of the cases, for travel parties consisting of nine or more people and parties without children the share of spring is 47.98%, and for trips with schoolchildren, with other children (0-5/15-19 years) and with unknown travel parties, the shares of the dominant spring season are respectively 45.56%, 50.81% and 67.78%. When two or more trips have already been scheduled in the summer, and the travel party is 'unknown' or 'alone', spring is the dominant action with 39.69%. The other sub-group arising from this split constitutes the exemplar decision rule (see above).

For reasons of economy, the remaining part of the decision tree and the other 99 decision rules will not be discussed here. Five of the condition variables that were entered into the exhaustive CHAID algorithm were not used in the decision rules, including 'civil status', 'the number of free days', 'level of urbanization', 'social class', and 'car'. The next sections will address the predictive performance of the induced set of 100 exclusive and exhaustive decision rules and contrast this to the three multinomial logit models.

The predictive performance of the rule-based model

To test the performance of the above described rule-based model, the tourists' choices of season of the training set were predicted. Secondly, the model was used to predict the choices of season for the validation set, consisting of the remaining 25% of the sample. Table 4 shows the resulting classification matrices. The columns in this table represent the observed choices of season for the 7121 trips in the two sets, and the rows represent the choices of season as predicted by the above described rule-based model. Consequently, the diagonal cells of the two matrices describe the correctly predicted choices of season, whereas the off-diagonal cells represent mis-classifications. Expressed as a percentage of the set in question, the model correctly predicted 56.5% of the training and 51.1% of the validation set, indicating that overfitting is not a serious problem. Finally, a comparison of the number of predicted and observed choices per season shows that the model seriously underestimates the number of autumn and winter trips, and overestimates the more popular spring and summer seasons. Hence, using the 'all-or-nothing' decision principle the rule-based model is not able to predict behaviour very accurately at the aggregate level.

Table 4 Classification Matrix for the CHAID-based Model (100 decision rules)

Pre-dict-ed Cat.	Actual Category									
	Training Set					Validation Set				
	Win.	Spr.	Sum.	Aut.	Total	Win.	Spr.	Sum.	Aut.	Total
Win.	**101**	62	41	27	231	**23**	38	14	10	85
Spr.	320	**1310**	380	414	2424	119	**405**	143	146	813
Sum.	172	484	**1486**	274	2416	63	169	**463**	101	796
Aut.	35	55	61	**125**	276	13	28	24	**15**	80
Total	628	1911	1968	840	5347	218	640	644	272	1774

Risk Estimate (s.e.): 0.4348 (0.0067) Correctly classified: **56.5%**	Risk Estimate (s.e.): 0.4892 (0.0118) Correctly classified: **51.1%**

Bold: Correctly classified
Risk Estimate: the proportion of misclassified cases

The MNL models

In order to compare the performance of the rule-based model to the traditional quantitative modelling approaches to tourist decision making, three MultiNomial Logit

(MNL) models were estimated on the same training set. For the first model – an MNL model without CHAID-pre-processing – the conditions in Table 2 were used without a categorization of condition states by the CHAID algorithm. Hence, continuous conditions like age and the number of previously scheduled days were entered as covariates and nominally and ordinally scaled variables were dummy coded and entered as factors into the MNL-model (SPSS 9.0 Nomial Regression). All factors and covariates were included in the utility function using alternative specific parameters and 'Autumn' was arbitrarily selected as the base alternative. In this model, missing values of factors were treated as a separate condition state. Missing values of the continuous condition variables (covariates) could, however, not be included in this model. This would have a dramatic effect on the number of valid trips because, on top of the 'normal' missing values, respondents younger than 16 years had not answered the additional questions on day-trips ('NDAYTRIPS') and numbers of free days ('FREEDAYS'). Similarly, people without a job had missing values on the 'FREEDAYS' variable. Since the condition 'WORKWEEK' included a state 'younger than 16 years old', it was decided to set the number of day-trips and the number of free days for trips made by this group of respondents at '0'. Similarly, the condition 'WORK' already included a dummy for the non-working situation, and the number of free days for these respondents was set at '0' too. Finally, 'real' missing values on these continuous condition variables were set at the average values over the other respondents, i.e. '37' (the round average of 36.5) for the number of free days and the value '4' (16-20 day-trips per year) for the number of day-trips (valid average was 16.7 day-trips per year). This model thus included 255 (df = 252) parameters and performed reasonably well as indicated by the pseudo Rho-squared = .175. Although not all the parameters proved to be significant, the entire model was used to predict the season for each trip in the two sets, the results of which are presented in Table 5.

Table 5 Classification Matrix for the MNL-Model without CHAID-pre-processing (255 parameters)

Pre-dicted Cat.	Actual Category									
	Training Set					Validation Set				
	Win.	Spr.	Sum.	Aut.	Total	Win.	Spr.	Sum.	Aut.	Total
Win.	**71**	65	21	26	183	**26**	23	14	9	72
Spr.	366	**1278**	454	455	2553	131	**413**	155	139	838
Sum.	151	496	**1436**	251	2334	48	172	**460**	89	769
Aut.	40	72	57	**108**	277	13	32	15	**35**	95
Total	628	1911	1986	840	5347	218	640	644	272	1774
	Correctly classified: **54.1%**					Correctly classified: **52.7%**				

Bold: Correctly classified

For the second model – an MNL model with CHAID-pre-processed condition states '*TREE*' – the condition states that appeared in the CHAID model described above were entered as alternative specific factors into a MNL model (again: 'Autumn' was the reference season). This implies that the condition variables and states that were not used in the CHAID model were also excluded from this second MNL model. This model included 201 (df = 198) parameters and performed reasonably well as indicated by McFadden's pseudo R-Squared = .176. Again, the entire model was used to predict the season for each trip in two sets, the results of which are presented in Table 6.

Table 6 Classification Matrix for the MNL Model with CHAID-pre-processed Condition States '*TREE*' (201 parameters)

Pre-dict-ed Cat.	Actual Category									
	Training Set					Validation Set				
	Win.	Spr.	Sum.	Aut.	Total	Win.	Spr.	Sum.	Aut.	Total
Win.	**69**	47	14	28	158	**26**	27	8	9	70
Spr.	334	**1248**	419	401	2402	115	**393**	147	132	787
Sum.	169	520	**1460**	264	2413	53	182	**467**	98	800
Aut.	56	96	75	**147**	374	24	38	22	**33**	117
Total	628	1911	1968	840	5347	218	640	644	272	1774
	Correctly classified: **54.7%**					Correctly classified: **51.8%**				

Bold: Correctly classified

Finally, for the third model – an MNL model with CHAID-pre-processed condition states '*SEPARATE*' – continuous conditions were categorized using the 'equal-frequency method' and each condition variable was entered into the exhaustive CHAID algorithm separately to obtain the most significant merger of states for this condition. Again, the resulting condition states were dummy coded and entered into an MNL model as alternative-specific factors and 'Autumn' was selected as the base alternative. This model included 228 (df = 225) parameters and McFadden's pseudo R-Squared equalled .165. Finally the entire model was used to predict the season for each trip in the two sets, the results of which are presented in Table 7.

Table 7 Classification Matrix for the MNL Model with CHAID-pre-processed Condition States '*SEPARATE*' (228 parameters)

Pre-dict-ed Cat.	Actual Category									
	Training Set					Validation Set				
	Win.	Spr.	Sum.	Aut.	Total	Win.	Spr.	Sum.	Aut.	Total
Win.	**61**	42	22	26	151	**20**	16	6	10	52
Spr.	363	**1282**	464	411	2520	121	**408**	171	137	837
Sum.	161	499	**1410**	269	2339	57	172	**451**	94	774
Aut.	43	88	72	**134**	337	20	44	16	**31**	111
Total	628	1911	1968	840	5347	218	640	644	272	1774
	Correctly classified: **54.1%**					Correctly classified: **51.3%**				

Bold: Correctly classified

The predictive performances compared

The Tables 5 to 7 show the classification matrices for the comparable MNL models applied to the same training and validation sets. With regard to the tree MNL models, the models without CHAID-pre-processing and with the individually merged condition states perform slightly worse on the training set than the other model while they include 24 or even 54 parameters more. However, the model without CHAID-pre-processing is very robust and it performs best on the validation set. In contrast, the model with the condition states that appeared in the CHAID tree-model performs most favourable on the training set and second best on the validation set – the differences in predictive performances are, however, very small. Comparing the three MNL models to the CHAID-based model (Table 4) indicates that the CHAID-based model outperforms the MNL models with regard to the training set (56.5% vs. 54.1%, 54.7% and 54.1% correctly classified cases), but that this advantage disappears when the models are tested on the validation set (51.1% vs. 52.7%, 51.8% and 51.3% correctly classified cases). Finally, comparing the number of predicted and observed choices per season for each model shows that the MNL models suffer from similar biases at the aggregate level in terms of overestimating spring and summer trips and underestimating the number of winter and autumn choices. The MNL models underestimate the number of winter trips more seriously, but perform slightly better on the aggregate number of autumn trips. In other words, none of the models clearly outperforms the other models, the rule-based model appears to be slightly less transferable to new sets of cases and the MNL model without CHAID pre-processing performs the best in terms of transferability – but, again, differences are very small.

Conclusion and Discussion

As an alternative to the more traditional utility-based approaches to modelling tourist choice behaviour, this paper proposed and tested a technique that represents tourist decisions by deriving decision rules from empirical data. More specifically, a tree-induction algorithm known as Chi-squared Interaction Detection (CHAID) was used to discover which actions (decisions) were taken under which conditions. This paper has shown that a set of 100 exclusive and exhaustive decision rules induced by a CHAID-based algorithm equalled the predictive performance of a multinomial logit model consisting of 255 parameters that was calibrated and tested on the same data-set (MNL-model without CHAID-pre-processing). Also, it was shown that the number of condition states that are entered in the MNL model can be reduced without decreasing the predictive performance of the model by using CHAID pre-processed condition states. Overall, however, it was concluded that none of the models clearly outperformed the other models, and that, in the present study, the CHAID-based model was slightly less transferable to new cases, although, again, the differences were insignificant. The MNL models, on the other hand, were much more complex than the rule-base model (201-255 parameters vs. 100 exclusive and exhaustive decision rules).

The proposed rule-based approach to tourist decision making relieves some of the limitations of the more traditional modelling approaches because it offers more flexibility in modelling tourist choice behaviour. In particular with regard to the model specification, rule-based models do not assume an a priori functional form of model, nor do they require the explicit inclusion of interactions (i.e. consciously deliberated relationships) between condition states. There are, however, three obvious difficulties in deriving and using rule-based models. One of the main disadvantages of sets of decision rules is that they can become rather large and it may sometimes be difficult to represent the set of exclusive and exhaustive decision rules economically. On the other hand, the utility-based models presented in this paper suffer from similar problems and can also become very complex. The advantages and disadvantages with regard to the communication and interpretation of the results of both approaches should be compared in future research. Secondly, at present, little is known about the possibilities of the various rule-inducing algorithms. With regard to the CHAID-based algorithm that was used in this paper it was concluded, for instance, that the transferability of the model should be considered carefully. Stricter stopping criteria may possibly relieve this problem. Future research should therefore focus on the optimal settings for this algorithm. In addition, the characteristics and effects of other rule-inducing algorithms such as C4.5 and CART could also be examined in the context of modelling tourist choice behaviour.

Third and finally, the proposed approach used deterministic decision rules to predict tourist choice behaviour. That is, observations complying with particular condition states were all assigned to the action with the highest confidence value. This can be a concern when the confidence values of the decision rules are rather low. Alternatively, the decisions can be interpreted as probabilistic rules, where the distribution over the actions (see, for example, Figure 2) is used rather than an all-or-nothing assignment to the dominant action. Future research should explore the application of both deterministic and probabilistic rule-based systems in tourism research.

Endnotes

[1] A decision table is a matrix-like representation of the decision-making process that consists of condition variables (left upper part), their levels or states (right upper part), actions or decisions (left bottom part) and rules that link condition states to actions (right bottom part) (Verhelst, 1993; Vanthienen and Wets, 1994; Witlox, 1995).

[2] It should be noted that, in order to reduce the task load for respondents, the CVO-quarterly measurements record detailed information on the two longest vacations of each quarter only. This implies that if people make three or more vacations in a particular quarter, only the most important information (dates of departure and return, destination, accommodation, means of transportation, expenses and the size of the travel party) is available for the third (and subsequent) vacation(s), and that there are missing values on a number of other vacation-related variables, including, for instance, the composition of the travel party and the activities.

[3] The trips pursued by a tourist during a particular year are subsequently scheduled in time. Evidently, the order in which these trips are scheduled will affect the results. To reduce the complexity of the model, the scheduling priority of each activity is first based on the duration (the longer the trip, the higher the priority) and second, if trip duration is identical, on the travel party (trips with schoolchildren have the highest priority; independent trips the lowest). The importance of a trip within the scheduling process thus reflects the idea that long trips often have a more extensive planning horizon, and establishes the commitment to other people and their schedules.

References

Arentze, T.A., Hofman, F. and Timmermans, H.P.J. (1997) Deriving Rules from Activity Diary Data: A Learning Algorithm and Results of Computer

Experiments. Paper presented at the Informs San Diego Conference, San Diego, USA, May 5-7 1997.

Arentze, T.A., Hofman, F., Van Mourik, H., Timmermans, H.J.P. and Wets, G. (2000) Using Decision Tree Induction Systems for Modelling Space-Time Behaviour. *Geographical Analysis* (in press).

Biggs, D., De Ville, B. and Suen, E. (1991) A Method of Choosing Multiway Partitions for Classification and Decision Trees. *Journal of Applied Statistics* 18, 49-62.

Breiman, L., Friedman, R.A., Olshen, R.A. and Stone, C.J. (1984) *Classification and Regression Trees*. Wadsworth, Belmont, CA.

Dellaert, B.C.G., Ettema, D.F. and Lindh, Ch. (1998a) Multi-faceted Tourist Travel Decisions: A Constraint-based Conceptual Framework to Describe Tourists' Sequential Choices of Travel Components. *Tourism Management* 19, 313-320.

Dellaert, B.C.G., Prodigalidad, M. and Louviere, J.J. (1998b) Using Conjoint Analysis to Study Family Travel Preference Structures: a Comparison of Day-trips and 1-week Holidays. *Tourism Analysis* 2, 67-75.

Goldberg, D.E. (1989) *Genetic Algorithms in Search, Optimization and Machine Learning*. Addison-Wesley Publishing Company, Reading, MA.

Greene, D.P. and Smith, S.F. (1987) A Genetic System for Learning Models of Consumer Choice. Paper presented at the *Second International Conference on Genetic Algorithms*, Massachusetts Institute of Technology, Cambridge, MA.

Jeng, J-M. and Fesenmaier, D.R. (1997) Facets of the Complex Trip Decision Making Process. Proceedings of the *28th Annual Conference of the Travel and Tourism Research Association*, Norfolk, Virginia, USA, June 15-18 1997, 31-41.

Kass, G.V. (1980) An Exploratory Technique for Investigating Large Quantities of Categorical Data. *Applied Statistics* 29, 119-127.

Lindh, C., Dellaert, B. and Ettema, D. (1995) Longer Term Activity Scheduling of Overnight Long Distance Trips: A Longitudinal Telephone Survey. Paper presented at the Workshop Activity Based Approaches: Activity Scheduling and the Analysis of Activity Patterns. Eindhoven, The Netherlands, May 25-28 1995.

Magidson, J. (1995) The CHAID Approach to Segmentation Modeling: CHI-Squared Automatic Interaction Detection. In: Bagozzi, R.P. (ed.) *Advanced Methods of Marketing Research*. Blackwell Publishers Ltd., Oxford, UK, pp. 118-159.

Mansfeld, Y. (1992) From Motivation to Actual Travel. *Annals of Tourism Research* 19, 399-419.

Oliver, J.R. (1994) Finding Decision Rules with Genetic Algorithms. *AI Expert* 9, 33-39.

Quinlan, J.R. (1993) *C4.5 Programs for Machine Learning*. Morgan Kaufmann Publishers, San Mateo, CA.

Richards, G. (1998) Time for a Holiday? Social Rights and International Tourism Consumption. *Time & Society* 7, 145-160.

SPSS (1998) *AnswerTree 2.0 User's Guide*. Chicago, IL.

Strambi, O. and Van de Bilt, K.A. (1998) Trip Generation Modeling Using CHAID, a Criterion-Based Segmentation Modeling Tool. *Transportation Research Record 1645*, nr. 98-0740, 24-31.

Thill, J.C. and Wheeler, A. (2000) Knowledge Discovery and Induction of Decision

Trees in Spatial Decision. In: Reggiani, A. (ed.) *Spatial Science: New Frontiers in Theory and Methodology*. Springer, Nuremberg (in press).

Van der Most, K. (1996) Continu Vakantie Onderzoek (CVO). In: *Handboek Recreatie en Toerisme*, pp. 1730-3-1730-12.

Vanthienen, J. and Wets, G. (1994) From Decision Tables to Expert System Shells. *Data and Knowledge Engineering* 13, 265-282.

Verhelst, N.P.M. (1993) *Beslissingstabellen*. Lansen Publishing bv, Leidschendam.

Wets, G., Vanhoof, K., Arentze, T. and Timmermans, H. (2000) Identifying Decision Structures Underlying Activity Patterns: An Exploration of Data Mining Algorithms. Paper presented at the *Annual TRB Meeting*. Washington DC, January 2000.

Witlox, F. (1995) Qualitative Housing Choice Modelling: Decision Plan Nets Versus Decision Tables. *Netherlands Journal of Housing and the Built Environment* 10, 209-237.

Woodside, A.G. and MacDonald, R. (1994) General System Framework of Customer Choice Processes of Tourism Services. In: Gasser, R. and Weiermair, K. (eds.) *Spoilt for Choice*. Kultur Verlag, Austria, pp. 31-59.

Chapter eight
Two Means to the Same End: Hierarchical Value Maps in Tourism – Comparing the Association Pattern Technique with Direct Importance Ratings

Andreas H. Zins
Institute for Tourism and Leisure Studies
University of Economics and Business Administration
A-1090 Vienna, Austria

Introduction

There are manifold cognitive approaches in the consumer behaviour theory which try to give detailed insight into the criteria influencing preference building and final buying decisions. One basic assumption for the development of a marketing theory is that transactions do not happen arbitrarily but purposely, guided by some particular objective. Hence, the regulating concept stimulating, restraining or blocking these exchange processes can be seen in the value attributed by the consumer (Kotler and Levy, 1969). Concepts such as motivations, benefits, product and service quality are useful instruments for modelling learning processes in general and in the field of tourism in particular. The common denominator of these concepts is the focus on value perspectives which differ in the level of abstractness and in the referred object of description (e.g. characteristics about the individual, the product, or the product-individual relationship).

Value is an abstract concept whose meaning is context specific (Sweeney, 1994). To mention only some views in the marketing field (see Patterson and Spreng, 1997 for an extended discussion):

- a relation or trade-off between all advantages received and disadvantages taken into account (e.g. Monroe and Krishnan, 1985; Buzzell and Gale, 1987; Monroe, 1990; Sweeney, 1994) or similar
- a weighted comparison between give- and get-characteristics (Sawyer and Dickson, 1984) or
- 'the consumer's overall assessment of the utility of a product based on perceptions of what is received and what is given.' (Zeithaml, 1988, p. 14)
- value is not to be reduced to its functional aspects but spans to social, emotional and epistemic components (Sheth *et al.*, 1991).

Holbrook (1994) developed a systematic taxonomy describing customer value by three dimensions (self-oriented – others-oriented; extrinsic – intrinsic; active – reactive). He defines value as 'an interactive relativistic preference experience of which the essence involves a process wherein all consumer products perform services that potentially provide value-creating experiences.' (p. 22). His approach of postulating statements about the character and evaluation of products in meta-normative way may be useful in adopting a broader view of marketing that is not reduced to the concepts of quality and price. Throughout the past decades researchers have argued that consumers do not decide upon products or product attributes but buy desired benefits and experiences (e.g. Lancaster, 1966; Urban and Hauser, 1993; Meffert and Perrey, 1997). Hilliard (1950, p. 42), for example, wrote 'Value is affectivity occurring in the relational contexture determined by the reaction of an organism to a stimulus object.'

Much more marketing oriented but in essence not really differently Woodruff 1997, p. 142 notes: 'Customer value is a customer's perceived preference for and evaluation of those product attributes, attribute performances, and consequences arising from use that facilitate (or block) achieving the customer's goals and purposes in use situations. ... it links together products with use situations and related consequences experienced by goal-oriented customers. This definition is anchored in a conceptual framework provided by a means-end type of model (Gutman, 1982; Woodruff and Gardial, 1996).' Hence, the subjective evaluation of the value of a product or service is based on an appraisal of the advantages associated with the purchase, the possession, the usage or the experience.

Means-end type models have their roots in cognitive psychology and neuro-psychology (e.g. Popper and Eccles, 1977; Grunert, 1990 for an overview) and have been adopted as hierarchical value concepts for marketing purposes (e.g. Rokeach, 1973; Gutman and Reynolds, 1983; Kahle, 1984). Kahle (1983) defines personal values in his 'social adaptation theory' as strategies to adopt someone's needs or the self to situations. Personal values support to appraise the potential of objects, situations and events to satisfy these needs. Consequently, personal values are linked to the consumer's evaluation of an object to be labelled as customer value.

The consumer's perception of the value of an exchange process is commonly measured with respect to the monetary price to be paid (value for money). The amount of monetary funds are shifted from an objective to the consumer's subjective level by this procedure. At this level one and the same monetary amount may weigh differently according to the varying financial standing, revenue prospects, and intrinsic value of money. However, it is necessary to consider the non-monetary contributions in an analogous manner; particularly in the context of highly individualized services with customer presence. The subjective evaluation of the psychological expenses (information search, appraisal and selection of alternatives) and the customer's time input must not be overlooked. Taking these elements into account it is not sufficient to calculate the requirements in absolute units (if possible at all) but to consider the various starting conditions. Following Kahnemann and Tversky's (1979) findings, the impacts of gains or losses have to be analysed in terms of their respective relative changes of benefits. Dowling and Staelin (1994) did incorporate this assumption in their risk behaviour model by introducing the concept of individual's 'wealth position' that can be understood as the ability to absorb losses.

At the phase of evaluating product (travel) alternatives the potential traveller may consult previous experiences, recommendations and stories from others, catalogues, brochures, videos, media reports and other sources (Schmoll, 1977; Mathieson and Wall, 1982; Moutinho, 1987; Goodall, 1991). He/She has some – more or less – vague perceptions about the particular travel elements (transportation, accommodation, catering, guides, sporting and recreation facilities). Nevertheless, the customer, first, anticipates his/her contribution to the entire production process and the consumption situation and, later, influences the realization. In contrast, the supplier/retailer sells implicitly not only the travel products and services but a situation as well: implicitly (e.g. climatic conditions) or explicitly (e.g. the atmosphere of a club resort). Consequently, evaluative processes – pre- or post-experience – on the part of the consumer are not restricted to the product and service attributes in a narrow sense.

Adopting such an extended conceptualization of products and services the question is raised to which degree traditional cognitivistic approaches (e.g. multi-attribute attitude models) for modelling choice and post-choice evaluation seem to be appropriate and efficient. According to Güthoff (1995) the various service quality models (e.g. Grönroos, 1984; Corsten, 1986) proposed in the literature are only apt to a limited degree to fully capture the complex service bundles. However, while these models strongly emphasize the characteristics of the services including process or interaction qualities, they neither consider explicitly the situational factors nor the customer contribution. Bitner (1992) shows theoretically in her servicescape framework that cognitive, emotional and physiological responses on the part of the customer and on the part of the employee are conceivable. These responses depend on environmental conditions (three dimensions of the servicescape) and are moderated by personal traits and situational factors. Though crowding phenomena are explicitly addressed within the spatial layout dimension, psycho-social influences deriving from foreign situations (e.g. different language, different habits and customs, multiple cultures represented by other consumers and/or employees) do not appear in her framework.

This study concentrates on two main issues. First, it tries to incorporate situational (atmospheric, environmental) factors at the product and the consequence level into the service evaluation process. Second, it compares two methodologies to derive subjectively based, meaningful value hierarchies. This will be done by applying two closed response formats to the same sample population. A direct rating format will be opposed to a fixed structure means-end instrument called association pattern technique (APT). The main characteristics of the means-end approach and the related methodologies will be outlined in the first section. The results from an empirical study will be presented and discussed in the following sections.

Means-End Chains

Basic principles

Means-end hierarchies aim at capturing the consumer's knowledge structures in a systematic way (Newell and Simon, 1972; Gutman, 1982). Gutman's theory is based on the idea that products and services are means to specific ends or objectives of consumers. These objectives are guided and controlled by personal values. Two assumptions underlie this concept: (1) Any consumer action is linked to consequences (2) Every consumer will learn to associate actions with particular consequences. These consequences may be positive or negative; they emerge directly from consumption of the product or later from the reaction of the consumption behaviour. It is postulated that consumers will act to endorse the desired consequences and at the same time to minimize negative ones (Gutman and Reynolds, 1983).

In-depth interviews have been developed called 'laddering' to discover such attribute-consequence-value chains. This method needs two steps. The first step tries to gather relevant product criteria (concrete attributes) applying a free elicitation task. During the second phase attributes are inquired why they are important to the individual. The on-going inquiry stops at the moment when answers become circular, when the respondent denies an answer despite various questioning techniques, or when the answer chain arrives at a terminal value.

After the data collection the coding process begins. The coding task aims at classifying each of the answers into an appropriate cognitive category (attribute, consequence, personal value) in a consistent way. Walker and Olson (1991) differentiated six categories: concrete and abstract attributes, functional and social-psychological consequences, instrumental and terminal values. To avoid subjective colouring of this procedure it is suggested to employ several judges independently. A continuous link between product attribute, consequence and personal value is labelled 'ladder'. The next step in the data processing tries to aggregate several individual ladders. From observing two interrelated category levels an implication matrix can be set up. From such an implication matrix a hierarchical value map can be derived which reflects the dominant cognitive structures of a group of consumers.

Referring to the validity of results from the laddering-technique Grunert and Grunert (1995) point to four criteria: (1) The cognitive structures and processes must not be biased by the researcher. This will be maintained predominantly by free elicitation techniques. Results derived from other investigations are seen to be tolerable. (2) The data collection should incorporate a minimal strategic perspective or at least a situation that comes very close to the real buying decision. The higher up the degree of abstract level the more cognitive processes will be triggered by the question mode which bias the original cognitive structures. (3) Coding should be done with cognitive categories which are familiar to the consumer, to the researcher and to the addressee of the results. This requirement can be met either by using strictly formalized coding procedures or by keeping purposely the criteria elicited by the consumer redundant. The latter option depends heavily on the amount of context information given during the interview. (4) Data aggregation should be managed theory-driven. A decision is to be made whether only the most important aspects of the cognitive structures of one group of consumers should be visualized or whether the focus is on the entire cognitive map of a sample. These objectives are handled by applying different rules for condensing the data (determination of a cut-off point, assumption of non-redundancy or economy-of-storage).

The association pattern technique (APT)

In-depth interviews are time consuming and a heavy work load for both interviewers and respondents. Hence, collecting data from larger samples, it is economically not very effective to use a completely open interviewing technique. Pieters *et al.* (1995) and Botschen and Hemetsberger (1998) demonstrate that the laddering technique can be successfully applied when adopting a self-administering format. This format is pre-structured with a limited number of boxes and arrows while respondents may fill in attributes and the reasons why the respective entries are linked.

A further step towards standardization of the data collection procedure is documented in the studies of ter Hofstede *et al.* (1998) and ter Hofstede *et al.* (1999). They apply a fully structured method for measuring the attribute-consequence (AC) and the consequence-value (CV) links which they call association pattern technique (APT). The first application demonstrates that compared to the traditional laddering technique the AC- and CV- links can be collected independently because they are unconditional to each other. In addition, the authors show that the hierarchical value maps derived from both techniques (laddering and APT) differ in content; however, the structures could not be identified as significantly different.

Applications in tourism

Means-end chains are seen to be highly relevant in the context of experience-based services. The texture for travel experiences seems to be very similar for quite a large variety of vacation trips: moving from one spot to another, change of the environment, stay in some accommodation, restaurants, beaches, sightseeing, events, friendly personnel. However, the travel motivations to be fulfilled by such travel activities are quite diverse and differently mixed for different travellers. The interpretation of the various product elements of a vacation trip has obviously many degrees of freedom which may be reduced to limited extent by situative, experiential, and personality factors.

Van Rekom (1994) illustrates the laddering technique for deriving means-end chains in the tourism context (e.g. for leisure attractions: Crotts and van Rekom, 1994). He stresses that hierarchical value maps are highly useful for the entire service chain which are necessary to convey and fulfil vacation experiences in a consistent manner. In many cases, it is not a single organization which is responsible for or delivers the entire tourism product and cares for the whole travel experience. Hence, it is even more difficult to guarantee a consistent positioning of travel products. Where the vertical integration cannot be realized effectively (Club Med is cited as an example) cooperations should envisage to enable consumers to perceive a viable, complete chain identity.

Klenosky *et al.* (1993) demonstrate the usefulness of the laddering technique by another example (choice of a ski destination). Three levels of abstractness have been differentiated: product attributes (n = 13), consequences (n = 7) and personal values (n = 4). They all emerged from free elicitation and were classified afterwards. The following categories for the level of personal values are similar to the list of values (Kahle 1983): 'sense of accomplishment', 'security', 'sense of belonging' and 'fun and excitement'. The remaining values ('self-respect', 'warm relationships with others', 'self-fulfilment' and 'being well-respected') were not used by the respondents. Clustering similar ladders into groups resulted in different typical explanations for the choice of a ski destination. The authors suggest further to draw different hierarchical value maps for routinized and novice skiers or to oppose HVM for skiers and non-skiers.

Another example for the laddering technique can be found in the context of transportation (rail travel; Bauer *et al.*, 1998). The objective of the study was among others to identify cultural differences between German and French rail travellers. These differences should be visualized by hierarchical value maps. Sixty respondents were interviewed; their answers were aggregated into 27 categories; eight of them represent personal values: five instrumental values (being successful, hedonism, living in a responsive manner, curiosity, sharing one's live with others) and three terminal values (joy of life, satisfaction, self-respect). Five value clusters were formed out of these eight personal values and described by additional characteristics.

Frauman *et al.* (1998) compared the laddering methodology with the interpretation of direct importance ratings for attributes, consequences and personal values; a comparative study with a similar objective to those of ter Hofstede *et al.* (1998). Research objects were pedagogical facilities and services for experiencing nature (e.g. information centres, guided walking tours, campfire programmes, overnight hikes, self-guided interpretive trails). The attribute lists (stemming from literature reviews and ad hoc discussions), consequences (developed predominantly from Drivers *et al.*'s 'Recreation Experience Preference Scales', 1991) and personal values (LOV) were condensed by factor analyses. The nine LOV items could not be reduced further. Correlation analyses were exercised at factor level. The cognitive levels revealed associations as strong as between 0.32 and 0.47. Some similarities in content could be detected between the results from the laddering technique and the correlation analyses. The derived hierarchical value maps differed, however, in some essential aspects. These differences were argued to stem partially from omitting the learn-dimension in the closed-format data collection. In their summary the authors recommend linking both techniques: As a first step, a small scale investigation will collect and identify the whole range of relevant criteria. The second step may be a larger scale investigation with a standardized measurement instrument.

Applied Methodology

The empirical study is designed to draw a comparison between the results from direct rating tasks and the association pattern technique. This approach will complement the findings from the design (correlation analyses versus laddering technique) applied by Frauman *et al.* (1998) and the design (laddering versus association pattern technique) applied by ter Hofstede *et al.* (1998). It is expected that the convergence of the two techniques will be much higher in the present experiment because of the strictly pre-structured response format; however, differences in the aggregated weight structure will not be surprising.

The following cognitive elements are used for this comparative approach (see Figure 1). Product attributes and travel consequences have been developed – partly from the literature, partly from own previous studies, partly from two rounds of focus group interviews. The point of the empirical research guaranteed that every respondent was already deeply involved in some kind of planning activities for the next summer holiday trip. Therefore, it was decided to have the product attributes (limited to 18) evaluated from the point of view of the expected degree of supply or personal experience. This cognitive category has to be distinguished from a subjective importance judgement. While the latter may express a general guideline for determining which alternative products are considered for detailed inspection the former category is much more bound to the particular offers, circumstances and present situation. Unconditional ratings for expressing someone's importance tend to lead to an overestimation of the pretensions. Addressing the expectations associated with a specific product that is already definitely chosen or at least in the choice set may reflect a more realistic picture of the evaluation process where tradeoffs have already been applied. The attribute expectation was handled as a point estimate represented on a 7-point Likert-scale ranging from 1 'does not apply at all' to 7 'applies exactly'.

	Intensity of attribution	
Temporal dimension	**ex ante**	**ex ante**
Cognitive category	**Expectation**	**Subjective importance**
Product attribute	▨▨▨	
Consequence		▨▨▨
Attribute– Consequence– relation		▧▧▧
Personal values		▨▨▨
Consequence– Personal values– relation		▧▧▧

Note: dark grey fields applied for direct rating task; light grey fields applied for the APT.

Figure 1 Cognitive elements for means-end hierarchies

Consequences are conceptualized as motivational forces associated with the product category of pleasure travel. These cognitive categories may act as guidelines for the evaluation of product characteristics. The direction of the valences is twofold: a motivation can be more or less important to achieve a favourable outcome or to avoid an unfavourable outcome of an action. The rating task was therefore based on importance judgements over 25 consequences; 12 of them had an unfavourable content. Each statement could be evaluated on a 7-point Likert scale ranging from 1 'does not apply at all' to 7 'applies exactly'. At the highest abstract level the nine items of the List of Values (LOV, Kahle, 1984) were used. The German translation was adopted from Grunert and Scherhorn (1990). For this cognitive category a complete ranking task seemed to be more appropriate and less effortful than a scale-based rating.

The direct measurement of the attribute-consequence (AC-) links and the consequence-value (CV-) links as constitutional elements for the APT was done in a dichotomous way. Conceptually, it is difficult to decide whether this kind of association measurement expresses an expectation or a subjective importance. In this particular experimental situation, it relates personal with object spheres, motivational aspects with product characteristics. As the majority of the respondents has already developed a concrete idea about the next vacation trip the recalled cognitive category is assumed not to be related to the abstract product class but to a real expected consumption situation. Respondents had to associate values and attributes only to the subjectively more important consequences. Therefore, the attribute-consequence link can be either interpreted as an important instrumentality or as the expectation that an attribute will lead to an important consequence in this particular trip. A similar perspective is applicable for the consequence-value association.

Technically, the direct ratings for travel attributes, travel consequences and personal values have been measured first. As the complete recording of all possible AC-links (m = 450) and CV-links (p = 225) would lead to an extreme time and cognitive effort the procedure was shortened. The detailed inquiry of unimportant travel consequences would be dubious and irritating for the respondents. It is for this reason that only the ten most important consequences were chosen individually to be presented for the APT sequence. This sequence of questions were introduced by the following screen (Figure 2).

For each consequence a screen with the range of 18 travel attributes (in abbreviated mode, Figure 3) was presented. After each consequence-attributes screen a second screen form with the nine LOV-items with reference to that consequence had to be completed (Figure 4). Respondents were free to click on all, several or none of the possible items expressing the appropriate number and content of AC- and CV-links.

Empirical Study

The field study was administered using the computer interview software Sensus (version 2.0) on five notebooks. A group of 25 graduate course students collected five to six interviews each in May 1999 with people who definitely intended to take a holiday trip between June and September of the same year. This convenience sample required no quotas and yielded the number of 137 respondents.

Table 1 gives a demographic overview of the sample population and compares the structure with two travel studies from a larger sample which are representative for the same geographic region. It is evident that the student's population is largely over-represented in this study sample. However, there is an almost equal share of males and females; other age and professional categories are not clustered.

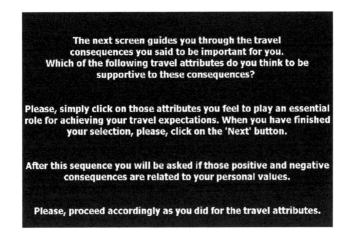

Figure 2 Introductory screen for the APT sequence

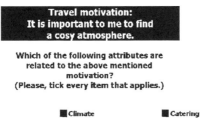

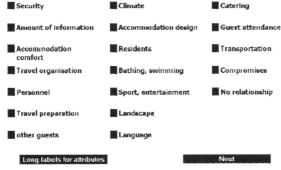

Figure 3 Computer interview screen assessing the attribute-consequence links

Figure 4 Computer interview screen assessing the consequence-value links

Table 1 Demographic Structure of the Convenience Sample

Structure	Sample	Travel Analysis 97	Travel Census 98
		in %	
Females	49	54	54
up to 20 years	5	3	3
up to 30 years	63	23	14
up to 40 years	12	21	21
up to 50 years	6	15	18
up to 60 years	8	15	19
up to 70 years	4	13	14
over 70 years	2	10	11
self employed	1	5	4
employed in advanced position	1	7	32
employed	10	26	
skilled worker	15	10	16
worker	7	6	
retired	11	27	24
household	2	6	6
student	2	8	15
no paid for occupation	53	6	3

Sources: Travel Analysis 1997 – Fessel – GfK; Travel Census 1998 – ÖSTAT 1999.

Results

Hierarchical value map from correlation analyses

In order to explain the relationships between product expectations, consumption goals and personal values one may consider to perform and interpret correlation analyses. Product attributes were mapped from the perspective of expectations about a concretely planned trip. By referring to such a real-life activity it is assumed to capture the cognitive content that is strongly associated with a much preferred travel product and the derived experience. Hence, the relationship between product expectations and favourable and unfavourable consequences can be interpreted as being instrumental. The links between travel consequences and personal values are considered to be less concrete. It is not obvious that consumption consequences for a particular product class are instrumental to one's personal values. However, it can be assumed that consumers, in general, do not decide to engage in consumption activities which are antagonistic to their personal values.

Pearson correlations show in total 72 significant links (at $p < 0.05$) between the 18 attributes and the 25 consequences. All attributes have at least one (and maximally 10) significant relationship. 22 out of the 25 travel consequences find an instrumental relationship to the used travel attributes. The aspects 'familiar atmosphere', 'feel free while on vacation' and 'distance from others' seem to be without connection to the predefined attributes. Figure 5 presents the significant correlations. Though, to keep the drawing uncluttered they had to be reduced in number. The correlations range between 0.17 and 0.36. One third of these associations are below 0.2 and are not shown in the figure. 60% have a range of between 0.2 and 0.29. Only correlations above 0.24 are added to the map to ensure a clear-cut interpretation. The bold-faced lines and numbers represent those few correlations above 0.3.

Additionally, the figure depicts the average importance of the respective cognitive category based on the direct rating task. Bold-framed fields signify values from the first third of the effectively used scale range, medium bold-framed fields are categories which lie in the medium range, and thin-framed fields are from the last third of the scale range representing aspects with relatively low priority. These descriptive elements apply for the relationships between consequences and values analogously. Yet, Spearman-correlations were computed considering the rank type rating of the personal values. Each of the nine items of the LOV shows significant correlations with 20 of the 25 consequences. In total, 41 links are available: 41% of them are below 0.2; 50% are in the medium range; only 5 of them above 0.24 are visualized in the figure. The remaining correlations exceed the 0.29 threshold.

By delimiting the interpretation to those correlations with an above average strength (>0.24) quite interesting insights can be derived. However, the filtered graphical representation should not imply that the remaining correlations are insignificant in a non-statistical sense. Much to the contrary, it turns out that the associations are manifold; and generally speaking, fulfilling particular consumption objectives is connected with a variety of product components.

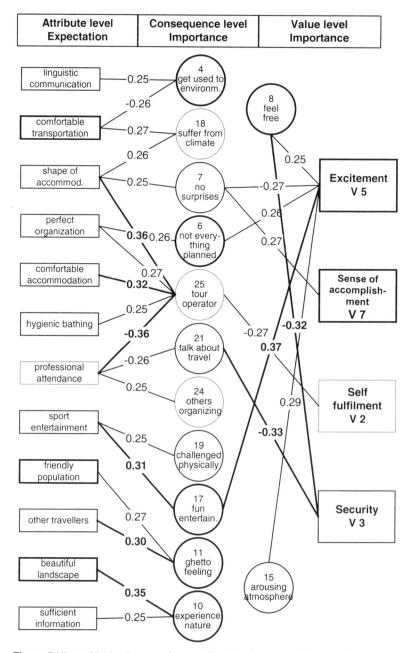

Figure 5 Hierarchical value map for vacation trips from correlation analyses

The interpretation of the means-end relationships is started from the most abstract level down to concrete product attributes. Considering the most important personal values, the search for a sense of accomplishment in the society is predominantly connected with the longing for control, avoiding surprises while on vacation. Less strong (not in the figure) but somehow consistent is the correlation with the expressiveness of travel experiences: what (relevant) other people think about my travel behaviour.

The personal value 'wishing to live an exciting life' shows the most strong associations to a variety of travel consequences: to have fun and entertainment, to get surprised (positively and negatively), to feel free, to have not everything planned in advance, to experience an arousing atmosphere, not to stay at remote and calm places and to be challenged physically. The personal value 'security' (at medium importance) is negatively associated with two travel consequences: the driving force for freedom and unrestrictedness as well as for expressiveness of the travel experiences, is counter-intuitive to the wish for living life in a secure environment. The somewhat weaker correlations fit into this scenario: avoiding surprises and an ever arousing surrounding, preferring to have a tour operator organizing the vacation trip.

Consequently, delegating these tasks means fewer possibilities to contribute to someone's self fulfilment. However, this personal value is supported by a sufficient distance from others, by specific challenges and by opportunities to talk and report about someone's experiences; maybe about some unintended adventures and surprises. Avoiding an ever arousing atmosphere or places and experiences with too much fun and entertainment seems to meet the desire for belonging, the feeling to be part of a well-known group to be accepted. Interestingly, the hedonic personal value of fun and entertainment does not show an instrumental relationship with travel experiences.

Following the means-end chains one level down several peculiarities are to be mentioned. On the one hand, there are travel consequences high in priority having no instrumental ability for any of the statements of personal values. On the other hand, correlations between very important personal values and travel consequences exist whose importance ratings were rather low. The first group is represented by statements such as 'to need several days to get acquainted to the unfamiliar environment', 'wishing to have not everything planned in advance', 'to accept something like a ghetto-feeling' and 'to experience nature consciously'. Values such as 'sense of accomplishment', 'security', 'sense of belonging' and 'fun and entertainment' adhere to the second group.

Wishing to have a tour operator planning and organizing the vacation trip is judged to be unimportant within this sample; however, for the relevant traveller segment this travel motivation has the strongest links with the following travel attributes: shape and design of the accommodation, comfortable accommodation, perfect organization, hygienic bathing facilities and professional guest services (yet with inverse sign). To meet the requirement for fun and entertainment it turns out to look for a sufficient sport and entertainment programme as well as for a friendly personnel. Taking the feeling of a vacation ghetto into account will be eased to some degree by a friendly population, by the undisturbed co-existence with other travellers, by a comfortable travel to and from the destination as well as by a sufficient quantity of information about the trip.

The very important aspiration to experience nature and wildlife is highly correlated with the product element 'beautiful landscape'. To have sufficient information available supports to achieve this experiential goal. The undisturbed co-existence of many travellers at one place helps to fulfil this objective to a somewhat reduced extent. For all those travellers looking for more degrees of freedom while on vacation ('having not everything planned in advance') the label 'perfect organization' appears to have an intimidating effect. However, deciding for a perfect travel organization may curb the effect of unfavourable surprises.

For all those who fear to suffer from the climate at their destination it is relieving to rely on a comfortable transportation, on an attractive design of the hotel complex, on the comfortable accommodation and on the perfect organization. The psychological and physiological effort to get acquainted to the unfamiliar environment seems to be reduced by fewer language barriers, by a friendly population, a perfect travel organization and by a pleasant co-existence with other vacationers. Surprisingly, a comfortable travel to and from the destination shows a negative correlation with the latter consequence. For those travellers for whom it is important to talk about their experiences to friends and relatives the focus is not on a professional organization of the local guest services (e.g. animation programmes).

In summary, for about half of the travel consequences significant correlations with travel attributes can be observed. Favourable and unfavourable (desires and fears) give a balanced picture. One third of the relatively important consequences ('interest in foreign cultures', 'tensions within travel party', 'no artificial scenery') does not appear in this means-end map reflecting only the stronger associations. Interestingly, intrinsic experiential goals – like 'feel free', 'arousing atmosphere' and 'fun and entertainment' – are not supported by concrete product elements.

Figure 6 summarizes the correlational means-end relationships on factor level. A factor analysis condensed the travel attributes to three spheres 'supply side', 'situation', and 'consumer' as it was suggested when applying an extended product perspective (see Appendix Table 2 for mean expectations and factor loadings). The travel consequences were factor analysed into eight dimensions (see Appendix Table 3 for mean importance ratings; factor solution omitted due to space limits): 1. psychological and physiological burden, 2. familiarity–strangeness, 3. fun–idleness, 4. degrees of freedom, 5. body consciousness, 6. social function, 7. authenticity, 8. self–other's organization. The content of these dimensions does not reflect clear counter-parts to the three spheres distinguished at product attribute level. The mean importance ranks for the list of values (LOV) are shown in Table 4 (see Appendix). Psychological and physiological burden stems from, supply-side product elements and from the environmental conditions. The authenticity dimension is associated with atmospheric elements (correlation $p < 0.10$) and with aspects stemming from the consumer. A similar split of contributions can be observed for the fun–idleness dimension: elements delivered by specific suppliers as well as by the traveller himself are responsible. With reference to the preference for self-organized or travel agency trips the correlations are clearly concentrated with the product and supplier's sphere.

In Figure 6 the links between travel consequences and personal values are extended by some weaker correlations (< 0.25) depicting all nine personal values. However, compared to the Figure 4, no other values than V2, V3, V5 and V7 turned out to have strong associations. The personal value 'sense of accomplishment' is strongly and positively linked with the social function of the travel experiences, while negatively with the burden factor and the search for authenticity. More self fulfilment may be achieved if the vacation trip is planned and organized by the traveller him- or herself.

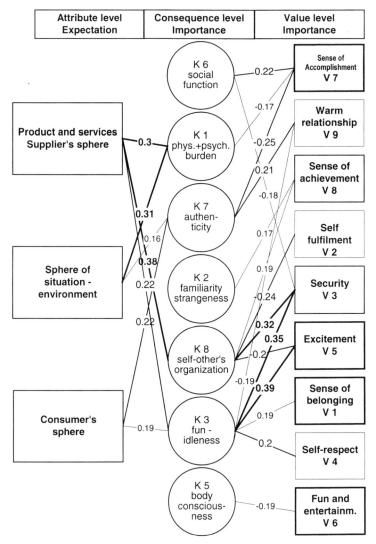

Figure 6 Hierarchical value map for vacation trips derived from correlations at factor level

Transferring the responsibility to somebody else (maybe a travel agency or tour operator) is not adverse to the need for security. However, if travellers seek to have a lot of fun and entertainment in life it is better to have their trips self-organized. Unexpectedly, this kind of personal value is positively correlated with the desire for experiencing calm and remote places.

The remaining personal values show significant links as well, however lower in strength (between 0.17 and 0.22). Warm relationships with others will be supported by authentic travel experiences as well as by the search for fun and entertainment. To go for unfamiliar settings is instrumental to experience the sense of achievement in one's life. Though, having someone's vacation organized by other people does not hamper this goal. Experiencing a sense of belonging as well as self-respect is not in conflict with looking for idleness while on vacation. The hedonic life value cannot be met by too much physical challenge.

Hierarchical value map from APT

The alternative approach to the means-end relationships derived from correlation analyses is based on the direct measurement of means-end sequences. The method of the association pattern technique (APT) starts with a limited set of means-end elements. In contrast, the laddering technique uses a completely free interviewing method which focuses on the instrumentality of two completely free elicited characteristics. The present empirical study inquires the instrumental character of various cognitive elements for the concrete intended vacation trip. Applying the APT, individual respondents could express this instrumental association only on a dichotomous basis.

The possible means-end combinations were restricted to ten subjectively most important consequences. This PC-controlled procedure not only reduced the cognitive effort but individualized to some degree the interviewing task. By this means the disadvantages of the closed response format compared to the free elicitation method could be compensated to some extent. Hence, the number of the theoretically possible AC-links was reduced from 450 to 180, for the possible CV-links from 225 to 90. Considering the total sample, 88% or 396 different AC-links were used at least once. The rate of exploitation for the CV-links amounts to 87% or 196 different combinations. The average response density has to take into account the number of maximally possible responses per respondent. The average usage rate is 30 AC-links and 15 CV-links. The number of links in both cases follows a normal distribution (see Figures 9 and 10 in the Appendix).

The graphical representation in a hierarchical value map is based on the more frequent links. More than 80% of the AC-links are quoted in less than 10% of the cases. Additionally 14% (or 61 AC-links) show a frequency between 11% and 19%. The remaining 27 links were inserted into Figure 7. Again, the frequency of occurrence was distinguished by the thickness of the lines: thin for frequencies between 20% and 25%, medium for 26% to 39% and thick for 40% to 72%. 80% of the CV-links are below a threshold of 10%. 11% of the links were cited in a range between 11% and 19% of the cases. Only nine CV-links have a frequency between 20% and 25%. As no other cognitive elements are addressed by this frequency category than by the remaining 5% of high frequency links, only the latter group was admitted for the graphical representation. The different frequencies are marked following the criteria for the AC-links. In addition, the different expectation and importance levels – as derived from the direct measurement task – for the cognitive elements are visualized by a different line-thickness of the field frames.

For each of the four personal values in Figure 7 at least one very important relationship with a travel consequence can recognized. The most frequent aspects instrumental to these personal values can be reduced to five: 'feel free', 'liking an arousing atmosphere', 'fun and entertainment', 'interest in foreign cultures' and 'self control'.

At the medium level 11 out of the 25 consequences show up among those with above average frequencies. On average, these 11 consequences were evaluated as most important (nine are rated in the highest third of the importance scale). This is not uniquely due to the pre-selection procedure of the most important 10 aspects. Because of the variation of the set of aspects from one respondent to another a configuration of consequences with a medium level of importance on average would be conceivable. Only the ghetto feeling does not find a frequently cited counterpart on a lower or higher abstraction level in the value chains. Yet, 13% associate the co-existence with other travellers and 12% the design of the hotel area with this kind of negative feeling. Four of the 18 travel attributes show a relative low frequency with respect to the pre-determined consequences: comfortable transportation, safe destination, sufficient travel information and comfortable accommodation.

The desire to learn about foreign cultures is the most intense reference for a number of travel attributes: the contact with the friendly population, a convenient climate, the beautiful landscape, no language barriers, and even food and beverages seem to play an important role for a cultural exchange. The second most significant argument focuses on the hedonic dimension of fun and entertainment. Obviously, this experience is nourished by a variety of sport and entertainment programmes, by the friendly population, by an undisturbed co-existence of many travellers, and by hygienic bathing facilities. A third, very frequent dimension concerns the conscious experience of nature. Travellers will benefit in this direction by a beautiful landscape, by pleasant climatic conditions, by a friendly personnel, and an attractive design of the resort. The fourth dimension with a high frequency of elicitation addresses the aspect of freedom, the possibility to live one's autonomy, free of narrowing rules and coincides with physical activity, the demand for a sufficient sport and entertainment programme, the professional guest attendance and good bathing facilities. 'To feel free' has additional links to the landscape and climatic factor.

The remaining consequences address negative aspects of a travel experience. They seem to be cognitively less strongly associated with other categories. However, they are represented in the list of highest frequencies with five elements. 'Not having everything planned in advance' is connected with the own intensive preparatory steps for the trip as well as with the desire for a perfect organization. To avoid an artificial scenery travellers want to get in touch with the friendly local population. This kind of social contact, the linguistic communication as well as the climatic conditions may help reducing the adaptation effort into the unfamiliar environment. Another element sometimes not to be avoided during a vacation trip is conflicts and tension among the travel party. This psychological burden is associated with the customer input factor of finding compromises together with the members of the travel party.

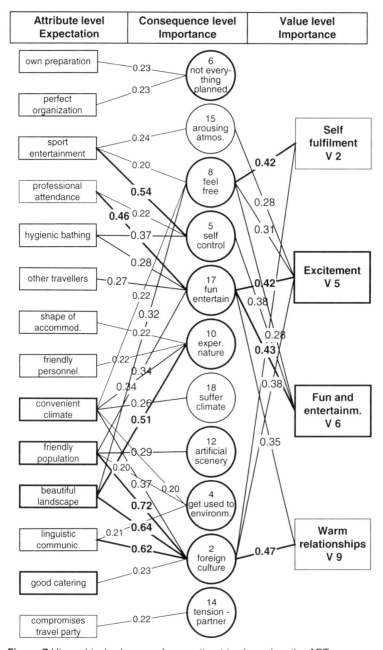

Figure 7 Hierarchical value map for vacation trips based on the APT

Discussion

Comparison of methods

The study of ter Hofestede *et al.* (1998) investigated the differences between laddering technique and the association pattern technique (APT) for four different products. The findings documented that both techniques converged in terms of the derived cognitive structure, however the content of the hierarchical value maps differed significantly. From their study the result that AC_i-links and C_iV-links are unconditional has been taken over as an implicit assumption for the product category of vacation trips. Fraumann *et al.* (1998) compared the laddering technique and direct importance ratings for attributes, consequences and personal values for guiding facilities in state parks. Their study implied that the cognitive representations derived from both methods differed significantly. This study is not designed to investigate structural differences as both applied techniques followed the same scheme of three levels of hierarchical values: attributes, desirable and undesirable consequences and personal values. Hence, the following comparison focuses on the differences in content.

Figure 8 is based on the average results from the APT for all respondents. The black-framed fields and black connecting lines depict those elements derived from the means-end analysis based on correlations (CA) which coincide with the APT findings. The grey shaped APT elements do not find an appropriate counterpart in the hierarchical value map from the CA. The remaining design characteristics follow the principles outlined for the previous figures. The CA features only six of the ten most important travel consequences whereas the APT elaborates nine. Three of the 13 consequences in the CA are relatively unimportant for the present sample. Yet, very important travel aspects such as 'learn about foreign cultures', 'to avoid artificially intact sceneries', 'maintaining someone's autonomy' and 'tensions with the travel partner' are not covered by the CA value map. Taking the almost negligible wish for package trips, the map from the CA specifies the most and strongest correlations. The cited travel elements are predominantly under the quality control of the tour operator. Hence, the correlations are consistent and plausible, however for this sample rather insignificant. Within the APT 14 out of the 18 travel attributes were cited very frequently which can be interpreted as high relevance or importance. In contrast, the CA characterizes only 12 out of the 18 attributes with significant correlations. Overall, five attributes are located in the top third of the used importance scale range. In the CA map only three of them, in the APT map four of these most important attributes are represented.

Apart from the modest matching of the hierarchical value maps from both techniques the APT delivers a much more dense net of relationships, especially for the most important travel motivations 'learn about foreign cultures', 'experience nature', 'having fun and entertainment', 'feel free' and 'not everything planned'. The CA map indicates that the supply of a variety of sport and entertainment programmes is sufficient to provide for the experience of the focal hedonic dimension for pleasure travel. The APT basically confirms this relationship, yet extends the plausible interpretation towards bathing facilities, the pleasant interaction with other travellers and with the friendly part of the population. In addition, the APT value map expands the insight that fun and entertainment seems to be not only instrumental to enjoy an exciting life but to the personal values of hedonism and warm relationships with others.

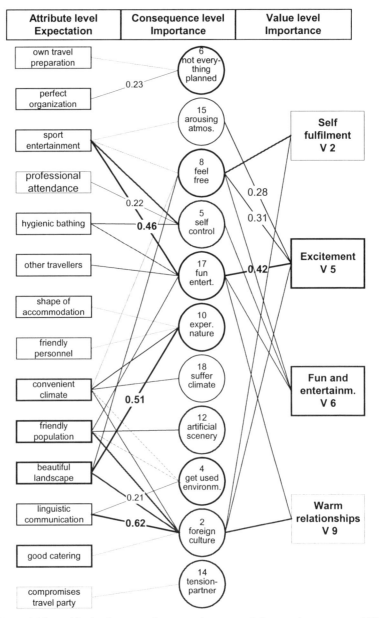

Figure 8 Hierarchical value maps in comparison: correlation analyses versus APT

A similar modest interpretation turns out for the experience of natural environments within the CA map. Beautiful, interesting landscapes are obvious prerequisites for the aspired nature-oriented experience. The sufficient information – as derived from the CA – may of course promote the intensity of experiences. However, only 1% of the respondents classify a direct instrumental relationship between these two issues. Furthermore, the desired conscious experience of natural environments has many more facets: e.g. the design factors of the resort, the pleasant climate, and even the friendly personnel are seen as mediators to this end.

The dominant motivation to experience freedom and spontaneity while on vacation turns out to have significant correlations only with some personal values. In contrast, the APT value map indicates clearly by what travel elements this strong feeling can be induced: by sports, entertainment, games, by the experience of the landscape as well as by climatic factors. The feeling of a piece of freedom during the vacation contributes not only to an exciting life but encourages a hedonic life and self fulfilment.

Implication and unresolved problems

From the comparison of the results it cannot be deduced that one of the applied techniques is wrong or right; though they are fairly distinct in their findings. It is the aggregation procedure that can be criticized which leads to a different cognitive picture. The direct rating task is more effortful compared to a dichotomous attribution of elements. Though, the number of evaluations is much more limited with the rating tasks ($i = 42$) compared to the APT ($j = 270$). Having more customer inputs – even on a low scaling level – turns into a more plausible picture about customers' valuation structures and provides a rich ground for interpretation and marketing planning purposes.

Both approaches substantiate that not only travel product elements for which a tour operator or different particular suppliers are responsible, but characteristics of the situation or environment as well as inputs from the traveller's personal sphere account for appreciating a travel experience (see Mattila, 1999 for similar results for business travellers). It was demonstrated that these spheres (identified as supply-side, situation and consumer) transcend via various mixed consequences into more abstract values. In turn, it can be argued that many travel motivations are linked to more than one particular travel element or attribute; sometimes to a multitude affiliated to different spheres of the entire travel experience. The consumer's sphere was represented only to a very small extent in this study. It is suggested to continue to go more into detail of this issue of customer integration into the service production process. It can be expected to contribute significantly to the explanation of product preferences, product choice, and finally of the satisfaction formation.

Finally, various methodological aspects are to be addressed. It would be worthwhile to test the assumption of unconditionality for the separated measurement of AC- and CV-links in the context of complex products and services; especially for services with customer presence like in tourism. If this assumption does not hold, the aggregation procedure is not that straightforward as with the applied APT and the complete value chains would have to be interpreted in a different way.

This study was based on a rather small convenience sample. No measure had been taken to look for a homogeneous sample structure. It can be assumed that the results between the two techniques would converge much more if the product variety would be smaller (taking e.g. only travellers to a selected destination, or only packaged-tour travellers, or city tourists). However, all these features are visible, behavioural aspects that do not guarantee a certain degree of homogeneity in terms of associated consumption goals or even personal values driving people to experience this or that particular product.

Another issue points to the cognitive categories referred to for this kind of investigation. Focusing on instrumental relationships means questioning why particular characteristics are important for the consumer. It is not evident that the value hierarchies would look the same if the consumer would have to reveal his/her expectations with respect to a concrete product or service to be purchased and consumed. Different reference categories remind about the extant literature in the context of service quality where different influences and conclusions have been drawn on this perspective. A comparative study with expectations and importance judgements could be fruitful. Another direction of extending this research agenda would be to investigate the hierarchical structure of the cognitive elements for travel experiences in more detail. The proposed six levels in the literature may act as a guideline. However, the problem of categorization of freely elicited notions in means-end-chain analyses is still a wide field of research.

Appendix

Table 2 Principal components analysis for 18 travel attributes

Product attributes	Expect-ation Mean	Spheres Factor loading Supply side	Situa-tion	Cons-umer
Extracted variance		35%	10%	8%
comfortable accommodation	4.8	0.90		
shape/design of accommodation	4.5	0.85		
professional guest attendance	3.8	0.79		
safe destination	5.1	0.69		
hygienic bathing facilities	5.1	0.66		
good catering, food and beverages	5.6	0.59		
comfortable transportation	5.2	0.58		
perfect organization	4.9	0.54		
friendly personnel	5.0	0.53		
sufficient sport facilities and entertainment	4.7	0.33		
friendly population	5.7		0.78	
undisturbed co-existence with other guests	5.1		0.70	
beautiful landscape	6.4		0.68	
convenient climate	5.7		0.63	
own intensive travel preparation	4.4			0.81
sufficient travel information	5.0			0.50
easy linguistic communication	4.8			0.33
many compromises within travel party	3.4	-	-	-

Table 3 Importance of 25 desirable and undesirable consequences

Desirable and undesirable travel consequences	Nr.	Desires, Fears	Intrinsic – Extrinsic	Subjective importance
I am very interested to learn about foreign cultures	2	+	E	6.0
On vacation I do not want to give up my autonomy	5	–	I	5.8
On vacation I want to feel really free	8	+	I	5.7
I like fun and entertainment while on vacation.	17	+	I	5.6
I deliberately accept a kind of 'ghetto' feeling	11	–	E	5.3
I cannot avoid tensions among travel party members while on vacation	14	–	E	5.2
I want to experience nature consciously during my holidays	10	+	E	5.1
I do not want to get in touch with an artificially intact scenery	12	–	E	5.0
It takes me some days to get acquainted to the unfamiliar environment	4	–	E	5.0
I do not want to have everything planned in advance	6	–	E	4.6
I will suffer from the climate at the destination	18	–	E	4.5
I want an arousing atmosphere at my destination	15	+	I	4.4
I want to come closer to my partner during the vacation	13	+	E	4.3
It is important to vacate at a reasonable price	23	–	E	4.3
On vacation I am longing for distance from others	9	+	E	4.2
I emphasize on talking to my friends and relatives about my travel experiences	21	+	E	4.2
On vacation I appreciate remote and calm places	16	–	I	4.1
I like a cosy atmosphere	1	+	I	3.6
I want to get physically challenged while on vacation	19	+	I	3.4
I do not want surprises while on vacation	7	–	E	3.3
I prefer to cut down my expenses around the year to allow for something special while on vacation	22	–	E	3.0
I like to have others care about the travel organization	24	+	E	2.7
It is important for me to have a tour operator organizing my trip	25	+	E	2.3
It is important for me what friends and relatives think about my travelling	20	+	E	2.3
It is strange and demanding to be surrounded by people who are so different	3	–	I	1.7

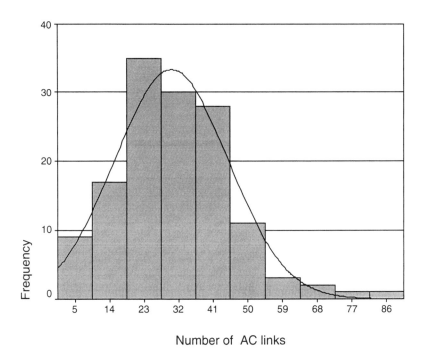

Number of AC links

Figure 9 Distribution density for AC links compared to normal distribution

Table 4 Subjective importance of personal values (LOV)

Personal Values (List of Values)	No.	Importance Rank
sense of accomplishment	7	6.7
excitement	5	5.9
fun and entertainment	6	5.7
sense of belonging	1	5.8
security	3	5.0
sense of achievement	8	4.7
self fulfilment	2	4.2
self-respect	4	4.1
warm relationship with other	9	3.2

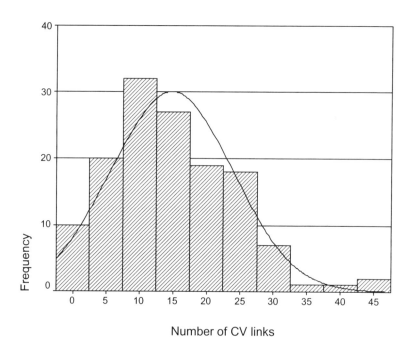

Number of CV links

Figure 10 Distribution density for CV links compared to normal distribution

References

Bauer, H.H., Huber, F. and Braunstein, C. (1998) Die Anwendung der means end-Theorie für die Produkt- und Werbegestaltung im Bereich des internationalen Personenfernverkehrs - Ergebnisse einer empirischen Studie zur interkulturellen Werteforschung. *Tourismus Journal* 2(2), 169-187.

Bitner, M.J. (1992) Servicescapes: The impact of physical surroundings on customers and employees. *Journal of Marketing* 56, 57-71.

Botschen, G. and Hemetsberger, A. (1998) Diagnosing means-end structures to determine the degree of potential marketing program standardization. *Journal of Business Research* 42, 151-159.

Buzzell, R. and Gale, B. (1987) *The PIMS Principles.* The Free Press, New York.

Corsten, H. (1986) Zur Diskussion der Dienstleistungsbesonderheiten und ihre ökonomischen Auswirkungen. *Jahrbuch der Absatz- und Verbrauchsforschung* 32 (1), 16-41.

Crotts, J.C. and van Rekom, J. (1994) Adding psychological value to visitor attractions. *Parks and Recreation* 29(9), 98-105.

Dowling, G.R. and Staelin, R. (1994) A model of perceived risk and intended risk-handling activity. *Journal of Consumer Research* 21, 119-134.

Driver, B. L., Tinsley, H. E. A. and Manfredo, M. J. (1991) The paragraphs about leisure and recreation experience preference scales: Results from two inventories designed to assess the breadth of the perceived psychological benefits of leisure. In Driver, B.L., Brown, P. J. and Peterson, G.L. (eds.) *Benefits of leisure.* Venture Publishing Inc., State College, PA, pp. 263-286.

Frauman, E., Norman, W.C. and Klenosky, D.B. (1998) Using means-end theory to understand visitors within a nature-based interpretive setting: a comparison of two methods. *Tourism Analysis* 2, 161-174.

Goodall, B. (1991) Understanding holiday choice. In: Cooper, C.P. (ed.) *Progress in Tourism, Recreation and Hospitality Management,* Vol. 3. Belhaven, London, pp. 58-77.

Grönroos, C. (1984) A service quality model and its marketing implications. *European Journal of Marketing* 18(4), 36-44.

Grunert, K. (1990) *Kognitive Strukturen in der Konsumforschung.* Physica, Heidelberg.

Grunert, K. G. and Scherhorn, G. (1990) Consumer values in West Germany: Underlying dimensions and cross-cultural comparison with North America. *Journal of Business Research*, 20(March), 97-108.

Grunert, K.G. and Grunert, S.C. (1995) Measuring subjective meaning structures by the laddering method: Theoretical considerations and methodological problems. *International Journal of Research in Marketing* 12(3), 209-225.

Güthoff, J. (1995) *Qualität komplexer Dienstleistungen. Konzeption und empirische Analyse der Wahrnehmungsdimensionen.* Deutscher Universitätsverlag, Wiesbaden.

Gutman, J. (1982) A means-end chain model based on consumer categorization processes. *Journal of Marketing* 46(Spring), 60-72.

Gutman, J. and Reynolds, T.J. (1983) Developing images for services through means-end chain analysis. In: Berry, L.L., Shostack, G.L. and Upah, G.D. (eds.) *Emerging Perspectives on Services Marketing.* American Marketing Association, Chicago, pp. 40-44.

Hilliard, A.L. (1950) *The Forms of Value: The Extension of Hedonistic Axiology.* Columbia University Press, New York.

Holbrook, M.B. (1994) The nature of customer value: An axiology of services in the consumption experience. In: Rust, R.T. and Oliver, R.L. (eds.) *Service Quality. New Directions in Theory and Practice.* Sage Publications, Thousand Oaks, CA, pp. 21-71.

Kahle, L.R. (ed.) (1983) *Social values and social change: adaptation to life in America.* Praeger, New York.

Kahle, L.R. (1984) *Attitudes and Social Adaption: a Person-Situation Interaction Approach.* Pergamon, Oxford.

Kahnemann, D. and Tversky, A. (1979) Prospect theory: an analysis of decision under risk. *Econometrica* 47(March), 263-291.

Klenosky, D.B., Gengler, C.E. and Mulvey, M.S. (1993) Understanding the factors influencing ski destination choice: A means-end analytic approach. *Journal of Leisure Research* 25(4), 362-379.

Kotler, P.J. and Levy, S.J. (1969) Broadening the concept of marketing. *Journal of Marketing* 33, 10-15.

Lancaster, K. (1966) A new approach to consumer theory. *Journal of Political Economy* 32, 132-157.

Mathieson, A. and Wall, G. (1982) *Tourism: Economic, Physical and Social Impacts.* Longman, London.

Mattila, A. (1999) Consumers' value judgments. *The Cornell Hotel and Restaurant Administration Quarterly* (February), 40-46.

Meffert, H. and Perrey, J. (1997) Nutzensegmentierung im Verkehrsdienstleistungs-bereich. *Tourismus Journal* 1(1), 13-40.

Monroe, K.B. (1990) *Pricing: making profitable decisions.* McGraw-Hill, New York.

Monroe, K.B. and Krishnan, R. (1985) The effect of price on subjective product evaluations. In: Jacoby, J. and Olson, L. (eds.) *Perceived Quality: How Consumers View Stores and Merchandise.* Lexington Books, Lexington, MA, pp. 209-232.

Moutinho, L. (1987) Consumer behaviour in tourism. *European Journal of Marketing* 21(10), 3-44.

Newell, A. and Simon, H.A. (1972) *Human Problem Solving.* Prentice-Hall, Englewood Cliffs, NJ.

Patterson, P.G. and Spreng, R.A. (1997) Modelling the relationship between perceived value, satisfaction and repurchase intentions in a business-to-business, services context: an empirical examination. *International Journal of Service Industry Management* 8(5), 414-434.

Pieters, R., Baumgartner, H. and Allen, D. (1995) A means-end chain approach to consumer goal structures. *International Journal of Research in Marketing* 12(3), 227-244.

Popper, K.R. and Eccles, J.C. (1977) *The Self and its Brain.* Springer International, Berlin.

Rokeach, M. (1973) *The Nature of Human Values.* Free Press, New York.

Sawyer, A.G. and Dickson, P. (1984) Psychological perspectives on consumer response to sales promotion. In: Jocz, C. (ed.) *Research on Sales Promotion: Collected Papers.* Marketing Science Institute, Cambridge, MA, pp. 1-21.

Schmoll, G.A. (1977) *Tourism promotion.* Tourism International Press, London.

Sheth, J.N., Newman, B.I. and Gross, B.L. (1991) Why we buy what we buy: a theory of consumption values. *Journal of Business Research* 22, 159-170.

Sweeney, J. (1994) *An Investigation of a Theoretical Model of Consumer Perceptions of Value.* School of Management and Marketing, Curtain University of Technology, Perth.

ter Hofstede, F., Audenaert, A., Steenkamp, J.-E.M. and Wedel, M. (1998) An investigation into the association pattern technique as a quantitative approach to measuring means-end-chains. *International Journal of Research in Marketing* 15(1), 37-50.

ter Hofstede, F., Steenkamp, J.-E.M. and Wedel, M. (1999) International market segmentation based on consumer-product relations. *Journal of Marketing Research* 36(February), 1-17.

Urban, G. and Hauser, J. (1993) *Design and marketing of new products.* Englewood Cliffs: Prentice-Hall.

van Rekom, J. (1994) Adding psychological value to tourism products. *Journal of Travel and Tourism Marketing* 3(3), 21-36.

Walker, B. and Olson, J.C. (1991) Means-end-chains: connecting products with self. *Journal of Business Research* 22, 110-122.

Woodruff, R.B. (1997) Customer value: the next source for competitive advantage.

Journal of the Academy of Marketing Science 25(2), 139-153.

Woodruff, R.B. and Gardial, S.F. (1996) *Know your Customer: New Approaches to Customer Value and Satisfaction.* Blackwell, Cambridge.

Zeithaml, V.A. (1988) Consumer perceptions of price, quality and value: A means-end model and synthesis of evidence. *Journal of Marketing* 52, 2-22.

Chapter nine
Segmenting Travel on the Sourcing of Information

Thomas Bieger and Christian Laesser
Institute for Public Services at the University of St. Gallen
Varnbüelstrasse 19, CH-9000 St. Gallen, Switzerland

Abstract

In this paper a market segmentation on the basis of information collection is presented. The study illustrates the important role of information in tourism. A successful strategy consists in providing convenience and in building up a relationship of trust between the tourist company and the tourist. Thus convenience is determined by quality of admission, availability of information and a customer-tailored presentation of information contents. A reliable source of information is not only provided by private relations (friends and relatives) but more and more by employees of travel agencies, tourist information and companies. One key goal of each information strategy lies in an optimal matching between human-oriented and technical-oriented sources of information.

Rationale: The Role of Information in Tourism (Theoretical Concept)

Tourist services are immaterial and intangible (Bieger, 1998). To begin with, this manifests itself as a mere promise of a potential performance on the part of the provider (Schertler, 1994). There is no prefabricated product, since the service can only be produced once provider and customers meet so that the original promise can be redeemed (*uno actu*).

In a competitive market such as tourism, consumer awareness, selection, and choice of tourism and hospitality products depend heavily on the information given to and used by the tourist (Moutinho, 1987; McIntosh and Goeldner, 1990; Fodness and Murray, 1997). From a guest's point of view, the quality and quantity of the risk which is linked to such a promise of performance is determined by information, which thus becomes the harbinger and initial indicator of the later, actual tourist service. It follows that the quality and quantity of the information that is available is an actual strategic success factor (Laesser, 1998). For this reason, it is necessary to have a more detailed knowledge of potential guests' information bases, and to make the right sources available to them at the right time in accordance with their information behaviour. The goal to be pursued here is to provide potential guests with a positive experience at the early stage of information gathering (which may, among other things, increase the probability of a booking being made) (Laesser, 1998). The information sources employed by tourists form the basis for vacation planning. Usually people in a travel group (travel situation) share in the information process and mostly, several sources of information are consulted in planning a trip.

Potential guests' identification of their intentions and their travelling decisions is the result of a variety of dimensions. The most important criteria of influence include (Snepenger et al., 1990; Laesser, 1998; Fodness and Murray, 1999):

- potential travellers' own intuition/desires;
- their own experience/satisfaction or dissatisfaction;
- information made available by the providers;
- information given by friends and relatives, recommendation by word of mouth;
- marketing influences such as information from guidebooks, press articles, TV programmes, TV/radio commercials and advertisements in the print media;
- the power or mystique of a brand or a brand name (geographical, topographical, potential travellers' predilections).

These criteria can also be perceived in the general structure of information sources used by Swiss travellers: the most important criterion for travellers from Switzerland is information given by friends and relatives (very important or important for 47%). Also of great importance are local and regional brochures (39%), tour operator catalogues (24%) and travel guides, books and journals (25%). Oral information by travel agents and tourist information offices occupies the middle ground (about 20%). What is interesting is the fact that the Internet (World Wide Web), at 5%, has drawn practically level with TV programmes and has already overtaken videotext! In this form, such a list of how information sources are utilized by all guest groups and in all travel situations does not allow for any conclusions regarding behaviour patterns.

Literature Review

Travel market segmentation is possible by several means. In the tourist industry, most producers will often have no practical choice but to deal with certain segments, mainly because of the location and nature of their business (Middleton, 1994). Possible segments include purpose of travel, buyer needs, user characteristics, demographic, economic or geographic characteristics, psychographic characteristics, price, etc. (Middleton, 1994; Bieger, 1998). Deriving from the contributions of Kotler (1984) or Chisnall (1985), it is necessary to focus on segments being discrete (clearly identifiable) and measurable (based on available market research data). From an implementing point of view, segments have further to be viable (the potential revenue being higher than the costs of the segment marketing mix) and appropriate (segments have to be compatible with the overall position of the service producer).

Research on information search behaviour is complex because of numerous factors involved. Also, information seeking is often coupled with a cultural (and therefore regionally different) background, which results in different patterns of behaviour (Dawar, 1993). However, several common denominators regarding information collection have been identified and published, at least in the Anglo-Saxon part of the world. Among those are (Snepenger *et al.*, 1990):

- the composition of the vacation group (which actually will not be confirmed for cases presented in this paper);
- the presence of family and friends at the destination (confirmed in the case of Swiss travellers; cf. Bieger and Laesser, 2000a,b);
- prior visits to the destination (still to be checked for Swiss cases);
- the degree of novelty associated with the destination (still to be checked for Swiss cases).

Empirically, the information sources construct has frequently been used as a segmentation variable in tourism literature. When used as a descriptor to profile the behaviour of tourists who have been segmented on some other basis, information search has provided valuable insights for planning marketing strategies and targeting marketing communications (Moutinho, 1987).

With increasing frequency, tourists have been directly segmented based on their search behaviour. In a recent study by Fodness and Murray (1997, 1999), the leisure tourism market was segmented on the basis of consumer search behaviours. Using behavioural data collected in a survey of 585 motoring travellers to Florida, analyses demonstrated that information search behaviour is meaningfully related to systematic tourism behaviour; information search and tourism context are the result of a number of situational, tourist and marketplace contingencies; information search is associated with tourism outcomes. Research on the collection and use of tourist information thus aims at individuals collecting information to help them make decisions concerning where to go (Um and Crompton, 1990; Mansfeld, 1992). Destinations, in particular, embrace this approach as they try to produce marketing-oriented information and participate in editorial communications, with the intent of attracting new visitors.

In the study presented here, another approach will be made, segmenting Swiss travel situations (and with them a saturated market) according to how travellers look for information. Understanding the interrelation between information sources and people's travel habits is crucial to predicting future travel patterns (especially in the upcoming information age). The purpose of this study is therefore to delineate the information sources Swiss pleasure travellers use when travelling domestically and abroad, using a cluster market segmentation approach. It is hoped that this study will provide tourism marketers with some insights regarding Swiss travellers, thus helping them plan the appropriate marketing strategies targeted at this market.

Segmenting Travel Situations on the Basis of Information Collection

Methodology

Introductory remarks
Previous research shows that socio-demographic characteristics are becoming less and less useful for the segmentation of guest groups: guests 'meander' and consume situatively, opportunistically, as it were, and detached from any norms, structures and/or

commitments. Reference is often made to 'hybrid' consumers, who 'zap' from one option to another in an almost incomprehensible manner; the structure of their selection is becoming increasingly blurred. It has therefore become almost impossible for direct conclusions to be drawn regarding certain behaviour patterns on the basis of age, income, education, profession, etc. (Schewe, 1990; Bieger, 1997, 1998; Bieger and Laesser, 1999; Romeiss-Stracke, 1999). Therefore, there must be other bases of patterns.

Deriving from the rationale of the study, the literature review and these short introductory remarks, we assume that there is an observable structure regarding the sourcing and collection of information. We further assume that there are a number of determining travel characteristics, which explain why any given person and specific travel situation can be assigned to a certain information segment.

We therefore formulate two explorative hypotheses: H_1: It is possible to segregate travellers by their pattern of information collection; H_2: The explanatory value of travel-related factors of information sourcing is larger than the value of socio-demographic factors.

Data collection

The study is based on data from the latest edition of the 'Swiss Travel Market' (Reisemarkt Schweiz), a project collecting data on Swiss leisure travel behaviour conducted by the Institute for Public Services and Tourism at the University of St. Gallen together with partners such as Switzerland Tourism, the Swiss Hotel Association, Touristik Union International (TUI), a number of foreign destination marketing offices (for example, France, Austria, Spain), and others. The project has been conducted for the past 25 years and is scheduled to be conducted every 2-3 years. The latest data collection took place in January and February 1999 on the travel behaviour of 1998. All leisure trips with one or more overnight stays have been covered.

The research tool was a written interview conducted within 1970 households on the basis of a structured questionnaire; 95% of the interviews are based on the 'consumer jury' – a panel of the IHA.GfM, a leading market research institute in Switzerland (German- and French-speaking population), 5% of the interviews are based on an ad hoc sample. Originally, 2578 households were contacted; 1970 (76.4%) returned the questionnaire. The goal of the data collection was to get an overall database of the travel behaviour of the Swiss and of assimilated foreign citizens in Switzerland. Therefore, not only the 'heads' of households, but all their members participated in that research project.

Questions covered factors such as: destination, number of participants during the trip (household and other), duration of trip, day and month of departure, reason for travel, travel motives, sources of information, travel organization, point and time of sale of different components, means of transport and accommodation, activities (sports and non-sporting), outlay, etc. Besides, each travel-related factor was underlined with household data, containing factors such as: number of persons in household, sex, date of birth, citizenship, education, profession, reasons for not travelling (filter), housing-situation, etc.

Thanks to this study, there is a representative database on the travel behaviour of 95% of Swiss (5.53 million) and 50% of foreign citizens (0.64 million), the major results of which were published in a short working paper (Bieger and Laesser, 1999).

Data selection

With the aim of being compatible with previous studies of all the above-mentioned partners, 16 possible sources of information were cooperatively developed and taken into consideration by asking the respondents to indicate on a scale from 1–4, how important any source was in their information sourcing process. Among these are:

- Destination Information Brochures
- Hotel Brochures/Hotel Guides
- Tour Operator Brochures
- Information by Travel Agencies
- Information by Rail Service
- Information by Tourist Info at Destination (oral)
- Information by Destination Sales Representatives in Switzerland (oral)
- Advertisements in Newspapers/Journals
- Travel Guides/Travel Books/Journals
- Video/CD-Rom
- Exhibitions/Fairs
- Radio Programmes
- TV Programmes
- Videotext/Teletext
- Internet
- Information given by friends and relatives (orally)
- Other Sources of Information.

Data analysis

The data analysis for this study consisted of three stages (Table 1). After possible information sources had already been summarized according to information factors when designing the questionnaire, a factor analysis to reduce the number of motivation items was deemed unnecessary.

For the further steps, the procedure recommended by Punj and Stewart (1983) was applied, not only because the authors offer recommendations from more than a dozen research-projects in marketing (mainly US) but also because that procedure has been used in several other similar research projects (for example, Lanz, 1999). Furthermore, results of research by Brogini (1998), and Backhaus *et al.* (1996), were considered when designing the research procedures (Table 1).

As a first step, a cluster analysis was performed on 10% of 11,600 cases (trips) to determine the number of homogeneous groups formed by the data. This analysis employed an agglomerative hierarchical technique. To order the objects, Ward's algorithm was used; apart from that, the squared Euclidian distance served as the measure of proximity (SPSS, 1998). Quick Cluster (k-Means Cluster), an algorithm using the nearest centroid sorting method of clustering, was used to form groups from the entire sample using individual responses on the basis of motivations. Quick cluster is normally used with large samples and may be employed after the number of clusters has been determined (Aldendefer and Blashfield, 1984; Jahnke, 1988; Kaufman and

Rousseuw, 1990). Second, differences among groups in terms of motivations associated with each group were identified by using SPSS multiple discriminant analysis (MDA). A multiple discriminant analysis with clusters as the dependent variable was performed to define cluster membership and characteristics. Third, cross tabulations with chi-square were employed to profile the clusters with regard to travel behaviour.

Table 1 Steps Involved in the Analysis

Step 1:	Cluster Analysis of respondents based on the predefined information sources
	Result: Identification of number of clusters
Step 2:	Discriminant analysis of information sources (MDA)
	Result: Identification of discriminating factors for each cluster
Step 3:	Chi-Square tests on different variables
	Result: Identification of significant cluster descriptors

Interpretation

When interpreting the results, one has to be aware that it is not the people of Switzerland who are being clustered but the travellers in Switzerland, both outbound and inbound. The underlying approach is therefore a situational one, i.e. it focuses on specifically observed travellers during a trip with specific characteristics.

Results

Cluster analysis

A cluster analysis was employed to identify groups of respondents based on similar responses to questions about the intensity of usage of certain information sources. An examination of the dendrograms suggested a 4-cluster-solution. The means for each of the sources of information – representing the intensity of the use of a specific source of information – for the members of each cluster were calculated (Table 2). The summarized information of the descriptive statistics reveals the importance of all factors for members of each cluster.

Table 2 indicates further that Destination Information Brochures, Information given by friends and relatives, Hotel Brochures/Hotel Guides and Travel Guides/ Travel Books/Journals are among the strongest sources of information in all clusters. On the other hand, the intensity of information used in cluster 3 is comparatively low (1.15), while in cluster 2 it is comparatively high (2.41).

The F-ratios as determined through an interpretation of the MDA-Printout indicate that all factors were significant in discriminating between the groups. However, the variables which differentiated the clusters most were 'Tour Operator Brochures', 'Destination Information Brochures' and 'Information by Travel Retail Offices'.

Discriminant analysis

Three discriminant functions were generated using MDA (Tables 3–6). Function 1 with an eigenvalue of 6.450 explained 70.0%, function 2 with an eigenvalue of 1.623 17.6%, function 3 with an eigenvalue of 1.137 12.3% of the variation. The classification matrix revealed that 94.6% of the cases were classified correctly. The Structure Matrix (Table 6) shows pooled within-groups correlations between discriminating variables and standardized canonical discriminant functions. The variables are classified by absolute size of correlation within function.

Table 2 Segmentation of Travel Situation on the Basis of Usage of Information Source (sample: persons aged 18+)
How to read this table : Cluster 3 includes 48.7% of all trips. The most important source of information in this cluster is 'Information given by friends and relatives' (1.99 on a scale from 1 to 4).

Sources of Information	Mean	Cluster 'Structure of information' (Share of all travel situations)			
		1 (17.4%)	2 (11.4%)	3 (48.7%)	4 (22.5%)
Mean values:		1.80	2.41	1.15	1.52
Destination Information Brochures	2.62	3.00	3.26	1.09	3.14
Hotel Brochures/ Hotel Guides	2.18	2.65	2.90	1.07	2.09
Tour Operator Brochures	2.15	3.39	2.92	1.07	1.20
Information by Travel Agencies	2.07	3.09	2.91	1.08	1.20
Information by Rail Service	1.45	1.36	2.14	1.06	1.22
Information by Tourist Info at Destination	1.89	1.47	2.88	1.10	2.09
Information by Destination Sales Reps in Switzerland	1.55	1.41	2.55	1.02	1.22
Advertisement in Newspapers/Journals	1.53	1.37	2.35	1.08	1.32
Travel Guides/ Travel Books/Journals	2.15	2.71	2.93	1.10	1.84
Video/CD-Rom	1.21	1.10	1.71	1.01	1.02
Exhibitions/Fairs	1.23	1.10	1.76	1.01	1.05
Radio Programmes	1.22	1.05	1.77	1.01	1.05
TV Programmes	1.41	1.23	2.25	1.03	1.14
Videotext/Teletext	1.20	1.05	1.71	1.02	1.03
Internet	1.26	1.23	1.65	1.05	1.12
Information given by friends and relatives	2.51	2.17	3.19	1.99	2.68
Other Sources of Information	1.65	1.29	2.01	1.81	1.47

Scale: 1=without any relevance to 4=very important
Source: Reisemarkt Schweiz, 1998

Chi-square tests: segments of travel behaviour

A number of cross-tabulation calculations were performed to provide a travel profile of each of the clusters (see Table 7). The chi-square statistic was utilized to determine if distribution differences were significant or due to chance variations. The results of the analysis revealed that all profile variables differ significantly between the clusters. Although it can be shown that there are interrelations between determining profile variables and the traveller's belonging to a specific cluster, the importance or relevance of that interrelation needs to be differentiated. This was achieved on the basis of calculating the symmetric measure Phi (shown in parenthesis).

Table 3 Tests of Equality of Group Means

Factor	Wilk's Lambda	F	Df1	Df2	Sig.
Tour Operator Brochures	0.255	8089.429	3	8294	.000
Destination Information Brochures	0.293	6666.625	3	8294	.000
Information by Travel Agencies	0.345	5253.300	3	8294	.000
Hotel Brochures/Hotel Guides	0.552	2244.807	3	8294	.000
Travel Guides/Travel Books/Journals	0.568	2103.904	3	8294	.000
Information by Dest. Sales Reps in Switzerland	0.579	2007.244	3	8294	.000
Information by Tourist Info at the Destination	0.615	1731.864	3	8294	.000
TV Programmes	0.618	1709.061	3	8294	.000
Radio Programmes	0.654	1460.567	3	8294	.000
Video/CD-Rom	0.689	1247.234	3	8294	.000
Videotext/Teletext	0.699	1189.903	3	8294	.000
Exhibitions/Fairs	0.730	1023.096	3	8294	.000
Advertisement in Newspapers/Journals	0.734	1003.611	3	8294	.000
Information by Rail Service	0.761	869.915	3	8294	.000
Internet	0.866	426.771	3	8294	.000
Information given by friends and relatives	0.898	315.578	3	8294	.000
Other Sources of Information	0.950	145.462	3	8294	.000

Table 4 Multiple Discriminant Analysis of Sources of Information

Discriminant Function	Eigenvalue	Canonical Correlation	Wilk's Lambda	Chi-Square	Sig.
1	6.450	0.930	0.024	31,240.025	.000
2	1.623	0.787	0.178	14,427.926	.000
3	1.137	0.729	0.468	6,356.354	.000

Table 5 Functions at Group Centroids

Cluster number	Function 1	Function 2	Function 3
Cluster 1	3.256	-2.098	-0.941
Cluster 2	4.812	1.342	2.046
Cluster 3	-2.104	-0.356	0.480
Cluster 4	0.118	1.708	-1.389

The analysis shows that the choice of destination, the type of trip taken and the degree of packaging are in a significant interrelation with the cluster of information sources. Also, the duration of trips differs between the clusters. Contrary to what has been suggested in the Anglo-Saxon literature (e.g. Woodside and Ronkainen, 1980; Gitelson and Crompton, 1983; Snepenger *et al.*, 1990), the information pattern is not relevantly influenced by the travel composition (size and persons)! The influence of socio-demographic factors is significant, but only trivial (Phi < 0.3). Among these are factors such as:

- Age (Phi: 0.154)

- Education, Job (Phi: 0.145), Income (Phi: 0.138)
- Area of Origin/'Home Town' (Phi: 0.090), Size of home town (inhabitants) (Phi: 0.069)

Their explanatory (deterministic) value is very small and therefore negligible.

Table 6 Structure Matrix*

Factor	Function 1	Function 2	Function 3
Tour Operator Brochures	0.615*	-0.550	0.001
Information by Travel Agencies	0.504*	-0.387	0.075
Hotel Brochures/Hotel Guides	0.347*	0.065	-0.165
Travel Guides/Travel Books/Journals	0.340*	-0.009	-0.089
Information by Tourist Info at Destination	0.229	*0.415*	0.026
Information given by friends and relatives	0.092	*0.191*	0.031
Destination Information Brochures	0.516	0.414	*-0.161**
Radio Programmes	0.196	0.222	*0.407**
TV Programmes	0.242	0.200	*0.388**
Videotext/Teletext	0.179	0.176	*0.387**
Video/CD-Rom	0.197	0.159	*0.368**
Information by Destination Sales Rep. In Switzerland	0.288	0.196	*0.329**
Exhibitions/Fairs	0.180	0.157	*0.317**
Information by Rail Service	0.190	0.126	*0.218**
Advertisements in Newspapers/Journals	0.200	0.170	*0.216**
Other sources of Information	-0.029	0.048	*0.195**
Internet	0.130	0.073	*0.170**

* Values in italics denote the largest absolute correlation between each variable and any discriminant function

Discussion

First of all, both hypotheses can be answered positively by accepting the zero-version, i.e. a segmentation on the basis of information sourcing is possible and the explanatory value of socio-demographic factors equals nil. Further discussion will be conducted from various angles, including information clusters, information channels, and special role played by friends and relatives.

'Information clusters' angle

To begin with, a look at the results of the various analyses enables us to note the following results from the point of view of information clusters:

- The information structure of the travel situations in **cluster 1** is characterized by the great importance of tour operator brochures and information provided by travel agents. The cluster combines 17.4% of all the travel situations, of which 80% are package tours. The preferred destinations are the entire Mediterranean, North and Central America, as well as Asia and Australia.

Table 7 Structure of Travel Profiles by Cluster (Selection)
How to read this table: 60% of all travellers in Cluster 3 travel to Switzerland.

Travel Profile (Phi; 0-1)	Cluster 1	Cluster 2	Cluster 3	Cluster 4	Total
Destination (Phi: 0.54):					
- Switzerland	5	23	60	49	43
- Austria	5	7	4	6	5
- Germany	4	6	6	5	6
- France	12	12	10	15	11
- Italy	12	12	9	12	10
- Spain	12	7	4	4	6
- Portugal	1	0	0	0	1
- Greece	7	5	0	0	2
- Other Mediterranean countries	4	3	1	0	1
- Northwest Europe	9	4	3	2	4
- Scandinavia	2	1	1	2	1
- Eastern Europe	2	2	1	0	1
- North Africa/Middle East	5	2	1	1	2
- North and Central America	11	9	1	1	4
- South America	1	1	0	0	1
- Africa (Central and South)	1	1	0	1	1
- Australasia	7	5	1	0	2
Type of trip (Phi: 0.54):					
- Vacation by the Sea/by a Lake	27	22	10	12	15
- City Trip	19	19	4	12	11
- Sightseeing Tour by Coach/Bus/ Rail	19	14	3	15	10
- Cruise	3	2	1	1	1
- Vacation in the Countryside	2	3	3	7	4
- Vacation in the Mountains (Summer)	2	3	8	7	6
- Health-oriented Trip	1	4	1	4	2
- Winter Vacation in the Snow	0	3	7	4	5
- Winter Vacation in Warm Areas	2	2	0	0	1
- Other Sports Trip	4	5	4	3	4
- Events Trip	4	4	8	6	6
- Visit to a Fun Park/Resort	4	2	0	1	1
- Study Tour	2	2	2	1	2
- Trip to learn a Language	1	1	0	0	0
- Shopping Trip	3	1	2	1	2
- Visiting Friends and relatives	2	11	35	13	21
- Other	7	5	11	12	10
Duration of trip (Phi: 0.296):					
- 1 night	3	3	17	11	11
- 2-3 nights	17	15	29	22	23
- 4-7 nights	34	36	29	37	33
- 8-14 nights	32	27	16	21	21
- 15-21 nights	10	14	5	7	7
- more than 21 nights	5	6	4	2	4
Degree of packaged tour (Phi: 0.534):					
- no package at all	22	46	84	77	67
- Single Package Tour	45	30	5	11	16
- Group Package Tour	17	9	4	4	7
- Group Package Tour without Travel Guide	7	5	3	4	4
- Other type of Package Tour	10	9	5	5	6

Errors in percentage total due to rounding; **bold**: Values in cluster relatively higher than in total.
Source: Reisemarkt Schweiz

- **Cluster 2** (11.4% of all travel situations) tries to obtain information in the comparatively most intensive manner. Partially, this cluster evinces similar information patterns to cluster 1; however, the local/regional brochures are the most important information source in this cluster. The second most important information source is information given by friends and relatives. The role played by tour operators and travel agents remains strong, but no longer as pronounced as in cluster 1. A prominent (substitute) role, however, is played by the tourist representation of the destination country, and information given by friends and relatives. In this cluster, the Internet achieves the highest (albeit still very low) rate of importance as an information channel. It does not come as a surprise that 46% of all trips in this segment are not package tours; most of them are made to Switzerland's neighbouring countries, in Switzerland itself and to other continents.
- **Cluster 3** (48.7% of all travel situations) is the cluster which gathers and requires the least amount of information. The very high proportion of domestic trips (60%) and the central role of visits to friends and relatives largely explain this characteristic. Further preferred types of travel are mountain holidays (not in winter), winter holidays in the snow, and event trips. The trips are comparatively short (46% with 3 and fewer nights); 84% of them are organized by the travellers themselves. Special mention must be accorded to the prominence of information given by friends and relatives as a source of information: in no other cluster does one single information source play such an isolatedly central role!
- In **Cluster 4** (22.5% of all travel situations), a majority of travellers obtain their information from local and regional brochures and from tourist information offices at their destination. Information given by friends and relatives also plays a role of above-average importance. The most important destinations are in Switzerland, Austria, France and Italy; the majority of the trips last 2-7 nights, and are not package tours.

'Information channels' angle

The following points can be noted from the point of view of information channels:
- **Brochures**, i.e. local and regional brochures, hotel brochures/hotel guides, tour operator catalogues, and information from travel agents and tourist information offices and tourist representations in the countries of origin remain the most widespread sources of information.
- The **print media** in the form of travel guides, books and journals and articles serve as a valuable information basis particularly for long-distance trips, regardless of whether those are package tours or individually organized trips.
- The **electronic media** (TV programmes, videotapes, CD-Rom; but also the Internet) are chiefly used for long-distance trips with a comparatively high degree of individual organization (individual organization requires more broadly based information). However, the proportion of such trips is comparatively low.

Table 8 Number of Important or Very Important Sources of Information

Parameter	Cluster 1	Cluster 2	Cluster 3	Cluster 4
Mean	4.8	7.7	0.9	3.2
Median	5	7	1	3

Source: Reisemarkt Schweiz 1998

Depending on the degree of organization and familiarity with the region of the destination, a varying number of information sources is used (cf. Table 8):

- Whereas in **cluster 1**, 50% of all the travellers refer to fewer than 5 sources of information, 50% of **cluster 2** make use of more than 7 sources. This fact must, in particular, be attributed to the varying degree of organization through other people (package tours) combined with a similarity of destinations.

- The low information requirement observed earlier in **cluster 3** also manifests itself in the low average and mean of the information sources judged important or very important. The most central role in this cluster is played by information given by friends and relatives.

- The number of the information sources used is also rather low in **cluster 4**. The comparatively low information requirement can also be explained in terms of the travellers' familiarity with their destinations and, in other cases, of the minimization of risk through booking a package tour.

Special role played by 'Information given by friends and relatives'

A special role is played by the source 'Information given by friends and relatives' (cf. Table 9): From the **travellers' point of view**, the importance of information given by friends and relatives increases in proportion to the growing number of information sources. The correlation is statistically significant and can, in particular, be explained through those persons' role as 'information filters'. From the **providers' point of view**, it must be noted that in more than 50% of the cases in which information given by friends and relatives is important or very important, reference was made to only 3 or fewer sources of information. By way of explanation of the central role of this information source, the following may be noted:

- Travelling is an area of consumption which possesses a very high emotional value and is closely connected with every individual's identity. Travelling also tends to create identity. Modern people in a world of rapid change consider the maintenance and reinforcement of their own identities ('I want to apprehend myself as a person in my own right.' / 'I want to have an impact.') to be increasingly important (Bieger and Laesser, 2000c). However, identity can be gained in a much more pronounced way through social interaction than through relationships with machines, which is why people are becoming even more important as 'consultants' for travelling decisions.

- Another essential factor is trust. Since travelling is a highly opaque product with great material and emotional risks, travelling is always a business that requires trust. However, trust can only be established and communicated through 'proxies' or 'guarantors' in the form of brands and persons. Also, trust must not be reduced to reliability. Trust also involves the conviction that my guarantor means well, is well-disposed toward me and, in terms of travelling, follows my thoughts, proactively tries to eliminate risks, offers additional benefits of his own will, and creates access to new things.

Table 9 The Importance of 'Information Given by Friends and Relatives' Related to the Number of Sources of Information

Number of Sources of Information	'important or rather important' among 'Number of Sources of Information'	'important or rather important' among 'Information given by friends and relatives'
1	46.2%	21.0%
2	58.6%	18.4%
3	59.2%	14.1%
4	55.8%	10.1%
5	62.9%	10.4%
6	70.8%	8.4%
7	80.7%	6.7%

Source: Reisemarkt Schweiz 1998

Conclusions for the Alpine Region in General and for Switzerland in Particular

The above analyses have brought to light a great number of results. For tourist marketing in Switzerland, these imply a number of conclusions, which are briefly outlined below. The information structure represented in the analysis calls for a corresponding update and adaptation of tourist information. From the inbound point of view, it must be noted that Swiss customers' information requirements are comparatively low, while the role of domestic guests as providers of turnover must never be underemphasized. From the outbound point of view, it must be indicated that depending on the type of trip, the information requirements may be completely different from other motivations, not only with regard to the contents but also with regard to the diversity and intensity of the sources. For this reason, it is not enough for a tour operator to make different catalogues available for different guest requirements. Rather, the operator himself ought to become active as an information filter and provide potential customers with concerted support in their selection of information sources (for instance, through a corresponding integration of retailers into an information concept, through cooperation with publishers, or by providing access to Internet links whose quality has been tested).

In most cases, information is gathered from persons, i.e. from travel agents, people in tourist information offices at destinations, or from friends/relatives. These persons are actual 'information filters' and thus assume an important supporting function; in particular, they lessen selection problems such as may arise from an excessively wide selection of information sources. These people, who help create – and sometimes broker – turnover, must be proactively integrated in the providers' marketing measures to a greater extent, say, through special customer relationship maintenance programmes, or through the creation of corresponding incentives. From the point of view of the Swiss providers (inbound), it is regular guests in particular who take over functions along these lines.

The media choice is primarily made on the basis of travelling distance, familiarity with a destination, and the degree of individual organization of the trip. The selection of suitable channels should therefore be made to a higher degree on the strength of specific elements, questions of scope, and the target markets. An orientation toward the guests' information requirements, which vary according to their decision-making situations, will not only improve their convenience but also make an essential contribution toward the establishment and maintenance of a relationship of trust between guests and providers.

References

Aldendefer, M.S. and Blashfield, R.K. (1984) *Cluster Analysis*. Sage, Beverly Hills.

Backhaus, K., Erichson, B., Plinke, W. and Weiber, R. (1996) *Multivariate Analyse-methoden*, 8th edn. Springer, Berlin.

Bieger, Th. (1997) *Tourismus Schweiz AG*. Discussion Paper des ITV-HSG, ITV, St. Gallen.

Bieger, Th. (1998) Neue Strukturen im Schweizer Tourismus. Das Konzept. In: Bieger, Th. and Laesser, Ch. (eds.) *Neue Strukturen im Tourismus. Der Weg der Schweiz.* Haupt, Bern/Stuttgart/Wien.

Bieger, Th. and Laesser, Ch. (1999) 'Sag mir, wie Du reist und ich sage Dir, wie Du bist'. NZZ, 09.12.1999.

Bieger, Th. and Laesser, Ch. (2000a) Segmentierung Reisemarkt Schweiz auf Basis von Motiven. In: *Schweiz Tourismus (2000) Länderbericht Schweiz*. Schweiz Tourismus, Zürich.

Bieger, Th. and Laesser, Ch. (2000b) Das Informationsverhalten der Schweizer Reisenden. In: Bieger, Th. and Laesser, Ch. (eds.) *Jahrbuch der Schweizerischen Tourismuswirtschaft*. IDT, St. Gallen.

Bieger, Th. and Laesser, Ch. (2000c) Persönliche Interaktion als Erfolgsfaktor. Wie kann der Wert der persönlichen Interaktion gesteigert werden? In: Belz, Ch. and Bieger, Th. (eds.) *Globales Service Management*. Thexis, St. Gallen.

Brogini, M. (1998) *Über Kundengruppen zur Marktstruktur. Das Modell der Segmentintensität.* Berner betriebswirtschaftliche Schriften Band 18, Universität Bern.

Chisnall, P.M. (1985) *Marketing: A Behavioural Analysis*, 2nd edn. McGraw-Hill, London.

Crandall, R. (1980) Motivations for Leisure. *Journal of Leisure Research* 12(1), 45-53.

Dawar, N. (1993) *A Cross-cultural Study of Interpersonal Information Seeking and Giving Behaviour*. INSEAD, Fontainebleau, Working Paper 93/01.

Fodness, D. and Murray, B. (1997) Tourist Information Search. *Annals of Tourism Research* 24(3), 503-523.

Fodness, D. and Murray, B. (1999) A Model of Tourist Information Search Behaviour. *Journal of Travel Research* 37(February), 220-230.

Gitelson, R.J. and Crompton, J.L. (1983) The Planning Horizons and Sources of

Information used by Pleasure Vacationers. *Journal of Travel Research* 21(Winter), 2-7.

Jahnke, H. (1988) *Clusteranalyse als Verfahren der schliessenden Statistik.* Vandenhoeck & Ruprecht, Göttingen.

Kaufman, L. and Rousseuw, P.J. (1990) *Finding Groups in Data. An Introduction to Cluster Analysis.* Series in Probability and Mathematical Statistics. Wiley, New York.

Kotler, P. (1984) *Marketing Management: Analysis Planning and Control*, 5th edn. Prentice Hall, London.

Laesser, Ch. (1998) *Destinationsmarketing im Zeitalter des Internet.* Haupt, Bern/Stuttgart/Wien.

Lanz, E. (1999) *Methodenzirkel zur Clusteranalyse.* FIF, Bern.

Mansfeld, Y. (1992) From Motivation to Actual Travel. *Annals of Tourism Research* 19, 399-419

McIntosh, R.W. and Goeldner, C.R. (1990) *Tourism: Principles, Practices, Philosophies.* Wiley, New York.

Middleton, V.T.C. (1994) *Marketing in Travel and Tourism.* Heinemann, Chichester.

Moutinho, L. (1987) Consumer Behaviour in Tourism. *European Journal of Marketing* 21, 5-44.

Punj, G. and Stewart, D.W. (1983) Cluster Analysis in Marketing Reserach: Review and Suggestions for Applications. *Journal of Marketing* 20(May), 134-148

Romeiss-Stracke, F. (1999) *Rechtzeitig auf Trends reagieren.* Address given on the occasion of the 'Attraktionspunkte' conference of 10 December 1999 at the University of St. Gallen, IDT, St. Gallen.

Schertler, W. (1994) Dienstleistungseigenschaften begründen Informationsgeschäfte – dargestellt an Tourismusdienstleistungen. In: Schertler, W. (ed.) *Tourismus als Informationsgeschäft.* Ueberreuther, Wien.

Schewe, Ch. (1990) Get in Position for the Older Market. *American Demographics* 12(6), 38-44.

Snepenger, D., Meged, K., Snelling, M. and Worrall, K. (1990) Information Search Strategies by destination-naive Tourists. *Journal of Travel Research* 29(1), 13-16.

SPSS (1998) *User Manuals SPSS Version 9.0*, SPSS Inc., Chicago.

Um, S. and Crompton, J.L. (1990) Attitude Determinants in Tourism Destination Choice. *Annals of Tourism Research* 17, 443-448.

Woodside, A.G. and Ronkainen, I.A. (1980) Vacation Travel Planning Segments. *Annals of Tourism Research* 7, 385-394.

Chapter ten
'Nowhere Left to Run': A Study of Value Boundaries and Segmentation Within the Backpacker Market of New Zealand

Irena Ateljevic and Stephen Doorne
School of Business and Public Management
Victoria University of Wellington
Wellington, New Zealand

Abstract

In the tourism literature the phenomenon of the 'long-term, budget' traveller has been conceptualized as a distinctive form of escape from mainstream 'institutionalized' tourism flows. A common characteristic of studies focusing on this market has been the tendency to treat these travellers as a homogeneous consumer group. In Australia and New Zealand these travellers are commonly referred to as the 'backpacker' market. Our study reveals heterogeneity within the backpacker markets in the Nelson and Marlborough regions of New Zealand. Our discussion of 'traditional long-term travellers' and 'mainstream' backpacker groups examines the diversity of underlying values influencing travel motivations and their respective forms of consumer behaviour. This paper contextualizes the discussion with respect to historical perspectives and the dynamics of associated industry development. We argue that the cultural context of globalization raises important implications for the study of travel motivations within this market.

Introduction

Tourism is currently the fastest growing industry worldwide, both internationally and domestically, reflecting a climate of change in the international community and corresponding changes in individuals. Through globalization and the movement of products, capital, technology, information and ideas around the world, people are experiencing more cultures through travel, imports, immigration, international organizations and the media. Economic restructuring, global economic competition, deregulation, new information technologies, and diverse and changing customer tastes are forcing a continuation of the restructuring process, ultimately affecting all peoples of the world.

Increasing concern for personal and environmental health has been joined by a rebirth in social activism. Quality of life issues, particularly the health of the individual and the state of the environment are emerging as widespread public concerns. Environmental degradation, the deterioration of public infrastructures, homelessness, racial tensions and increasing global poverty are some of the issues present.

As an industry, tourism in an integral part of all of these changes. Embroiled in the analysis of its industry are the expectations, desires, and motivations of individuals (tourist and host), as well as the interaction of industrial sectors. In terms of travel motivations these issues have been conceptualized with respect to an 'escape' from everyday life (Krippendorf, 1987; Mannel and Iso-Ahola, 1987; Urry, 1990; Rojek, 1993). This need to escape is a characteristic common to all tourist markets. The packaging and commodification of escape opportunities through economies of scale and market diversification have underpinned the industrialization process, which has resulted in tourism today being arguably the world's largest industry.

The institutionalization of travel, on the other hand, has created demand for escape opportunities outside 'mass tourism' typified by the now global tourism industry complex. From the visitor market perspective this trend has been variously referred as 'craft tourism' (Rodenburg, 1980), as practised by 'drifters' (Cohen, 1973), 'wanderers' (Vogt, 1976), 'budget travellers' (Riley, 1988), and most recently with respect to South-East Asia and Australasia, as 'backpackers' (Pearce, 1990; Wilson, 1997). Accompanying this literature are emerging observations of parallel industrialization within the now coherent backpacker industry (Hampton, 1998).

Aiming to shed more light on an area which Hampton identifies as 'yet to receive serious academic study' (1998, p.639), this paper seeks to address the following: firstly, to reveal the complexity (heterogeneity) of what has been widely perceived as a homogeneous tourist consumer group; secondly, to explore changing needs and travel aspiration as reflecting an evolving socio-cultural context; and thirdly, to provide a historical perspective by contextualizing the dynamics of this evolving market. We base our discussion on research projects conducted over 2 years in the Nelson and Marlbourough regions of New Zealand's South Island.

The paper begins with a review of relevant literature which chronologically examines the conceptualization of what is now known as the backpacker phenomenon. Following this we outline our study and methodology and proceed to present our findings and observations. The paper concludes with a discussion of salient issues and presents a contemporary conceptualization of the dynamics of consumption within this market.

Literature review: Conceptualizing 'backpackers/long-term budget travellers'

The term 'backpacker' has only recently come into vogue as a description less derogatory than 'drifter' and yet more succinct than 'budget traveller'. As a term which has essentially followed the phenomenon, it is now commonly used to define a wide spectrum of people, some whose movements are more representative of the conventional 'tourist' than their 'drifter' predecessors, and others whose expenditure patterns preclude them from the categorization of 'budget travellers'. The term backpacker is also representative of traveller styles where the emphasis is on movement and mobility. The backpack as a luggage item facilitates these actions far more effectively than, for example, the suitcase.

Adler (1985) argues that contemporary tourism originates from the 'Grand Tour' taken by young European aristocrats in the 17th and 18th centuries. She goes on to identify the modern low-budget, extended-period travel phenomenon with 'tramping', an 18th and 19th century religious or labour related travel practice which provided opportunities for sightseeing, adventure, and education through first-hand experience. Tramping was the Grand Tour of the lower classes and provided the opportunity for individuals to gain and share skills by plying their craft from village to village while finding accommodation at inns or labour-related societies. Although the practice was commonly associated with work, it also functioned as a rite of passage to full (usually male) adulthood through separation from home and family. By the 1930s tramping had all but passed as a labour-related practice and began to be viewed as socially-deviant behaviour. As Adler (1985, p. 341) comments, 'their mobility was conceived as a social problem, and their motivation explained in individual, psychological terms as 'Wanderlust'.

In the 1970s, Cohen (1972, 1973, 1974) and Vogt (1976) provided definitions of wanderlust travellers in the 1960s and 1970s. Cohen presented a typology of tourist roles with two major distinctions: institutionalized and non-institutionalized travellers. Institutionalized roles are typified by the organized mass tourist displaying a preference for being confined to an 'environmental bubble' in which decisions are made on behalf of the traveller and needs are met by the tourist infrastructure. Institutionalized roles also feature the individual mass tourist who makes arrangements for transportation and accommodation through an agency though chooses low risk, familiar situations when planning itineraries.

Non-institutionalized roles identified by Cohen include the 'explorer' and the 'drifter'. The primary shared values of these groups are novelty, spontaneity, risk, independence, and a multitude of options (Vogt, 1976, p. 27). The primary distinction between the two centres around the drifter's lack of a fixed itinerary and a more limited budget. The drifter is also seen as more of a risk taker than the other groups. Cohen based these classifications on observations from the late 1960s. He also noted how drifting assumed the status of a major trend in tourism which could be closely associated with a counterculture which is, 'institutionalised on a level completely segregated from, but parallel to, ordinary mass tourism' (Cohen, 1973, p. 90).

Vogt (1976) prefers the term 'wanderer' and, though accepting Cohen's differentiation between institutionalized and non-institutionalized forms of tourism, prefers to view them as a continuum placing at opposite ends the stereotypical American 'bubble' tourist, and the wanderer. Wanderers, he notes, are a product of affluent society and often represent a reaction to it. Other characteristics identified by Cohen displayed by travellers in this group tend to include escapism, hedonism and anarchism. These travellers also frequently emerge from middle- or upper-class family backgrounds. He goes further to suggest links between drifting and drug culture though is cautious not to infer all drifters view drugs as the purpose of travelling. Here Cohen's descriptions appear more based on the stereotypical 'hippie' of the 1960s as popularized in contemporary fiction such as James Mitchener's *The Drifters*.

Cultural, economic and political factors also motivate participation in the drifter 'sub-culture' (Cohen, 1973). In particular, he identifies three primary factors motivating participation as cultural, economic and political forces. With respect to culture, Cohen's drifters sought to engage with 'exotic, primitive' cultures to satisfy spiritual and emotional needs. Economic factors include the desire to avoid routine work (or unemployment). Drifting allows for that interim period to be extended and also provides acceptable circumstances under which avoidance of major life decisions can take place. Politically, this form of travel represented a rejection of prevailing political situations (e.g. the Vietnam war). In this respect the travellers' alienation assumes an anarchistic dimension in which 'drifting is both a symptom and an expression of broader alienative forces current among contemporary youth' (Cohen, 1973, p. 94).

Contemporary definitions of the backpacker

The budget traveller today differs in many respects from earlier observations. Riley's study (1988) provides useful sociological insights into 'long-term budget travellers' and the psychology behind this travel phenomenon. In broad terms she describes this travel group as consisting of 'college graduates, delaying the transition into the responsibilities associated with adulthood in western society, or taking leave between jobs' (1988, p. 313). The term 'budget' is useful in this definition in that it adequately describes the day-to-day functioning of individuals committed to extending their travels beyond that of a cyclical holiday. In this respect, backpackers differ greatly from other tourist groups in their desire to seek out new and relatively 'unexplored' areas. When indulging in travel to this end, the individual is released from the roles with which he or she is identified in the home environment. The traveller is able to enjoy 'playing with identity' as the middle-class person assumes the role of a 'learned beggar' (Adler, 1985, p. 347). The traveller allows the opportunity to observe local behaviour from within. In rejecting Cohen's (1972, 1973, 1974) earlier definitions, Riley (1988, p. 326) asserts that 'today's typical youthful traveller is not accurately described as a 'hippie', a 'bum', or an adherent to 'counter-culture'. Western society has undergone some major changes and the contemporary long-term traveller reflects them'. Riley's study has significantly changed the conceptualization and 'negative' connotations associated around 'drifters'. She described these individuals (1988, p. 326):

> *'as likely to be middle class, at a juncture in life, somewhat older than the earlier travellers on average, college educated, and not aimless drifters. They travel under flexible timetables and itineraries. Most expect to rejoin the work force in the society they left.'*

Riley's observations are further supported by Pearce (1990) who similarly observes the 'contemporary backpacker' by identifying three key motivations: related to extending one's education; travel as escape from pressing life choices; and 'occasional work' to extend travel time. Most significantly, Pearce identifies a fourth theme related to the emergence of a subculture focused on the pursuit of health and outdoor activities. Pearce attributes the growth of this market specifically to the development of a corresponding industry in the form of the Youth Hostel Association in Australia throughout the 1990s. Most recently, Firth and Hing (1999) have examined the relationship between markets and industry focusing on backpackers and youth hostels. Their study pays particular attention to both producers' and consumers' perspectives of sustainability. They questioned the 'small is beautiful' notion, observing a 'superficial' approach to environmental sensitivity amongst industry operators.

Hampton (1998) provides the most recent review of backpacker tourism focusing on a detailed discussion of industry dynamics with respect to backpacking in Lombok, Indonesia. Hampton observes the consolidation of industry sectors catering specifically and exclusively to backpacker markets. His observations of the relationship between backpacker markets and the small business environment provide a useful contribution of our understanding of the sector. His conceptualization of the 'backpacker' as a market group reflects an evolving lineage of the concept in which people involved in the phenomenon are generally regarded as a homogeneous group. This paper seeks to broaden the concept of this market segment by demonstrating a clear polarization within it. Our study focuses on the values of individuals which, from a motivational perspective, illustrate the dynamics of the sector. Drawing on our research we argue that motivational values reflect the cultural and political environment of an increasingly globalized world, values which are expressed in distinctively different behaviour patterns.

Case Study

Context

The 'long-term budget traveller' phenomenon in New Zealand is now regarded as a significant element in the New Zealand tourism industry. Its emergence parallels the observations of Pearce and Hampton noted above with respect to role of the Youth Hostel Association, and the subsequent development of the industry sub-sector over the last decade (Parr, 1989; Ware, 1992; Garnham, 1993). A number of different features of the backpacker phenomenon have been studied. Parr (1989), for example, examined behavioural characteristics and decision making amongst free independent travellers. Similarly, Ware (1992) explored decision-making processes amongst off-season backpackers engaging with the adventure tourism industry. The Department of Conservation and Tourism Resource Consultants (1993) have examined the exchange of information amongst backpackers emphasizing the significance of word-of-mouth as an influence in decision-making. Cloke and Perkins' (1998) study of the marketing images of the adventure tourism industry in New Zealand illustrates the extent to which the corresponding backpacker market now features as a core element in the New Zealand tourism industry. The characteristic demand for flexibility and independence amongst this market in the late 1980s and early 1990s saw the emergence of backpacker transport networks, namely Kiwi Experience and Magic Bus. Initially, the concept was based on the idea of travellers being able to create spontaneous itineraries in which they can get off and on buses at will, using a pass system.

Doorne's (1994) analysis of their expenditure patterns and the corresponding industry development, however, describes dynamics of their integration within backpacker industry over time. He observes how over the previous decade transport has played a pivotal role in shaping the tourism industry relating to backpackers in New Zealand by providing the link between the tourist, the place, and the product. Over time the growing demand for this form of travel transformed the 'flexible pass' arrangement into a more structured tour format. These relationships facilitated the rapid growth of a new short term holiday market by creating products which could be consumed during holidays from regular on-going employment. The integration process also facilitated additional demand via economies of scale and the introduction of packaging. These observations provide significant historical background upon which we will develop our conceptualization of the dynamics within this market.

Method

Our study draws on a project spanning 2 years in the Marlborough and Nelson regions of the central part of New Zealand. A series of 106 in-depth interviews with free-independent travellers were conducted together with five focus backpacker groups as part of a wider 'Centre Stage' research project. 'Centre Stage' is a strategic marketing initiative, comprising regional tourism organizations from the Nelson, Marlborough, Wellington and Wairarapa Regions. The aim of this part of the research was to gain greater insight into the profile of visitors to the regions of Nelson and Marlborough for purposes of strategic tourism marketing and planning. Traditionally, these regions have been peripheral to mainstream international tourist routes, their industry structure reflecting a dominance of small and micro enterprises.

The interviews with free-independent travellers were conducted in December 1998 to February 1999 in a wide range of settings across the region. A broad cross-section of respondents was interviewed in order to highlight a range of relevant issues relating to various market segments. Focus groups with backpackers were conducted towards the end of the project in the year 2000. Fieldwork was supported by participant observation which was informed by extended periods of immersion in community case study areas. The focus of the study was not to demonstrate representativeness to the tourist population, but to identify and contextualize the issues relating to the travel experience. The focus of the qualitative research was to answer questions of 'how' and 'why' certain travel characteristics are exhibited. Our research identified a significant segmentation of what has been traditionally regarded as a homogeneous consumer group of backpacker/long-term budget travellers.

The interviews and focus groups focused specifically on establishing the profile of visitors, examining their motivations for travel, their perceptions of products and experiences. Focus groups explored the underlying values and attitudes influencing visitor behaviour. The following sections discuss the polarization of the backpacker market by focusing on two extreme ends of the spectrum. First, traditional long-term budget travellers are discussed with respect to the above issues. Following this, by contrast, we present a similarly structured overview of the more 'industrialized' end of the market, referred to as 'mainstream backpackers'.

Study findings: Traditional, long-term budget travellers

Profile

These travellers are generally well-travelled and experienced and regard themselves as 'real travellers' as distinct from 'tourists'. Frequently their visit to New Zealand occurs as part of a round-the-world ticket for extended periods of up to a year, commonly visiting other destinations in Asia such as Thailand, Fiji, and Australia. In contrast to their regular annual holiday (generally within Europe) this long-haul trip is considered as a 'travelling', as one respondent explained: 'there is a difference between travelling to holiday spots and these long trips where you live with citizens of the country'. These visitors generally travel on a low budget, their average expenditure amounts to approximately NZ$40-45 per day although they often stay for long periods in desirable destinations. Their time-frame makes budget a significant consideration in travel behaviour in which the richness of experience (cultural immersion, social relations, 'back to nature') is of primary importance. In order to extend their stay many combine travel with work, and engage in so-called WWOOF (willing workers on organic farms) programmes increasingly oriented towards a growing interest from these travellers. Within New Zealand these travellers commonly seek to avoid 'the beaten track' and commonly use public transport (train, bus), hitch-hike, cycle or have a private vehicle bought for travel purposes. These travel modes facilitate the spontaneity they seek; freedom and flexibility are regarded as crucial for the whole experience. The following quotes illustrate the above issues:

'The whole thing about this trip is no booking in advance. I don't know what I am going to do next, or who you are going to meet, I mean I could have booked it but I met Garry and he had just bought a car...we stayed in Picton for few days and will stay here as long as we like' (female, 30s, Israel).

'I spent a year and a half and I hitched from Cape Town up to Northern Africa, I hitched up there with a girlfriend. I hitched South Africa, I hitched across America. And then after my trek in Africa then I went to .... living in London ...... but I have never been this far, and I can't make up my mind whether to stay a bit longer in NZ and work and then go to Australia, I might do that. Australia is so big though. The joy of NZ is that it is little and easy to go around' (male, 20s, South Africa).

'New Zealand is not a holiday...it is a country for travel...and I don't plan really, I just go ahead' (female, 30s, Germany).

'Travel is my lifestyle. I have been doing it for eight years. It was just after I had covered most of South East Asia, United States, Canada, Mexico... I don't own very much, a backpack and a bike and some clothes and that is it. That is how I do it. If I owned much else it would be a burden. It would be hard to do' (male, 20s, USA).

Motivations

These travellers are motivated by feelings of dissatisfaction with their home societies and the pressures of everyday life. They generally see travel as a form of escape and personal growth, as one respondent explained:

'I was just becoming stagnant. I felt I needed a change. To broaden my mind, to feel freedom...work commitments were getting a bit serious at home' (male, 30s, Ireland).

By travelling for long periods and meeting other people (primarily locals and other travellers) these visitors hope to broaden their minds and gain a fresh perspective on their way of life. A common group in this respect were single women travellers experiencing 'life crises' in their early/mid 30s and using travel to find a new meaning for life. As one woman from the England explained: 'It was a junction in my life. I had to start thinking about the direction, so I decided to make a break'.

These individuals commonly seek to escape from long-term ('boring') relationships. The absence of social expectations and work pressures in the long-term travel experience were regarded as a way of 'buying time... to stop and think'. Independent travel represents a key factor in the search for a 'new identity' away from familiarity (family and friends), as the following quotes illustrate:

'I think I have lots of reasons for travelling, a break in my job, I had had a pretty traumatic personal life and I decided now was a good time to go off and do something that I wanted to do'(male, 30s, Canada).

'At home I felt very stuck. My life kind of crumbled up, I lost my job and the place where I was living and I had to make a new start, and I didn't want to do that. I have to find a new profession and everything just seems to be so heavy, so complicated, and travelling I meet so many people, get some new ideas. I meet a lot of people in similar situations, a lot of people who are travelling had the major change in their lives that set them loose, at least at my age (male, 30s, UK).

Generally, this market segment perceives long-term travel as a process of transformation, as an opportunity to stop a hectic life, hoping for a change to their lifestyle once being back home again, as one respondent explained:

'You are so busy the whole time you never get a chance to actually appreciate here and now, this minute, not worrying about tomorrow, not looking at yesterday, but today. I find when I go off and do other things I get involved with each day rather than worrying about what is happening at the weekend or next week. What happened yesterday, it is a good centering thing, it gets you back in yourself, it is good, enjoying sitting here now talking to you rather than worrying about what I am going to have for supper tonight. I wanted to get back in my own skin rather than worrying about this or doing that. You get quite frantic. I hope to change that when I go back' (female, 30s, UK).

Focus groups identified some further issues more closely related to the cultural and political values of individuals and reflecting the contemporary condition of global society and development. The 'meaning' of travel is related to unexpected things, everyday life is too predictable, as one respondent described: 'travel is about mystery'. It is also considered as a very good educational process when you can learn first-hand about other cultures and places. For young people it is an opportunity to take that freedom of no serious responsibilities, to go travelling at that age when 'you really don't know what to do anyway...travel is an important life experience...the best way to learn'.

The focus groups stressed an 'increasing dissatisfaction with the Western way of life' which pushes people into other countries that are more 'laid back and relaxed like New Zealand....different than most of Europe and North America'. These people generally felt pessimistic about the economics and lifestyle of the West, felt the pressure of globalization and a loss of control over their lives; restructuring, competition, environmental degradation, big profits, greed, stress and consumerism were words commonly associated with it. Through travel, the majority of people are searching for life meaning, trying to explore other ways of life, felt sick of urbanization and crowded places, and search for solitude, as two respondents explained:

> *'I have been living in the big city (London) for a long time...for me it's quite important to get away from people and New Zealand is good for that...I think most people who come here enjoy that side...it's so easy to find solitude if you want...'*
(male, 30s, Ireland).

> *'I needed to take a breath... this urban, global and over technological world in which I live makes me very depressed ...'* (female, 40s, UK).

Most of these people were long-term travellers trying to 'step out' of visitor perspectives to learn more about local culture, to feel 'integrated' as one respondent (female, 20s, Germany) working on a farm explained: '...you experience life of the family and Kiwi people living together...you don't feel like a visitor, you feel like someone who lives here'. Feeling overwhelmed by 'corporate' culture and alienation of their own society, respondents agreed that they use travel as a form of nostalgia, seeking the reassurance of traditional lifestyles, a personal human touch and 'direct contact with nature'. The fear of increasing globalization, the 'take over of big companies', and uncertainty are key issues, which one respondent (male, 40s, UK) attributed to the 'so-called free-market evil that kills small businesses and local culture'. All respondents stressed motivations with respect to the escape from everyday life, as one respondent noted 'to get a perspective from a distance, to find a meaning which you might lose in a comfortable routine'.

Perceptions of the regions and their experiences

Interviews initially gravitated towards perceptions of New Zealand and the respective research areas (Nelson and Marlborough region). Their responses reflected general expectations related to the image of country as 'beautiful, clean and green'. As the interviews unfolded, deeper concerns emerged reflecting value positions of individuals and their perceptions of the political and cultural environment at both the global and local levels. The majority noticed that whilst the overall environmental awareness of the New Zealand population is 'very strong', generally the actions did not correspond, as low population creates less necessity for more environmentally responsible behaviour, as one respondent explained: 'New Zealanders are aware of it but not carrying it out at the same pace'. One respondent made a comparison between Europe and New Zealand, recognizing the difference of green awareness in New Zealand as fairly limited to 'small "market niches" who can afford to be interested in "green politics" and buy organic produce...I've noticed that the majority of people buy their food in supermarkets....' Another respondent remarked on the fact that New Zealand, despite its 'clean and green image', is getting a reputation in Europe of being not 'self-sustained', with agriculture and farming industries using high levels of sprays and preservatives. One respondent expressed concern about the long-term implications of such practices and suggested how New Zealand would be even more attractive to Europeans if it developed its self-sufficiency and its reputation of being a 'completely natural alternative to the rest of the developed world'. Everyone recognized that environmental concerns and awareness are stronger at the 'claiming' level, but less in reality and actions. One respondent from Germany noted how all shoppers get so many bags for their groceries. One respondent observed the inevitability of globalization when he was buying food in a local organic shop and saw organic beans grown in

England. He was surprised to see that, expecting to see locally made produce.

Tourism and its development emerged as an area of concern for these travellers. Both interview and focus group respondents expressed fear of further 'touristy' development, recognizing the paradox of their presence in the area having the possibility of introducing a dependence on tourism for the local economy. There were frequent desires for 'the place to stay as it is at the moment' accompanied by questions as to whether it was possible, reflecting a generally pessimistic attitude about the future ('the world' as well as New Zealand).

Another important issue to emerge in the course of interviews and focus groups was this group's perception of 'other backpackers'. Respondents frequently sought to distance themselves from the more commercial, mainstream backpacker market, focusing on their respective differences related to ideology and behaviour. Respondents recognized the commercialization of the Kiwi Experience transport network and the different type of travellers that use it, as one respondent noted: 'they are party animals, very loud, mainly young, having late night parties and sleeping on the bus during the day'. Another respondent agreed by noting: 'they do not come to see New Zealand, they come to have good time; they are a completely different set of people from those who stay in place like this'.

Another respondent noted that Kiwi Experience although claiming to be independent and flexible, stop where they want 'which might be the place where I wouldn't like to stop and to go where I want to go, as for example here in Golden bay where Kiwi Experience doesn't come...so I decided to buy my own car and it feels great...I've come here to what I would otherwise miss...'.

Respondents who had visited New Zealand before noted that the Kiwi Experience network used to be 'much smaller', more flexible and personal but over time got bigger in terms of buses and routes. Often these travellers choose this travel pattern after first rejecting the travel packages offered by backpacker transport networks, as one respondent explained:

> *'New Zealand is ideally set up for backpacking...One of the impressions we have had as we have watched the Kiwi Experience go by is the desperately lethargic people sitting on a bus. Why don't they get off the bus and onto a bicycle or whatever it might be'* (male, 40s, UK).

The majority of respondents agreed that only by owning a car, hitchhiking or using public transport can they achieve the desirable flexibility and freedom. These travellers sought to stay in backpacker places with small dormitories, as one respondent explained: 'where the people who own and run it are actually there on the premises all the time, like here they come in everyday, spend some time with us as opposed to the large, impersonal places where you never see those people who own it'.

Study findings: 'Mainstream backpackers'

Profile

This market segment is characterized by two major traveller types: 'mature' and/or older holiday-makers seeking a more flexible travel experience, and younger adults (often students and 'party animals') experiencing international travel in 'budget form'. For these visitors meeting other travellers and creating friendships are seen as important elements of a 'global lifestyle' accompanied by a corresponding disinterest in 'local culture'. Their visit to New Zealand occurs as part of an organized regional travel experience (e.g. 'Down Under'/Pacific). Their travel within New Zealand occurs via well-established backpacker transport networks (e.g. Kiwi Experience), they generally stay together as a group and participate in the attractions and facilities that are linked to the transport network. The duration of travel within New Zealand is from 2-3 weeks up to 3 months. The shorter timeframe and the prepaid component of their travel budget means that these people often have more disposable income for activities in which peer pressure to participate/consume features strongly. Activities are normally outdoor oriented and/or adrenaline based. Service quality (e.g. bus drivers, friendliness of reception, standard of facility) is an important evaluative factor for this group. The comfort of an 'easy cruise' within the 'bubble' of Western/global culture is important because 'travel is sort of hard work...and can include many hard decisions'. The influences this group is exposed to are largely determined by the itineraries of the networks they travel with.

> *'I am traveller or a backpacker. I never use anything else. I have got insurance which covers well for backpackers. You do what you want to do, and you save up for other things...I travel on the Magic Bus and I had to book it in the hostel here...It is a safe place to stay, good base. Magic Bus I must say is excellent, good drivers, friendly, good service, excellent'* (male, Scotland, 60s).

> *'Here for three weeks altogether. Started booking with the Kiwi Experience tours, for the first trip to the Bay of Islands then we went onto the Magic Bus and went to Rotorua, Tongariro, Wellington and then crossed on the ferry ...I think it is a very good system because it is sort of open that you can stop off at certain places for a few days if you want to. And they will book your accommodation, which is really good. They bring you to the door, so you don't have to carry any luggage around too far. It is really difficult to travel, you know. Hard work'* (Mother, 40s and daughter, 20s, travelling together, UK).

> *'I left home a month ago. I might stay for another month in New Zealand and then I am going to Australia. I travel by buses on this magic network. I've come to Nelson because it is part of the route. I went to the Abel Tasman track...I like doing the adventure activities. I learned the kayaks here and it was disappointing because it was too slow. I like wild things. I am going to try rafting. Activities are very expensive so you can't do many things...I am leaving Nelson tomorrow. It is a very small quiet city. Too quiet for my taste'* (female, Israel, 30s).

Motivations

'Mainstream backpackers' generally seek a change from everyday life and a chance to pursue certain recreation activities or simply to see 'different things, doing things that I haven't done before. You meet so many different people, mainly my motivation is to experience' (female, USA, 20s). For younger people (mainly students) travel presents a form of excitement, away from responsibilities and not part of their normal lifestyle, as a few respondents commented:

> *'Travelling is not reality. Not living the real life, and I don't think very much great things about real life. That is what I feel like and that is the reason'* (male, USA, 20s).

> *'I always have a wish to see a little bit more from the world. Not just a holiday, a little bit more time, which is also a relaxing time. I think a life-span is too short to say I will do it, I am retired, 65 years, I won't be able to kayak for one day or even two or three days or hiking'* (male, UK, 60s).
>
> *'It is an instant generation. I think a lot of it I had to find out, I want to do things now, not later. Instant. It means like instant coffee. Now not later. Modern term in Europe. There is something true about it'* (male, Germany, 30s).

Overcoming the traditional image of retired passive sightseers is for many older travellers an important decision-making factor. The pursuit of outdoor (and often adventure) activities, such as trekking, mountain biking or mountaineering is important when deciding on a destination. Flora, fauna and the general outdoor life of New Zealand is a great appeal, as one retired traveller/backpacker (in his 70s) from Scotland explained:

> *'I had picked specific things to do, in each country I go to, I try to keep to a minimum, everything else I do is a bonus. This is important for me ...I always wanted to see an albatross, and I was in ... South America for six months, but I didn't see any albatrosses. When I heard they had been seen here, ... I thought that is excellent I will go to NZ. One of the reasons I went to Dunedin. I actually saw them flying... it was wonderful. It just filled something up in my life, which is difficult to explain. The second one, I really wanted to go to the geysers and muddy waters just outside Rotorua, ... And the third one was the bungy jump. I did the three things I wanted to do'* (male, Scotland, 70s).

Perceptions of the regions and experiences

This market group similarly expressed their perceptions of physical environment and made reference to clean and green landscapes. Defining characteristics of these travellers, however, was their desire to interact with landscape through consumption of commodified products usually in the form of various outdoor activities.

Adventure tourism products dominated the activities of these backpackers and were generally regarded as expensive. They were, however, seen as unique experiences and therefore value for money. The following comments from backpackers illustrate issues present in activity consumption and reveal underlying value system.

> *'These things are expensive but I will do them anyway – only in New Zealand. I wouldn't do them anywhere else'* (male, 20s, Switzerland).
>
> *'It is the first time I have done any of these things and they are in such good locations. By staying in hostels I can afford to do some of the more expensive things. I pay for the more expensive activities on my visa card'* (female, 20s England).
>
> *'The prices vary a lot – from one extreme to another – but I will still do them. Mainly I have never done any of these things before which is why I want to do them – one off things'* (male, 20s, Zimbabwe).

The more expensive products are often known to the traveller prior to arrival at the destination as are details of operators, costs and the experience itself. Many of these 'mainstream' backpackers who were aware of particular activities before arriving in New Zealand were often eager to purchase the product in the 'authentic' place. Many of these activities were associated with the Queenstown area, such as, bungee jumping, skiing, jet boating and white-water rafting. They were reluctant to consume similar products elsewhere, considering them to be inferior in quality, as one respondent (male, 20s, Denmark) noted: 'One of the reasons I came here was to bungee in Queenstown. Other places just don't measure up'.

Similar issues surround the pricing of adventure tourism products. Commonly, similar products are evenly priced and this price is perceived as the 'going rate' for that experience. More cheaply priced activities are often shunned by backpackers who consider them to be inferior products. The best product is desired for 'once in a lifetime' experiences, as one respondent (female, 20s, Scotland) explained: 'Some of these cheap places look a bit dodgy. If I'm going to spend that sort of money I want the best'.

Consumption patterns of these travellers with respect to food illustrate some interesting contrasts to the previously discussed group. Food is commonly not a high priority in the 'mainstream' backpacker budget, often being regarded simply as 'fuel'. The most common pattern for them is to buy food and cook in the hostel kitchen. Food is commonly bought every few days because limited luggage precludes bulk purchasing. Supermarkets are favoured if they are conveniently located to the hostels. As with other areas of expenditure there is considerable variety in the types of food consumed. The most frugal backpackers buy 'no frills' items from supermarkets and will often stock up in urban centres on dried goods to minimize costs. The following comments illustrate this behaviour:

'I always buy food at a supermarket even if I have to walk miles to get there'. (female, 20s England).

'I buy the cheapest food I can find, usually in a tin'. (male, 20s, Ireland).

'I will walk anywhere up to 20 mins to get to a supermarket in the city and I usually stock up if I know there won't be another one for a while'. (female, 20s, England).

The desire for cheap food has lead to many hostels offering free shuttles to local supermarkets. Backpacker transport networks frequently stop at supermarkets for passengers to buy food as part of their service. The hostels associated with these transport companies often include cafés, restaurants or bars where food is commonly discounted to pass holders. Cooking facilities in these hostels are often limited so the travellers are encouraged to buy food on the premises. Food in this form or takeaways often form the staple of these backpackers:

'If there is a place to eat at the hostel we usually will have a discount with the Kiwi Experience pass so we will eat there. Sometimes we go to MacDonalds. Otherwise we get some food from the shop (two female friends, 20s, Denmark).

'I usually just buy some food wherever it is convenient and I don't usually cook myself. That is probably the same for most of the people on the bus' (male, 20s, USA).

'The bus sometimes stopped at supermarkets for us to buy food but other times the bus only stopped at expensive type shops. We tend to eat out during the days but usually cook in the hostel in the evenings' (two female friends, 20s, Israel).

In contrast to the previously discussed group of long-term budget travellers, this group did not seek to compare themselves with other 'backpacker' markets. Their awareness of travelling culture was, for the most part, limited to their immediate social environment and the group they were travelling with. However, this group were anxious

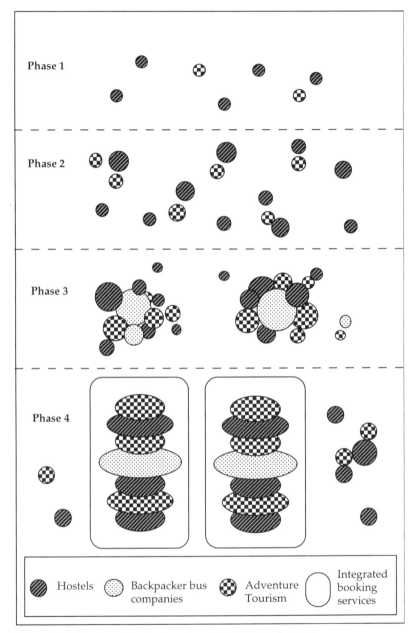

Figure 1 Polarization of the backpacker market in New Zealand

to distinguish themselves as 'travellers' from the stereotypical 'mass-tourist', emphasizing distinctions between their focus on outdoor activities as distinct from a more 'passive' form of tourism.

Discussion: Issues and Implications

Implicit in our discussion so far has been the observation that relationship between markets and industry is dynamic and has undergone significant changes over time. In this section, we discuss how the industry has developed over time, how that development produces distinctive patterns of consumer segmentation and the emergence of polarization of the two market groups discussed above. Following this we will examine the perceptions of the two markets identified above with respect to the industry, values, and each other. In order to facilitate this discussion we present a model of the evolution of consumer-producer relationship in this sector and following this examine the issues and implications model raises.

Against the historical background discussed earlier in the contextual discussion, the development of the backpacker tourist industry is presented in Figure 1, showing the nature of the relationships between the various backpacker industry sectors in four phases.

The model illustrates the process of evolutionary change affecting businesses in the backpacker tourist industry in New Zealand. The model is not designed to represent a strict chronology of the industry but is representative of the trends which have occurred over time. It should be noted that all four phases may exist simultaneously in different areas of New Zealand depending on the local tourism industry's level of involvement with the backpacker market. The shading for each sector shown in Figure 1 shows that throughout the process of integration, ownership of individual businesses remains sectorally distinct. Figure 1 is examined as follows.

Phase 1 represents the tourist industry in the early stages of a relationship with the backpacker. The accommodation sector represents the dominant industry activity along with adventure tourism enterprises. There are few if any linkages between the two sectors and the backpacker transport sector is non-existent.

Phase 2 shows newly established adventure tourism businesses emerging alongside the existing hostel market. Those hostels close to adventure tourism businesses experience growth in patronage. The establishment of new businesses in both sectors illustrates the existence of backpackers as a separate but distinct tourist market.

Phase 3 shows accommodation and adventure tourism enterprises developing an association with newly formed backpacker transport companies. The increased economic activity generated by the relationship brings mutual growth to those involved. Other adventure tourism, accommodation and transport businesses continue to operate on a lesser scale, independent of industry integration.

Phase 4 is representative of the more developed elements of the backpacker industry during this study's research period. The integration process has advanced to include the packaging of products via relationships between industry sectors. Booking services are common to those involved, and each complex surrounding the transport network is clearly defined and operates parallel, but separately to the others.

Growth continued in all businesses associated with the dominant transport networks. Other smaller transport operations similarly fused products in competition with the larger networks. Surrounding these, are clusters of associated sectors similar to those in Phase 3. Backpacker transport services no longer exist in isolation of activity or accommodation sectors. As the volume of backpackers increases, remote accommodation and activity businesses continue to survive in isolation of transport connections by appealing to a traditional long-term budget traveller niche within the wider market which rejects the 'mainstream' backpacker industry. New activity and accommodation enterprises enter and depart depending on their ability to integrate with transport networks. In Phase 4, those businesses more closely associated with the transport network grow most strongly, whereas those businesses with secondary and tertiary relationships with the network grow less quickly.

Whilst, in theory, all four phases in Figure 1 can exist simultaneously, as the industry as a whole develops new businesses entering the industry are more likely to enter in the advanced stages of the model. The thresholds of entry, over time, necessarily include elements of the integration process. New enterprises are more likely to be inspired by existing activity resulting in spatially concentrated backpacker industry conglomerations. New enterprises are also more likely to be sectorally diverse in responding to perceived market demand.

Drawing on the interview data presented earlier, the perspective of market groups (traditional 'long-term, budget travellers' and 'mainstream backpackers') towards each other illustrate some interesting issues from consumers perspectives. The diagrammatic representation of the industry in Phase 4 articulates an issue raised by a focus group of long-term budget travellers who observed how the development of backpacker industry in New Zealand can be seen to resemble a backpacker 'tourist hamburger'. As noted earlier, these travellers generally displayed an awareness of the values underpinning particular forms of tourism consumption. Respondents noted how these 'so-called independent networks' were not flexible in reality and rather reflected mainstream tourism activity by catering to shorter-stay, high-consumption 'tours'. Focus group respondents identified how each ingredient of the product is stacked vertically and integrated into one package. Indeed, the analogy can also be extended to areas of marketing, consumption, digestion and concepts of satisfaction. The product is readily available, quickly consumed, balanced in content, although in the final analysis, is a substitute for 'the real thing'. A range of products using the same concept are available from numerous outlets to suit a variety of travel tastes.

To explore this concept further still; backpacker tourist products in New Zealand can, at present, be seen as representative of a 'pre-MacDonalds' backpacker industry. That is, the product is available from local independent operators (e.g. Kiwi Experience, akin to the suburban hamburger bar) and is, although similar in concept, unique to the producer. If the development of the fast food industry is indicative of the backpacker industry, the future will see the emergence of efficiently marketed, vertically integrated, transnational corporate structures offering a range of standardized products to backpackers throughout the world.

On the other hand respondents from group B were less conscious of the wider development context, instead, displaying a focus on the group, the status of the activities they consume. This group maintained a distinction between themselves and 'mass-tourist' markets emphasizing their identity as a 'new generation' of global companionship. Whilst traditionally the profile of mainstream backpackers has reflected global youth culture, our research suggests a rapid broadening of the demographic profile of visitors to whom this integrated industry structure can provide 'global standards' of service and quality.

With respect to global culture this issue was also significant to long-term budget travellers. What appears as a significant transformation of the motivation of long-term, budget travellers noted earlier (Adler, 1985; Riley, 1988) is the reduced significance of nation-state boundaries in providing a delineation between cultures. The perceived homogenization of global culture represents a clear push factor for these travellers seeking to remove themselves from the pervasive values of an overarching capitalist system. In doing so, these individuals actively seek to associate themselves with both travellers and business operators sharing these values. In the Nelson region and Golden Bay in particular, this process of dislocation from global culture, symbolically represented by the integration of the mainstream backpacker tourism industry, was still achievable through physical, spatial removal from that system.

Conclusion

This paper has sought to reveal the complexity of what has been widely perceived as an homogeneous tourist consumer group of 'backpackers'. Our study has displayed a significant segmentation of this market, particularly with respect to consumer behaviour and the underlying cultural values which guide that behaviour.

By focusing on two opposite ends of spectrum of what could be more accurately described as a continuum we have demonstrated the significance of global cultural change in influencing the value positions of consumers within this market. With respect to changing needs and travel aspirations, the pessimistic perceptions of global capitalism and its associated lifestyle are significant push factors for long-term budget travellers, the same context however facilitates and attracts mainstream backpackers to engage in travel activities. Despite what we suggest as a significant transformation in cultural context, there remain similarities with earlier observations of long-term, budget travellers. Cohen's observations of a hierarchy of values distinguishing 'real travellers' from 'lesser' forms of travel are exemplified by tourists, and in this case mainstream backpackers. Riley's study of long-term travellers as being middle class, educated professionals remains characteristic across the continuum of the backpacker market.

The historical insight we provide, however, suggests the inevitability of 'industrialization' and integration of 'alternative' forms of travel into the 'mainstream' model. The sheer volume of the participants in international tourism and the rapid segmentation across markets appears to have a mass and momentum sufficient that any activity in the tourism industry will inevitably gravitate towards increasing levels of integration.

With respect to future research we suggest the underlying values influencing travel motivations and respective form of tourism consumption we have identified, present significant implications for industry development studies, market research, local policy environment and wider debate surrounding tourism sustainability.

References

Adler, J. (1985) Youth on the Road: Reflection on the History of Tramping. *Annals of Tourism Research* 12, 335-354.

Cloke, P. and Perkins, H. (1998) 'Cracking the canyon with the awesome foursome': Representations of Adventure Tourism in New Zealand. *Environment and Planning D. Society and Space* 16, 185-218.

Cohen, E. (1972) Toward a Sociology of International Tourism. *Social Research* 39, 164-182.

Cohen, E. (1973) Nomads From Affluence: Notes on the Phenomenon of Drifter-Tourism. *International Journal of Comparative Sociology* 14, 89-103.

Cohen, E. (1974) Who is a Tourist? A Conceptual Classification. *Sociological Review* 22, 527-555.

Department of Conservation and Tourism Resource Consultants (1993) *Word of Mouth Information Systems – How backpackers learn about what to do in New Zealand and on Department of Conservation tracks.* Dpt. of Conservation: New Zealand.

Doorne, S. (1994*) Symbiosis, Integration and the Backpacker Tourist Industry.* Unpublished Masters thesis. Victoria University of Wellington.

Firth, T. and Hing, N. (1999) Backpacker hostels and their guests: attitudes and behaviours relating to sustainable tourism. *Tourism Management* 20, 251-254.

Garnham, R. (1993) *A Backpacking Geography of New Zealand.* New Zealand Geography Conference Proceedings, Wellington.

Gray, P.H. (1981) Wanderlust Tourism: Problems of Infrastructure. *Annals of Tourism Research* 7, 285-290.

Hampton, M.P. (1998) Backpacker Tourism and Economic Development. *Annals of Tourism Research* 25, 639-660.

Krippendorf, J. (1987) *The Holidaymakers.* Heinemann, London.

Mannel, R.C. and Iso-Ahola, S.E. (1987) Psychological Nature of Leisure and Tourism Experience. *Annals of Tourism Research* 14, 314-331.

Parr, D.K. (1989) *Free Independent Travellers: The Unknown Tourists.* MA dissertation, University of Canterbury, Lincoln College.

Pearce, P.L. (1990) *The Backpacker Phenomenon Preliminary Answers to Basic Questions.* Department of Tourism, James Cook University of North Queensland.

Riley, P.J. (1988) Road Culture of International Long Term Budget Travellers. *Annals of Tourism Research* 15, 313-328.

Rodenburg, E. (1980) The Effects of Scale in Economic Development: Tourism in Bali. *Annals of Tourism Research* 7, 177-196.

Rojek, C. (1993) *Ways of Escape: Modern Transformations in Leisure and Travel.* The Macmillan Press, London.

Urry, J. (1990) *The Tourist Gaze.* Sage, London.

Vogt, J. (1976) Wandering: Youth and Travel Behaviour. *Annals of Tourism Research* 4, 25-40.

Ware, M.P. (1992) *Been There Done That: A Study of Winter Backpackers in New Zealand.* Bachelor of Arts dissertation, Jesus College, Cambridge, UK.

Wilson, D. (1997) Paradoxes of Tourism in Goa. *Annals of Tourism Research* 24, 52-75.

Chapter eleven
Using Internet Technology to Request Travel Information and Purchase Travel Services: A Comparison of X'ers, Boomers and Mature Market Segments Visiting Florida

Mark A. Bonn
Florida State University, College of Business
Department of Hospitality Administration, Tallahassee, Florida

H. Leslie Furr
Georgia Southern University, Hotel and Restaurant Management
Statesboro

Angela Hausman
Lewis College of Business
Management/Marketing Division, Marshall University
Huntington, West Virginia

Introduction

Travel and tourism contributes substantially to the economy in Florida, where 48.7 million people chose to spend their 1998 vacation dollars. Of all the visitors to Florida that year, almost 8 million were foreigners (Visit Florida Inc., 1998). The economic impact of these visitors is substantial. In 1997 alone, Florida visitors spent over $40 billion and tourism directly employed almost 800,000 Floridians (Florida Department of Revenue, 1998).

Many visitors to Florida choose to visit major destination cities that offer a concentrated vacation experience, such as the theme parks in Orlando, golf in famous West Palm Beach clubs or water sports in the Florida Keys. Others select areas with a more diverse selection of activities, including Tampa, which attracted over 12 million visitors, 11.5% of them foreign, in 1998 (THCVA, 1999). Understanding how visitors choose and utilize information sources in their destination-selection process is vital to marketing managers who are responsible for allocating resources for promotional campaigns.

In addition, profiling visitors to an area is important as it serves to identify target markets, thereby guiding appropriate marketing strategies (Court and Lupton, 1997).

Thus, segmentation leads to efficiencies, allowing higher returns on promotional activities (McQueen and Miller, 1985).

This paper identifies and investigates three specific visitor groups of consumers of travel products and services according to their generation: Generation X'ers, Baby Boomers, and Mature Travellers. For the purposes of this paper, Generation X'ers are defined as adult visitors between the age of 24 and 35 years old. Baby Boomers are those visitors between the ages of 35 and 54 years of age. Matures are visitors over the age of 54 years old. The paper further compares the groups based upon their geographical categories of either United States (US) residents or Non-US residents (foreigners). Profiles are created for these group classifications based upon their use of the Internet to (a) request destination information and (b) purchase travel-related services (i.e. air, lodging, auto rental, and attractions' tickets). The paper identifies statistically significant differences in terms of party size, age, on-site expenditures, length of stay, trip purpose and travel mode. These profiles are intended to demonstrate the utility of segmenting travellers by their willingness to use Internet technology, according to generations, which will contribute to promotional efficiencies.

Review of Literature

Variables commonly used to profile travel segments include: (1) demographic characteristics (Court and Lupton, 1997); (2) geographic distance (Etzel and Woodside, 1982; Dagostar and Isotalo 1992); (3) motivation (Snepenger1987; Cha *et al.*, 1995); and (4) behavioural descriptors (Ronkainen and Woodside, 1980; McQueen and Miller, 1985; Mills *et al.*, 1986).

Demographic characteristics, such as age, help facilitate media selection for each target market segment (cf. Woodside and Pitts, 1976; McQueen and Miller, 1985). However, traditional market research using age has recently begun to assume categories associated with generations such as Generation X'ers, Baby Boomers, and Matures (National Leisure Travel Monitor, 1998). This is based in part on the assumption that different generations may in fact possess different psychographic characteristics based upon society's changing life styles and behaviours. This new trend in age research has been especially supported by leading travel industry corporations desiring to obtain competitive consumer behaviour data for use in advertising campaigns (National Leisure Travel Monitor, 1999). Geographic distance has been studied with respect to distant vs. near-home travellers (Etzel and Woodside, 1982) and as a continuum representing increasing expenditures of time and money as a function of location (Dagostar and Isotalo, 1992). Behavioural descriptors commonly employed to distinguish between market segments are consumption patterns, length of stay, number of previous visits, and activities chosen.

Recent studies explored segmentation among visitors to areas who used the Internet for requesting pre-trip information and for purchasing travel-related services (Schonland and Williams, 1996; Furr and Bonn, 1998; Bonn *et al.*, 1999). These results suggest Internet users' characteristics differ significantly from non-Internet users in terms of selected travel characteristics such as preference for length of stay, on-site expenditures, and travel mode.

Methodology

During 1996-1998, professional surveyors completed 13,490 personal interviews with travellers during their recent trip to Tampa using a randomized day/site/time sampling technique. Visitors answered queries from a standard questionnaire regarding their recent trip, including motivational factors, prior experience with the Tampa area, activities engaged in during their visit, spending patterns for food, lodging, and activities, importance of various factors influencing their decision to visit Tampa. Of those contacted, 45.3% (n = 6117) indicated they would request trip-related information about the destination using the Internet. An additional 29.5% (n = 3976) indicated they would purchase travel-related services using the Internet.

Analysis and Results

Data collection efforts throughout 1996-1998 produced 13,323 usable surveys. The completed surveys contained 1357 (approximately 10.1%) foreign visitors, and 12,123 (approximately 89.9%) US residents. The top four countries of origin for foreign tourists (in order of frequency) were England, Canada, Germany, and Brazil.

First, the data were divided into two groups based on origin of visitors; foreign vs. US. The demographic data indicate that foreign visitors were significantly less likely than other visitors to use the Internet for information or as a tool for buying travel services. Notice specifically in Table 1 that only one of every four foreign visitors would book travel services on the Internet while nearly one in three of their new-world counterparts would book travel services via the Internet.

Table 2 represents another division of the data to highlight generational differences in attitudes and behaviour. 'Baby Boomer' travellers were consistently the most likely users of Internet services in the travel arena. As one could assume, the Mature Travellers were least likely to use the Internet to book a trip.

Figure 1 illustrates that the trend lines for X'ers and Baby Boomers seem to predict a growing willingness for members of these two age groups to expand their use of the Internet in the future. The Mature Travellers' indicates nearly flat growth in this area. Future growth in Internet interest for the Mature Traveller will probably occur with the maturation of the population rather than from the changing behaviour patterns of the Mature Travellers.

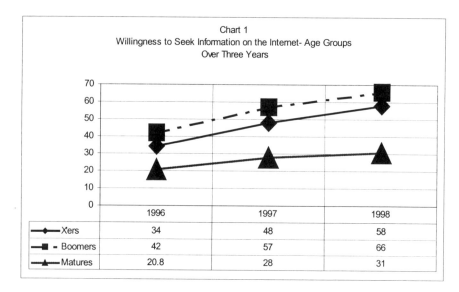

Figure 1 Willingness to seek information on the Internet

Table 1 Chi-square Analysis of Pleasure Travellers of different Origins

Variables	Number and Per cent of Respondents Who Would (or Would Not) Seek Travel Information on the Internet				χ^2 Value	df	p	eta
	Yes		No					
Origin, $\underline{N}$ = 7061	$\underline{n}$	%	$\underline{n}$	%	56.250	1	.000	.089
USA	2839	49.7	2869	50.3				
Foreign Visitors	521	38.4	835	61.6				
	Number and Per cent of Respondents Who Would (or Would Not) Book a Travel Trip on the Internet				χ^2 Value	df	p	eta
	Yes		No					
Origin, $\underline{N}$ = 7061	$\underline{n}$	%	$\underline{n}$	%	29.804	1	.000	.065
USA	1847	32.4	3857	67.6				
Foreign Visitors	336	24.8	1021	75.2				

A stepwise one-way analysis of variance was employed as a data reduction tool to determine the most salient behavioural variables of visitor's behaviour that define the difference between foreign and US visitors to Tampa. These results indicate that nine behavioural factors (shopping expenditures, number of nights spent in Tampa, number in the travel party, lodging expenditures, attractions admission fees, total average daily expenditures, transportation fees, evening entertainment fees, and food expenditures) best identify behavioural differences between the behaviour of foreign tourists and US tourists in the Tampa area. Note the comparison of means for foreign and US visitors in

Table 3 for these behavioural items (listed above) that support marketing opportunities for the Tampa area. For example, foreign shoppers spend a daily average of $69.68 compared to the daily average US shopper's $39.84. In addition, foreign travellers spend an average of $51.01 on attraction admissions per day compared to the US traveller who spends $35.70 each day.

Table 2 Chi-square Analysis of Pleasure Travellers of Three Age Groups

Variables	Number and Per cent of Respondents Who Would (or Would Not) Seek Travel Information on the Internet				χ^2 Value	df	p	eta
	Yes		No					
Age, $\underline{N}$ = 6089	$\underline{n}$	%	$\underline{n}$	%	205.392	2	.000	.065
X'ers	1554	48.2	1671	51.6				
Boomers	1466	57.2	1100	42.8				
Mature Travellers	312	30.7	704	20.3				
	Number and Per cent of Respondents Who Would (or Would Not) Book a Travel Trip on the Internet				χ^2 Value	df	p	eta
	Yes		No					
Age, $\underline{N}$ = 6805	$\underline{n}$	%	$\underline{n}$	%	97.458	2	.000	.061
X'ers	1038	32.2	2183	67.8				
Boomers	934	36.4	1633	63.6				
Mature Travellers	197	19.4	820	80.6				

	Travel Mode							
Variables	Air		Roadway		χ^2 Value	df	p	eta
Age, $\underline{N}$ = 6089	$\underline{n}$	%	$\underline{n}$	%	49.144	2	.000	.065
X'ers	1969	76.8	596	23.2				
Boomers	1935	77.4	566	22.6				
Mature Travellers	638	66.5	322	33.5				

Discussion

Clearly, utility exists for analysing visitor data according to their generation groupings (X'ers, Boomers and Matures) and geographic location (i.e. domestic vs. foreign). This study documents numerous differences between foreign visitors and non-foreign visitors. When examining attitudinal and behaviour differences between the groups, marketing managers would be prudent to observe foreign visitor characteristics such as level of expenditures for particular activities. For example, foreign visitors, in this particular market, are more likely to spend more money in shorter time periods than US travellers. Also note that the X'ers are more likely to travel by air than their grandparents (see Table 2). At a minimum, marketing executives should devise strategies that create packages of opportunities within each market segment that take into account generations and place of origin. Significant contributions to existing consumer behaviour issues is possible through generation groupings compared with traditional demographic market research using age as absolute values.

Table 3 Number of Respondents, Means, and Standard Deviations, Total Average Expenditures, Shopping Expenditures, Transportation Fees, Evening Entertainment Fees, Event Admission Fees, Food Expenditures, Lodging Expenditures, Travel Party Number, and Number of Nights in Tampa

		Daily Average	Lodging	# Nights in Tampa	Travel Party #	Event Fees
Foreign	Mean	253.04	27.79	1.74	3.32	51.01
	n	1357	1357	1353	1349	1357
US	Mean	218.04	37.93	2.41	2.84	35.70
	n	5780	5769	5780	5780	5780

		Shopping	Transport Fees	Evening Entertain.	Prepared Food
Foreign	Mean	69.68	20.85	9.43	46.89
	n	1357	1357	1357	1357
US	Mean	39.04	21.38	9.22	45.68
	n	5780	5780	5780	5780

References

Bonn, M.A., Furr, H.L. and Susskind, A.M. (1999) Predicting a Behavioral Profile for Pleasure Travelers on the Basis of Internet Use. *Journal of Travel Research* 37(4), 333-340.

Cha, S., McCleary, K. and Uysal, M. (1995) Travel Motivations of the Japanese Overseas Travelers: A Factor-Cluster Segmentation Approach. *Journal of Travel Research* 33(Summer), 33-39.

Court, B. and Lupton, R.A. (1997) Customer Portfolio Development: Modeling Destination Adopter, Inactive, and Rejecters. *Journal of Travel Research* 20(Spring), 10-14.

Dagostar, B. and Isotalo, R. (1992) Factors Affecting Time Spent by Near-Home Tourists in City Destinations. *Journal of Travel Research* 30(Autumn), 34-39.

Etzel, M. and Woodside, A. (1982) Segmenting Vacation Markets: The Case of the Distant and Near-Home Traveler. *Journal of Travel Research* 36(4), 16-24.

Florida Department of Revenue (1998) www.census.gov/ftp/pub/indicator/www/indicat.html

Furr, H.L. and Bonn, M.A. (1998) The Internet and the Hospitality Marketing Profession. *Journal of Applied Hospitality Management* 1, 60-69.

McQueen, J. and Miller, K. (1985) Target Market Selection of Tourists: A Comparison of Approaches. *Journal of Travel Research* 23(Summer), 24.

Mills, A., Couturier, H. and Snepenger, D. (1986) Segmenting Texas Snow Skiers. *Journal of Travel Research* 25(Autumn), 19-23.

National Leisure Travel Monitor (1998) Yankelovich Monitor's ME.2. National Leisure

Travel Monitor (1999), Yankelovich Monitor.

National Leisure Travel Monitor (1999) Yesawich, Pepperdine and Brown and Yanklovich Partners, Inc.

Ronkainen, I. and Woodside, A. (1980) First Timer Versus Repeat Visitors: Analysing Multiple Travel Market Segments. *The Travel and Tourism Assocation's Tenth Annual Conference Proceedings*. Bureau of Economic and Business Research, University of Utah, Salt Lake City, UT, pp. 97-101.

Schonland, A.M. and Williams, R. (1996) Using the Internet for Travel and Tourism Survey Research: Experiences from the Net Traveler Survey. *Journal of Travel Research* 35(Autumn), 81-87.

Snepenger, D. (1987) Separating the Vacation Market by Novelty-Seeking Role. *Journal of Travel Research* 26(Autumn), 8-14.

THCVA (1999) 1998 Annual Visitor's Study for Tampa/Hillsborough County, Florida.

Visit Florida (1998) Florida Visitor Study 1997. Visit Florida, Tallahassee, FL.

Woodside, A. and Pitts, R. (1976) Effects of Consumer Lifestyles, Demographics, and Travel Activities on Foreign and Domestic Travel Behavior. *Journal of Travel Research* 14(Winter), 13-15.

Chapter twelve
Which Determines Our Leisure Preferences: Demographics or Personality?

Robyn L. McGuiggan
School of Marketing, University of Technology Sydney
Sydney NSW 2007, Australia

Introduction

Does the purchase of leisure products differ from the purchase of other types of products? Foxall (1984) and Dimanche *et al.* (1991) suggest that 'the consumption of leisure can be seen as a subset of broader patterns of consumption and thus can be understood through the theories of consumer behaviour. ... That decisions to purchase leisure goods and services are comparable to decisions to purchase other products' (Dimanche and Samdahl, 1994, p. 120). This does not mean that the more 'traditional models' of consumer choice necessarily explain leisure choice, nor, for that matter, the choice of other products.

Although numerous authors have proposed various models of consumer choice, the most common models in the literature today rely on understanding the decision-making process through an information processing, or problem-solving, approach. This is particularly evident in the orientation of the more prominent models, which primarily use logical flow models of bounded rationality to explain consumer behaviour (Holbrook and Hirschman, 1982). Much of the research underlying the development of these models has focused on the purchase of durable products and the tangible benefits they provide. More recently, a number of researchers have suggested that these models view consumption too narrowly failing to take into account the choice of products for more hedonic reasons. Consumers may purchase products in anticipation of having fun, to fulfil fantasies, or simply for the emotions or feelings the products generate (Woods, 1981; Holbrook *et al.,* 1984; Shimp, 1993). To account for these choices, as well as impulse purchasing and variety seeking behaviour, the traditional information processing model has been broadened into what Holbrook and Hirschman (1982) and Mowen (1988) refer to as the 'experiential view' of consumer choice. In a recent paper by Bernd Schmitt (1999) it is argued that this 'experiential view' of consumer decision making may now be a better representation of consumer choice than the more traditional models for all types of products. He suggests that with current changes in the business environment – information technology, increasing importance of branding, and the omnipresence of communication and entertainment – consumer interest is not restricted to purely functional benefits, but to purchasing a total experience. If this is in fact true, then it is important that the information processing perspective of consumer choice be expanded to include more of the hedonic aspects of consumption – fantasies, feelings and fun.

In their paper, comparing the information processing and experiential views of consumer behaviour, Holbrook and Hirschman (1982) suggest that this requires the rethinking of the relative importance of various aspects of environmental and consumer inputs, the actual choice process, the evaluation of the consumption experience, and the feedback and consumer learning process. They argue that, as all products may carry symbolic meaning, the study of 'experiential' products, such as the arts, entertainment and leisure, can add a new dimension to our understanding of consumer choice in general.

The aim of this paper is to expand the knowledge of hedonic consumption by examining the relative influence of demographic characteristics and personality on leisure choice preferences. Holbrook and Hirschman (1982, p. 136) suggest that although personality has shown relatively poor performance in predicting consumer behaviour, the 'investigation of experiential consumption appears to offer considerable scope for the revival of personality' research. Although they acknowledge that all individual differences are important in determining choice, they suggest that personality may be a better predictor of choice than demographics, for experiential products.

Leisure choice

Numerous demographic and sociological variables have been studied singularly and in combination in an attempt to determine which have the greatest influence on the choices of consumers. There is no shortage of 'explanatory' studies of this type in the leisure literature. Explanation of leisure activity choice, provided by studies using one variable, or combinations of variables, is limited. Kamphorst (1987) suggests that correlation coefficients between a specific form of leisure behaviour and a single sociological variable of 0.25 and greater, are the exception rather than the rule. Furthermore, he states that multiple correlation coefficients between a set of typical sociological variables and a specific form of leisure activity very seldom exceed 0.35. This means that, on average, only 5-10% of the differences in leisure activities between people can be explained by sociological variables (Kamphorst, 1987, p. 195).

The results of personality studies are no better, with most of the correlation coefficients falling in the range 0.1 to 0.3, with an occasional coefficient reaching 0.4 or 0.5 in studies utilizing attributes rather than specific activities (McGuiggan, 1996, p. 50). Despite results to date, authors such as Barash (1997) agree with Holbrook and Hirschman (1982) regarding the relative influence of personality and demographics. In fact Barash (1997, p. 4) suggests that marketplace behaviour in general is far more likely to be influenced by 'personality, temperament, character, values, ethos, mythos, and specific individual circumstances than by any combination of accumulated demographic data'.

The warnings of Iso-Ahola should be born in mind. He suggests that personality may predispose an individual towards certain leisure satisfactions, but he qualifies this, stating that 'any isolated concept (e.g., biological dispositions, personality, childhood-adulthood socialization, optimal arousal, and intrinsic motivation) is insufficient and inadequate to fully explain the "whys" of leisure behaviour' (Iso-Ahola, 1984, p. 100).

The aim of this study was not to prove that only one variable requires consideration when investigating leisure choice, but rather to establish the relative importance of personality and demographics in that choice. The importance of personality with regard to leisure choice was studied in relation to the importance of the most common demographic variables cited in the leisure literature.

The following provides a brief overview of the personality and demographic variables utilized in this study. An attempt has been made to discuss the effects of the different variables on leisure choice in isolation from other variables. Many of these variables are interrelated, so this is not always possible. This categorization is therefore artificial and is used simply as a mechanism for organizing the discussion.

Culture

It is generally agreed that leisure activity is a product of a particular culture – learned in ways peculiar to that culture (Kelly, 1982, p. 207). Hirschman and Holbrook (1982, p. 99) suggest that part of cultural socialization is learning the appropriate emotional and imaginal responses to various products. An individual learns to treat a product from the perspective learnt from his/her ethnic group. Culture is not fixed or static, but changes over time. Authors, such as Lynch and Veal (1996, p. 3), see leisure as being both shaped by, and a shaper of, culture.

In many studies, differences in what people do and how they do it are self-evident between cultures. Differences in a country's resources, cultural values and the form activities take, mean that activities seen as central to leisure in one community may not even be considered as leisure in another (Kelly, 1983).

Although most authors will agree that leisure cannot be studied outside of its cultural context, there has been a distinct lack of attention to the role of ethnicity in the study of leisure (Kelly and Godbey, 1992, p. 159). It is also evident that culture is interwoven, and inseparable from, the effects of other elements such as family, education and occupation.

Family life-cycle

Stage in the family life-cycle affects not only which leisure activities are undertaken, but why, and with whom. There is widespread agreement that the family is a key variable in the determination of leisure involvement – the most common forms of leisure activity taking place in the home, in the company of other family members (Kelly, 1982; Glyptis, 1987). The family acts as a stimulus and provides opportunity for leisure learning, but also restricts the choice of activities and the time available to partake of them (Kelly, 1987). Not all activities involving family members may be considered leisure by all participants. Freedom of choice and the extent of obligation involved need be considered when investigating family leisure (Orthner and Mancini, 1980). Parents constrain each others' choices and those of their children, and children in turn constrain the choices available to their parents (Iso-Ahola and Mannell, 1985). With the advent of children, not only do leisure activities outside the home decrease, but also certain leisure activities within the home, such as listening to music and reading books (Smith, 1987). Smith found this decrease in activities to be more pronounced for women than for men, as did Iso-Ahola and Mannell (1985).

Traditionally age and stage in the family life-cycle were highly correlated, thus allowing age to be used as a surrogate variable in the measurement of family life-cycle. In recent years, later marriage, smaller families and rising divorce rates – leading to an increase in older single households and one parent households as well as second marriages – suggests that the traditional progression through family life-cycle stages is no longer applicable. The relationship between age and stage in the family life-cycle is no longer clearly defined, and marketing research has indicated that, in terms of market segmentation, life-cycle performs better than age (Moschis, 1981). Some research in the leisure area also supports this conclusion. For example, King (1965) found 80% of campers had children, and of these, 49% were in the 6 to 12 year age group, regardless of the age of the parents.

Although there are many aspects to family life-cycle, it would appear, from the literature, that children living in the household have a major impact on the leisure activities undertaken by all members of the family.

Age

Although it is difficult to isolate the effects of age from other variables, such as culture and stage in the family life-cycle, there are significant but predictable shifts in leisure participation related to age (Hendee and Burdge, 1974; Kelly 1980; Smith 1987; Iso-Ahola and Jackson, 1994). Increasing age is associated with a shift away from physical activity and a shift toward home-based activities and social interaction (Hendee and Burdge, 1974). A number of age related leisure changes have been described in the literature. In particular, the older the respondent, the lower the general level of leisure activity, the narrower the range of activities, the less 'intense' and physically demanding its forms, and the more likely that it is based within the home (Baley, 1955; Schmitz-Scherzer, 1976; Iso-Ahola and Jackson, 1994). Schmitz-Scherzer (1976) also found that older people seldom take up totally new activities, variety being achieved through changing the pattern of existing activities.

Although previous studies have consistently found a decreasing involvement in active leisure pursuits with age, changes in family life-cycle may result in age becoming less important in the determination of leisure choice. For example, a father, at 60 years of age, may be found playing cricket or tennis with his 10-year-old son or even taking his son rock climbing.

Gender

Most people would agree that gender has a major influence on choice of leisure activities. Gruber (1980) found males' and females' sex-type activities similarly – activities being seen as either masculine, feminine or neutral. He found knowledge of, and interest in, activities to be highly correlated with gender – games and sports involving skills, competition and contact being associated with males rather than females. Kirkcaldy and Furnham (1991) also found significant differences between the sexes. Males scored highest on contact, combative sports with a potentially aggressive component (e.g. wrestling and boxing) and male-stereotyped ball games such as handball and football. Females scored higher on creative/craft type activities such as dancing, painting and handicrafts. These findings are consistent with previous studies conducted by these and other authors. It appears that social and cultural activities are least likely to show sex differences (Deem, 1988).

Smith (1987) points out, as does Bialeschki and Henderson (1986), Deem (1988) and Shaw (1994), that women tend to engage in fewer leisure activities than men, and that the activities chosen are more likely to be home based and domestic in nature – especially during the child raising years. Kelly (1983, p. 223-225) suggests that these and other differences seen in leisure choice between the sexes is a reflection of the expectations of society – that these choices are related to sex-role socialization. Iso-Ahola and Mannell (1985, p. 114) agree with Kelly that gender, rather than being a determining variable, may be regarded as a social constraint. But casual observation, for example the introduction of men's rules basketball for women into the Olympic games, would indicate that cultural change and the changing role of women is gradually altering society's view of acceptable leisure activities for women. Yet it is still true that 'while sports opportunities have increased for girls and women in recent years, some sports are still more socially acceptable than other sports for females' (Shaw, 1994, p. 13).

Education

The few studies that have looked at the influence of education on leisure choice seem to suggest that the relationship between education and leisure participation is relatively weak (Roberts, 1970; Kelly, 1978). Roberts (1970) hypothesized that this may be due to the narrow definition of education, i.e. years of formal education. Although later studies by Kelly (1980), Hendee and Burdge (1974), and Jamrozik (1986) did find that decreased education leads to a decrease in outdoor recreation, they suggest that this may be a reflection of income rather than education.

Neulinger (1974) points out that education is an indicator of social class, and thus variation in activity choice could be due to social class pressure, rather than a direct result of education. In fact, it is possible that education does not directly influence leisure activity choice, but exerts its effect indirectly through occupation and income. Education may provide opportunity for leisure learning and the ability to earn higher income, thus allowing involvement in more, and more expensive, leisure pursuits.

Occupation

The demographic that has been most extensively studied in relation to leisure is work. These studies have led to the formulation of three different work/leisure hypotheses: spillover or congruence, compensation or contrast, and neutrality or segmentation. Authors such as Kornhauser (1965), Meissner (1971), Rousseau (1978), Zuzanek and Mannell (1983) and Liou *et al.* (1990) support the spillover hypothesis, which asserts that there is consistency between behaviour at work, and leisure. Skills, attitudes and personality attributes are carried over from one area of behaviour and experience to another. In the compensation explanation, 'desirable experiences' – behaviour or psychological states that are catered for adequately in the work situation – are pursued in non-work time. Little empirical support for this view can be found in the literature. Most comes from studies which look at the alienation of workers in monotonous occupations (Grubb, 1975), or under-employed workers (Spreitzer and Snyder, 1987), or those employed in stressful occupations such as coal mining (Dennis *et al.,* 1956) and fishing (Tunstall, 1962). The third hypothesis claims that work and leisure are two different entities and are not interactive. Studies by Snyder and Spreitzer (1974), Kabanoff and O'Brien (1980, 1982), Kabanoff (1982) and Poole and Cooney (1986) have provided some support for this proposition.

Although the studies carried out by Kabanoff and O'Brien (1980, 1982) and

Kabanoff (1982) found no evidence of a strong relationship between work and leisure attributes, their results do not wholly support the segmentation approach, but may in fact uphold a joint determination approach, whereby work and leisure are both influenced by other factors. Kabanoff and O'Brien (1980, 1986), and other researchers such as Iso-Ahola (1980), have suggested that the relationship between work and leisure may not be clear because of moderating variables, such as stress levels, differences in cognitive processes, social status, reference group influence, cultural differences or personality characteristics. Furthermore, because of the reciprocity between the two domains, it is extremely difficult to assign 'cause and effect' and separating the effects of occupation from education, social status and prestige is almost impossible (Iso-Aloha, 1980, p. 361).

Even if work does not directly influence leisure activity choice, it will certainly have an influence in terms of availability of time, income level, and social status in society, all of which affect access to certain leisure experiences and opportunities.

Income
In general people believe that income has considerable influence over their choice of leisure activities. This has not been born out by the research. In spite of the differences in incomes and financial resources, the leisure pursuits adopted throughout society are remarkably similar (Roberts, 1970, p. 15). Obviously, low income can filter out costly recreation, in particular that requiring extensive travel. But in terms of the quantity of leisure engaged in, many individuals with low incomes have just as many, or more, leisure interests as those with high incomes (Deem, 1988, p. 96). The inequalities in income and wealth are reflected only in the extent to which people can indulge their leisure interests: for example, fishing in the local stream or deep-sea fishing off the Alaskan coast (Roberts, 1970). Contrary to the findings of Roberts (1970), Kelly (1980) and Deem(1988), Nias (1985) noted that an increased income was associated with an increased involvement in home life, household tasks, and a wider repertoire of leisure activities. An increase in physical recreation and membership of more clubs and associations has also been found with increasing income (Hendee and Burdge, 1974; Cheek and Burch, 1976). However, in these studies other variables such as education level or personality were not controlled.

From the above studies it seems fair to conclude that, in general, income alone is not a good predictor of actual leisure choice, and may be better considered as a constraining variable – 'Money does not form tastes, it limits their expression' (Cheek and Burch 1976, pp. 47-48).

Personality
Literally hundreds of studies have been completed looking at the relationship between personality and leisure choice. The studies have predominantly focused on participation in sport and to a lesser extent on recreational activities. Very little research has focused on the more common, and more frequently engaged in, home and family based leisure activities. Very few conclusions can be drawn regarding the influence of personality on leisure choice, due to the great diversity of studies published, their methodological problems, and the often conflicting results.

It would seem that extraversion is associated with a greater general interest and participation in leisure activities (Kirkcaldy, 1985; Furnham, 1990). Extraverts tend to gravitate towards more social leisure situations and team sports, and seek more variety in their leisure activities (Furnham, 1982; Kirkcaldy, 1990). They also appear to have a greater interest in single, competitive sports than introverts (Kirkcaldy, 1990). Part of this is claimed to be due to the extravert's need for constant stimulation (Furnham, 1982). Studies using Zuckerman's sensation seeking scale (Zuckerman, 1983) show that people high on this scale tend to seek out new activities. Whether people who score high on sensation seeking engage in more activities involving higher risk appears to depend on the activities studied. It has been suggested that any increase in involvement is due to the sensation seeker underestimating the risk level of an activity, rather than consciously seeking out a risky activity (Kirkcaldy, 1985). Evidence suggests that introverts gravitate towards individual activities (Peterson *et al.*, 1970; Kirkcaldy and Thom, 1983). Studies also imply that introverts are more likely to choose certain variations of a sport – for example middle and long distance running (Clitsome and Kostrubala, 1977; Gontang *et al.*, 1977), or activities requiring accuracy, but providing time for preparation, for example prone rifle shooting rather than rapid-fire moving target shooting (Kirkcaldy, 1985).

Furnham (1990, pp. 228-229) claims that both average and superior sports persons are more likely to be extraverted because of their higher pain thresholds, sensation-seeking, assertiveness, competitiveness and speed of reaction. They tend to be low on neuroticism but high on psychoticism because of the aggressiveness, egocentricity and competitiveness associated with tough-mindedness. The sport being measured seems to be of importance – for example Schurr *et al.* (1977) found individual sport players to be less anxious than team sport players. He also found players of aggressive team sports to be more extraverted and anxious than players of non-aggressive team sports. Research to date has been unable to categorically establish personality differences between average and superior performers in sports, or other leisure activities such as chess, but there is some evidence to suggest that excellence in sport is related both to extraversion and stability (Eysenck *et al.*, 1982).

Most of the findings of previous studies relate to involvement in specific activities, making generalizations as to the level and type of influence personality has on leisure choice impossible to evaluate. Studies such as that undertaken by McGuiggan (1996, 2000) suggest that generalizations are possible, if many of the pitfalls of previous studies are avoided and leisure attributes rather than specific activities are measured. For example, the desire to plan leisure, as well as the seeking of variety and risk, the desire for competition and the need to engage in activities with others, were highly correlated with personality type (explanatory power varying between 21-46%).

Conclusion

From the above discussion, it is evident that no single variable can explain as complex and hedonic a consumption choice as leisure activity. The question is not one of establishing the determinants of leisure choice, but rather considering the elements that influence that choice, realizing that the choice will never be fully predictable. Secondly, it is necessary to establish the relative influence of the various elements on leisure choice. This study takes a first step in establishing the relative influence of socio-demographic variables and personality on leisure attribute preference.

Method

Choice of personality indicator

The choice of personality indicator has been a major criticism of past research (McGuiggan, 1996, 2000). Although the Myers-Briggs Type Indicator (MBTI) has been used only to a very limited extent in consumer research, Shank and Langmeyer (1994, p. 162) concluded from their study that, despite the fact that they found only a weak relationship between MBTI type and product/service image attributes, 'in fact, the Myers-Briggs Type Indicator would seem to be the ideal personality inventory for marketers'.

The MBTI describes a person's personality on four dichotomous dimensions, indicating a person's preference for source of psychological energy (extraversion vs. introversion), perception (sensing vs. intuition), making judgements (thinking vs. feeling), and orientation to the outer world (judging vs. perceiving). The MBTI questionnaire is a forced-choice, self-report inventory, virtually self-administering and designed for use with normal subjects. Countless papers have been written reviewing the reliability and validity data on the MBTI. Generally, these support the view that the four MBTI scales have construct validity and measure important dimensions of personality (Coan, 1978; Murray, 1990). In addition the MBTI questionnaire is readily available, simple to administer and score and is the most widely used personality questionnaire in America for non-psychiatric populations (Murray, 1990).

A limited number of studies have been completed in the leisure area using the MBTI. Most have focused on determining the personality type of people engaged in very specific leisure activities. Although the results do not show overwhelming support for a relationship existing between MBTI type and leisure activity, considering the limitations of the studies (see McGuiggan, 1996) – for example choice of subjects, and activities (rather than attributes) – the results indicate that a relationship may exist. Gontang *et al.* (1977) found that marathon runners were more likely to be introverts and judging types, while Clitsome and Kostrubala (1977) also found them to be more likely to be introverts but to have a preference for sensing. In contrast, Franzoi (1985) found that cross-country runners have an overwhelming preference for perception, with some indication that a preference for extraversion, intuition or feeling may encourage participation in this sport. In addition, Schurr *et al.* (1988) found that sensing types were more likely to attend male basketball games, and Morehouse *et al.* (1990) that extroverts exhibit a greater desire for activity in general. Sensing types appear to watch more television than intuitive types, and programme preference has also been related to MBTI type (Nolan and Patterson, 1990).

McGuiggan (1996, 2000) utilized the MBTI in the study of leisure attribute preference. Significant correlations were found ranging from 0.12 to 0.68 between leisure attribute preferences and MBTI preferences. In particular, in their leisure time people with a preference for extraversion like to seek out others, look for variety, and prefer team sports. Sensing people like to plan their leisure and prefer home based activities, whereas intuitive people prefer to undertake a variety of activities, especially those they identify as involving some level of risk. A preference for judging was overwhelmingly associated with leisure planning, and perceiving with variety seeking, risk, and engaging in activities with others. The findings of this study, and others previously discussed, support the contention that a relationship exists between MBTI type and leisure preference. For this, and other reasons submitted by McGuiggan (2000), the MBTI was chosen for this study.

Questionnaire development

The MBTI literature was scanned to discover any predictions regarding the relationship between type and leisure preferences. Other MBTI type characteristics that might be applicable to leisure attribute preference were also noted. For example, it could be anticipated that people preferring to function as a team member in the workplace would also prefer team leisure activities.

One hundred and twenty forced choice questions were developed under 25 broad headings suggested by the literature (see Table 1). These groupings were later used in the analysis, to form leisure scales. Since MBTI questions are presented in forced choice format, the leisure questions were developed to replicate this. The intention was to make questionnaire completion easier for the respondent and to minimize completion time. (For a full description of the development of the actual questions, see McGuiggan (1996).)

Table 1 Broad Headings Used to Develop Leisure Questions

Planning:	Variety:
Vacation planning	Variety of vacations
Leisure planning	Variety of activities on vacation
Acceptability of changes to plans	Level of comfort on vacation
Carry through with plans	Variety of sports
Complete planned projects	Variety of leisure activities
Follow rules	Risk involved in sports
People:	Sports:
Number of people vacation with	Watching or engaging in sports
Number of people spend leisure with	Pace of activities engaged in
Depth of involvement in activities	Team or contact sports
Length of vacation	Competition
Reading:	Household tasks
General questions	Traditional or modern activities
Preferred type of reading	Other aspects of leisure

A sample of 103 undergraduate business students was used to pre-test the questions. After skewed (non-discriminating) questions were deleted and highly correlating questions either deleted or reworded, 101 leisure questions remained. The final questionnaire contained these 101 questions, the 94 scoring questions from the MBTI Form G, and demographic questions to establish the respondent's sex, age, marital status, whether children lived with them, highest level of education, usual occupation, country of origin, and the household income.

Data collection

A purposive sample was sought, with the aim of achieving a large sample made up of a relatively even distribution of the 16 MBTI types. Personal drop off and collection of the questionnaire was the preferred method of data collection, because of the length of the questionnaire and also the concern that the forced choice format might increase the number of questionnaires returned with missing data. To achieve enough respondents of each type, data was collected in two phases.

Undergraduate students, completing the subject Marketing Research at UTS, were required to collect data for this study as part of their course requirement. Each student needed to have six questionnaires completed by appropriate respondents. Instruction on respondent suitability was provided in an attempt to maximize the variation in respondent personality type. In this way 782 useable questionnaires were obtained. After establishing the MBTI type of the respondents, it was found that 12 of the MBTI types contained fewer than 30 respondents, with 4 of the types having less than 20. Further respondents were sought to boost the numbers in these groups.

A list of possible participants of 'known' MBTI type in each of the 12 groups sought was provided by the Director of The Institute for Type Development, Sydney, on the understanding that the list would be destroyed upon completion of data collection and that respondent questionnaires would be anonymous. A package, including a copy of the questionnaire, a reply paid envelope and a covering letter on Institute for Type Development letterhead, signed by the Director, requesting their help with the project, was mailed to each of these people. Approximately 50% of the questionnaires were returned and, after checking, a further 126 cases were added to the data bank, resulting in a total sample size of 908 cases.

Men comprised 49% of the sample, and the mean age was 35-39 years (range 18-65+ years). Seventy two per cent were born in Australia and 50% had obtained at least a trade qualification. Of the 70% who were working, 58% worked full-time and 12% part-time, contributing to an average household income of $65,000 per year. In comparison with the general Australian population, the sample had a higher percentage of respondents who worked and was skewed towards the upper quartile of household income brackets. This was not unexpected, considering the method of sample selection.

Results

SPSS, a statistical package for the social sciences, was used to analyse the data. Data reduction of the 101 leisure questions was achieved by utilizing the original 25 leisure attribute categories from the literature. Three of these groups were dropped from the analysis since correlation analysis indicated that the questions within these groups were not closely related. The individual question scores in each of the remaining leisure categories were added together to create 22 new variables. Factor analysis was utilized to determine whether any of these 22 scales should be combined, and reliability analysis used to improve the internal consistency of the scales. The final outcome was the formation of 11 simple additive scales utilizing 79 of the 101 leisure questions. (For a full description of the data reduction process and the actual questions in each of the scales see McGuiggan, 1996). These scales were correlated with the four MBTI continuous scales (created as described in the MBTI Manual (Myers and McCaully, 1992, p. 9)) and the demographics. The length of vacation scale showed no significant relationship with any of the MBTI scales or demographics, and was therefore excluded from further analysis. The reliability of the remaining ten scales is presented in Table 2.

With the exception of the People scale, the internal reliability of these scales is above Nunnally's (1967) cut-off value of 0.5.

Table 2 Reliability of the Leisure Scales - Cronbach's Alpha

Leisure Scale	Number of items in scale	Cronbach Alpha
Planning	14	.69
Follow through	6	.53
Variety	18	.73
People	6	.43
Team sport	5	.55
Risk	3	.61
Household tasks	4	.52
Pace of activities	5	.73
Modernity	8	.61
Involvement	8	.53

To determine the relative influence of MBTI personality type and demographics on leisure attribute preference, two sets of nested multiple regression analyses were undertaken, with the dependent variables being the leisure attribute scales. The full model for both sets of analysis included the four MBTI continuous scale scores plus the demographic variables – age, household income, education level, gender, children under 18 years living in the household, usual occupation and cultural heritage (dummy variables having been created for the cultural heritage variable). In the first set of regressions the four MBTI continuous scale scores were used as the independent variables in the nested equation, while in the second the demographic variables were utilized. In each case the change in R^2 and F-value was examined to determine the relative contribution to exploratory power provided by the two sets of variables. The results are presented in Table 3.

From Table 3 it is evident that the power of the MBTI to explain the variability in the leisure scales differs greatly from a low of 6.5% for the Involvement scale, to a high of 46.6% for the Planning scale. For five of the leisure scales, Planning, Variety, Risk, People and Team sports, more than 20% of the variance could be explained by the MBTI scales alone. Taking demographics alone, the variability explained varies from a low of 4.5% for the Planning scale to a high of 23.8% for the Modernity scale. For the three scales Risk, Pace of activities and Modernity, more than 20% of the variance could be explained by demographics. From these results it would appear that personality, as measured by the MBTI, is in fact a better predictor of leisure preference than demographics. However, examination of the full model and the change in R^2 and

F-value, indicates that the explanatory power of all the leisure scales, except that of planning, could be better explained by a combination of both personality and demographics.

Table 3 Change in R^2 and F value for Nested Regression Analyses

Leisure Scale	R^2			Total model change of R^2 (F-value) over	
	Demo-graphics	Personality	Demo-graphics + Personality	Demo-graphics alone	Personality alone
Planning	.045	.466	.470	.425 (163.281)***	.004 (.711)
Follow through	.048	.116	.145	.096 (22.946)***	.029 (3.102)***
Variety	.149	.261	.311	.163 (48.055)***	.050 (6.629)***
People	.134	.236	.281	.147 (41.677)***	.045 (5.603)***
Team sport	.165	.230	.305	.140 (41.137)***	.075 (9.796)***
Risk	.224	.214	.322	.098 (29.508)***	.108 (14.353)***
Household tasks	.183	.141	.238	.055 (14.619)***	.097 (11.547)***
Pace of activities	.212	.123	.251	.039 (10.635)***	.128 (15.421)***
Modernity	.238	.134	.285	.047 (13.348)***	.151 (19.154)***
Involve-ment	.053	.065	.091	.037 (8.291)***	.026 (2.566)**

***F change significant at .001; ** F change significant at .01

From Table 3 it can be seen that for the Planning scale, demographics add nothing to the explanatory power of the equation – in fact the judging-perceptive scale alone accounts for the full 46.6% of the variability. For a further four of the scales – Follow through, Variety, People and Team sport – personality provides a much better explanation than demographics alone (although adding demographics leads to a statistically significant increase in explanatory power of between 2.9 and 7.5 percent). Personality is also a better predictor of Involvement in activities than demographics, but this scale is poorly predicted by all variables measured (9.1%). For the Risk scale, personality and demographics, when used separately, have approximately equal predictive power (21.4% and 22.4% respectively), but by combining them, the explanation of variability in the scales is greatly enhanced (32.2%). At the other end of the continuum, Household tasks, the Pace of activities and Modernity scales are best described in terms of the demographic profile of the respondent (18.3%, 21.2% and 23.8% respectively), although adding personality leads to a significant increase in explanatory power (5.5%, 3.9% and 4.7% respectively).

Therefore, in all but the Planning scale, it appears that both demographics and personality are necessary to explain leisure attribute preference. The significant standardized β values for the full equations are presented in Table 4.

From Table 4 it would seem that people with a preference for judging are more likely to plan their leisure time. Younger males are likely to have a favourable attitude towards risk-taking in their leisure activities, especially if they have a preference for extraversion, intuition, thinking or perceiving. Younger males in more professional occupations, who do not have children and have a preference for extraversion, intuition, or perception, are also more likely to prefer variety in their leisure activities. Young males with children, with a preference for extraversion or perception, are more likely to watch, or participate in, team sports in their leisure time. Modern culture seems more likely to be preferred over traditional culture by young males with less formal education in more prestigious occupations, who also have a preference for extraversion, perceiving or sensing. Young singles in less prestigious occupations, with a preference for either extraversion or perception, are more likely to spend their leisure time with other people. Younger single males in more professional occupations appear to have a preference for faster paced, competitive leisure activities, especially if they also have a preference for extraversion, thinking or perception. People who are likely to occupy their leisure time with tasks around the house are generally older and married, with a below average household income and have a preference for sensing, feeling or judging. Older people (perhaps of Asian or European decent), employed in more professional types of occupations with a preference for extraversion, sensing or judging, are more likely to follow through with their leisure plans. Although the association is weak, males with a preference for thinking or intuition score higher on the involvement in activities scale.

Discussion

In all cases except the Planning scale, explanation was improved by use of both demographic and personality variables. The combination of personality and demographic variables explained 20% or more of the variance in eight of the ten leisure scales. Even though using the two types of variables significantly improved explanation in all cases except the Planning scale, the improvement varied considerably. By adding demographics to the personality only model, explanation was improved from 2.6% to 15.1%, while adding personality to the demographics only model led to between 3.7% and 16.3% improvement in explanation. It appears from the results, that some attributes of leisure are better explained by personality (Planning, Follow through, Variety, People and Team sport), others (Household tasks, Pace of activities and Modernity) by demographics and still others (Risk) equally by the two. It is apparent that neither personality nor the demographic variables used in this study are appropriate for determining the level of involvement in activities, nor the preferred length of vacation. It is also evident that both demographics and personality contribute to the explanation of leisure attribute preference.

Table 4 Full Regression Model – Standardized Significant β Values

Planning scale		Risk scale		Pace of activities scale	
JP scale	-.668***	Age	-.243***	Age	-.252***
		Sex	-.210***	Sex	-.212***
Follow through scale		JP scale	.163***	EI scale	-.166***
JP scale	-.234***	SN scale	.192***	JP scale	.108**
SN scale	-.139***	EI scale	-.143***	Work	.085*
EI scale	-.113***	TF scale	-.068*	Marital status	-.079*
Asian	.168**			TF scale	-.074*
Work	.115**	People scale			
Age	.099**	EI scale	-.349***	Team sport scale	
European	.133*	JP scale	.174***	EI scale	-.371***
		Marital status	-.103**	Age	-.214***
Variety scale		Work	-.097**	Children	-.106***
EI scale	-.336***	Age	-.084*	JP scale	.111**
SN scale	.191***			Sex	-.076*
Age	-.189***	Modernity scale			
Work	.099**	Age	-.396***	Household tasks scale	
JP scale	.092**	JP scale	.172***	Marital status	.208***
Children	.062*	EI scale	-.141***	JP scale	-.188***
Sex	-.062*	SN scale	-.137***	Age	.160***
		Sex	-.121***	SN scale	-.112**
Involvement scale		Work	.104**	House Income	-.084*
TF scale	-.188***	Education	-.087	TF scale	.076*
Sex	-.145***				
SN scale	.120**				

*** significant at .001; ** significant at .01; * significant at .05

A possible explanation for the variability in the proficiency of both the personality and the demographic variables in explaining leisure attribute preference, could be the reliability of the various leisure scales. As demonstrated in Lastovicka and Joachimsthaler's (1988) paper, the coefficient of determination is as dependent on the reliability of the dependent variable as it is on the reliability of the independent variables. Therefore further research needs to be undertaken to improve the internal reliability of the leisure attribute scales, which may in turn enhance the explanatory power of the MBTI and demographics. Other explanations for the variation in explanatory power are possible. For example, the leisure attribute may not be related to personality, nor to demographics. Other demographic variables not measured in this study may be better predictors of leisure preference. Alternatively, the respondent may not see the attribute as leisure, and therefore lower correlations might be expected.

Conclusion

The results of this study provide support for Holbrook and Hirschman's (1982) contention that personality should be considered an important influence in the choice of experiential products such as leisure. The study also indicates that not all attributes of leisure are equally likely to be influenced by personality. In some cases demographics may provide a better explanation. This study suggests that both demographic and personality variables play an important role in the formation of preferences for experiential products such as leisure.

References

Baley, J.A. (1955) Recreation and the aging process. *Research Quarterly* 26, 1-7.

Barash, R. (1997) The dumbing-down of America. *Marketing News* 31(22), 4.

Bialeschki, D.M. and Henderson, K. (1986) Leisure in the common world of women. *Leisure Studies* 5, 299-308.

Cheek Jr., N.H. and Burch Jr., W.R. (1976) *The social organisation of leisure in human society*. Harper and Row Publishers Inc., New York.

Clitsome, T. and Kostrubala, T. (1977) A psychological study of 100 marathoners using the Myers-Briggs Type Indicator and demographic data. *Annals of the New York Academy of Science* 301, 1010-1019.

Coan, R.W. (1978) Review of the Myers-Briggs Type Indicator. In: *The Eighth Mental Measurements Yearbook*. Gryphon Press, Highland Park, New Jersey, pp. 970-975.

Deem, R. (1988) *Work, Unemployment, and Leisure*. Routledge, London.

Dennis, N., Henriques, F. and Slaughter, C. (1956) *Coal is our life: an analysis of a Yorkshire mining community*. Eyre and Spottiswoode, London.

Dimanche, F., Havitz, M.E. and Howard, R. (1991) Testing the involvement profile (IP) scale in the context of selected recreational and tourism activities. *Journal of Leisure Research* 23(1), 51-66.

Dimanche, F. and Samdahl, D. (1994) Leisure as symbolic consumption: a conceptualization and prospectus for future research. *Leisure Sciences* 16(2), 119-129.

Eysenck, H.J., Nias, D.K.B. and Cox, D.N. (1982) Sport and personality. *Advances in Behavior Research and Theory* 4(1), 1-56.

Foxall, G. (1984) The meaning of marketing and leisure: issues for research and development. *European Journal of Marketing* 18(2), 23-32.

Franzoi, S. (1985) Personality characteristics of the cross-country hitchhiker.

Adolescence 20(79), 655-668.

Furnham, A. (1982) Psychoticism, social desirability and situation selection. *Personality and Individual Differences* 3, 43-51.

Furnham, A. (1990) Personality and demographic determinants of leisure and sports preference and performance. *Journal of Sport Psychology* 21(3), 218-236.

Glyptis, S. (1987) Leisure and the home. In: Graefe, A. and Parker, S. (eds.) *Recreation and Leisure: An Introductory Handbook.* Venture Publishing Inc., Palo Alto, CA. pp. 253-255.

Gontang, A., Clitsome, T. and Kostrubala, T. (1977) A psychological study of 50 sub-3-hour marathoners. *Annals of New York Academy of Sciences* 301, 1020-1028.

Grubb, E.A. (1975) Assembly line boredom and individual differences in recreation participation. *Journal of Leisure Research* 7, 256-269.

Gruber, K.J. (1980) Sex-typing of leisure activities: A current Appraisal. *Psychological Reports* 46, 259-265.

Hendee, J.C. and Burdge, R.J. (1974) The substitutability concept: implications for recreation research and measurement. *Journal of Leisure Research* 6, 157-162.

Holbrook, M.B. and Hirschman, E.C. (1982) The experiential aspects of consumption: consumer fantasies, feelings, and fun. *Journal of Consumer Research* 9(Sept), 132-140.

Holbrook, M.B., Chestnut, R.W., Oliva, T.A. and Greenleaf, E.A. (1984) Play as a consumption experience: the roles of emotions, performance, and personality in the enjoyment of games. *Journal of Consumer Research* 11(Sept), 728-739.

Iso-Ahola, S.E. (1980) *The Social Psychology of Leisure and Recreation.* Wm.C. Brown Company, Dubuque, Iowa.

Iso-Ahola, S.E. (1984) Social psychological foundations of leisure and resultant implications for leisure counseling. In: Dowd, E.T. (ed.) *Leisure Counseling: concepts and applications.* Charles C. Thomas, Springfield, Illinois, pp. 97-125.

Iso-Ahola, S.E. and Jackson, E. (1994) Starting, ceasing, and replacing leisure activities over the life-span. *Journal of Leisure Research* 26(3), 227-249.

Iso-Ahola, S.E. and Mannell, R.C. (1985) Social and psychological constraints on leisure. In: Wade, M.G. (ed.) *Constraints on Leisure.* Charles C. Thomas, Springfield, Illinois, pp. 111-151.

Jamrozik, A. (1986) Leisure as a social consumption: some equity considerations for social policy. In: Castle, R., Lewis, D.E. and Mangan, J. (eds.) *Work, Leisure and Technology,* 1st edn. Longman Cheshire, Melbourne, Australia, pp. 184-209.

Kabanoff, B. (1982) Occupational and sex differences in leisure needs and leisure satisfaction. *Journal of Occupational Behaviour* 3, 233-245.

Kabanoff, B. and O'Brien, G.E. (1980) Work and leisure: a task attribute analysis. *Journal of Applied Psychology* 65(5), 596-609.

Kabanoff, B. and O'Brien, G.E. (1982) Relationships between work and leisure attributes across occupational and sex groups in Australia. *Australian Journal of Psychology* 34(2), 165-182.

Kabanoff, B. and O'Brien, G.E. (1986) Stress and the leisure needs and activities of different occupations. *Human Relations* 39(10), 903-916.

Kamphorst, T.J. (1987) The underlying dimensions of leisure activities: the example of watching television. *Society and Leisure* 10(2), 195-208.

Kelly, J.R. (1978) Leisure style and choices in three environments. *Pacific Sociological*

Review 21(2), 187-207.

Kelly, J.R. (1980) Outdoor recreation participation: a comparative analysis. *Leisure Sciences* 3(2), 129-154.

Kelly, J.R. (1982) *Leisure*. Prentice Hall, Inc., Englewood Cliffs, New Jersey.

Kelly, J.R. (1983) *Leisure Identities and Interactions*. George Allen and Unwin, London, UK.

Kelly, J.R. (1987) Leisure and the family. In: Graefe, A. and Parker, S. (eds.) *Recreation and Leisure: An Introductory Handbook*. Venture Publishing, Inc., Palo Alto, CA, pp. 197-202.

Kelly, J.R. and Godbey, G. (1992) *The Sociology of Leisure*. Venture Publishing, Inc., Palo Alto, CA.

King, D.A. (1965) Some socioeconomic comparisons of Huron and Manistee National Forest family campers with market populations. *Papers of the Michigan Academy of Science, Arts, and Letters* 50, 49-65.

Kirkcaldy, B. (1985) The value of traits in sport. In: Kircaldy, B. (ed.) *Individual Differences in Movement*. MPT Press Limited, Lancaster, UK, pp. 257-277.

Kirkcaldy, B. (1990) Gender and personality determinants of recreational interests. *Studia Psychologica* 32(1-2), 115-121.

Kirkcaldy, B. and Furnham, A. (1991) Extraversion, neuroticism, psychoticism and recreational choice. *Personality and Individual Differences* 12(7), 737-745.

Kirkcaldy, B. and Thom, E. (1983) Personality, aggressivity and recreational preference in behaviourally disturbed and nondisturbed boys. *School Psychology International* 4, 203-208.

Kornhauser, A. (1965) *Mental Health and the Industrial Worker*. Wiley, New York.

Lastovicka, J.L. and Jaochimsthaler, E.A. (1988) Improving the detection of personality-behavior relationships in consumer research. *Journal of Consumer Research* 14(March), 583-587.

Liou, K.T., Sylvia, R.D. and Brunk, G. (1990) Non-work factors and job satisfaction revisited. *Human Relations* 43(1), 77-86.

Lynch, R. and Veal, A.J. (1996) *Australian Leisure*. Addison Wesley Longman Australia Pty Ltd., South Melbourne, Australia.

McGuiggan, R.L. (1996) *The relationship between personality, as measured by the Myers-Briggs Type Indicator, and leisure preferences*. Ph.D. diss., Macquarie University, Australia.

McGuiggan, R.L. (2000) The Myers-Briggs Type Indicator and leisure attribute preference. In: Woodside, A.G., Crouch, G.I., Mazanec, J.A., Oppermann, M. and Sakai M.Y. (eds.) *Consumer Psychology of Tourism, Hospitality and Leisure*. CABI Publishing, UK, pp. 245-267.

Meissner, M. (1971) The long arm of the job: a study of work and leisure. *Industrial Relations* 10, 239-260.

Morehouse, R.E., Farley, F. and Youngquist, J.V. (1990) Type T personality and the Jungian classification system. *Journal of Personality Assessment* 54(1and2), 231-235.

Moschis, G.P. (1981) Socialization perspectives and consumer behaviour. In: Enis, B.M. and Roering, K.J. (eds.) *Review of Marketing*. American Marketing Association, Chicago, pp. 43-56.

Mowen, J.C. (1988) Beyond consumer decision making. *The Journal of Consumer*

Marketing 5(1), 15-25.

Murray, J.B. (1990) Review of research on the Myers-Briggs Type Indicator. *Perceptual and Motor skills* 70, 1187-1202.

Myers, I. and McCaulley, M.H. (1992) *Manual: A Guide to the Development and Use of the Myers-Briggs Type Indicator.* Consulting Psychologists Press, Inc., Palo Alto, CA.

Neulinger, J. (1974) *The Psychology of Leisure: Research Approaches to the Study of Leisure.* Charles C. Thomas, Springfield, Illinios.

Nias, D.K.B. (1985) Personality and recreational behaviour. In: Kirkcaldy, B. (ed.) *Individual Differences in Movement.* MTP Press Ltd., Lancaster, England, pp. 279-292.

Nolan, L.L. and Patterson, S.J. (1990) The active audience: personality type as an indicator of TV program preference. *Journal of Social Behavior and Personality* 5(6), 697-710.

Nunnally, J.C. (1967) *Psychometric Theory.* McGraw-Hill Book Company, New York.

Orthner, D.K. and Mancini, J.A. (1980) Leisure behaviour and group dynamics: the case of the family. In: Iso-Ahola, S.E. (ed.) *Social Psychological Perspectives on Leisure and Recreation.* Charles C. Thomas, Springfield, Illinois, pp. 307-328.

Peterson, S.L., Weber, J.C. and Lonsdale, W.W. (1970) Personality traits of women in team sports vs. women in individual sports. In: Morgan, W.P. (ed.) *Contemporary Readings in Sport Psychology.* Charles C. Thomas, Springfield, Illinois.

Poole, M.E. and Cooney, G.H. (1986) Work and leisure relationships: an exploration of life possibilities during adolescence. *Journal of Youth and Adolescence* 15(6), 475-486.

Roberts, K. (1970) *Leisure,* 1st edn. Longman Group Limited, London.

Rousseau, D.M. (1978) Short notes: relationship of work to nonwork. *Journal of Applied Psychology* 63(4), 513-517.

Schmitt, B. (1999) Experiential Marketing. *Journal of Marketing Management* 15, 53-67.

Schmitz-Scherzer, R. (1976) Longitudinal change in leisure behavior of the elderly. *Contributions to Human development* 3, 127-136.

Schurr, K.T., Ashley, M.A. and Joy, K.L. (1977) A multivariate analysis of male athlete personality characteristics: sport type and success. *Multivariate Experimental Clinical Research* 3(2), 53-68.

Schurr, K.T., Wittig, A.F., Ruble, V.E. and Arthur, S.E. (1988) Demographic and personality characteristics associated with persistent, occasional, and non-attendance of university male basketball games by college students. *Journal of Sports Behaviour* 11(1), 3-17.

Shank, M.D. and Langmeyer, L. (1994) Does personality influence brand image? *The Journal of Psychology* 128(2), 157-164.

Shaw, S.M. (1994) Gender, leisure, and constraint: towards a framework for the analysis of women's leisure. *Journal of Leisure Research* 26(1), 8-22.

Shimp, T.A. (1993) *Promotions Management and Marketing Communications,* 3rd edn. Harcourt Brace and Company, Marrickville, NSW.

Smith, J. (1987) Men and women at play: gender, life-cycle, and leisure. *The Sociological Review Monograph* 33, 51-85.

Snyder, E.E. and Spreitzer, E. (1974) Orientations toward work and leisure as predictors of sports involvement. *Research Quarterly* 45(4), 398-406.

Spreitzer, E. and Snyder, E.E. (1987) Educational–occupational fit and leisure orientation as related to life satisfaction. *Journal of Leisure Research* 19(2), 149-158.

Tunstall, J. (1962) *The Fisherman*. McGibbon and Kee, London.

Woods, W.A. (1981) *Consumer Behavior*. North-Holland, New York.

Zuckerman, M. (1983) Sensation-seeking and sports. *Personality and Individual Differences* 4, 285-293.

Zuzanek, J. and Mannell, R. (1983) Work-leisure relationships from a sociological and social psychological perspective. *Leisure Studies* 2, 327-344.

Chapter thirteen
A New Psychographic Segmentation Method Using Jungian MBTI Variables in the Tourism Industry

John Y. Gountas and Sandra (Carey) Gountas
School of Business, University of Ballarat, Mt. Helen Campus
Ballarat, Victoria, Australia

Abstract

This paper discusses the psychographic methods of segmentation for tourists. It analyses the various theories, criteria and methods of classifying tourists; a new approach to tourism segmentation based on Jung's personality theory is proposed. The findings of an initial survey conducted with a major UK charter airline are introduced and discussed.

Introduction

The broad methods of segmenting consumer demand are based on geodemographic characteristics, psychographic, behavioural and destination product attributes. The overall effectiveness of segmentation is influenced by all the above criteria. Tourist segmentation using geodemographic, behavioural and destination product characteristics is concerned with questions of who travels, where they go, what they do and so on, which are purely descriptive data of the consumers. Geodemographics do not give comprehensive insights into *why* certain products and activities are chosen. However, in some cases, characteristics like gender, income and life cycle stages provide insights into consumer's behaviours.

Due to the intense competition currently facing both destinations and tourism principals (tour operators, accommodation providers, transport companies and destination attractions) it is even more crucial to understand tourists' motivations accurately. It is not sufficient to know the tourists' behaviour in relation to their life cycle stages, geodemographics and behavioural characteristics but also in terms of who they are as decision-makers and the procedures they follow in making choices. Some of the key questions on why tourists choose a destination or type of holiday are only possible to answer by looking at the internal psychological factors correlated with the external situational factors. The market intelligence gained by providing more insightful answers to questions of decision influences and processes would clearly be invaluable for aspects of marketing, e.g. product development, segmentation and target marketing, promotions and competitive differentiation.

Some tourism psychographic segmentation typologies are based on motivation, personality types, attitudes, values and other sociological, cultural and psychological variables. In the tourism literature a large number of tourism typologies are a mixture of psychographic and other segmentation methods, mostly geodemographics and/or the attributes of tourist destinations.

According to Denby (1989), who is credited with inventing the term, psychographic segmentation is the 'use of psychological, sociological and anthropological factors such as benefits, desires, self concept and lifestyle'. Psychographics attempt to segment the market into distinct groups of individuals by focusing on their reasons for making a particular decision about products, services, persons, ideologies and/or otherwise the reasons for holding an attitude or/and have specific preferences.

The term psychographics is often used interchangeably with lifestyles which uses activities/attitudes, interests and opinions (AIO) as the research variables. It is assumed to be a shorter and easier method of trying to uncover the core issues of *why* and *how* consumers choose a particular brand as opposed to another. AIOs have been used extensively because they are closer to the needs of marketing practitioners, who need to predict behavioural outcomes. It is possible to correlate past behaviour, socioeconomic and geodemographic variables with AIOs in order to develop a more comprehensive picture of the consumers' likely behaviour.

Lifestyle segmentation is also more desirable than geodemographics, because it examines the reasons that influence the decision-making. Attitudes and opinions are assumed to be the influencing factors preceding the action stage for the consumers. AIOs do not delve on the assumed/hypothesized cognitive processes, nor into the particular personality characteristics/traits and values which are a bit too general, abstract and therefore at a 'greater distance' from the actual behaviour/action stage. However, the lack of any underlying consumer theories and constructs is probably one of the main weaknesses. It is not possible to test relevant hypotheses and also to interpret the findings in a systematic way.

Empirical findings about what consumers do, think, and are interested in doing, cannot by themselves explain adequately why the consumers behave in a particular way. The main weakness is the limited options that are available to the respondents. There are many differences in preferences that the individuals would like to express and explore but the opportunities are not available. This may be because their preferred brands/activities are not available and therefore not aware of them; or/and the research methodology does not ask the right questions.

Without testable assumptions that can be developed into a tentative theory, consumer behaviour according to the AIO's paradigm is confined to the variables that are included in the questionnaire. The list of AIO variables are assumed to be hypothetical reasons for their actual behaviour. The emerging typologies of consumers are therefore restricted to the AIO's research design parameters. In other words, consumers consist of Actions/Attitudes, Interests and Opinions according to the frequently observed characteristics and causal assumptions by the researchers. The drawback with the AIO is that it does not have the ability to describe adequately the various psychographic and geodemographic causes that influence the tourism consumers' decisions.

Some studies are much more specific, attempting to understand the motives of different groups of people going to particular destinations (Henshall *et al.*, 1985; Cha *et al.*, 1995). Motivation as a construct has been used extensively by many researchers (London *et al.*, 1977: Crompton, 1979; Crandall, 1980; Dann, 1981; Iso-Ahola and Allen, 1982; Kale and Weir, 1986). Many more studies directly or indirectly relating to tourism motivation have also been published with a variety of motivational inventories. Some attempt to be all encompassing by referring to cultural and sociological influences (Cohen, 1973; Crompton, 1979; Dann, 1981). Dann (1981) argues that the 'push' factors precede 'pull' factors and that they are responsible for tourists' choices and actions.

However, the problem of interpreting tourists' minds is one of the most difficult tasks (Dann, 1981). His view is that a pluralistic perspective may help in improving some of the weaknesses between the vastly different hypotheses and procedures that the various researchers adopt.

Recent research within the UK Tour Operating industry, conducted by Carey and Gountas (1999), suggests that the *push and pull* factors are of equal relevance for the more mature and experienced tourists participating in organized tour packages.

The various motivational constructs used to develop tourist typologies provide a lot of useful information, which somewhat clarifies our understanding, of why tourists travel, but they are unable to comprehensively map out the motives for travel behaviour. There is not any overall or individual motivational theory that can be used in market segmentation with all types of products/services. Psychographics do not use many of the motivational typologies because they are difficult to relate to the actual behaviour and also there is not enough evidence to support claims that motives are adequate predictors of complex/high involvement decisions such as purchasing holidays. The lack of a testable theory of motivation may be one of the reasons for the inadequate understanding of tourism motivation.

Value Based Segmentation Methods

The psychographic segmentation studies using values as the main construct suggest that values precede motives, attitudes and behaviour (Boote, 1981). Some of the well-known studies on values attempt to integrate motivational theories with social and psychological factors (Rokeach, 1973). One of the instruments that is widely used to measure values is the 'Values and Lifestyles' (VALS).

VALS classifies consumers into nine lifestyles (Mitchell, 1983), according to their overall life-orientation values that are based on the values relating to Riesman *et al.*'s (1961) ideas of the inner, outer and tradition oriented consumers. The VALS typology of three broad categories of consumers, the need driven, the outer directed and the inner-directed, includes a range of behavioural and geodemographic characteristics are claimed to increase the predictability of consumers' behaviour.

The List of Values (LOV), on the other hand, is another well-known research instrument for values and was developed as a shorter version of the terminal values from the Rokeach Value Survey (RVS) by a team of researchers (Kahle, 1983). The respective research instruments of VALS and LOV produce clusters of lifestyle segments which are considered to be representative of the whole of the USA market. The variables that VALS uses are: values, socio-demographic and behavioural characteristics. An international version comparing the lifestyles of the UK, Germany, France, Sweden and Italy was published which produced similar lifestyle segments in all of these developed countries (Mitchell, 1983). The overall reliability and validity was tested for both the VALS and LOV typologies (Kahle *et al.*, 1986; Novak and MacEvoy, 1990). The results favour LOV over VALS if they are used with demographic characteristics too.

Attempts have been made to develop an international value-based typology of tourists/consumers (Schwartz and Bilsky, 1987; Segal *et al.*, 1993; Kamakura and Mazzon, 1991). Claims about the existence of universal values were made using a variety of values, RVS and universal needs of a biological, interpersonal and societal nature (Schwartz and Bilsky, 1987). Muller (1991) attempted to identify distinct international tourism segments using the List of Values (LOV) and destination attributes. It should be possible to segment tourism markets on the basis of value differences but it is not clear how values influence decisions; this is an area for further research.

The conceptual distance in the consumers' decision-making processes, between the cognitive beliefs and the end benefits/outcomes that values may have been the instrumental causes, is very big, because there is no inclusion of the formation of attitudes that may also influence behaviour extensively. Methodological and conceptual issues need to be addressed in order to improve overall validity especially in international tourism markets (Muller, 1991).

The claims that values are reliable segmentation variables because they are more stable than attitudes, have been based on the notion that values are more central to an individual's cognitive system (Rokeach, 1973; Rokeach and Ball-Rokeach, 1981). This is still a hypothesis without any robust evidence. The assertion that values are more efficient as a measurable set of variables because they are smaller in number has been based on the assumption that LOV, RVS and other lists are true constructs existing in the consumers' minds in identical ways. However, it is difficult to establish a clear understanding of what is meant by an RVS terminal value such as a 'comfortable life' within a sample of tourists because the meaning is an entirely individualistic and subjective notion and therefore impossible to test in an objective manner (Pitts and Woodside, 1986).

Likewise for a number of other values which are tested on tourists from a cultural group, the differences due to the subjective interpretation of the individual meanings become impossible to measure when one considers the various sub-cultural differences, religions and levels of education. There is a great deal of semantic ambiguity in the meanings that values represent in the minds of the consumers, which makes it impossible to establish an objective yardstick for empirical measurement and validation studies to be carried out. Values are useful in describing what tourists may think about abstract principles but do not explain why they prefer a particular tourist product from another. For instance, the RVS instrument has been used extensively in a number of studies but reliability and validity has not been proven sufficiently and therefore it is not yet suitable for market segmentation applications (Vinson *et al.*, 1977; Kamakura and Mazzon, 1991; Luk *et al.*, 1993). Criticisms also have been raised about the validity and representativeness of values because hardly any test/retest study has been carried out using the same methodology and using the value constructs on their own (Kamakura and Novak, 1992).

In order to improve the overall reliability of the tourists' values in predicting the relative influence on decision making such as destination choices and other behavioural outcomes, many marketing and situational influences also need to be taken into account such as product attributes, benefits, preferences and demographics (Gutman, 1982). Psychographics' failure to predict what consumers want has led researchers to look for more robust methods of prediction.

Values have been seen as a possible substitute which is hypothesized to identify higher order of beliefs reflecting generic concepts of what is a good, desirable and ultimately ideal outcome. However, most studies conclude with a cautious reservation, that general/core values and vacation specific values lend support to the central theme of the theory which contends that *values can act as predictors of travel behaviour* (Pizam and Calantone, 1987). Trying to apply cultural values to issue-specific applications is useful but not adequate if used alone without any other constructs and geodemographic variables (Madrigal and Kahle, 1994).

The plurality of values is evident and possible conflicts arise when considering specific issues of marketing applications, therefore looking for the isolation of few values to predict decisions and segment markets is an elusive task (Tetlock, 1986).

Personality Based Segmentation Methods

People/consumers think and consider travel issues, not only on the basis of their values, but also as an integrative process, which includes a bundle of benefits, behaviours, motives and cognition altogether. Since value variation is partly due to individual differences, considering values together with personality types may result in a more accurate understanding of what the consumer's needs and behaviours may be.

Psychographic segmentation, based on personality types may improve the overall effectiveness of tourism markets more than all the other constructs so far. Pearce and Stringer (1991) comment that personality, as a topic, does not feature as much as other psychological constructs in the tourism literature.

However, personality as a construct has been considered as a possible predictor of leisure differences. Iso-Ahola (1983) studied personality traits to predict leisure activities with some success. A number of studies have attempted to identify and test individual personality dimensions, but the correlations have been modest for leisure and sport preferences (Mannell, 1984; Furnham, 1990).

Plog's (1974) typological continuum, of allocentric and psychocentric personality types, has attracted a lot of attention in the tourism literature. Plog linked personality types with choice of destination, but strong criticism arose of whether his theory was robust enough as a result of a validation study by Smith (1990a). Smith's test on a sample of international tourists failed to support the hypothesis of Plog's personality types and destination preferences (Smith, 1990a). Plog, naturally, refuted the findings by Smith (Plog, 1990; Smith, 1990b). However, the debate of whether personality characteristics are valid and reliable predictors has not been conclusively settled, yet.

There are a plethora of studies focusing on the individual personality characteristics and tourist preferences as predictors of behaviour. In some cases, *personality types* are assumed and seem to be equated with, the *tourist roles.* International tourism roles have been developed to segment tourists using Cohen's tourist role typology (Mo *et al.,* 1994). The instrument has been developed rigorously and it is capable of producing standardized, reliable and valid data, but it needs to be tested and retested by other researchers to establish more accurately the degree of reliability and validity.

Yiannakis and Gibson (1992) investigated tourists' preferences using demographics, benefits/attributes and psychographic characteristics and have identified a number of personality types that are largely assumed to be the causal factor of the consumers' behaviour. However, the absence of replication studies makes it difficult to accept the finding's empirical validity.

A number of other approaches, research instruments and models have been developed to predict tourism behaviour, but the stated roles are not robust enough to be used as segmentation categories because they lack the empirical evidence of behavioural outcomes related to each role (Cohen, 1972; Yiannakis and Gibson, 1992). On the other hand, Zuckerman's (1983) examination of the influence of sensation, as an individual trait, in the leisure and sports fields proved to be useful in describing what happens to different types/levels of sensation that consumers are seeking. However, this does not explain fully all the reasons why people engage in various activities.

The personality trait/motive of involvement has received extensive coverage in the literature but there seem to be no examples of measuring the relationship of the tourists' involvement and the perceived attractiveness of a destination. The meaning of involvement may be ambiguous for many consumers because it may be associated with motivation, interest, curiosity arousal and something that has the ability to drive/influence individuals (Dimanche *et al.,* 1991; Madrigal and Kahle, 1992). It is tenuous to argue that this trait could be used consistently in tourism research and to claim that the interpretations of the findings are valid and representative for all these studies.

Consumer typologies can help practitioners and research to understand more comprehensively the reasons why consumers do something and how they make their decisions. The major drawback is that the existing typologies are based on subjective and hypothetical methods of clustering the research findings into particular groups, without a theoretical guide/basis of how consumers operate overall/globally and how the entire decision-making process is carried out.

Often the techniques used predetermine the results of the analysis. The linkage between the overall picture of what the consumers are as human beings and the individual traits and behaviours is missed out. Instead, the emphasis is placed on the examination of the individual traits to identify the person's preferences and behaviours as though they are separate from and capable of indicating the person's personality and lifestyle. It is important to see the overall picture of consumer decision making, as well as the individual behaviours, and the underlying personality preferences, in order to test more comprehensively the hypotheses of possible lifestyle patterns and relationships between behaviours and personality constructs.

The dynamic and simultaneous interaction of behaviour, situational factors and personality characteristics is missing from the tourism literature. The assumption that individual personality traits or variables can be identified, then isolated and tested as the possible predictors of behaviour needs to be reconsidered. The focus of research needs to be widened by including the general/overall personality types with the situational factors that may influence the consumer's decision process and actions

Every major personality theory has been explored in consumer research including Jung's theory on personality types. However, there is no, single study in the tourism literature that effectively uses Jung's typology. Jung (1921) postulated the existence of four broad types: The Thinking, The Feeling, The Intuitive and The Sensation Seeking, with each type displaying distinct characteristics and traits of Extraversion and Introversion. Few studies have actually developed, in detail, the full range of characteristics for every Jungian of personality type for applied research purposes. The issue/area that has received a lot of attention by numerous researchers is the traits of extraversion and introversion (Eysenck and Eysenck, 1969).

The Jungian personality types attempt to provide a global picture of how individuals deal with themselves and the world around them. It attempts to pull together different types of personalities and organize/group them into four general ones. Myers and Briggs developed a personality inventory, the Myers-Briggs Type Indicator; (MBTI) based on the Jungian types and added two more dimensions, the Perceiving and Judging (Myers and McCaulley, 1992).

The MBTI's conceptualization is based on the four pairs of dimensions which aim to identify (a) the person's source of energy (extraversion-introversion), (b) the mode of perceiving stimuli (sensing-intuition), (c) how decisions/judgements are made (thinking-feeling) and (d) how they relate/orient themselves towards the outside world (judging-perceiving). The types were developed through extensive observations, tests, and surveys over a long period of time.

The MBTI is a forced-choice, self-report inventory and very easy to administer and score personality test. It is one of the most widely used tests in the USA for normal subjects (Murray, 1990).

The usage of the Myers-Briggs Type Indicator (MBTI) has a long track record of research and a theoretical basis to support its validity and reliability (Steele and Kelly, 1976; Cloan, 1978; Levy and Padilla, 1982; Tzeng *et al.,* 1984; Sipp *et al.,* 1985; Thompson and Borrello, 1986; Wiggins, 1989; Murray, 1990). Many advocates state that the MBTI is capable of predicting a relationship between the occupational preference and the personality type/characteristics. The assertion is that people with similar personality types should exhibit similar preferences for jobs/occupations and many other things in life, for example decision styles of executives in organization (Kroeger and Theusen, 1988; Provost, 1990).

Although the MBTI has been used mainly for personnel management issues with considerable success, Shank and Langmeyer (1994) go one step further and suggest that the MBTI could be used and adapted equally well by marketers for consumer research. A small number of studies have been done in the leisure area trying to find out whether there is any relationship between the personality types and the leisure activities. The results are not as robust as they are in the area of career choices. The results are somewhat inconsistent, but encouraging and suggest that the relationships between leisure activities and personality types could be improved (Gontang *et al.,* 1977; Franzoi, 1985; Morehouse *et al.,* 1990).

A recent study by McGuiggan (1996) tested the predictability of the MBTI and demographics variables regarding the preference of leisure activities. The study adapted the MBTI inventory to suit the leisure preferences and concluded that personality types are better explanatory variables for issues like planning, follow through, variety, people and pace of activities. Demographics, on the other hand, indicated a stronger correlation for household tasks, team sports and modernity. Both variables could predict equally well, the element of risk taking. Neither personality type nor the demographic variables could predict the level of involvement. McGuiggan's study lends support to Holbrook and Hirschman's (1982) suggestion that personality should be considered as an important influence in the choice of experiential products/services such as leisure and tourism.

Research methodology

In order to avoid the criticism of assembling individual personality traits/parts and then trying to find the personality type that fits the data, the authors adopted the Jungian personality types theory and the MBTI inventory as the basis for the conceptualization of the consumers as a whole person. The MBTI items were tested and refined to reflect the travelling consumers' preferences. The research, qualitative and quantitative, has been conducted over a two-year period. The early exploratory and qualitative research concentrated on identifying the primary/original four major personality types now identified as *Thinking/logically* oriented, *Sensing/materially* oriented, *Feeling/affectively* oriented and *Perceptive/intuitively* oriented.

The reason for the simplified format is that the extensive research output on Extraversion and Introversion is inconclusive and the main reason that Jung added them on was because these two traits were very prominent ideas in his epoch. The exploratory research found the MBTI additions of Perceiving and Judging to have no sound foundation as separate orientations. They appear to fit more accurately into the Perceptive/Intuitive and Thinking/Logical orientations respectively. The authors found the original four Jungian types, which were postulated by the ancient Greeks, were much easier to work with than the MBTI. The exploratory research was conducted through a series of depth interviews and focus groups with normal subjects of all ages and social, economic and educational levels who had participated in travel.

The four orientations, their motivations and preferences were tested and retested through a number of inventories that emerged from the literature review and the field work. A clearer list of items was developed, indicating that there are distinct characteristics between each of the orientations differentiating consumers in terms of how they see the world and behave. A self-completion questionnaire was constructed in 1998 and tested on a sample of holiday-makers in the Greek Ionian Islands. The results tentatively supported the hypothesis of the four reformulated orientations, but the sampling method and the administration of the survey needed to change to improve the rate of responses and level of representativeness. A new and shorter, 50-item inventory/questionnaire was developed and pilot tested with a sample of travelling consumers. The results were deemed reliable enough to justify a larger survey.

The survey findings

A leading UK charter airline, Air 2000 collaborated with the survey. The questionnaire consisted of 50 questions about the preferences, interests and attitudes of the four orientations. Also, 12 questions regarding the satisfaction levels for the airline purposes were added, using a five-point Likert scale. Three thousand questionnaires were distributed amongst in-bound and out-bound sectors of flights from 11 UK airports to a variety of European and long-haul destinations. Nearly 800 questionnaires were returned and from that, 775 (N=775) were fully completed and suitable for factor analysis. Recognizing that seasonality may affect the nature and motivation of tourists, the researchers are conducting replication surveys in winter and summer 2000 to capture the entire year around travelling public. The test of sampling adequacy is high, 0.947 and therefore satisfies the requirements for the factor analysis (see Table 1).

Table 1 KMO and Bartlett's Test*

Kaiser-Meyer-Olkin Measure of Sampling Adequacy:	.947		
Bartlett's Test of Sphericity:	Approx. Chi-Square:	11,184.503	
	df:	325	
	Sig.:	0.000	

* Based on correlations

The principal component factor analysis with Varimax rotation produced four factors with a cumulative variance explained of 61.652% (see Table 2). The Scree Plot (Figure 1) shows how the eigenvalues of each factor relate to the overall explanation of variance.

The orthogonal structure of the Varimax factor analysis does not take into account the potential factor inter-correlations. A Promax oblique factor rotation represents the clustering of variables more accurately because the rotated factors axis is now closer to the respective group of variables. The Promax factor rotation produced four more easily interpretable factors.

Table 2 Total Variance Explained

Raw Component Nr.	Initial eigenvalues		
	Absolute	% of variance	Cumulative%
1	15.749	41.937	41.937
2	3.831	10.202	52.140
3	1.935	5.151	57.291
4	1.638	4.361	61.652

The four factors that emerged using the Promax oblique rotation method are highlighted in Table 3. The first factor which was hypothesized to be the Sensing /material orientation clusters with the Feeling/affective orientation. The Perceptive/intuitive factor is split into factors 2 and 3. Factor 4, the Thinking/logical has emerged as hypothesized. The Pearson correlation for Factors 2 and 3 is .603, (2-tailed, significant at .000). This strong correlation indicates that these two factors share some common characteristics.

The correlation matrix (Table 4) indicates that there is a high correlation between all four factors ranging from .361 to .610. This indicates that there are common characteristics within all four factors as expected. The alpha values for all factors are very high: Factor 1, alpha coefficient is .9135; Factor 2, alpha coefficient is .8644; Factor 3, alpha coefficient is .8559 and Factor 4, alpha coefficient is .8468. This indicates that the reliability of all factors is very high.

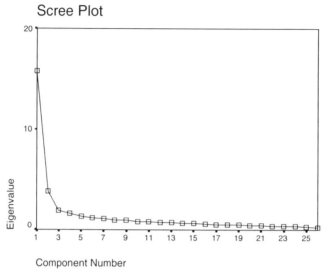

Figure 1 Scree plot

Discussion

The four personality orientations, hypothesized through the exploratory research, emerged with some variance on the overall configuration of characteristics and preferences. The hypothesized characteristics of Factor 1 (Sensing/materially oriented) and Factor 2 (Feelings/affective oriented) have emerged as one orientation. The possible reason for this is the close relationship/similarity for the variables ascribed to these orientations. In order to differentiate between the two, it may be necessary to modify the survey tool in order to avoid semantic confusion. Another contributory factor may be the shared motives of most holiday consumers such as good weather, relaxation, to be pampered and social interaction. Whilst these motivations are very useful in practical marketing terms, accurate targeting depends on a more precise and comprehensive understanding of the consumers. These common motivations may be regarded as generic and form only part of the overall cluster of motives. The other two factors predicted are strongly supported by the findings.

Factor 1 – Sensing/materially oriented and Feelings/affective oriented, underlying characteristics
This orientation seems to value the material world, is pragmatic, likes order and certainty and considers itself to be pragmatic in its decisions/choices. The preferred holiday/leisure activities would, most likely, include the enjoyment of all tangible/material attributes, the natural world that can be experienced primarily with the

physical senses.

Table 3 Structure Matrix

Items related to each factor:	Rescaled Components			
	1	2	3	4
Q29: I like certainty/facts in life	.768	.337	.459	.506
Q30: I like order in my life	.766	.279	.446	.401
Q31: I am a realistic person	.762	.506	.265	.485
Q36: I am a logical person	.711	.506	.184	.627
Q26: I am a practical person	.701	.458	.145	.422
Q34: I am confident about my feelings	.689	.565	.158	.578
Q28: I value material possessions	.689	.290	.562	.462
Q32: I am self sufficient	.681	.555	.175	.553
Q35: I value experience more than ideas	.661	.499	.330	.463
Q33: I am a doer	.642	.582	.209	.501
Q25: I am down to earth	.635	.536	.169	.318
Q40: I think before I act	.615	.451	.300	.585
Q27: The pleasures of food/eating are important	.513	.399	.334	.291
Q43: I am sensitive to others	.501	.793	.394	.425
Q44: I often put other people first	.493	.763	.380	.394
Q45: I have a very good imagination	.416	.747	.378	.581
Q42: I like to mix with other people	.422	.713	.344	.411
Q46: I am very perceptive	.549	.697	.383	.585
Q48: I make mountains out of molehills	.392	.353	.888	.383
Q49: My heart rules my head	.368	.464	.826	.315
Q47: I depend on other people	.401	.401	.808	.376
Q50: It is important to spend time daydreaming	.283	.548	.732	.456
Q39: I am very interested in new inventions, discoveries, and the future	.440	.426	.321	.885
Q37: I prefer to understand the meaning of how and why things work or are	.559	.381	.289	.780
Q38: I am very objective	.611	.571	.320	.751
Q41: I am an ideas person	.525	.673	.380	.750

Extraction Method: Principal Component Analysis.
Rotation Method: Promax with Kaiser Normalization.

Table 4 Component Correlation Matrix

Component	1	2	3	4
1	1.000	.551	.372	.610
2	.551	1.000	.361	.581
3	.372	.361	1.000	.365
4	.610	.581	.365	1.000

Extraction Method: Principal Component Analysis.
Rotation Method: Promax with Kaiser Normalization.

The issues relating to emotion and feelings driven experiences would be of primary importance. People and issues regarding the ego enhancement are the centre of the activities. Action and direct experiential exploration of the world is the medium of making sense of their lives.

Factors 2 and 3 – The Perceptive/Intuitives
The ability to perceive the external world through their intuition gives them a distinct perspective of the objective and subjective world. The are likely to be interested in the imagined past civilizations, the new possibilities and the sensitive treatment/relationships between themselves and others.

Factor 4 – Thinking/Logical
The main emphasis is on the understanding of how things work, what is the best way to deal with any situation and learning about the new cultures, places and people. Mind is the driving force and using logical/rational thinking is the process. The findings indicate clearly the existence of the four factors. There is some supporting evidence from the MBTI research for a large number of the items in the new inventory. The work by Hermann (1973) which proposed the 'whole brain' theory divides the brain into four parts. Each part prefers or responds more strongly to a different type of stimuli: rational, safekeeping, experimental and feeling.

Hermann's research shows that most people have a preferred style of thinking and avoid the other styles. Jung's general personality types are rather vague but the new inventory gives a clear idea of what are the salient issues and modes of operation for each orientation.

The behavioural patterns are less clear at this stage of the research because they depend on a number of factors such as the disposable income, the lifecycle stages and the range of available product/services in the culture that they live.

Zajonc's (1983) postulation of a feeling domain provides sufficient evidence to support some of the feeling-affective orientation type of personality. There is strong empirical support for modified Jungian types of personalities but the challenge is to develop a more detailed and effective research instrument, which will identify the personality types and the behaviours more reliably. The next stage of this research is to develop the detailed tourism behavioural inventories for each orientation and test them empirically.

References

Boote, A.S. (1981) Market Segmentation by Personal Values and Salient Attributes. *Journal of Advertising Research* 21, 29-35.

Carey, S. and Gountas, Y. (1999) Changing attitudes to 'mass tourism' products – The UK outbound market perspective. *Journal of Vacation Marketing* 6(1), 69-76.

Cha, S., McCleary, K.W.and Uysal, M. (1995) Travel Motivations of Japanese Overseas Travelers: A Factor Cluster Segmentation Approach. *Journal of Travel Research* (summer), 33-39.

Cloan, R.W. (1978) *Review of the MBTI: In the Eighth Mental Measurement Yearbook.* Gryphon Press, Highland Park, New Jersey, pp. 970-975.

Cohen, E. (1972) Towards a Sociology of International Tourism. *Social Research* 39, 164-182.

Cohen, E. (1973) Nomads From Affluence: Notes On The Phenomenon of Drifter Travel. *International Journal of Comparative Sociology* 14, 89-103.

Crandall, R. (1980) Motivations for Leisure. *Journal of Leisure Research* 12, 45–54.

Crompton, J. (1979) Motivations for Pleasure Vacation. *Annals of Tourism Research* 6, 408-424.

Dann, G.M.S. (1981) Tourist Motivation: an Appraisal. *Annals of Tourism Research* 8(2), 187-219.

Denby, E.H. (1989) Psychographics Revisited: The Birth of a Technique. *Marketing News* (January) 2, 21.

Dimanche, F., Havitz, M. and Howard, D.R. (1991) Testing the Involvement Profile (IP) Scale in the Context of Selected Recreational and Touristic Activities. *Journal of Leisure Research* 23(1), 51-66.

Eysenck, H. and Eysenck, S. (1969) *Personality Structure and Measurement.* Routledge and Kegan, London.

Franzoi, S. (1985) Personality Characteristics of the Cross-country Hitchhiker. *Adolescence* 20(79), 655-668.

Furnham, A. (1990) Personality and Demographic Determinants of Leisure and Sports Preference and Performance. *International Journal of Sport Psychology* 21, 218-236.

Gontang, A., Clitsome, T. and Kostrubala, T. (1977) A psychological study of 50 sub-3-hour Marathoners. *Annals of New York Academy of Sciences* 301, 1020-1028.

Gutman, J. (1982) A Means-End Chain Model Based on Consumer Categorization Processes. *Journal of Marketing* 42, 60-72.

Henshall, B.P., Roberts, R. and Leighton, A. (1985) Fly Drive Tourists: Motivation and Destination Choice Factors. *Journal of Travel Research* 1, 23-27.

Hermann, N., in Kyrianky, J. (1973) Advertising For The Whole Brain – American Advertising. *International Journal of Comparative Sociology* 14, 89-103.

Holbrook, M.B. and Hirschman, E.C. (1982) the experiential aspects of consumption: consumer fantasies, feelings, and fun. *Journal of Consumer Research* 9, 132-140.

Iso-Ahola, S. and Allen, J. (1982) The Dynamics of Leisure Motivation: The Effects of Outcome on Leisure Needs. *Research Quarterly For Exercise And Sport* 53, 141-149.

Iso-Ahola, S. (1983) Toward a Social Psychology of Recreational Travel. *Leisure Studies* 2, 45-56.

Jung, C.G. (1921) Psychological Types. In: Reid, H., Fordham, and Adler, G., revised by Hull, R.F.C. (eds.) *The Collected Works.* Routledge and Kegan, London.

Kahle, L. R. (1983) *Social Values and Social Change: Adaptation to Life in America.* Praeger, New York.

Kahle, L.R., Beatty, G.E. and Homer, P. (1986) Alternative Measurement Approaches to Consumer Values: The List of Values (LOV) and Life Styles (VALS). *Journal of Consumer Research* 13, 405-409.

Kale, S.H. and Weir, K.M. (1986) Marketing Third World Countries to the Western Traveller: the Case of India. *Journal of Travel Research* 25(Fall), 2-7.

Kamakura, W.A. and Mazzon, J.A. (1991) Values Segmentation: A Model for the Measurement of Values and Value Systems. *Journal of Consumer Research* 18, 208-218.

Kamakura, W.A. and Novak, T.P. (1992) Value System Segmentation: Exploring the Meaning of LOV. *Journal of Consumer Research* 19, 119-132.

Kroeger, O. and Theusen, J.M. (1988) *Type talk: the 16 personality types that determine how we live, love and work.* Bantam Doubleday Dell Publishing Group Inc, New

York.

Levy, N. and Padilla, A.Z. (1982) A Spanish translation of the Myers-Briggs Type Indicator Form G. *Psychological Reports* 51, 109-110.

London, M., Crandall, R. and Fitzgibbons. (1977) The Psychological Structure of Leisure: Activities, Needs, People. *Journal of Leisure Research* 9, 252-263.

Luk, S., Leon, C. and Leong, F. (1993) Value Segmentation of Tourists' Expectations of Service Quality. *Journal of Travel and Tourism Marketing* 2, 23-38.

Madrigal, R. and Kahle, L.R, (1992) Predicting Vacation Activity Preferences on the Basis of Value-System. *Journal of Travel Research* 19, 119-132.

Madrigal, R. and Kahle, L.R. (1994) Predicting Vacation Activity Preferences on the Basis of Value-System Segmentation. *Journal of Travel Research* 32(3), 22-28.

Mannell, R. (1984) Personality in Leisure Theory: The Self as Entertainment Construct. *Society and Leisure* 7(1), 229-240.

McGuiggan, R.L. (1996) *The relationship between personality, as measured by the MBTI, and leisure preferences.* Ph.D. dissertation, Macquarie University, Australia.

Mitchell, A. (1983) *Nine American Lifestyles: Who are we and where are we going?* MacMillan, New York.

Mo, C., Havitz, M.E. and Howard, D. (1994) Segmenting Travel Markets With The International Tourism Role (ITR) Scale. *Journal of Travel Research* 3, 24-31.

Morehouse, R.E., Farley, F. and Younquist, J.V. (1990) Type T personality and the Jungian classification system. *Journal of Personality Assessment* 54(1and2), 231-235.

Muller, T.E. (1991) Using Personal Values to Define Segments in an International Tourism Market, *International Marketing Review* 8, 57-70.

Murray, J.B. (1990) Review of research on the MBTI. *Perceptual and Motor skills* 70, 1187-1202

Myers, I. and McCaulley, M.H. (1992) *Manual: A Guide to the Development and Use of the MBTI.* Consulting Psychologists Press Inc., Palo Alto, California.

Novak, T.P. and MacEvoy, B. (1990) On Comparing Alternative Segmentation Schemes: The List of Values (LOV) and Values and Lifestyles (VALS). *Journal of Consumer Research* 17, 105-109.

Pearce, P. and Stringer, P. (1991) Psychology and Tourism. *Annals of Tourism Research* 18, 136-154.

Pitts, R.E. and Woodside, A.G. (1986) Personal Values and Travel Decisions. *Journal of Travel Research* 25 (summer), 20-25.

Pizam, A. and Calantone, R. (1987) Beyond Psychographics – Values As Determinants of Tourist Behaviour. *International Journal of Hospitality Management* 6(3), 177-181.

Plog, S. (1974) Why Destination Areas Rise And Fall In Popularity. *The Cornell Hotel and Restaurant Administration Quarterly* 14(4), 55-58.

Plog, S. (1990) A Carpenter's Tools: An Answer To S. Smith's Review of Psychocentrism/Allocentrism. *Journal of Travel and Tourism* (Spring), 43-44.

Provost, J.A. (1990) *Work, play and Type.* Consulting Psychologists Press, Inc., Palo Alto, California.

Riesman, D., Glazer, N. and Denney, R. (1961) *The Lonely Crowd.* Yale University Press, USA.

Rokeach, M. (1973) *The Nature of Human Values.* NY Free Press, USA.

Rokeach, M. and Ball-Rokeach, S.J. (1981) Stability and Change in American Value Priorities. *American Psychologist* 44, 773-784.

Schwartz, S.H. and Bilsky, W. (1987) Toward a Universal Psychological Structure of Human Values. *Journal of Personality and Social Psychology* 53(3), 550-562.

Segal, M.N., Segal, U.A. and Niemczycki, M.A. (1993) Value Network for Cross-National Marketing Management: A Framework For Analysis And Application. *Journal of Business Research* 27, 65-83.

Shank, M.D. and Langmeyer, L. (1994) Does personality influence brand image? *The Journal of Psychology* 128(2), 157-164.

Sipp, G.J., Alexander, R.A. and Friedt, L. (1985) Item analysis of the MBTI. *Educational and Psychological Measurement* 45, 789-796.

Smith, S. (1990a) A Test Of Plog's Allocentric/Psychocentric Model: Evidence From Seven Nations. *Journal of Travel Research* (Spring), 40-43.

Smith, S. (1990b) Another Look At The Carpenter's Tools: A Return To Plog. *Journal of Travel Research* (Autumn), 50-51.

Steele, R.S. and Kelly, T.J. (1976) Eysenck Personality Questionnaire and Jungian MBTI of Extraversion-Introversion. *Journal of Consulting and Clinical Psychology* 44, 690-691.

Tetlock, P. (1986) A Value Pluralism Model of Ideological Reasoning. *Journal of Personality and Social Psychology* 50(4), 819-827.

Thompson, B. and Borrello, G.M. (1986) Second-order Factor Structure of the MBTI: a Construct Validity Assessment. *Measurement and Evaluation in Counselling and Development* 18(4), 148-153.

Tzeng, O.C.S., Outcault, D., Boyer, S.L., Ware, R. and Landis, D. (1984) Item Validity of the MBTI. *Journal of Personality Assessment* 48(3), 255-256.

Vinson, D.E., Scott, J.E. and Lamont, L.M. (1977) The Role of Personal Values in Marketing a Consumer Behaviour. *Journal of Marketing* (April), 44-50.

Wiggins, J.S. (1989) *Review of MBTI.* In: Conoley, J.C. and Kramer, J.J. (eds.) *The Tenth Mental Measurement Yearbook.* University of Nebraska Press, Lincoln, New England, pp. 537-538.

Yiannakis, A. and Gibson, H. (1992) Roles Tourists Play. *Annals of Tourism Research* 19, 287-303.

Zajonc, R.B. (1982) Affective and Cognitive Factors in Preferences. *Journal of Consumer Research* 9, 123-131.

Zuckerman, M. (1983) Sensation-Seeking and Sports. *Personality and Individual Differences* 4, 285-292.

Chapter fourteen
K-Means vs. Topology Representing Networks: Comparing Ease of Use for Gaining Optimal Results With Reference to Data Input Order

Alexandra Ganglmair and Ben Wooliscroft
Department of Marketing, University of Otago, Dunedin, New Zealand

Introduction

Market segmentation, as a tool for targeting homogeneous sub-groups of the market, is aimed at increasing efficiency and profitability (Markin, 1982). Segmentation has been widely used in tourism (McIntosh *et al.*, 1995). Since the 1950s numerous statistic tools for market segmentation have been developed (Wedel and Kamakura, 1998).

K-Means clustering analysis is the best known and most frequently used statistical segmentation technique (Wedel and Kamakura, 1998). The following discussion of K-Means refers to its implementation in the most popular statistical data analysis program (Bruehl and Zoefel, 1996); SPSS (SPSS, 1999a)[1].

Backhaus *et al.* (1996) suggested that this implementation of K-Means is sensitive to the input order of data. However, a comprehensive literature search including the SPSS manual (SPSS, 1999b,c) produces no empirical studies to support the suggestion about sensitivity to the order of input data. If changes in the input order of data lead to different results, changes in segments in follow-up surveys could be due to actual changes in the structure or attitude of consumers or the result of a change of the data input order.

Topology Representing Network (TRN) is a sophisticated Neural Network program for data segmentation. It does not impose rigorous assumptions on the data and is supposed to produce more stable results than traditional clustering methods (Dolnicar *et al.*, 1999).

The purpose of this paper is to provide supporting evidence that TRN can offer more stable solutions for clustering procedures than the well known K-Means/SPSS clustering with regard to changes to the order of input data. TRN comes to these more stable results without major transformation of the data or extensive use of other subjective analysis techniques prior to the segmentation. To provide maximum validity for practitioners real-world data as well as real-world data analysis procedures have been used and reference has been made to popular data analysis texts for procedures.

The first part of the paper deals with market segmentation and its implications in a managerial context. K-Means cluster analysis and TRN are discussed in the subsequent section. A dataset from a survey of 430 Germans considering travelling to New Zealand is used to show how the order of input data can affect the stability of segments with K-Means and TRN, respectively.

Market segmentation

Tourism managers develop different strategies for dealing with market segments and thereby build a more customer oriented targeting approach (Markin, 1982).

> 'In contrast with other social science disciplines looking into tourism the marketing researcher has no ambition to seek the "one-and-only" or the "true" typology of tourists. The "type generating" technique of market segmentation itself becomes an instrument of competitive strategy. ... The marketing analyst "invents" them and tailors them according to the service provider's objectives.' Mazanec, 1999, p.219)

In order to find appropriate segments, the researcher can choose from an abundant range of clustering techniques. Ten years ago Dickson reported more than 400 clustering and latent class analysis techniques (Chaturvedi et al., 1997). This paper deals with one of the most popular, K-Means/SPSS, and a representative of Neural Networks, Topology Representing Networks (TRN).

K-Means clustering

MacQueen's K-Means and its variants are the best known and most frequently used clustering techniques for market segmentation (Chaturvedi et al., 1997). The method was introduced in the 1950s with later development in the late 60s and mid 70s and has since been documented in an abundance of literature (Garcia-Escudero and Gordaliza, 1999).

The principles of K-Means are the following: After seed points or initial cluster centres have been chosen each observation is assigned to the nearest cluster centre. Once all cases are assigned to an initial cluster, out of the average of all cases a new cluster centre is computed. Cases may then be reassigned in order to reduce the total squared Euclidean distance between cases and the cluster centre. Once the impact of an exchange of cases is below a specified threshold the process is stopped (Huettner and Schwartnig, 1997).

Steps in clustering procedures

Running a cluster analyses with a traditional technique such as K-Means in SPSS makes a number of considerations necessary. Hair et al. (1998) mentioned several steps. Table 1 lists the steps appropriate for K-Means clustering analysis.

There are no guidelines about the right way to cluster with K-Means, instead the appropriate options depend on the context and are subject to the researcher's judgement while having a severe impact on the outcome of the analyses. There are numerous possible ways to perform K-Means clustering as implemented in SPSS. Many practitioners do not have the technical (statistical) knowledge to come to 'the best' solution possible using K-Means in SPSS.

Table 1 Important Considerations for Running a Cluster Analysis

	Suggested steps	Suggested procedures
1	unnecessary variables	Hair *et al.* (1998) point out that the inclusion of one irrelevant variable can alter the result considerably. Variables that do not differ significantly across clusters should be eliminated.
2	check for outliers	In high dimensional data the detection of outliers is somewhat problematic, especially when the number of clusters has to be specified in advance. Observations of outliers have to be checked for their representativeness of the population as they might represent sub-groups if the number of clusters chosen is large enough (Garcia-Escudero and Gordaliza, 1999). Hair *et al.* (1998) also mention that outliers might be not easily detected for large numbers of observations or variables and require special tests.
3	standardize data	Hair *et al.* (1998) list several possible ways of standardization: e.g. z-scores or within-case standardization without giving any specific recommendations when to choose which procedure. Deciding on the appropriate form of standardization depends on the researchers' judgement. However, choosing the right form of standardization can have a considerable inpact on the outcome.
4	multi-collinearity	While cluster analysis is less sensitive to violation in normality, linearity and homoscedasticity of the data than other techniques, multicollinearity is an important issue as it becomes a weighting instrument. Hair *et al.* (1998) therefore encourage the researcher to examine variables for 'substantial multicollinearity'.

A number of other drawbacks are discussed in the literature. Firstly, the segmentation method is scale dependent and different solutions may be obtained when the data are transformed. Furthermore, the performance depends heavily on the starting partition (number of clusters) chosen (Wedel and Kamakura, 1998) and is sensitive to outliers (Garcia-Escudero and Gordaliza, 1999).

A major concern is the dependence of K-Means on the order of data-input and its sensitivity towards local instead of global optimum-solutions (Backhaus *et al.*, 1996). This is due to the choice of seed points that leads to SPSS settling into a local optimum. SPSS uses a parallel threshold method to select seed points (initial cluster centres) amongst all cases that Hair *et al.* (1998) suggest somewhat reduces the impact of the input order, when the seed points are not specified by the analyst.

However, the impact of seed points cannot be overstated as once specified the solution will replicate exactly regardless of the data order, and stability cannot be consulted as an indicator for good clustering results. E.g. if the analyst puts randomly generated seed-points in K-Means will also provide a stable solution, regardless of the data input order, as long as the seed points are not changed. However, few practitioners have the knowledge to generate optimal seed points.

It is suggested that one way that may improve K-Means clustering is by combining this method with a hierarchical clustering solution (Hair *et al.*, 1998; SPSS, 1999a). It is suggested that a preceding hierarchical clustering procedure helps in determining the number of clusters most appropriate. By using the final cluster centres of a hierarchical cluster run as initial seed points for K-Means/SPSS the problems with choosing appropriate seed-points may be overcome. However, hierarchical segmentation techniques themselves depend on a number of assumptions and subjective judgements that might exceed the statistical ability of many practitioners as the K-Means solution itself depends substantially on the appropriateness of the result of the hierarchical clustering. Furthermore, hierarchical cluster are computational intensive and therefore not suitable for large data-sets (Hair *et al.*, 1998). If only a random sample is chosen the question of representativeness of the chosen sample from the original sample has to be considered (Hair *et al.*, 1998). Conducting hierarchical cluster analysis before K-Means overcomes the problems only partially and introduces many others.

Considering these acknowledged shortcomings of K-Means it is predictable that the academic community has sought segmentation methods that rely on less assumptions and subjective judgements.

The K-Means clustering procedure in this paper has been conducted with reference to the SPSS Manual (SPSS, 1999a,b) using all core steps specified.

Classification with a neural network

Interest in the topic of Artificial Neural Networks has experienced a substantial increase in recent years (Krycha and Wagner, 1999). Neural Networks have frequently been used for duplicating traditional statistical data-analysis tools but extend their applicability, especially to their non-linear alternatives (Natter, 1999).

Most applications are still in the area of computer science and mainly in Japan. However, a survey conducted in 1999 examined Artificial Neural Network applications in a managerial context (especially market response and classification) and found 25 Neural Network publications in the area of marketing between 1990 and 1996 (Krycha and Wagner, 1999).

Krycha and Wagner (1999) analysed applications that compare performance of Neural Networks with traditional analysing techniques and found that Neural Networks outperformed all tested traditional methods (e.g. Discriminant Analysis, Logit Regression, Multiple Regression, Multiple Competitive Interaction Model, etc.).

Topology Representing Network

TRN is a non-parametric method for segmentation, based on topology sensitive vector quantization (Dolnicar *et al.*, 1999). These topology preserving maps can be found in various parts of nervous systems as well as in Artificial Neural Network models, e.g. Kohonen's feature maps. The information-processing task consists of the exploitation of neighbourhood and topological relations between patterns (Martinetz and Schulten, 1994).

TRN uses the 'Neural Gas' algorithm by Martinez and Schulten (1994) to perform a topology sensitive vector quantization (TRN32 © J.A. Mazanec may be downloaded from ftp://charly.wu-wien.ac.at/pub/software/).

In essence TRN undertakes the following steps: during training, a specified number of prototypes are repeatedly exposed to input vectors randomly selected from the data-set. The most similar prototype (according to the Euclidean distance) becomes the *winner* and is allowed to *learn*, e.g. it is updated towards the input vector. The second- and/or third-most close prototypes are also updated according to the learning rule Martinetz *et al.* (1993). The small weights that were initially distributed randomly and acted as start co-ordinates are adapted in a way that the system *learns* to adapt its weight structure according to the distribution pattern of the input data. This weight update follows the learning rule and each prototype learns to take responsibility for a homogeneous set of data vectors (Dolnicar *et al.*, 1999).

The Neural Gas algorithm has been tested in comparison with K-means clustering and Kohonen's Self Organizing Maps (SOM). By co-updating adjacent prototypes (best, second- and third-best-prototype) it has been shown to optimize an explicit cost function. TRN thereby outperforms K-Means as well as SOMs. Its algorithm converges faster and reaches smaller distortion errors (Martinetz *et al.*, 1993). However, problems associated with ordering and K-Means were not explicitly discussed.

Methodology

The data used was collected as part of a major survey of *Expectations and Satisfaction of Tourists coming to New Zealand*. New Zealand faces distinct challenges when dealing with prospective visitors from overseas, especially in terms of actual and emotional distance, time and money involved because a vast majority of visitors to New Zealand arrive via long-haul flights. Having a thorough understanding of their expectations is essential for a successful tourism industry. However, the 'average tourist' does not exist. People differ in their expectations regarding a trip to New Zealand. Revealing distinctive visitor segments assists tourism managers in tailoring marketing activities directly to the visitors' needs and thereby increasing the possibility of turning an intention to maybe visiting New Zealand into an actual visit.

Four hundred and thirty German respondents were segmented according to their response to 48 expectation statements using K-Means as well as TRN clustering procedure. The 48 expectation statements were evaluated on 7-point itemized-category scales (Aaker *et al.*, 1995). The polar categories were labelled with 1='strongly disagree', 7='strongly agree', 4 was labelled 'neutral'.

In order to examine if K-Means and TRN segmentation provide results that differ in their stability, five K-Means and five TRN segmentations were run on the same data, the only change being input order. For every re-run the data-set was sorted differently. The results of these two segmentation methods are compared in order to reveal differently placed cases. It should be noted that repeated K-Means clustering of the data in the same input order produced the same results.

In non-hierarchical segmentation procedures choosing the number of clusters is a critical issue. Various possibilities have been suggested in addition to the check of face validity to choose the right number of clusters, e.g. the use of hierarchical clusters, the use of hold-out samples, etc. (see e.g. Backhaus *et al.*, 1996 or Hair *et al.*, 1998). However, for the purpose of this paper it was considered sufficient to check the results for their face validity. A four-segment solution offered the highest face validity for K-Means clustering. When using TRN it is possible to run several replications of the analysis (holding the number of clusters constant) and to compare the results in order to examine its reproducibility.

TRN was also trained with three to nine segments. A four and a six-segment solution provided the best robustness over replications. Robustness refers to a reported measure for reproducibility. Frequencies are counted for each pair of data points and whether they are attributed to the same cluster or not. In order to receive a meaningful comparison the four-cluster solution was used for the following analyses.

The benchmark segmentation, as is common practice in market research, was run while the data was sorted according to increasing identification number (ID). The result of this original solution is used as standard of comparison. Results for a four segment solution with TRN and with K-Means show segments with a highly comparable face validity.

Comparative performance and choice of the cluster algorithm

In comparison, neural networks in general and TRN in particular do not imply such rigorous assumptions on the data (Dolnicar *et al.,* 1999). Therefore it is assumed that this procedure performs better without major transformation of the data, irrespectively of a change of input order of the data and randomly chosen seed points. In the following cluster analyses the issues have been dealt with as follows:

1. Irrelevant variables were detected by checking for low variances between observations. These variables were not considered for the segmentation.
2. The data has been standardized within every case in order to compensate for different usage of a 7 point scale.
3. Multicollinearity has been checked with a factor analysis. The underlying dimensions are predominantly represented by 4 to 6 variables. A stronger (or weaker) weighting of the dimensions represented by more (or less) variables has been considered for the interpretation of the results.

Comparison over re-runs

Subsequently four additional K-Means and four TRN-analysis were run. Three repetitions were run on the same data, the only difference being input order of the data. The data-set was sorted according to decreasing ID, increasing age and decreasing age. In a fourth run only a randomly selected 50% of the data was used in order to check for stability in reduced data-sets.

The face validity of the original cluster solution was comparable to the newly computed results for TRN and K-Means. With all cluster solutions there were segments that could be described as Dreamer, Adventurer, Group Traveller and Uncertain segments. The cluster membership of the four test results (sorted by decreasing ID, increasing and decreasing age and the 50% sample) was compared to the original result (sorted by increasing ID) and the shifting-behaviour of unstable cases analysed.

Results

Overall the Neural Network showed a considerably more stable result. Between 92 and 100% of the cases are assigned to a segment that would be interpreted the same way. A 50% random sample could still place between 70 and 87% of all cases in the same segments.

Table 2 Interpretation of the Original Cluster Solution (K-Means and TRN)

Rational, Demanding Group Traveller	Price Conscious Adventurer	Dreamer	Uncertain
Size: TRN: 28% K-Means: 31%	Size: TRN: 26% K-Means: 25%	Size: TRN: 24% K-Means: 28%	Size: TRN: 22% K-Means: 17%
• organized tour preferred	• highest knowledge about NZ	• New Zealand is paradise on earth	• have not made up their mind
• perfect organization and luxury expected	• outdoor facilities very important	• excellent:	• limited knowledge
• do not look for thrilling experience	• no doubts about going	- tourist facilities +	• in need of a holiday
• some doubts about NZ	+ know when	- perfect outdoor opportunities +	• want to escape daily routine
• worried about language	• will live without luxury	- good value for money	• NZ is less advanced
	• lowest income →	• could imagine to live in NZ	• worried about language
	• price conscious	• BUT: no concrete plans yet	• NZ not top-of-mind

K-means analysis assigned between 51 and 95% of all cases into the segment that would be interpreted the same way when the sample was re-sorted and between 49 and 95% when a 50% random sample was used.

Table 3 TRN Segmentation: Stable Cases in %

	TRN results: stable cases in %			
	ID decreasing	age decreasing	age increasing	50% sample
Uncertain	98%	95%	100%	87%
Dreamer	96%	97%	93%	70%
Adventurer	97%	98%	96%	81%
Group Traveller	92%	92%	94%	74%
	96% average			78% average

The comparison of Table 3 and Table 4 shows that TRN placed an average of 96% (78% for the smaller random sample) in the same cluster. K-Means clustering assigned an average of 77% to the right cases. For the smaller random sample the hit-rate with K-Means clustering is 62%. As can be seen for re-runs with the full datasets, TRN placed an average of 19% more cases into the segments they were originally assigned to. For the 50% random sample TRN still placed an average of 16% more cases correctly than K-means did.

Table 4 K-Means Clustering: Stable Cases in %

	K-Means: stable cases in %			
	ID decreasing	age decreasing	age increasing	50% sample
Uncertain	84%	84%	95%	56%
Dreamer	51%	68%	65%	49%
Adventurer	75%	90%	89%	91%
Group Traveller	73%	78%	66%	52%
		77% average		62% average

In a next step the flow of unstable cases was analysed. The original segmentation (according to increasing ID) acted as standard of comparison once again. Results are summarised in Table 5 and Table 6.

Table 5 shows that the most unstable TRN segment is the Group Traveller. An average of 7% of all cases was placed in segments different from the original one when the whole sample was re-sorted. With a random sample containing only 50% of the cases 26% of those cases were placed in clusters other than the one they were originally assigned to. The floating cases were most likely to drift into the Dreamer and the Adventurer, respectively.

Less than 5% of the Dreamers were drifting into different cases (with a random sample of 50% this number goes up to 30%). Most likely they could be found as part of the Adventurer or Uncertain. Only 3% of all Adventurer and Uncertain had a tendency to drift to different segments.

Except for the Group Traveller, cases were floating between similar segments, especially Dreamer and Uncertain or Adventurer. However for the Group Traveller there are some cases that drifted into a completely different segment like the Adventurer.

The TRN solution is relatively insensitive to the order of the input data, however the 50% random sample solution has some stability problems. Table 6 highlights cases that have drifted between segments during the K-Means segmentation. As can be seen, instability is a far bigger issue in this case.

The considerably less stable results which emerged in Table 4 are reflected in the detailed analyses undertaken in Table 6. While the most unstable TRN segment showed an average of 7% of all cases moving between segments, the least stable K-Means segment contains 38% cases that tend to drift towards other segments when the segmentation is re-run with a different input order of the data.

Of particular interest is that with a certain order of the input data (decreasing ID) 30% of the cases originally part of the Dreamer are found in a completely different cluster: the Group Traveller

Cases in the Group Traveller also show the tendency to float around segments with an average of 28% drifting mostly to Dreamer or Adventurer. It is important to notice that a majority of these drifting cases are ending up at a segment with a completely different face validity.

Table 5 TRN: Stability in Comparison to Original Solution

		TRN: Stability in comparison to result (ID increasing)			
		% of unstable cases	shifting to: Uncertain	shifting to: Dreamer	shifting to: Adventurer	shifting to: Group Traveller
Uncertain	ID decreasing	2%		1 (1%)	1 (1%)	
	age increasing	0%				
	age decreasing	5%			3 (3%)	2 (2%)
	entire dataset, unstable cases: 2.3% on average					
	50% sample	13%		5 (11%)		1 (2%)
Dreamer	ID decreasing	4%			2 (2%)	2 (2%)
	age increasing	7%	5 (5%)			2 (2%)
	age decreasing	3%			3 (3%)	
	entire dataset, unstable cases: 4.7% on average					
	50% sample	30%			17 (29%)	1 (1%)
Adventurer	ID decreasing	3%	1 (1%)	2 (2%)		
	age increasing	4%	2 (2%)	2 (2%)		
	age decreasing	2%	1 (1%)	1 (1%)		
	entire dataset, unstable cases 3% on average					
	50% sample	19%	3 (5%)	4 (6%)		5 (8%)
Group Traveller	ID decreasing	8%	1 (1%)	5 (4.5%)	4 (3.5%)	
	age increasing	6%	3 (2.5%)	1 (1%)	3 (2.5%)	
	age decreasing	8%		8 (6%)	2 (2%)	
	entire dataset, unstable cases: 7.3% on average					
	50% sample	26%	1 (2%)	15 (23%)	1 (2%)	

Uncertain and Adventurer are the most stable cases with only 13% and 15% drifting into other segments, respectively. Nevertheless this figure is still twice as high as the least stable TRN segment (7% Group Traveller).

Table 6 K-Means stability in comparison to original solution*

K-Means: Stability cases in comparison to result (ID increasing)

		% of unstable cases	shifting to: Uncertain	shifting to: Dreamer	shifting to: Adventurer	shifting to: Group Traveller
Uncertain	ID decreasing	16%		7 (11%)	2 (3%)	1 (2%)
	age increasing	5%		1 (1.6%)	1 (1.6%)	1 (1.6%)
	age decreasing	17%			9 (15%)	1 (2%)
	entire dataset, unstable cases: 12.7% on average					
Dreamer	ID decreasing	49%	9 (9%)		12 (12%)	30 (28%)
	age increasing	35%	18 (18%)		15 (14%)	3 (3%)
	age decreasing	31%	2 (2%)		15 (14%)	16 (15%)
	entire dataset, unstable cases: 38.3% on average					
Adventurer	ID decreasing	25%		21 (23%)		2 (2%)
	age increasing	10%	1 (1%)	4 (4%)		5 (5%)
	age decreasing	9%	4 (4%)	5 (5%)		
	entire dataset, instable cases: 14.6% on average					
Group Traveller	ID decreasing	26%	4 (3%)		27 (23%)	
	age increasing	35%		39 (34%)	1 (1%)	
	age decreasing	23%	1 (1%)	2 (2%)	23 (20%)	
	entire dataset, unstable cases: 28% on average					

* When only 50% of the respondents were segmented, K-Means clustering comes to a completely different result!

Conclusion

Although segmentation does not strive for a single truth, using the same segmentation method on the same dataset should lead to the same or at least very similar results. The research found that the K-Means clustering procedure as implemented in SPSS is very sensitive to changes in the input order of the data. In comparison a Neural Networks approach to segmentation such as the Topology Representing Network showed considerably less sensitivity for the same changes.

This outcome is especially noteworthy because K-Means clusters are not only less stable but they also tend to drift into clusters that have completely different face validity, e.g. Dreamer to Group Traveller. A 50% random sample segmented with TRN came to a considerably less stable result. However, clusters are still comparable by face validity. If the same 50% random sample is clustered with K-Means/SPSS, the resulting segments differ in their basic characteristics.

K-Means clustering remains the most widely used method of segmentation and yet it is at best an inexact method of segmentation. While TRN is not 100% stable it offers considerable advantages over K-Means for market segmentation. The advantages include a reduction in the number of choices/steps in the analysis process, a reduction in the number of assumptions required and a stable face valid result.

Endnotes

[1] referred to as: K-Means/SPSS

References

Aaker, D.A., Kumar, V. and Day, G.S. (1995) *Marketing Research,* 5th edn. John Wiley and Sons, New York.

Backhaus, K., Erichson, B., Plinke, W. and Weiber, R. (1996) *Multivariate Analyse-Methoden; eine anwendungsorientierte Einführung,* 8th edn. Springer Verlag, Berlin.

Bruehl, A. and Zoefel, P. (1996) SPSS fuer Windows Version 6.1. 3rd edn. Addison-Wesley-Logmann, Bonn.

Chaturvedi, A., Carroll, D.J., Green, P.E. and Rotondo, J.A. (1997) A feature based approach to market segmentation via overlapping K-centroids clustering. *Journal of Marketing Research* 34(3), 370-377.

Dolnicar, S., Grabler, K. and Mazanec, J.A. (1999) A Tale of Three cities: Perceptual Charting for Analysing Destination Images. In: Woodside, A.G., Crouch, G.I., Mazanc, J.A., Opperman, M. and Sakai, M.Y. (eds.) *Consumer Psychology of Tourism, Hospitality and Leisure.* CAB International, Wallingford, pp. 39-62.

Garcia-Escudero, L.A. and Gordaliza, A. (1999) Robustness Properties of K-Means and Trimmed K-Means. *Journal of the American Statistical Association* 94, 956–969.

Hair Jr., J.F., Anderson, R.E., Totha, R.L. and Bloch, W.C. (1998) *Multivariate Data Analysis,* 5th edn. Prentice-Hall, Englewood Cliffs, New Jersey.

Huettner, M. and Schwartnig, U. (1997) *Grundzuege der Marktforschung,* 5th edn. R. Oldenburg, Muenchen.

Krycha, K.A. and Wagner, U. (1999) Applications of artificial neural networks in management science: a survey. *Journal of Retailing and Consumer Services* 6(4), 185-203.

Markin, R.J. (1982) *Marketing, Strategy and Management.* John Wiley and Sons, New York

Martinetz, T.M. and Schulten, K. (1994) Topology Representing Networks. *Neural Networks* 7(3), 507-522.

Martinetz, T.M., Berkovich, S. and Schulten, K. (1993) Neural Gas Network for Vector Quantization and its Application to Time-Series Prediction. *IEEE Transactions on Neural Networks* 14(4), 558-569.

Mazanec, J.A. (1999) Simultaneous positioning and segmentation analysis with topologically ordered feature maps: a tour operator example. *Journal of Retailing and Consumer Services* 6(4), 219-235.

McIntosh, R.W., Goeldner, C.R. and Ritchie, J.R.B. (1995) *Tourism Principles, Practices, Philosophies*, 7th edn. John Wiley and Sons, New York.

Natter, M. (1999) Conditional market segmentation by neural networks: a Monte Carlo study. *Journal of Retailing and Consumer Services* 6(4), 237-248.

SPSS for Windows (1999a) *Standard Version 10.0.5.* SPSS Inc.

SPSS Base 10.0 Users Guide (1999b) SPSS Inc.

SPSS Base 10.0 Application Guide (1999c) SPSS Inc.

Wedel, M. and Kamakura, W.A. (1998) *Market Segmentation; Conceptual and Methodological Foundations*. Kluwer Academic Publishers, Boston.

Chapter fifteen
Behavioural Market Segmentation Using the Bagged Clustering Approach Based on Binary Guest Survey Data: Exploring and Visualizing Unobserved Heterogeneity

Sara Dolnicar
Institute for Tourism and Leisure Studies
Vienna University of Economics and Business Administration
Vienna, Austria

Friedrich Leisch
Department of Statistics, Probability Theory and Actuarial Mathematics
Vienna University of Technology
Vienna, Austria

Introduction

Binary survey data from the Austrian National Guest Survey conducted in the summer season of 1997 was used to identify behavioural market segments on the basis of vacation activity information. The bagged clustering methodology applied overcomes a number of difficulties typically encountered when partitioning clustering algorithms are applied to large binary data-sets. Besides rendering more stable results in the sense of reproducibility and making the yet unsolved question of the correct number of clusters to choose less important by a hierarchical step of analysis at the end of the procedure, the bagged clustering approach eases interpretation of segment profiles as classically given by the mean variable values per segment and thus markedly improves the investigation and visualization of unobserved heterogeneity within the field of exploratory market segmentation.

Three developments relevant to the analysis of data for marketing purposes motivate this paper. First, the general acceptance for the need to account for consumer heterogeneity when taking e.g. marketing action on the marketplace (going hand in hand with the wide use of different kinds of both exploratory and confirmative techniques to identify market segments) has been increasing since the introduction of the market segmentation concept in the late 1950s. Second, importance of binary data in social sciences is growing. The reasons for later development are manifold. Yes-no questions are simpler and faster to answer for respondents. Not only does this fact increase the chances of the respondents finishing the questionnaire and answering it in a concentrated, spontaneous and motivated manner, binary question format also allows the designer of the questionnaire to pose more questions, as the single answer is less tiring. This is especially important for studies, where attitudes towards a multitude of objects are questioned, thus dramatically increasing the number of answers expected from the respondents as it is typically the case with guest surveys within the field of tourism. Thirdly, these developments lead to an increasing number of medium to large empirical binary data-sets available for data analysis.

Turning to the field of market segmentation, empirical binary survey data-sets exclude a number of clustering techniques viable for analysis due to their size, which seems to be too large for hierarchical and too small for parametric approaches. Most parametric approaches require very large amounts of data in relation to the number of variables, growing exponentially. For the use of latent class analysis, Formann (1984) recommends a sample size of 5×2^d, a very strict requirement, especially when item batteries of d=15 to 20 items are not unusual, as it is the case in market segmentation, be it with demographic, socioeconomic, behavioural or psycho-graphic variables. Unless these huge[1] data-sets are available, exploratory clustering techniques (e.g. Anderberg, 1973) will broadly be applied to analyse the heterogeneity underlying the population sample. Among the classical clustering approaches, the hierarchical techniques – as mentioned before – require the data-sets to be rather small, as all pairwise distances need to be computed (and either stored in memory or re-computed at every step). This leaves us with partitioning approaches within the family of exploratory cluster analytic techniques.

Bagged clustering tries to take advantage of the strengths of both the hierarchical and the partitioning clustering approaches, that are summarized by Myers and Tauber (1977, p. 80) in their milestone publication on market structure analysis: hierarchical clustering better shows how individuals combine in terms of similarities and partitioning methods produce more homogeneous groups.

The Bagged Clustering Approach

The central idea of bagged clustering is to stabilize partitioning methods like K-means or learning vector quantization (LVQ, e.g. Ripley, 1996) by repeatedly running the cluster algorithm and combining the results. K-means is an unstable method in the sense that in many runs one will not find the global optimum of the error function but a local optimum only. Both initializations and small changes in the training set can have big influence on the actual local minimum where the algorithm converges.

By repeatedly training on new data-sets one gets different solutions which should on average be independent from training set influence and random initializations. We can obtain a collection of training sets by sampling from the empirical distribution of the original data, i.e. by bootstrapping. We then run any partitioning cluster algorithm – called the *base cluster method* below – on each of these training sets.

Bagged clustering simultaneously explores the independent solution from several runs of the base method in an exploratory way using hierarchical clustering. The results of the base method are combined into a new data-set which is then used as input for a hierarchical method. This allows the researcher to identify structurally stable (regions of) centres which are found repeatedly.

The algorithm works as follows:

1. Construct B bootstrap training samples $X_N^1,..., X_N^B$ by drawing with replacement from the original sample X_N.
2. Run the base cluster method (K-means, LVQ, ...) on each set, resulting in $B \times K$ centres $c_{11},c_{12},...,c_{1K},c_{21},...,c_{BK}$ where K is the number of centres used in the base method and c_{ij} is the j-th centre found using X_N^i.
3. Combine all centres into a new data-set $C^B=C^B(K)=\{c_{11},...,c_{BK}\}$.
4. Run a hierarchical cluster algorithm on C^B resulting in the usual dendrogram.
5. Let $c(x)$ in C^B denote the centre closest to x. A partition of the original data can now be obtained by cutting the dendrogram at a certain level, resulting in a partition $C_1^B,...,C_m^B$ of set C^B. Each point x in X_N is now assigned to the cluster containing $c(x)$.

The algorithm has been shown to compare favourably to several standard clustering methods on binary and metric benchmark data-sets (Leisch, 1998); for a detailed analysis see Leisch (1999).

Behavioural Segmentation

Summer tourists – outline of the segmentation base

As a basis for identification of behavioural market segments among summer tourists visiting Austria for a holiday, a data-set including 5365 respondents and 12 variables was used. The respondents were tourists spending their vacation in the rural area of Austria during the summer season of 1997. These visitors were questioned in the course of the Austrian National Guest Survey. The variables used for behavioural segmentation[2] purposes included the following vacation activities: cycling (30% stated to do cycling during their stay), swimming (63%), going to a spa (15%), hiking (76%), going for walks (93%), organized excursions (22%), excursions (77%), relaxing (80%), shopping (72%), sightseeing (78%), museums (45%) and using health facilities (14%).

In addition to these variables used as segmentation base, a number of demographic, socioeconomic, behavioural and psycho-graphic background variables is available in the extensive guest survey data-set. A detailed description of selected variables is provided in Table 1. Keep in mind, that city tourists are excluded from the sample.

Especially the monetary variables expenditures and income have a strongly skewed distribution with large positive outliers (as expected), such that we give the robust measures median together with 1st and 3rd Quartile in Table 1. For all categorical variables we give percentage of observations in each category.

Bagged clustering parameters

For this data-set we used learning vector quantization with $K=20$ centres as base method. The base method was applied on $B=50$ bootstrap samples, resulting in a total of 1000 centres, which were then hierarchically clustered using Euclidean distance and Ward's agglomerative linkage method (e.g. Kaufman and Rousseeuw, 1990). These parameters were chosen because they performed best in empirical studies (Leisch, 1998) on simulated artificial data with similar characteristics as the present data-set (Dolnicar *et al.*, 1998).

Table 1 Description of Background Variables. For metric variables we list the 25%, 50% (Median) and 75% Quartiles, for categorical variables the percentage of people per category

Variable	Type	% per level or		
		Q1	Med	Q3
Age (metric)	Years	38.0	49.0	59.0
Daily expenditures per person (metric)	EUR	37.2	53.3	74.6
Monthly disposable income (metric)	EUR	1547.9	2267.4	3069.7
Length of stay (metric)	days	7.0	10.0	14.0
intention to revisit Austria (4 ordered categories)	definitely		31.6	
	probably		31.5	
	probably not		16.5	
	definitely not		20.4	
Intention to recommend Austria (5 ordered categories)	definitely (1)		73.0	
	2		19.6	
	3		5.7	
	4		1.2	
	5		0.2	
	definitely not (6)		0.3	
Prior vacations in Austria (3 ordered categories)	never		7.5	
	once		5.9	
	twice and more		86.6	
Sources of information (8 nominal categories)	brochures		14.0	
(one variable each)	media ads		2.8	
	friends and relatives		21.1	
	travel agent		7.1	
	local and regional tourism bureau		7.0	
	Internet		0.4	
	no information needed		37.9	

All computations and graphics were done using the R software package for statistical computing (see http://www.R-project.org). R functions for bagged clustering can be obtained from the authors upon request.

How many behavioural segments to choose?

Figure 1 depicts the dendrogram resulting from the bagged clustering analysis. The dendrogram looks well-structured and the partitions with either three or five clusters seem to be worth thorough investigation. The three cluster solution renders a very rough outline of the tourist structure when investigated in detail: besides the identification of a clearly characterized health tourist group, the remaining tourists were only divided in either active or inactive visitors. So, for every organization not focusing on health tourism, the three cluster solution would be evaluated as being too imprecise. Hence, the five cluster solution was chosen and is discussed in detail below.

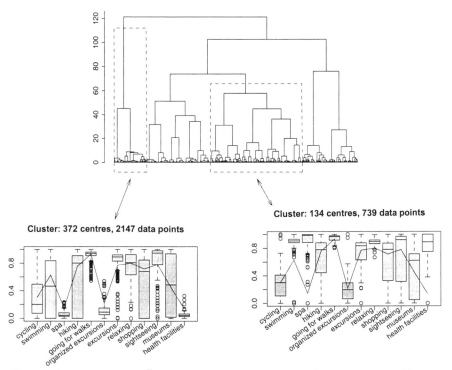

Figure 1 Bagged clustering dendrogram together with box plots for segments 5 and 2

Of course, bagged clustering is in general less concerned about the number-of-clusters problem, as the same bagged clustering solution can arbitrarily be explored for different numbers of tourist segments. Exploring the bagged clustering solutions allows exploration in the sense of stepwise splitting and thus increased insight into the unobserved heterogeneity structure inherent to the survey data.

A positive side-effect of using the bagged clustering methodology becomes visible when discussing the number of clusters to choose: identifying niche segments causes less difficulties for the two-step bagged clustering procedure that it was shown to cause when using classical partitioning algorithms as e.g. K-means or learning vector quantization by Weingessel *et al.* (forthcoming). This fact is well-illustrated here, as the health tourism niche segment consists of only 13.8 per cent of the respondents and is already identified in the three-segment solution.

Activity segments among summer tourists – interpretation and visualization

The visualization of segment 2 and 5 in Figure 1 gives the mean segment agreement with single activities, the distribution of answers within the groups and, as indicated by the line, the sample average. This distribution information clearly cannot be given for segment solutions based on classical partitioning algorithms for binary data, where only the mean value can be used for interpretation, the distribution always lying between 0 and 1. The intermediate step of calculating a multitude of centres within the bagged cluster framework thus adds valuable information to the segment interpretation step.

Box plots supporting the evaluation of variables are provided in Figure 2. The following conclusions about the behavioural tourist segments among the visitors of Austria during the summer season of 1997 can be drawn on the basis of the box plots for this particular bagged clustering solution:

Segment 1: 'Active individual tourists'

This group consists of 24% of the respondents and is best described by the high level of general activity in both cultural activities and sports. Three activities are of little importance to this group: the members of segment 1 are very homogeneous in their avoidance of spas and health facilities and participating in organized excursions is not their favourite leisure time activity either, although the opinions concerning this third issue vary to a higher extent as can be seen from the quantile range as indicated in the box plot in Figure 2. Cycling and visiting museums also deserve special treatment. Obviously these activities are bad descriptors for this segment as the behaviour of the segment members vary strongly.

Segment 2: 'Health oriented holiday-makers'

This niche segment represents a very stable and distinct interest group with profile and membership remaining unchanged as compared to the three-cluster solution. Clearly, these tourists spend their vacation swimming and relaxing in spas and health facilities. Also, they all seem to enjoy going for a walk (after the pool is closed?). As far as the remaining activities are concerned, homogeneity decreases as indicated by the large dispersion of mean values.

Segment 3: 'Just hanging arounds'

Except for the two items health facilities and relaxation all activities are undertaken far less often than in the average tourist population of Austria in summer by this niche segment including only 9% of the respondents. The highest extent of agreement in this group exists concerning the absolute avoidance of spas, organized excursions, health facilities and museums.

Segment 4: 'Tourists on tour'

Passive activities are characteristic for this segment that represents 13% of the respondents. Sightseeing, shopping and going for walks – probably mostly within the framework of organized excursions – are the common passions of the members of this segment. Concerning these interests the group also demonstrates very strong homogeneity.

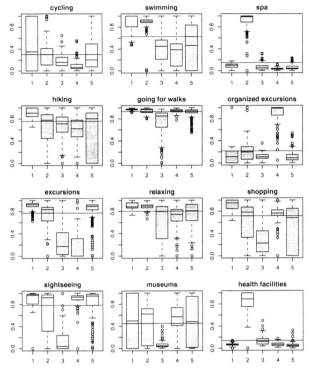

Figure 2 Variable box plot of the five cluster solution

Segment 5: 'Individual sightseers'

This largest segment (40% of the tourists questioned) has a clear focus when visiting Austria: they want to hop from sight to sight. Therefore both the items sightseeing and excursions are strongly and commonly agreed upon in this group. Neither sports nor shopping are of central importance, although some members do spend some of their leisure time undertaking those activities. Well reflecting the individualist character of this group is the heterogeneity of this segment concerning a number of activities, as e.g. swimming, hiking, shopping or visiting museums.

The results of the analysis of the background variables are provided in Table 2. Segment 4 (tourists on tour) demonstrates some very typical features of culture tourists: short stay, low intention to revisit, low prior experience with Austria and high use of travel agents for the organized vacation. Segment 3 ('just hanging arounds') on the other hand seems to have spent decades of summer holidays in Austria. With an 89% proportion of regular visitors and 43% of the group members needing no information whatsoever, this group makes the impression of coming to a well-known holiday destination and enjoying life without any kind of excitement or action. The active tourist group (Segment 1) is characterized by a generally high activity level and represents the youngest segment with an average age of 45 years. They spend the lowest amount of money in Austria per person. Their prior experience is relatively low. The second active group (Segment 5) focuses on the sightseeing part of possible holiday activities. This rather young group of travellers is fond of Austria and intends to revisit the country to a high extent.

Table 2 Description of Background Variables for the Five Cluster Bagged Clustering Solution

	seg.1	seg.2	seg.3	seg.4	seg.5	p-val
Age	45.00	53.00	53.00	55.00	48.00	2e-16
daily exp. per person	47.76	68.01	52.4	56.02	52.43	2e-16
monthly dispos. Income	2325.53	2380.76	1901.09	2180.19	2267.39	2e-09
length of stay	12.00	10.00	8.00	7.00	9.00	2e-16
intention to revisit A.:						0.002
definitely	30.58	35.51	32.06	26.03	33.65	
probably	36.82	32.93	27.39	44.13	35.29	
probably not	17.71	19.59	14.65	16.83	15.91	
definitely not	14.90	11.97	25.90	13.01	15.15	
intent. to recommend A.:						0.011
definitely (1)	70.67	72.32	66.03	70.85	67.35	
2	23.58	22.25	23.84	22.96	25.78	
3	4.73	4.88	7.81	4.79	5.28	
4	0.70	0.41	1.69	1.13	1.21	
5	0.23	0.00	0.42	0.14	0.09	
definitely not (6)	0.08	0.14	0.21	0.14	0.28	
prior vacations in A.:						2e-16
never	13.93	7.99	6.53	23.52	11.18	
once	11.69	6.10	4.84	13.52	8.48	
twice or more	74.38	85.91	88.63	62.96	80.34	
sources of inform. used:						2e-16
no information needed	30.70	34.91	44.21	20.11	35.21	
brochures	19.26	17.32	12.21	22.22	19.98	
travel agent	11.29	6.50	8.42	22.08	8.80	
media ads	4.72	4.60	4.42	5.06	4.19	
friends and relatives	23.12	26.93	22.95	20.68	22.12	
local tourism bureau	6.96	6.50	5.47	6.89	7.08	
Internet	3.94	3.25	2.32	2.95	2.61	

As could be seen from this interpretation and visualization section, bagged clustering substantially eases interpretation of results based on binary data, both in terms of variable evaluation and identification of marker variables for the segment description. To visualize the improvement reached by applying bagged clustering, take a look at Figure 3 which includes the information resulting from non-hierarchical clustering algorithms, only showing the sample average (line) and the segment-wise mean variable values (bar height).

Conclusions

There is no doubt, that market segmentation represents one of the most powerful strategic tools in tourism industry, be it on organizational or destination level. Besides the decision, which data base to choose for segmentation, the clustering tool applied strongly influences the result. In this paper behavioural variables were chosen and a powerful partitioning procedure, the bagged clustering approach was introduced and illustrated.

Cluster 1: 779 points (14.52%)

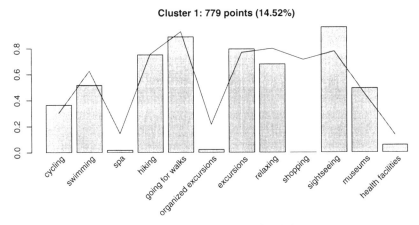

Figure 3 Bar plot of segment 1 of the five cluster LVQ solution

The bagged clustering approach offers tourism managers numerous advantages, some of which are of general interest, others especially favourable for analysts confronted with binary survey data. Due to the steps of the bagged clustering procedure, results are less dependent on the starting solution and more stable when replicated. Also, a priori choice of the number of clusters is not crucial. After exploring the dendrogram, a starting partition can be chosen. More detailed solutions can easily be generated by splitting the starting segments.

From the interpretation point of view, this same splitting possibility turns out to be very helpful in exploratory analysis, giving additional insight into the data structure. Another major advantage is the ability of the bagged clustering approach to identify niche segments directly. Finally, interpretation of results based on binary survey data is eased dramatically by the intermediate step of generating metric prototypes and thus enabling the box plot visualization of segments and variables. Including this range information in the variable evaluation and segment description reduces the probability of misinterpretation as compared to mere mean values used as segment descriptors.

Acknowledgement

This piece of research was supported by the Austrian Science Foundation (FWF) under grant SFB#010 ('Adaptive Information Systems and Modelling in Economics and Management Science').

Endnotes

[1] E.g., $5 \times 2^{15} = 163,840$, $5 \times 2^{20} = 5,242,880$
[2] Of course, the bagged clustering approach is not limited to behavioural segmentation approaches. The

data analysed here are used for demonstration purposes and torn out of context. In case of a segmentation study conducted for a destination or tourism attraction, the respective segmentation (geographic, demographic, behavioural or psycho-graphic) would have to be chosen thoroughly.

References

Anderberg, M.R. (1973) *Cluster Analysis for Applications.* Academic Press Inc., New York, USA.

Dolnicar, S., Leisch, F. and Weingessel, A. (1998) *Artificial Binary Data Scenarios.* Working Paper, Nr. 20, SFB Adaptive Information Systems and Modelling in Economics and Management Science, http://www.wu-wien.ac.at/am

Formann, A.K. (1984) *Die Latent-Class-Analyse: Einführung in die Theorie und Anwendung.* Beltz, Weinheim.

Kaufman, L. and Rousseeuw, P.J. (1990) *Finding Groups in Data.* John Wiley and Sons, Inc., New York, USA.

Leisch, F. (1998) *Ensemble Methods for Neural Clustering and Classification.* Ph.D. thesis, Institut für Statistik, Wahrscheinlichkeitstheorie und Versicherungs-mathematik. Technische Universität Wien, Austria.

Leisch, F. (1999) *Bagged Clustering.* Working Paper, Nr. 51, SFB Adaptive Information Systems and Modeling in Economics and Management Science, http://www.wu-wien.ac.at/am

Myers, J.H. and Tauber, E. (1977) *Market Structure Analysis.* American Marketing Association, Chicago.

Ripley, B.D. (1996) *Pattern Recognition and Neural Networks.* Cambridge University Press, Cambridge, UK.

Weingessel, A., Dimitriadou, E. and Dolnicar, S. (forthcoming) An examination of indexes for determining the number of clusters in binary data-sets. *Psychometrika.* Accepted for publication.

Chapter sixteen
Mastering Unobserved Heterogeneity
in Tourist Behaviour Research

Josef A. Mazanec
Institute for Tourism and Leisure Studies
Vienna University of Economics and Business Administration
Vienna, Austria

Abstract

According to what the philosophy of science considers to be a scientifically relevant undertaking, tourist behaviour research should be based on explicit hypotheses or–even better–on a system of interconnected relationships (a 'model'). The models are subject to empirical testing to assess their explanatory and predictive capabilities. As in any other sub-field of behavioural science a sample of tourists used for model testing is often heterogeneous in terms of variable values and association between variables. Therefore, the results gained for bivariate or multivariate relations may be artefacts due to spurious correlations. Heterogeneity is found to appear on different levels of tourist behaviour model building. It is easier to control if there are explicit assumptions about moderator variables. However, it becomes particularly troublesome if the hypothesized cause-effect relationships are subject to variation over an unknown structure of sub-groups. Examples are discussed to portray these cases.

The Heterogeneity Concept

Heterogeneity in tourist behaviour research emerges in different forms. The two fundamental forms are (A) model heterogeneity and (B) parameter heterogeneity. (A) originates either from (A1) interpersonal or from (A2) intrapersonal changes in the tourists' decision processes. Under (A1) various sub-groups of a consumer/tourist population follow a different explanatory system, say, an attitude, image, or perceived risk model (Mazanec, 1978). (A2) accounts for the fact that the same tourist evaluates a travel destination according to an (emotion-driven) image model during the early stages of his decision-making process, but later on–once he has collected more factual knowledge–switches to an attitudinal assessment behaviour. Under (B) the basic explanatory structure fits the tourist population, but the parameter values may vary widely in different sub-groups. Three forms of (B) may be termed (B1) cause heterogeneity, (B2) effect heterogeneity, and (B3) cause-effect heterogeneity. In marketing research (B3) is called 'response-based' heterogeneity (Jain *et al.*, 1994; Jedidi *et al.*, 1997). It is the most challenging of these forms and may be either explicit or implicit. If the analyst has sufficient prior knowledge to make an assumption regarding one or more grouping variables he may be able to control a substantial portion of this explicit type (B3) heterogeneity. If he lacks such knowledge the unobserved heterogeneity remains totally implicit. Popular examples for (B1) are motivational or attitudinal typologies where tourists are classified into sub-groups with homogeneous bundles of travel motives or attitudes toward a destination or tourist service provider. (B2) is easily described by travel activity types where behavioural patterns and habits appear in symptomatic combinations (see recent examples discussed by Dolnicar and Mazanec, 2000). Behaviours are assumed to be explained by psychographics and thus a more advanced model is likely to comprise both domains of traveller characteristics. However, the way the psychographics get transformed into verbal and actual behaviour is also group-specific. With (B3) the influence of the predictors on the major dependent variables such as choice of destination, spending patterns, or word-of-mouth varies over partly known (the 'explicit' case) or unknown (the 'implicit' case) tourist sub-groups.

If the analyst is clever and lucky enough to rely on a well-corroborated theory he will be able to identify (some of) the crucial sources of cause-effect heterogeneity. Travel experience or loyalty to a destination are typical examples of very powerful sources of cause-effect heterogeneity. The same amount of disappointment experienced in a service encounter leads to fairly different reactions of a first-time visitor compared to a repeat visitor or a highly loyal guest. Besides the well-known pathways of tourist behaviour theory, however, the number and the size of heterogeneous cause-effect sub-groups is unknown and must be inferred from the data. Over the last decade a number of analytical tools have been developed to uncover heterogeneity in cause-effect relationships. Merging the classical concepts of latent class analysis with multidimensional scaling or unfolding techniques has generated new segmentation instruments in marketing science. Generalized linear models have been elaborated to respect heterogeneity leading to random coefficient and mixture regression modelling (Fahrmeir and Tutz, 1994; Wedel and DeSarbo, 1994; Wedel and Kamakura, 1998). A second-generation structural equation modelling instrument has also been developed in psychometric research (Muthén, 1984; Muthén, 1998; Muthén and Muthén, 1998). To avoid the distributional assumptions required in these parametric approaches radically new ideas of nonparametric (adaptive, data-driven) methodology emerged recently (Mazanec and Strasser, 2000). The next section is going to demonstrate the detection of explicit heterogeneity. It will outline the consequences of ignoring heterogeneous cause-effect relationships and discuss the danger of arriving at erroneous conclusions. Empirical examples for the analysis of tourist service quality and destination choice will be presented.

Capturing Explicit Heterogeneity – an Example for Loyalty as a Moderator

Imagine an ordinary model which relates direct measures of trip satisfaction to perceived service quality (PSQ). PSQ is split into a service part called 'compositional' quality and a 'value-for-money' part. Both latent constructs are multidimensional and assumed to induce tourists to make favourable statements about their overall degree of satisfaction. Considering the criticisms brought forward against the 'disconfirmation' approach (Fick and Ritchie, 1991; Buttle, 1995; Ryan, 1995, pp. 88-95) a performance-based 'after-only' measurement design was adopted for this study of visitors to Austria during the 1997/98 winter season. To capture the evaluative aspects the measuring instrument asked the tourist about the extent to which his or her expectations have been met. The ratings on a number of 'quality performance' criteria build a compositional measure which should correlate significantly with overall and direct (unidimensional) indicators of satisfaction.

The tourists' performance judgments relate to what is offered and to how much one has to pay. Therefore, the expectations about the level of prices are included. Seventeen items described the fulfilment of expectations by a leisure trip to an Austrian winter resort ('exceeded', 'met', 'not met my expectations'). After excluding the city travellers[1] 2,900 respondents remained in the winter sample of the Austrian National Guest Survey 1997/98. They commented on

- landscape,
- picturesqueness of the resort,
- peace and quite,
- furnishing and pleasantness of the accommodation,
- service in the accommodation,
- cuisine and catering,
- friendliness of the staff in restaurants and inns,
- friendliness of the locals,
- entertainment facilities,
- shopping facilities,
- opening hours of shops,
- walking and hiking paths,
- offerings for families with children,
- cleanliness of the resort,
- quality of the skiing runways,
- comfort of the lifts and cable ways,
- waiting time and queuing for the ski lifts.

These 17 observational variables made up the aggregate latent construct termed the 'compositional perceived quality'.

Four consumption items were thought to be indicative of how the winter tourists perceive the fairness of prices. Respondents compared their price expectations and experiences again in four categories, i.e. for

- drinks,
- meals,
- accommodation, and
- ski lifts.

The attitudinal variable named 'value for money' resulted from these four judgements. It was hypothesized that the 'compositional perceived quality' in conjunction with the 'value-for-money' builds the 'overall satisfaction' indicated by a 'lump' judgment of general performance (with three categories), a direct question about satisfaction (a five-point rating scale), and the willingness to recommend Austria to a friend (a six-point rating scale).

The popular software packages such as LISREL make structural equation modelling (SEM) an easy and straightforward exercise. This is tempting and, therefore, many applications ignore the rigorous distributional assumptions (see Baumgartner and Homburg, 1996). Given the qualitative variables prevailing in tourist behaviour analysis a second-generation SEM is preferred. Bengt and Linda Muthén's *Mplus* (1998) system is used here to account for the properties of the data. (1) A guest survey normally must employ a disproportional sampling procedure as the distribution of the visitor nations in the tourist population is heavily skewed. On the other hand, a minimum number of respondents is required to warrant conclusions about the individual countries of origin. *Mplus* accepts a weighting factor to correct the proportions in the master sample. (2) The service quality indicators being categorical variables are inadequate for assuming multivariate normality. *Mplus* overcomes this deficiency by replacing each three-categorical observational measure y by a continuous latent variable y^* where two threshold parameters t_1 and t_2 (to be estimated from the data) govern the translation into the observed categories $c=0,...,2$:

$$y=c \quad if \ t_c < y^* \le t_{c+1}, \quad c=0,1,2, \quad t_0=-\infty, \ t_3=\infty.$$

(3) Muthén's robust (mean and variance-adjusted) weighted least squares estimator replaces the maximum likelihood estimation which is unfeasible due to non-normality.

Figure 1 exhibits the structural part of the simple quality-satisfaction model. The diagram shows the three continuous latent variables and some selected observables. The 'overall satisfaction' is measured with three indicators: (1) a categorical variable stating the respondent's perceived degree of global fulfilment of trip expectations, (2) a five-points 'smiling faces' scale expressing overall satisfaction in a nonverbal manner, and (3) the respondent's stated propensity to recommend the winter destination Austria to a friend. The two composite measures i.e. perceived quality and value-for-money, explain 44% of the variance of the overall satisfaction construct. All coefficients in the structural and measurement sub-models are highly significant with an estimate/standard-error ratio ranging between 16.1 and 76.5 (the values in parentheses accompanying the parameter estimates). The parameters shown are standardized with respect to the variances of the latent variables. Quality perceptions are more influential than the price level judgments. This is in accordance with the results of another empirical investigation of the relative influence of quality versus price gained from an European non-guest sample in 1995 (Mazanec, 1997; Davies *et al.*, 1999). As fine as these results appear to be, they are misleading if one starts extrapolating them indiscriminately to the total guest population. Some decent amount of unobserved heterogeneity may be made explicit by accounting for an elementary moderator variable such as guest loyalty[2].

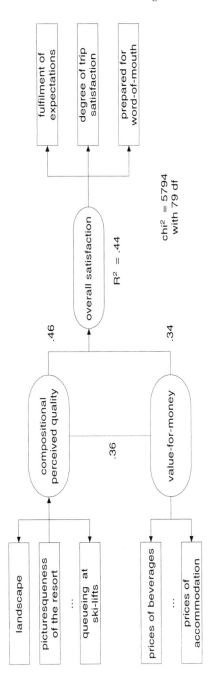

Figure 1 Perceived quality and satisfaction

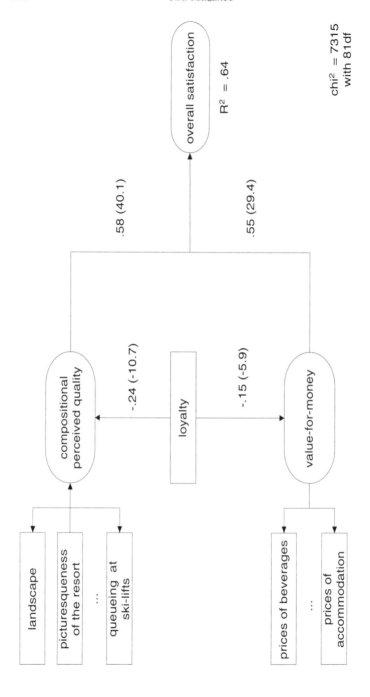

Figure 2 Building overall satisfaction with loyalty-mediated perceived quality

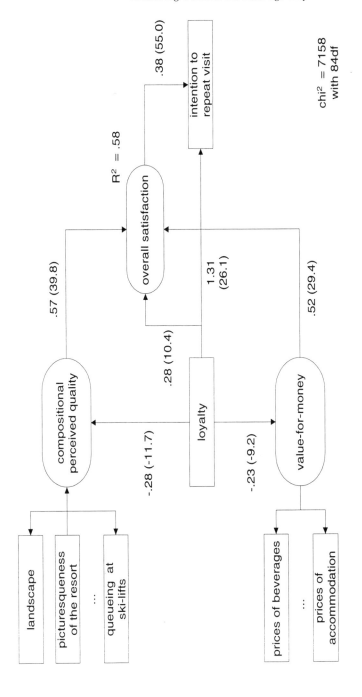

Figure 3 The loyalty-mediated explanation of the intention to repeat visit

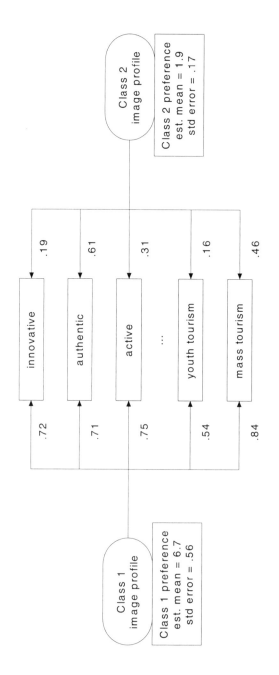

Figure 4 The Vienna city image in two latent classes

Figure 2 incorporates loyalty as an exogenous variable. Loyalty is expected to influence the interplay between the latent variables, i.e. tourists' quality and price perceptions, the overall satisfaction judgements, and also the intention to repeat visitation. If one assumes that loyalty even acts upon the measurement sub-models, additional relationships can be introduced between loyalty and the quality/value-for-money/satisfaction indicators. This is customary in MIMIC modelling (multiple causes, multiple indicators) to capture across-group heterogeneity in measurement intercepts (Muthén, 1989). To underline the loyalty mediation the two sub-groups of first-time visitors versus second-time repeat visitors were selected. The smallest group of first-time repeaters was excluded. A moderator effect of loyalty which is sometimes amazing for practitioners and tourist marketers now becomes clearly visible. The loyal and experienced guests are more critical than the first-time visitors and express a lot of disappointment. The 'compositional quality perceptions' as well as the 'value-for-money' judgment receives a negative impact from the loyalty variable. Without a direct relationship between loyalty and overall satisfaction the variance explained of the satisfaction construct increases to 64%. The question now is if the repeaters tend not to change their travel habits and continue to patronize the old places despite their criticism. Also, the first-time visitors may be more strongly motivated by variety-seeking and, therefore, less loyalty-prone or inclined to repeat visitation.

Figure 3 complements the picture by introducing repeat visitation into the causal chain. It is measured by the respondent's stated intention to return to the same resort within the next three years giving a qualitative variable with four ordered categories. The perceived quality–satisfaction substructure does not change much, though a direct influence of loyalty on satisfaction is also permitted. As a very distinct result, the satisfaction impact is far smaller (.38 with an estimate/std error-ratio of 55.0) than the influence of the loyalty pattern (1.31; 26.1).[3] Uncovering more of the unobserved heterogeneity is equivalent to expanding the structural system. Additional moderator variables other than loyalty are likely to disturb the link between satisfaction and repeat visitation. Consider psychographics such as purpose of trip, product comprehension, vacation style, or activity and spending patterns.

Implicit Heterogeneity – an Example for Perceptions-Based Preference

How do you proceed if there is no theoretical guidance regarding further moderator variables to capture heterogeneity? Consider an example from city tourism. During the 1997 summer season visitors to Vienna were asked to attribute various image criteria to this destination and at the same time to their 'ideal' city they had long desired to travel to. (Budapest and Prague were also analysed, but this is for the next step.) Suppose there is no prior indication of some obvious grouping in the data. Thus a finite mixture model seems to be appropriate to search for differences in the image formation process. 'Response-based' heterogeneity is involved as the number of matching attributes of the 'real' and the 'ideal' city images are indicative of the tourists' height of preference for the destination. Note that the image attributes are binary ('fit', 'don't fit') and, therefore, make a perfect raw material for latent class analysis (LCA). The structural equation modelling framework recently has been extended to incorporate LCA via categorical latent variables (Muthén, 1998).

The 20 image criteria are the observational class indicators. Figure 4 outlines the case of two latent classes meaning that the Vienna city image emerges in two different setups. The image attributes are binary variables in a logistic regression on the latent classes. The number of matches between the Vienna and the 'ideal' city profiles serves as a measure for preference. Consequently, two separate values are estimated for the height of preference in the two latent groups of tourists with a distinct image profile each (Table 1).

Table 1 City Image Attributes in Two Latent Classes (in probability scale)

image items	class 1	class 2
innovative	.72	.19
authentic	.71	.61
active	75	.31
quiet	.44	.42
modern	.45	.34
old-fashioned	.52	.32
exciting	.54	.18
exclusive	.75	.41
expensive	.75	.58
relaxing	.55	.34
nostalgic	.87	.66
friendly	.88	.56
extraordinary	.48	.18
up-to-date	.55	.24
secure	.95	.78
popular	.94	.70
unique	.76	.23
for senior travellers	.71	.42
for the youth	.54	.16
mass tourism	.84	.46
av. height of pref.	6.7	1.9
class size	46%	54%

Class 1 visitors exhibit a significantly higher preference of 6.7 (std. error = .56) than class 2 visitors (1.9; std. error = .17). Comparing the probability values for the class indicators assists in judging which image criteria are more crucial than others in building preferences. (Increasing the number of classes to three leads to a negligible drop in the sample-size adjusted BIC information criterion and a third class does not capture more than 8.4% of the cases.) Figure 5 shows the discretized bivariate distribution of the posterior probabilities denoting class membership corresponding to a fuzzy clustering. The reader easily verifies that the two classes are fairly well separated.

Three potential *a priori* segmentation criteria have been examined regarding their correlation with the posterior probabilities for classes 1 and 2: frequency of past visits, intention to re-visit, and nationality. There is no association with past behaviour. Only the strongest intensity of the intention to repeat visit is over-represented among class 1 tourists. Swiss, Dutch, Belgians, and, particularly, Italians are over-represented among class 2 visitors; Americans and British are biased in favour of class 1 image profiles. There is no 'theory' or prior knowledge which might have predicted these findings.

Recognizing that a fair amount of heterogeneity prevails in the one-city profiles, how should one deal with the joint database of the three-cities? Repeated measurements must now be taken into account for Budapest, Prague, and Vienna[4]. Latent class analysis with a second-generation structural equation model allows for more flexibility, as the latent classes may be considered to be dependent variables in a multinomial regression on exogenous factors x_i. If three 0-1 dummy variables x_1, x_2 and x_3 account for the fact that each respondent rated three cities, only two are needed in the analysis. Figure 6 exhibits again a solution for two latent classes. (The decrease in the information measure for three classes is negligible (the sample adjusted BIC = 36954) and a fourth class would only capture 4% of the respondents.) The average height of preference recorded for the class 1 city profiles is four times the value for the class 2 profiles. All coefficients are in logit scale. The class indicators (except #3, #6, and #8 for class 1) and the coefficients differentiating the Budapest base profile from the Prague and Vienna image profiles are statistically significant (p < .05). The city impact factor for Vienna (x_3) raises the (logit) value for the high-preference class 1 almost ten times as much as x_2 does for Prague. While Budapest and Prague do not differ much, Vienna is more likely to generate high-preference image profiles. 45% of all city profiles are associated with the high-preference class, 55% are of the low-preference type.

Though the latent class analysis uncovers two distinctly different levels of the height of preference for the city image profiles, it cannot be considered a 'response-based' market segmentation. It is true that the latent class variable with its two values is responsible for generating two different image profiles. The image criteria, however, do not influence the height of preference in a direct and class-specific manner. A mixture regression model is appropriate if the analyst assumes that the sample of city travellers is heterogeneous in terms of image criteria leading to weak or strong preference for an urban destination. In this case the 20 image items x_{i1k}, x_{i2k},...x_{i20k} attributed to Budapest, Prague, and Vienna ($k=1,2,3$) by respondent i from the latent segment s are repeated measurements in a preference (y_{ik}) building process such as

$$y_{iks} \approx \hat{y}_{iks} = \sum_{j=1}^{20} \beta_{js} x_{ijk} + \beta_{0s} .$$

For each unknown segment s these linear predictors are equivalent to the means μ_{sk} of assumed normal distributions of the y_{ik}. With the parameter vectors $\beta_s = (\beta_{s0},...,\beta_{s20})$, the mixture proportions π_s, and σ_s denoting the variance of the y-observations in segment s the preference values are then distributed according to

$$f(\mathbf{y}_i \mid \pi,\beta,\sigma) = \sum_{s=1}^{S} \pi_s f_s (\mathbf{y}_i \mid \beta_s,\sigma_s).$$

A maximum likelihood estimation of the parameters may be obtained by the EM algorithm, where a tentative number of latent segments must be pre-specified (Wedel and Kamakura, 1998, 107ff.; Wedel, 1997). The city data are not perfectly suited for demonstrating the mixture regression approach, as the dependent preference variable lacks a normal distribution. The advantage of comparing with the results presented earlier, however, justifies this attempt relying on the robustness of the EM estimates. The information and goodness-of-fit criteria suggest three latent preference-building segments.[5] Figure 7 portrays the model specification. The image attributes contribute to building preference, but the pattern of this contribution varies by segments 1 to 3.

Table 2 lists all the regression parameters. Only two of the segment 1, seven of the segment 3, but almost all of the segment 2 coefficients are not significant on $p<.05$. Segment 1 members value an image of authenticity and uniqueness; segment 2 tourists seek activity and popularity not adequately delivered by the three cities under consideration; segment 3 seek the extraordinary, activity and excitement when forming a preference calibrated against their 'ideal' urban destination.

Table 2 The Effect of City Image Attributes on City Preference in a Mixture Regression for Three Segments

image items	segment 1	segment 2	segment 3
innovative	.52	-.04	.54
authentic	1.15	.25	.35
active	.61	.42	.94
quiet	-.07	-.16	-.17
modern	.37	-.07	-.02
old-fashioned	1.12	.05	.02
exciting	1.10	.26	.68
exclusive	.51	-.09	.38
expensive	.44	-.14	.06
relaxing	.82	.12	.05
nostalgic	1.08	.08	.48
friendly	.30	.04	.23
extraordinary	.44	.15	1.09
up-to-date	.64	.00	.42
secure	.27	.05	.03
popular	.69	.61	.85
unique	1.25	.11	.72
for senior travellers	.72	.07	.30
for the youth	.93	.24	.28
mass tourism	.58	-.19	.64
intercept	-.06	.05	.06
segment size	27%	35%	38%

The respondents may be classified by using the posterior probabilities of segment membership. The segments are well separated. Figure 8 exhibits the discretized distribution of the posterior probabilities for segments 1 and 2; where both segments 1 and 2 have close to zero values segment 3 (not shown) has the highest membership probabilities. Again, the membership in a 'preference-building' segment is uncorrelated with the number of previous stays in Vienna as well as with the intention to repeat visit. Travellers from the US are over-represented in segment 1, Italians and French are under-represented. Domestic travellers exceed their fair proportion in segment 3 considerably. For some other countries of origin the sample size is too small to further pursue the association between preference-building and nationality.

While in Figure 6 the city represented an 'experimental' factor with a separate influence on the latent class variable–and thus indirectly on the height of preference measured for this class–the mixture regression in Figure 7 yields three segment-specific sets of coefficients which are the same for each city. Given a unique image profile x_{ks} for a city, however, also makes the ensuing height of preference differ from the less distinct destinations. Budapest and Prague exhibit a similar preference pattern which contrasts highly with the Vienna results.

Table 3 Height of Preference by Cities and Segments

Segment	Mean height of preference for ...		
#	Budapest	Prague	Vienna
1	4.45	4.99	8.43
2	.52	.57	.86
3	2.03	2.11	4.23
average	2.12	2.30	4.12

To sum up, there are at least two markedly distinct patterns of how tourists built preferences by judging the three urban destination images. These patterns could be uncovered by tackling the heterogeneity in the sample, even without any prior hypotheses about moderators of tourist information processing or decision styles. One must admit, however, that tourist behaviour research so far has not done more than scratched the surface of heterogeneity phenomena. The analyst becomes rather helpless if model and parameter heterogeneity are interwoven in a data-set. If, for example, the nice linearity assumption in the preference-building ('utility') function does not hold and an unknown but substantial portion of tourists follow a non-compensatory cognitive algebra, the analytical output may get out of control. There are no other remedies than the principles of scientific pluralism and a portfolio of rivalling theories, models and methods.

Endnotes

[1] Actually, this step also corresponds to a 'theory-guided' but rather crude measure of avoiding heterogeneity in one's data base.

[2] This is loyalty vis-à-vis an individual destination. Only recently multiple destination loyalty has been picked up by tourism analysts (see Baloglu and Erickson, 1998a, the commentary by the late Martin Oppermann, 1998, and the rejoinder by Baloglu and Erickson, 1998b).

[3] It might be mentioned here that the same effect has been proven with a completely different methodology based on combining topology-sensitive vector quantization with conventional contingency tabulation (Mazanec, 1996).

[4] Readers interested in a nonparametric version of this 'tale of three cities' are referred to Dolnicar, Grabler and Mazanec (1999).

[5] The BIC decreases from 4467 (2 segments) to 4239 (3 segments) and only 4215 (4 segments); the corresponding R^2 values are .82, .91, and .92.

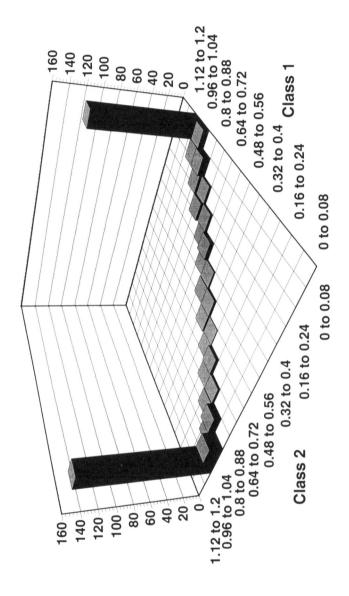

Figure 5 Bivariate distribution of the class membership probabilities

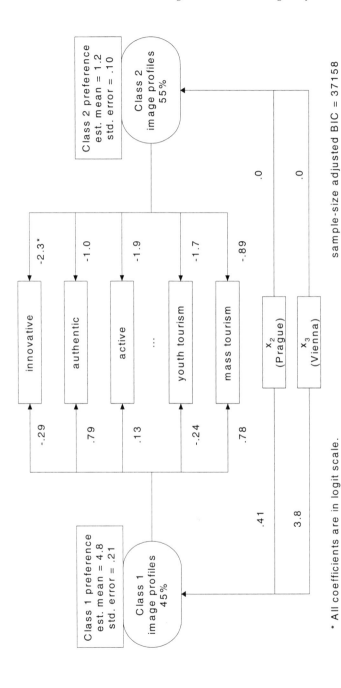

sample-size adjusted BIC = 37158

* All coefficients are in logit scale.

Figure 6 Image profiles with two latent classes and a city effect

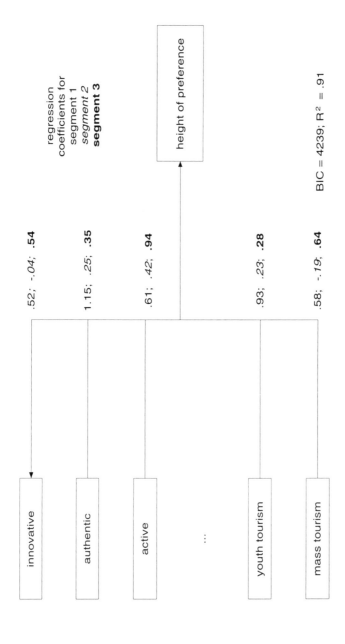

Figure 7 Mixture regression of city preference on image attributes (with three unobserved segments)

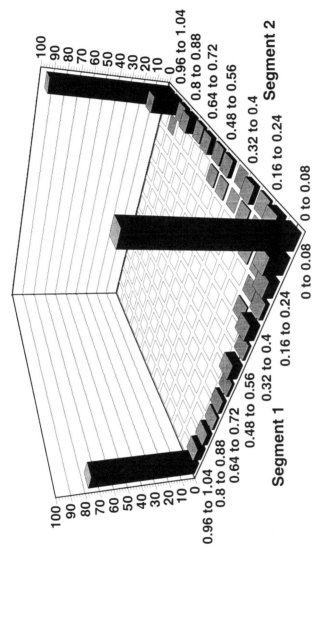

Figure 8 Distribution of the membership probabilities for segments 1 and 2

References

Baloglu, S. and Erickson, R.E. (1998a) Destination Loyalty and Switching Behavior of Travelers: A Markov Analysis. *Tourism Analysis* 2(2), 119-127.

Baloglu, S. and Erickson, R.E. (1998b) Destination Loyalty and Switching Behavior of Travelers Revisited. *Tourism Analysis* 3(2), 117-118.

Baumgartner, H. and Homburg, Chr. (1996) Applications of Structural Equation Modeling in Marketing and Consumer Research: A Review. *International Journal of Research in Marketing* 13, 139-161.

Buttle, F.A. (1995) What Future for SERVQUAL? In: 24th EMAC Conference Proceedings, vol. I. ESSEC, Cergy-Pontoise Cedex, pp. 211-30.

Davies, F.M., Goode, M., Mazanec, J.A. and Moutinho, L. (1999) LISREL and Neural Network Modelling: Two Comparison Studies. *Journal of Retailing and Consumer Services. Special Issue on Marketing Applications of Neural Networks* 6(4), 249-261.

Dolnicar, S. and Mazanec, J.A. (2000) Holiday Styles and Tourist Types: Emerging New Concepts and Methodology. In: Gartner, W.C. and Lime, D.W. (eds.) *Trends in Outdoor Recreation, Leisure and Tourism*. CAB International, Wallingford, pp. 245-255.

Dolnicar, S., Grabler, K. and Mazanec, J.A. (1999) A Tale of Three Cities: Perceptual Charting for Analyzing Destination Images. In: Woodside, A.G., Crouch, G.I., Mazanec, J.A., Oppermann, M. and Sakai, M.Y. (eds.) *Consumer Psychology of Tourism, Hospitality and Leisure*. CAB International, Wallingford, pp. 39-62.

Fahrmeir, L. and Tutz, G. (1994) *Multivariate Statistical Modelling Based on Generalized Linear Models*. Springer, New York.

Fick, G.R. and Ritchie, J.R.B. (1991) Measuring Service Quality in the Travel and Tourism Industry. *Journal of Travel Research* 29, 2-9.

Jain, D.C., Vilcassim, N.J. and Chintagunta, P.K. (1994) A Random-Coefficients Logit Brand-Choice Model Applied to Panel Data. *Journal of Business and Economic Statistics* 12(3), 317-328.

Jedidi, K., Jagpal, H.S. and DeSarbo, W.S. (1997) Finite-Mixture Structural Equation Models for Response-Based Segmentation and Unobserved Heterogeneity. *Marketing Science* 16(1), 39-59.

Mazanec, J.A. (1978) *Strukturmodelle des Konsumverhaltens*. Orac, Vienna.

Mazanec, J.A. (1996) Guest Satisfaction Tracking: Eine Analyse am Beispiel der Sommerurlauber in Österreich. In: Fischer, G. and Laesser, Ch. (eds.) *Theorie und Praxis der Tourismus- und Verkehrswirtschaft im Wertewandel*. Haupt, Bern, pp. 97-115.

Mazanec, J.A. (1997) Preisniveau oder Angebotsqualität? Ursachenanalyse der Attraktivitätseinbuße Österreichs als Sommerurlaubsland. *Wirtschaftspolitische Blätter*, nr. 2, 1-9.

Mazanec, J.A. and Strasser, H. (2000) *A Nonparametric Approach to Perceptions-Based Market Segmentation*. Vol. I: Foundations, Springer, Vienna.

Muthén, B.O. (1984) A General Structural Equation Model with Dichotomous, Ordered Categorical, and Continuous Latent Variables. *Psychometrika* 49(1), 115-132.

Muthén, B.O. (1989) Latent Variable Modeling in Heterogeneous Populations. *Psychometrika* 54(4), 557-585.

Muthén, B. (1998) Second-Generation Structural Equation Modeling with a Combination of Categorical and Continuous Latent Variables: New Opportunities for Latent Class/Latent Growth Modeling. Forthcoming in: Sayer, A. and Collins, L. (eds.) *New Methods for the Analysis of Change.* APA, Washington.

Muthén, L.K. and Muthén, B.O. (1998) *Mplus, User's Guide.* Muthén and Muthén, Los Angeles.

Oppermann, M. (1998) Destination Loyalty and Switching Behavior of Travelers Revisited. *Tourism Analysis* 3(2), 115-116.

Ryan, Ch. (1995) *Researching Tourist Satisfaction: Issues, Concepts, Problems.* Routledge, London.

Wedel, M. (1997) *GLIMMIX User's Manual.* ProGamma, Groningen.

Wedel, M. and DeSarbo, W.S. (1994) A Review of Recent Developments in Latent Class Regression Models. In: Bagozzi, R. (ed.) *Advanced Methods of Marketing Research.* Blackwell, Cambridge, pp. 352-381.

Wedel, M. and Kamakura, W.A. (1998) *Market Segmentation, Conceptual and Methodological Foundations.* Kluwer Academic Publishers, Boston.

Chapter seventeen
The Consumption of Tour Routes in Cultural Landscapes

Tove Oliver
Centre for Tourism and Visitor Management
Nottingham Business School
Burton Street
The Nottingham Trent University
Nottingham NG5 2DT, UK

Introduction

The paper reviews a number of interrelated topics that are relevant to the study of tourists' experiences of cultural landscapes through the medium of the organized tour. The aim is to examine these, with the specific objective of identifying fruitful directions for future research in this area. Additionally, it poses that the cultural landscapes of tourist consumption are socially constructed, as they continually acquire new meanings for tourists as well as local inhabitants. The value of the latter group has been explored, particularly with regard to managing cultural destinations, while tourists' contributions have been largely ignored (Ringer, 1998a). In fact, meaningful interactions between tourists and their destinations are often assumed to be minimal, the organized tour in particular having been compared to 'a bubble', in the sense that it isolates tourists from their external environments, and integrates them into the social environment of the tour (Schmidt, 1979; Schuchat, 1983; Quiroga, 1990). The tour itinerary consists of activities and experiences that are fixed in time and space (Dann, 1999). Seeking and acquiring knowledge about the tour destination by way of a set itinerary is of critical importance to the levels of satisfaction experienced by cultural tour members (Dunn-Ross and Iso-Ahola, 1991). However, empirical information about the degree to which this requirement is satisfied is almost absent, as most tour evaluations have focused on service encounters in preference to the actual process of consumption. The concept of destination image, its formation and measurement, has been principally used as a marketing tool to influence consumer behaviour. While it can be used to identify environmental preferences (MacKay and Fesenmaier, 1997), and therefore has particular relevance in this review, the investigation of tourists' understanding of transient destination images makes the concern one of environmental cognition. 'Route mapping', an approach developed in this area, is considered to have specific application here and therefore it is explored in some depth (Pearce, 1981; Spencer *et al.*, 1989).

Organizing Tourist Space and Consuming Culture

'If there is one dominant and recurrent image in the annals of the modern tour, it
is surely that of the beaten track, which succinctly designates the space of the
"touristic" as a region in which experience is predictable and repetitive, all
cultures and objects mere "touristy" self-parodies'.   (Buzard, 1993, p. 4)

'Tourists visit the signified vantage points of designated places, realising that
there is nothing in between. They are transported to a destination through the
periphery to the center and, in the very act of being carried, they reject travel. For
them, it is a meaningless exercise to gaze out of a vehicular window, since there is
only emptiness to behold. Instead, tourists chatter, read their guidebooks, or else
simply fall asleep through boredom. As mob-ile, tourists constitute a sense-less
mob'.   (Dann, 1999, p. 168)

Contrary to the above, somewhat stereotypical images of the organized tour, tourism is
an important medium by which meanings are given to the spatial contexts of travel
(Hughes, 1998). Such meanings may change as tour itineraries form well-trodden routes
and bring less existential forms of travel (Cohen, 1979). There is no question that as
places become embedded in the dialogue of tourist consumption their existing cultural
and physical characters are reshaped (Hughes, 1998). However, almost since the
inception of modern, organized tourism, the extent to which these consumed places and
cultures are authentic and meaningful has been disputed, for as tourist 'sights' their
descriptions may deny the depths of their cultural and political origins (*ibid;*
MacCannell, 1973). The risks involved in presenting heritage to international tourists
seem especially great, for, as Boniface and Fowler (1993) point out, such interpretations
can homogenize and corrupt culture. Boorstin, an early and influential writer on the
subject, denounced the ubiquity of tourism for the masses as an example of the
adaptation of 'real experiences' into superficial 'pseudo events':

'All over the world now we find these "attractions" – of little significance for the
inward life of a people, but wonderfully saleable as a tourist commodity'.
                                                                    (Boorstin, 1964, p. 103)

The idea that culture is consumed by tourists 'drenched by commodity fetishism'
has frequently been articulated by observers of tourist behaviour (Selwyn, 1996b, p. 15).
In particular, the 'commoditization' of social and ritual events was originally thought to
lead to an erosion of their cultural meaning (Greenwood, 1978).

In contrast to this, Cohen has argued that cultural productions for tourists may in
fact 'acquire new meanings' that supplement more traditional values (Cohen, 1988, p.
383). Earlier, MacCannell (1976) had viewed the tourism attraction as being imbued
with meaning specifically through tourist consumption. Richards (1996, p. 263) takes
this further arguing that tourism has become 'one of the most powerful modern
traditions' where attractions are themselves pivotal cultural experiences. Urry (1994)
states that tourism is culture, and in the new culture of tourism, areas such as theme

parks, heritage attractions, and literary landscapes, have been specially designed to assist tourists in their search for meaning (Richards, 1996). Other writers have acknowledged that tourists on organized tours can express interest in many dimensions of their host cultures and societies, even adopting certain behaviours, such as enacting traditional rituals, in their attempts to experience culture directly (see Selwyn, 1996b, p. 14-15). Increasingly sophisticated tourist expectations are clearly emerging in the cultural segment of the organized tours markets (Hughes, 1991). Not only is the concept of culture as commodity itself complex, but in the past it seems frequently to have been inextricably linked to researchers' own consumer milieus (Selwyn, 1996b).

Recently Prentice has attempted to conceptualize the consumption of cultural tourism as 'a process of co-operation between facilitators (for example, tour operators) and consumers (tourists)' (Prentice, 1999, p. 1). To be useful in theoretical and practical settings, he stresses the need for the simultaneous requirement of both etic and emic approaches (the most common definition for these being the 'outsider' versus 'insider' view, Headland, 1999), thus linking academic discourse to the perceived realities of tourists (Prentice, 1999). There is a need for empirical studies that dissect the process of cultural consumption by tourists in their settings, specifically those that bring the tourist as the consumer sharply into focus (Selwyn, 1996a).

Destination image

The image of a tourist destination is the collective sum of a tourist's beliefs, ideas, impressions, and expectations (Crompton, 1979). Tourists may perceive many images, and these can in turn influence their behaviour as consumers (Ahmed, 1996). Image marketing therefore can alter behaviour, first-time visitors usually responding to more generalized images than those with a greater experience of a destination (*ibid*; Schreyer *et al.*, 1984) who develop more complex associations (MacKay and Fesenmaier, 1997). The components of destinations that make up their overall image are thought of as tourism products for marketing purposes, but tourist destinations are also subjectively valued cultural landscapes that are created by their inhabitants and by visitors (Ringer, 1998b). It is thought that the consumption experience of these landscapes can be significantly influenced, not only by the nature of the consumers thought likely to patronize them, but also by interactions of the other consumers present (Ahmed, 1996; Oliver, 2000).

The consumption of destinations produces images that are based on the tangible components of these environments as well as service encounters and atmosphere. These images strongly influence tourists' perceptions of quality and value (Murphy *et al.*, 2000). Evaluating tourists' perceptions of these environmental elements is fundamental to understanding the formation of their destination images and can powerfully predict preference (MacKay and Fesenmaier, 1997). An individual's cognitive and affective images derived from information sources about destinations, and coupled with their socio-psychological motivations to travel, appear to a great extent, to form their actual intention to visit (Baloglu, 1999).

The cultural landscape of the tourist destination can convey powerful historical and geographical images (Ringer, 1998b). In discourse addressing the 'Disneyfication' of tourism landscapes, writers have advocated the need for the identification and a respect for such places, arguing that 'improved knowledge of the nature of place can contribute to the maintenance and manipulation of existing places and the creation of new places' (Relph, 1976, p. 44). As Ringer (1998b) argues, this requires that the destination be understood in terms of personal experience, as well as attractiveness, claiming that recognition of the socially constructed destination helps to clarify the individualized landscapes of tradition and subjective attachment perceived by people (*ibid*).

> 'Through such representations, a wealth of social and psychological information, both informed and sensed, is revealed regarding the destination as attraction and habitat, and the emotional degree to which that space is individually humanised through direct experience and intimacy'.   (*ibid,* pp. 5-6)

Conway and Ruddy (1999) take the idea a stage further, emphasizing that while the components of an image are frequently used in tourism product positioning strategies, the tourists themselves do not visit a place with a set of objective destination features, but instead select activities and experiences to fulfil highly subjective needs.

The destination bubble

Closely linked to the concept of destination image is the study of consumer behaviour. This is frequently defined as a process including activities directly involved in obtaining, consuming and disposing of products and services (Moutinho, 1987; Mowen, 1995). When applied to tourism, the central part of this process is the directly experiencing a destination or multiple destinations, and likely to provide the bulk of the tour experience (Hanefors and Larsson-Mossberg, 1998). Many studies have used the analogy of a tourist or environmental 'bubble' to describe this temporal and spatial span in the consumption process (Hanefors and Larsson-Mossberg, 1998). Despite this, there is no consensus as to what is actually meant by the notion, nor whether it can in some way be defined in spatial terms. Smith (1978, p. 6) describes it as a means of fulfilling 'social needs ... thereby creating their own reality – their "tourist bubble" – of being physically "in" a foreign place but socially "outside" the culture'. Cohen suggests the bubble is an all-embracing 'tourist space'; Dumazedier refers it as a region that is '..."cooked" up solely for the benefits of tourists'; while Sampson discusses what happens there by referring to 'the cruise liner effect'; Farrel calls it an, 'enclave of familiarity' (see Hanefors and Larsson-Mossberg, 1998, p. 151); and according to Graburn (1978, p. 31) this tourist enclave is a 'home-grown "bubble" of their [the tourists'] life style'; it gives people the confidence to travel (Hudson, 1999). It appears that the destination bubble therefore, is meant to convey the sense of physical and cultural isolation, as well as the way in which tourists create meaning through their social integration to the tour group (Schmidt, 1975; Gorman, 1979; Hanefors and Larsson-Mossberg, 1998). For Hanefors and Larsson Mossberg, the bubble offers tourists almost unlimited opportunities for challenging or changing the norms controlling their everyday life, and this could include assuming a new role or identity. In other words, 'the tourist is anywhere rather than somewhere, articulating his escape motives in a tourist environment – the bubble' (*ibid,* p. 151).

It therefore seems ironic, that in the organized cultural tours segment, often characterized as the epitome of the destination bubble, it is the 'seeking' motive that is usually the most significant in peoples' decisions to travel. Several studies have demonstrated that for participants, the acquisition of knowledge about their destination is more important than any form of social interaction on sightseeing tours (Quiroga, 1990; Dunn-Ross and Iso-Ahola, 1991; Geva and Goldman, 1991; Duke and Persia, 1996).

Tour itineraries are often well established, forming well-worn circuits or 'beaten tracks'. In Europe for example, many can be traced back to the Grand Tour of the 17th and 18th centuries. Although the general subject of destination itineraries is one that is under researched (Dahl, 1999), and sadly left much poorer by the untimely death of one of its main contributors (Oppermann, 2000), it is known that analysis of tour itineraries tends to provide insights into the operators' perception of a destinations' tourism resources and what they consider to be of interest to their market, rather than providing input from customers (Oppermann, 1995). The homogeny of available itineraries requires that tour operators are forced to find their competitive edge in service encounters as it is these that differentiate one service company from another (Hanefors and Larsson-Mossberg, 1998). Therefore, tour personnel are seen as a strategic resource that can be used to fulfil tourists' expectations while they are in their destination bubble (*ibid*). However, this approach is not without its problems, for as Geva and Goldman (1991) have shown, while the success of a tour may be attributed to its personnel, in the minds of participants the companies themselves are not necessarily accredited with the success of a tour.

The cultural tours experience

Whether academic or commercial, most customer-focused tour evaluations have addressed the service aspects of tours in preference to the consumption of the tour route itself, although some writers have included the itinerary as a significant variable for study. An itinerary includes both nodal and more spatially diffuse attractions, such as scenery, positioned in a sequence along a route. In their study of the changes in the perception of organized tours during their consumption, Geva and Goldman (1989) found the itinerary increased in importance. This finding is thought to demonstrate the significance of an individual directly experiencing the tour environment. If this is the case, then using methods by which respondents rate an entire service setting by proxy, such as evaluating a picture in which certain quality variables have been manipulated, seems of limited value when seeking to explain the relationship between tour members and setting (Chadee and Mattsson, 1996).

Duke and Persia (1996) conclude from their study of 'consumer-defined' dimensions of importance in the escorted tours segment, that tour planners should continually improve itineraries as well as ensuring that personal enjoyment aspects, such as social issues, are satisfied. Earlier, in their study of foreign and domestic escorted tour members' expectations, they found that the tour destination and the associated attractions were the most important factors (Duke and Persia, 1994).

While focusing on motivation and satisfaction as central concepts in their study to understand the behaviour of sightseeing tourists, Dunn-Ross and Iso-Ahola (1991) found that knowledge seeking, in particular learning about the history of the destination, in this case Washington DC, was the most significant variable determining behaviour. In their view, the success of the tour itinerary is of critical importance, as it will radiate positive effects to other dimensions, including social interaction (*ibid*).

Given that cultural tour participants tend to seek information, how much of a destination bubble is the environment of an organized tour? Selwyn in his observation of an Israeli walking tour (*tiyoulim*) draws attention to the influence of the guide on tour participants' experiences. In particular, he describes the concept of 'boundary hopping' that is prevalent in the presentation of the countryside, where tours involve a mixture of 'scientific' and 'magical' experiences where 'the traveller is propelled' at great speed, oscillating from one plane to the other (Selwyn, 1996a, pp. 156-157). Weightman (1987) found that the landscape experiences of tourists on package tours of India have little coincidence with the experiential reality of the country, as visitors are isolated and encapsulated in vehicles and hotels. Furthermore, it is noted that the itineraries emphasize monuments from the past, to the exclusion of everyday events and activities of contemporary society. She concludes that tour planners who are genuinely interested in promoting international understanding should design tours which provide 'opportunities for discovering the meaning of landscape and capturing a sense of place' (*ibid*, p. 237).

The increasing demand for customized and special interest tours will eventually lead to a more diversified supply of tour packages worldwide, in an environment that is already highly competitive (Oppermann, 1995). Duke and Persia (1994) suggest that the increasing use of specialized tours may in addition help provide for the apparently conflicting needs of some tour participants' requirements for comfort, security, and adventure. An innovative move towards the inclusion of 'new' attractions may be crucial to secure the future success of many cultural tour operators (Oppermann, 1995). The advancement of a framework with which to explore tour members' experiences of their touring environments and the significance of the destination bubble would greatly assist in this objective.

Route maps

The investigation of tourists' understanding of transient destination images makes the concern one of environmental cognition (Spencer *et al.*, 1989). This field is extremely fertile in methods to elicit both recall and/or recognition of environments, and approaches have highlighted links between environmental legibility and attraction (Lynch, 1960). Cognitive mapping is one of these techniques that has been used to assess tourists' spatial knowledge mainly in relation to urban contexts (Pearce, 1977a; Page, 1997). The utility of the method has been linked to assessing the commercial viability and promotion of attractions, as well as enhancing tourists' way-finding in unfamiliar environments (Walmsley and Jenkins, 1992).

A cognitive sketch map is the instrument by which spatial knowledge can be externalized, and a linear form of this is the strip map. These have been used for many centuries, predominantly to represent routes between a place of origin and destination, and a variety of which was used by the Ancient Egyptians to depict the route the dead would follow to 'the beyond' (*Yaru*) (Bell, 1999, 1). In more recent times, very little work has been done in this area, although the technique has particular utility for rural areas and across extensive tracts of landscape, although works by Pearce (1977b, 1981) and more recently Young (1999), are notable exceptions in the tourism literature. Pearce (1977b) pioneered a modern variation of the strip map technique that he later termed 'route maps' (Pearce, 1981), in his study of American students travelling between London and Oxford. These maps consist of a summary statement of travellers' memories and perceptions and facilitate a more objective approach than the synthesis of aesthetic judgements (Pearce, 1977b). The technique was subsequently used to gain independent tourists' accounts of a touring route in North Queensland (Pearce, 1981). The particular emphasis that subjects gave to specific environmental categories and experiential elements (i.e. landmarks, districts, paths, texture and social activity) appears to form the basis of a route map typology reflecting individuals' different experiences of the same route (*ibid*).

By applying the concept of route maps to touring landscapes, Pearce's main contributions have been to extend studies of the responses of travellers as they move across large-scale environments. These are frequently linked to environmental design and concerned with the patterns and structures of the environment as seen by commuters travelling along highways. For example, Appleyard *et al.* (1964) asked subjects to make rapid sketches of what they perceived as they travelled over designated road sectors. A second frequently quoted study is that of Carr and Schissler (1969) who examined travellers' eye movements and free recall over the same route, and reported considerably less attention to the road itself than Appleyard *et al.* In addition, the amount of time that an object was observed was highly correlated to item recall and the degree of correlation among what different subjects observed was high (*ibid*).

Pearce concluded from his work on route maps that comparative work with organized tours would assist in understanding tourists' 'response to alternative transport strategies' (Pearce 1981, p. 154). The different vantage points usually experienced by tourists travelling independently by car and by those in a coach, would invalidate a study that primarily compares the visual phenomena recalled by these two groups. However, a much better comprehension of tourists' environmental preferences and informal learning associated with their destinations could be obtained by focusing on the organized tours segment. Two studies have begun to explore the relationships between learning in unfamiliar environments and the sources of information used (Beck and Wood, 1976a; Guy *et al.*, 1990) although both assessed escorted tourists in a city, rather than addressing the wider cultural landscape. Despite the advances made by such pioneering works, empirical studies using the technique still face a number of challenges (Walmsley and Jenkins, 1992). Although a full review of these is beyond the scope of this paper, the technique can be used to reveal meanings that are attached to places, and great confidence is placed on the development of mapping 'languages' which can improve communication and expression of environmental experiences (Beck and Wood, 1976b; Wood and Beck, 1976). Combining or 'triangulating' findings from route mapping with those from other research methods, including closed-question survey, observation, diary keeping, and depth-interviews, will help verify the qualitative elements produced by the technique (Beck and Wood, 1976a; Guy *et al.*, 1990; Oliver, forthcoming; see Decrop, 1999). This parallels Echtner and Richie's (1991) recommendation for the combined use of structured and unstructured methodologies, to enable the more complete capture of the components of destination image (*ibid*). The methodological innovations made by Lynch and others over 40 years ago need not be relegated to academic history, as they offer a way forward for the current interest in exploring the relationships between tourists' experiences and their environments (Pearce and Fagence, 1996). The potential that cognitive mapping techniques have for tourism has not been fully realized to date (*ibid*; Hall and Page, 1999; Oppermann, 2000). There is particular scope for application in segments where gaining informal knowledge about a destination is an important part of the experience, such as cultural tours, and where participants may readily engage in cognitive recall after their trip (Oliver, forthcoming). Such behaviour is perhaps less apparent after more extraordinary hedonic experiences (Arnould and Price, 1993).

Conclusions

Cultural tourism is a growth area not least because it can fulfil a range of requirements for diverse markets from those simply taking one or two cultural tours, to those for whom it is a 'serious' hobby (Richards, 1996; Stebbins, 1996). Cultural landscapes are therefore increasingly consumed by tourists. One of the main media for experiencing cultural destinations is the organized tour, and these are often characterized as the epitome of 'the destination bubble'. While the tour itinerary and acquiring knowledge about the destination are of critical importance to cultural tour members, the extent to which tour participants interact and learn about these landscapes and the consumption process itself are little understood. The destination as configured in the tourist's mind differs from that perceived by the tour operator, and a greater emphasis on customer-focused approaches is required to redress the balance in tourism research. The investigation of tourists' understanding of transient destination images makes the concern one of environmental cognition. Route mapping is presented here as an especially relevant approach that can begin to penetrate the 'destination bubble' experienced by tourists, by gaining insight into the degree to which their desire for knowledge about their tour destination is satisfied. It is encouraging to see studies providing renewed vigour to a methodology established almost half a century ago, with the express purpose of addressing contemporary research issues in the consumer psychology of tourism (Young, 1999; Oliver, forthcoming).

References

Ahmed, Z.U. (1996) The need for the identification of the constituents of a destination's tourist image: A promotion segmentation perspective. *Journal of Professional Services Marketing* 14, 37-59.

Appleyard, D., Lynch, K. and Meyer, J.R. (1964) *The View from the Road*. MIT Press, Cambridge, Massachusetts.

Arnould, E.J. and Price, L.L. (1993) River Magic: Extraordinary experience and the extended service encounter. *Consumer Research* 20, 24-45.

Baloglu, S. (1999) A path analytic model of visitation intention involving information sources, socio-psychological motivations, and destination image. *Journal of Travel and Tourism Marketing* 8, 81-90.

Beck, R. and Wood, D. (1976a) Cognitive transformation of information from urban geographic fields to mental maps. *Environment and Behaviour* 8, 199-238.

Beck, R. and Wood, D. (1976b) Comparative developmental analysis of individual and aggregated cognitive maps of London. In: Moore, G. and Golledge, R. (eds.)

Environmental Knowing. John Wiley, New York, pp. 173-184.

Bell, S. (1999) *Cartographic presentation as an aid to spatial knowledge acquisition in unknown environments.* Ph.D thesis, University of California at Santa Barbara, Santa Barbara, USA. Retrieved February 29, 2000 from the World Wide Web: http//www.geo.ucsb.edu/~bell/thesis/chap3.html.

Boniface, P. and Fowler, P.J. (1993) *Heritage and Tourism in 'The Global Village'.* Routledge, London.

Boorstin, D. (1964) *The Image: A Guide to Pseudo-events in America.* Harper and Row, New York.

Buzard, J. (1993) *The Beaten Track: European Tourism, Literature, and the Ways to Culture 1800-1918.* Clarendon Press, Oxford.

Carr, S. and Schissler, D. (1969) Perceptual selection and memory in the view from the road. *Environment and Behaviour* 1, 7-35.

Chadee, D.D. and Mattsson, J. (1996) An empirical assessment of customer satisfaction in tourism. *The Service Industries Journal* 16, 305-320.

Cohen, E. (1979) A phenomenology of tourist experiences. *Sociology* 13, 179-201.

Cohen, E. (1988) Authenticity and commoditisation in tourism. *Annals of Tourism Research* 15, 371-86.

Conway, A. and Ruddy, J. (1999) Consumer behaviour, motives and perceptions when selecting a destination. In: Ruddy, J. (ed.) *Tourism Destination Marketing: Gaining the competitive edge.* The 1999 European Conference of the Travel and Tourism Research Association, 29-30 September and 1-2 October 1999. TTRA, Dublin, pp. 1-9.

Crompton, J.L. (1979) An assessment of the image of Mexico as a vacation destination and the influence of geographical location upon image. *Journal of Travel Research* 17, 18-23.

Dahl, R. (1999) Tracing complex travel behaviour. In: Ruddy, J. (ed.) *Tourism Destination Marketing: Gaining the competitive edge.* The 1999 European Conference of the Travel and Tourism Research Association, 29-30 September and 1-2 October 1999. TTRA, Dublin, pp. 10-16.

Dann, G. (1999) Writing out the tourist in space and time. *Annals of Tourism Research* 26, 159-187.

Decrop, A. (1999) Triangulation in qualitative tourism research. *Tourism Management* 20, 157-161.

Duke, C.R. and Persia, M.A. (1994) Foreign and domestic escorted tour expectations of American travelers. *Journal of International Consumer Marketing* 6, 61-77.

Duke, C.R. and Persia, M.A. (1996) Consumer-defined dimensions for the escorted tour industry segment: expectations, satisfactions, and importance. *Journal of Travel and Tourism Marketing* 5, 77-99.

Dunn-Ross, E.L. and Iso-Ahola, S. (1991) Sightseeing tourists' motivation and satisfaction. *Annals of Tourism Research* 18, 226-237.

Echtner, C.M. and Richie, J.R.B. (1991) The meaning and measurement of destination image. *Journal of Tourism Studies* 2, 2-12.

Geva, A. and Goldman, A. (1989) Changes in the perception of a service during its consumption: the case of organised tours. *European Journal of Marketing* 23, 44-52.

Geva, A. and Goldman, A. (1991) Satisfaction measurement in guided tours. *Annals of*

Tourism Research 18, 177-185.

Gorman, B. (1979) Seven days, five countries. The making of a group. *Urban Life* 7, 469-491.

Graburn, N.H.H. (1978) Tourism: The sacred journey. In: Smith, V.L. (ed.) *Hosts and Guests. The Anthropology of Tourism.* Basil Blackwell, Oxford, pp. 17-31.

Greenwood, D. (1978) Culture by the pound: An anthropological perspective on tourism as cultural commodification. In: Smith, V.L. (ed.) *Hosts and Guests: The Anthropology of Tourism.* Basil Blackwell, Oxford, pp. 129-1.

Guy, B.S., Curtis, W.W. and Crotts, J.C. (1990) Environmental learning of first-time travellers. *Annals of Tourism Research* 17, 419-431.

Hall, C.M. and Page, S.J. (1999) *The Geography of Tourism and Recreation. Environment, Place and Space.* Routledge, London.

Hanefors, M. and Larsson-Mossberg, L. (1998) The tourism and travel consumer. In: Gabbott, M. and Hogg, G. (eds.) *Consumers and Services.* John Wiley and Sons, Chichester, pp. 141-161.

Headland, T.N. (1999) Emics and Etics: The Insider/Outsider Debate, reprinted from Emics and Etics: The Insider/Outsider Debate. In: T.N. Headland, Pike, K.L. and Harris, M. (eds.) Sage Publications, London. Retrieved February 26, 2000 from the World Wide Web:
http://www.sil.org/sil/roster/headland-t/ee-intro.html

Hudson, S. (1999) Consumer behaviour related to tourism. In: Pizam, A. and Mansfeld, Y. (eds.) *Consumer Behaviour in Travel and Tourism.* The Haworth Press, Inc., Binghamton, New York, pp. 7-32.

Hughes, G. (1998) Tourism and the semiological realisation of space. In: Ringer, G. (ed.) *Destinations. Cultural Landscapes of Tourism.* Routledge, London, pp. 17-32.

Hughes, K. (1991) Tourist satisfaction: a guided cultural tour in North Queensland. *Australian Psychologist* 26, 166-171.

Lynch, K. (1960) *Image of the City.* MIT Press, Cambridge, Massachusetts.

MacCannell, D. (1973) Staged authenticity: arrangements of social space in tourist settings. *American Journal of Sociology* 79, 589-603.

MacCannell, D. (1976) *The Tourist: A New Theory of the Leisure Class.* Macmillan, London.

MacKay, K.J. and Fesenmaier, D.R. (1997) Pictorial element of destination in image formation. *Annals of Tourism Research* 24, 537-565.

Moutinho, L. (1987) Consumer behaviour in tourism. *European Journal of Marketing* 21, 5-44.

Mowen, J.C. (1995) *Consumer Behaviour.* Prentice Hall International, Englewood Cliffs, New Jersey.

Murphy, P., Pritchard, M.P., and Smith, B. (2000) The destination product and its impact on traveller perceptions. *Tourism Management* 21, 43-52.

Oliver, T. (2000) Watch this Space: Observing patterns of tourist behaviour on a cultural tour. In: Robinson, M., Long, P., Evans, N., Sharpley, R. and Swarbrooke, J. (eds.) *Motivations, Behaviour and Tourist Types.* Sunderland Business Education Publishers Ltd, pp.321-330.

Oliver, T. (forthcoming) *Altered images? The case of the cultural tour route.* Ph.D thesis, Nottingham Trent University, Nottingham, UK.

Oppermann, M. (1995) Comparative analysis of escorted tour packages in New Zealand and North America. *Progress in Tourism and Hospitality Research* 1, 85-98.

Oppermann, M. (2000) Where psychology and geography interface in tourism research and theory. In: Woodside, A.G., Crouch, G.I., Mazanec, J.A., Oppermann, M. and Sakai, M.Y. (eds.) *Consumer Psychology of Tourism, Hospitality and Leisure.* CAB International, Wallingford, pp. 19-37.

Page, S. (1997) Urban tourism: analysing and evaluating the tourist experience. In: Ryan, C. (ed.) *The Tourism Experience.* Cassel, London/New York, pp. 112-135.

Pearce, P.L. (1977a) Mental souvenirs: a study of tourists and their city maps. *Australian Journal of Psychology* 29, 203-210.

Pearce, P.L. (1977b) *The social and environmental perceptions of overseas tourists.* D.Phil. Thesis, University of Oxford, Oxford, UK.

Pearce, P.L. (1981) Route maps: a study of travellers' perceptions of a section of countryside. *Journal of Environmental Psychology* 1, 141-155.

Pearce, P.L. and Fagence, M. (1996) The legacy of Kevin Lynch. Research implications. *Annals of Tourism Research* 23, 576-598.

Prentice, R. (1999) Conceptualising cultural tourism. In: Ruddy, J. (ed.) *Tourism Destination Marketing: Gaining the Competitive Edge.* The 1999 European Conference of the Travel and Tourism Research Association, 29-30 September and 1-2 October 1999. TTRA, Dublin, pp. 1-23.

Quiroga, I. (1990) Characteristics of package tours in Europe. *Annals of Tourism Research* 17, 185-207.

Relph, E. (1976) *Place and Placelessness.* Pion, London.

Richards, G. (1996) Production and consumption of European cultural tourism. *Annals of Tourism Research* 23, 261-283.

Ringer, G. (ed.) (1998a). *Destinations. Cultural Landscapes of Tourism.* Routledge, London.

Ringer, G. (1998b) Introduction. In: Ringer, G. (ed.) *Destinations. Cultural landscapes of tourism.* Routledge, London, pp. 1-13.

Schmidt, C.J. (1975) The guided tour: insulated adventure. Paper presented at the 6th Annual Conference Proceedings of the Travel Association, UK.

Schmidt, C.J. (1979) The guided tour. Insulated adventure. *Urban Life* 7, 441-67.

Schreyer, R., Lime, D., and Williams, D.R. (1984) Characterizing the influence of past experience on recreation behavior. *Journal of Leisure Research* 16, 34-50.

Schuchat, M. (1983) Comforts of group tours. *Annals of Tourism Research* 10, 465-477.

Selwyn, T. (1996a) Atmospheric notes from the fields: Reflections on myth-collecting tours. In: Selwyn, T. (ed.) *The Tourist Image: Myths and Myth Making in Tourism.* John Wiley and Sons, Chichester, pp. 147-162.

Selwyn, T. (1996b) Introduction. In: Selwyn, T. (ed.) *The Tourist Image. Myths and Myth Making in Tourism.* John Wiley and Sons, Chichester, pp. 1-32.

Smith, V.L. (1978) Introduction. In: Smith, V.L. (ed.) *Hosts and Guests. The Anthropology of Tourism.* Basil Blackwell, Oxford, pp. 1-14.

Spencer, C., Blades, M. and Morsley, K. (1989) *The Child in the Physical Environment. The development of spatial knowledge and cognition.* John Wiley and Sons, Chichester.

Stebbins, R.A. (1996) Cultural tourism as serious leisure. *Annals of Tourism Research* 23, 948-950.

Urry, J. (1994) *The Tourist Gaze. Leisure and travel in contemporary society*. Sage, London.

Walmsley, D.J. and Jenkins, J.M. (1992) Tourism cognitive mapping of unfamiliar environments. *Annals of Tourism Research* 19, 268-286.

Weightman, B.A. (1987) Third world tour landscapes. *Annals of Tourism Research* 14, 227-239.

Young, M. (1999) Cognitive maps of nature-based tourists. *Annals of Tourism Research* 26, 817-839.

Chapter eighteen
Evaluating Heritage Visitor Attractions from the Consumer Perspective: A Focus on Castlefield Urban Heritage Park in Manchester, UK

Peter Schofield
School of Leisure, Hospitality and Food Management
University of Salford
Salford M6 6PU, UK

Introduction

The general aims of a destination's tourism strategy are typically to match the strengths of the place with the market opportunities, to avoid threats from environmental forces, particularly competitive elements, and to remedy any weaknesses in the destination's 'product'. Clearly, the strengths and weaknesses of a destination should be analysed from the consumer perspective, but more often they are determined from a supply-side perspective, that is, from the situational analysts' and/or destination attraction and amenity managers' point of view because of the lack of expertise and/or resources. In some cases, this has resulted in a tendency to emphasize and develop certain aspects of the destination, which are considered to be important from the management perspective. Moreover, these features are often highlighted by the agents responsible for creating and transmitting the 'official' image of the destination whilst other aspects, which may be more relevant to the consumer, are neglected.

Notwithstanding the effect of tourists' 'organic' images of a destination, this 'official' image (Gunn, 1972) is likely to have a significant impact on the tourists' destination choice process. It may also have an important effect on their evaluation of the destination experience because, according to the logic of the expectation-disconfirmation paradigm in consumer research, visitor satisfaction is a function of expectations and disconfirmation, with expectations used as the standard of comparison (Yi, 1990; Chon, 1991). Planners and marketers therefore require information about what is perceived to be important from the consumer perspective. This data will facilitate the determination of their likes and dislikes regarding various features of the destination and/or aspects of their experience (Haywood and Muller, 1988).

Heritage visitor attractions are no exception to this general scenario. Heritage sites and artefacts are important economic resources and capital assets (Edwards, 1989;

Johnson and Thomas, 1990). They are also important motivating factors for educational visits (Thomas, 1989). Moreover, nostalgia has 'lengthened' and 'deepened' to the extent that more mundane 'everyday histories' have become progressively more inclusive both in time and in content (Lowenthal, 1985), which has extended the range of opportunities for tourism product development. The objective of the study was therefore to evaluate, from the consumer perspective, Castlefield Urban Heritage Park, a day-trip destination in the city of Manchester, in order to inform the destination's product development strategy. This involved an examination of the issues of importance in this market from the consumer perspective together with an analysis of visitor perceptions of, and levels of satisfaction with, the destination.

Castlefield Urban Heritage Park

Castlefield, a corruption of 'Castle in the field', a Georgian reference to the remains of a Roman fort constructed to take advantage of the strategic importance of the site, is situated in the south west corner of Manchester at the confluence of the Rivers Medlock and Irwell and occupies an area of approximately 200 acres. From the outset, it has been of major significance in the historic development of the city from its Roman origin as 'Mamucium' ('breast shaped hill') through its industrial evolution to its present regeneration as a post-industrial leisure environment. Following the example of Lowell in Massachusetts, the former textile town designated as an 'urban heritage park' in 1975, Castlefield Urban Heritage Park came into being in 1982 after being given Conservation Area status in 1979. Castlefield Conservation Committee, representing all major organizations and land interests in the area, was also formed in 1982. The object of these declarations was to preserve and interpret the history of the area, to control development and to attract special allocations of funds to make improvements to the area particularly for tourism and recreation. Castlefield is a complex 'product' with an eclectic combination of different architectural styles and features such as Granada Studios Tour, a television theme park, in which the main elements of the core attraction are the 'Coronation Street', 'Downing Street' and 'Baker Street' sets. These inauthentic, media creations are juxtaposed with Castlefield's authentic heritage. This is comprised of the site's architectural and artefactual history in the form of an ancient Roman monument; the country's first 'true cut' canal, completed in 1764; and the world's first passenger railway station which opened in 1830, together with the collections housed within the Greater Manchester Museum of Science and Industry.

The Conceptual Basis of the Study

Given the complexity of tourism destination 'products' (Jefferson and Lickorish, 1988; Gunn, 1988; Middleton, 1994), it is difficult to manage those elements, which contribute to a satisfactory destination experience without identifying, from the consumer perspective, the components of the 'product' and their importance (Echtner and Ritchie, 1993). The initial stage of the study was therefore concerned with the development of a consumer attitude scale with which to examine day-trip destinations; the scale was then used to evaluate Castlefield Urban Heritage Park. Attitude, in this context, was defined as a psychological tendency that is expressed by evaluating a particular entity on a cognitive, an effective or a behavioural basis (Eagly and

Chaiken, 1993).

The study forms part of a longitudinal research project, which examined the position of Castlefield in three-dimensional 'product' space relative to competitors in the day-trip market. To this end, an expectancy-value multi-brand, multi-attribute model (after Scott *et al.*, 1978) was used as the conceptual framework for the analysis (Figure 1). This model represents an extension of the Fishbein and Ajzen's (1975) model of reasoned action. The original expectancy-value model (Fishbein, 1967) and that part of the extended model the researcher is concerned with in this paper, describes a predicted relationship between the consumer's attitude towards some object or action, Aij, and two variables: Bijk, 'belief' about whether a particular object or action (j) possesses a given quality (k), and Vik, 'value' placed on the desirability of the ith quality, to predict the attitude or opinion a person holds about a particular choice. Thus, an individual's attitude toward, or opinion about, an object is a composite of his/her evaluation of that object in terms of attaining certain goals, weighted by the relative importance or saliency of the goals. Following the logic of the model, if both 'importance' and 'evaluative' components of the consumer's attitude towards a destination can be identified, then theoretically, the destination's strengths and weaknesses, from the consumer perspective, can be determined. This technique has been used widely (Scott *et al.*, 1978; Tourism Canada, 1988; Ryan, 1995).

The Development of the Measurement Instrument

In designing the measurement instrument, the researcher compared empirically, and determined the convergent validity among, a number of alternative methods of attitude scale construction in an effort to identify attributes that were relevant in this context. First, as a basis for the comparison, a review of the pertinent literature was conducted to identify the attributes that had been found to be relevant in previous research (Perry *et al.*, 1976; Goodrich, 1977; La Page and Cormier, 1977; Var *et al.*, 1977; Pizam *et.al.*, 1978; Scott *et al.*, 1978; Pearce, 1982; Calantone and Johar, 1984; Sternquist-Witter, 1985; Bojanic, 1991; Gartner, 1986; Haahti, 1986; Shih, 1986; Haywood and Muller, 1988; Reilly, 1990; Um and Crompton, 1990; Chon, 1991; Driscoll *et al.*, 1994; Glasson, 1994). These attributes were used to construct an a priori construct. The vast majority of these studies focused on vacations, but many of the variables were considered by the researcher to be generally applicable, although their specific relevance to the day-trip market was unknown at that stage.

In the second approach, a repertory grid test, based on Kelly's (1955) personal construct theory, was used to obtain relevant attributes. The test was conducted using the subjects' 'evoked set' (Howard and Sheth, 1969) of day-trip destinations as the 'stimuli of interest'. The objective was to identify the constructs that the subjects used to describe similarities and differences between day-trip tourist attractions and thereby determine the attributes which were relevant from their perspective.

Finally, attributes were obtained from subjects using the technique of free elicitation. Like the repertory grid test, this technique was used to enable subjects to describe the stimulus in their own terms rather than responding to the researcher's predetermined dimensions or those derived from either relevant published research or from a management perspective. The elicitation measure was derived from the open-ended question, 'what 10 words would you use to describe the things you are looking for when you go out for a day trip?' (They may be 'things' or 'feelings'). By using this procedure, the problems associated with sampling from a more detailed text such as recorded interviews, or lengthy statements from a more open-ended questionnaire format, were avoided. Seventy-four attributes, in total, were produced from the three techniques. They formed the basis of the composite scale, which was presented, within a questionnaire, to a sample of 320 subjects who were asked to rate each attribute on a 7-point Likert scale in terms of its importance for a day-trip. They were then asked to rate Castlefield Urban Heritage Park, after visiting this day-trip destination, in terms of how much or how little of each attribute they thought the destination had. A random sample of 40 subjects were also interviewed following their visit to Castlefield. For a full discussion of the scale construction, see Schofield (2000).

$$BI_{ij} = A_{ij} \sum_{j=1}^{m} \sum_{k=1}^{n} (B_{ijk} V_{ik} PPK_{ij})$$

Where:
- i = Consumer
- j = Brand or product
- k = Attribute or product characteristic
- n = Number of attributes
- m = Number of brands/products
- BI_{ij} = Consumer i's behavioural intention toward brand j
- A_{ij} = A unidimensional measure of consumer i's attitude toward brand j
- B_{ijk} = The strength of consumer i's belief that attribute k is possessed by brand j
- V_{ik} = The degree to which attribute k is desired by consumer i
- PPK_{ij} = Proportional product knowledge of consumer i for brand j

Figure 1: An expectancy-value multi-brand, multi-attribute model adapted from Scott *et al.* (1978).

Results and Discussion

The objective of the research was not to calculate an overall score for Castlefield by aggregating the individual scores from each attribute but to examine the data in disaggregated form in order to identify the destination's strengths and weaknesses against a benchmark of attributes which are considered to be important from the consumer perspective. The identification of attributes, which are considered to be important and yet absent from Castlefield, may inform the destination's product development strategy. Additionally, substantial features of the destination which are currently considered, by potential consumers, to be unimportant could be addressed by the promotional strategy in an attempt to change their perceptions. The disaggregated form of the data also overcomes, at least in part, a number of objections relating to the following issues: the nature of the relationship between the component parts, the validity of univariate scores produced by component summation, and the process of component compensation and its relationship with attitude formation (Ryan, 1991).

The 'importance' component: day-trip destination choice

The subjects' mean ratings for the 74 attributes, on a 7-point Likert-type scale, in terms of their importance for a day trip are shown in Figure 2. The 10 highest rated attributes were 'clean toilets' (mean: 6.28), 'toilet facilities' (6.17), 'good atmosphere' (6.06), 'a good reputation' (6.05), 'having something for everyone' (6.05), 'a fun place to visit' (6.03), 'good value for money' (5.99), 'many interesting things to do' (5.95), 'a clean environment' (5.94) and 'a safe place to visit' (5.92). The importance attributed to 'clean toilets' probably reflects their use as an indicator of the overall quality of the amenities provided by a tourist destination. Nevertheless, it is interesting that the common functional facilities (the secondary features of destinations) and not the distinctive or unique attractions (the primary elements of place) were perceived as being most important (Schofield, 2000). Moreover, in addition to the tangible features of destinations, the 'psychological' elements (Echtner and Ritchie, 1993) are also represented.

At the other end of the scale, 'historical attractions' (3.77), 'distinctive local features' (3.87), 'opportunities for walking' (4.02), 'attractive buildings' (4.13), 'a waterside location' (4.15) and 'special interests e.g. museums' (4.16) were considered to be of relatively little importance to the subjects when choosing a day-trip destination. This is significant in that these attributes are some of Castlefield's most prominent features.

The 'evaluative' component: Castlefield's product attributes

The respondents' post-visit evaluation of Castlefield on the attitude scale's 74 attributes (in terms of how much or how little the destination was thought to have of each item) is shown in Figure 3. The 10 highest rated items indicate that Castlefield is perceived as a destination offering 'a convenient location' (mean: 5.56) and 'dry weather facilities' (5.54) with 'special interests e.g. museums' (5.48), 'historical attractions' (5.41), 'educational value' (5.34), 'heritage trails and information' (5.30) and 'distinctive local features' (5.26). It is also seen as 'an all year round attraction' (5.26) as 'not being overcrowded' (5.21).

By contrast, the destination is not perceived to have much in the way of 'fairground rides' (2.44), 'boat trips' (3.24), 'beautiful gardens' (3.28), 'scenic beauty' (3.35), 'quality shopping facilities' (3.32), 'nightlife' (3.58) or 'markets' (3.62).

Castlefield's strengths and weaknesses from the consumer perspective

The post-visit 'evaluative' scores represent the features or qualities Castlefield is perceived to have or not have, but make no reference to their *importance* from the subjects' point of view. The subjects' mean 'importance' and 'evaluation' ratings on each of the 74 attributes were, therefore, plotted using Excel 97 to produce the distribution given in Figure 4. Castlefield is perceived as a destination, which offers little of the attributes featured in the bottom, left quadrant. These are not considered to be weaknesses with respect to day-trip destination choice, however, because the subjects considered them to be among the least important attributes.

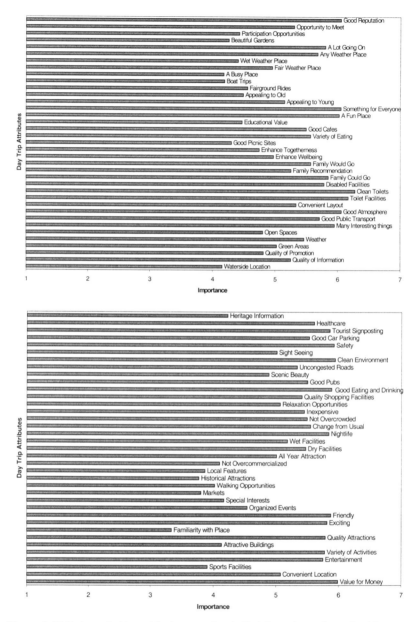

Figure 2 Attributes rated by subjects according to their importance for a day trip

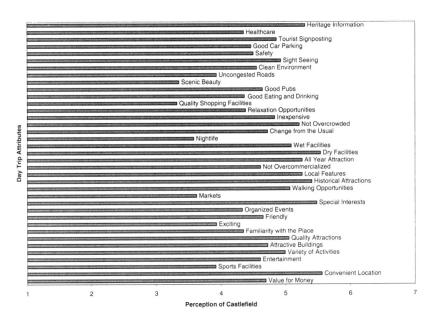

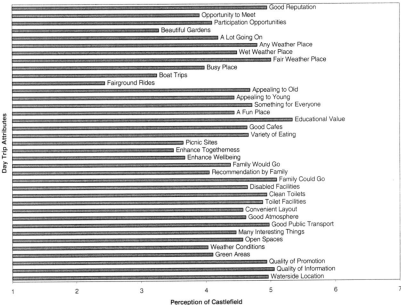

Figure 3 Castlefield rated by subjects on the attributes of importance

By comparison, Castlefield does not offer much of the attributes which are clustered in the top, left quadrant, but these are considered to be important for selecting day-trip destinations. As a result, the destination could be perceived as being weak in terms of 'nightlife', 'excitement', 'quality shopping facilities', 'opportunities to meet people' and 'uncongested roads'. These attributes were also listed as weaknesses by subjects in the post-visit qualitative research.

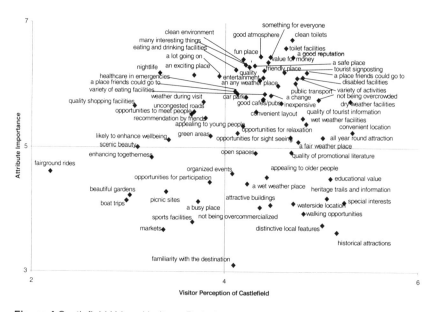

Figure 4 Castlefield Urban Heritage Park: Importance versus visitor perception

Castlefield is perceived to offer much of the attributes which occupy the top, right quadrant and these elements are also considered, by subjects, to be important. These strengths include, among others, the following: 'a friendly place', 'entertainment', 'a variety of activities', 'a good atmosphere', 'a good reputation', 'a change from the usual', 'quality attractions and tourist information', 'good pubs and cafes', 'something for everyone', 'value for money', 'clean toilet facilities', 'a fun place', 'a safe place', 'a convenient location' and dry and wet weather facilities'.

The destination is seen to provide much of the attributes in the bottom, right quadrant, but these are among the least important from the perspective of the consumer. It is interesting to note that 'educational value', 'heritage trails and information', 'attractive buildings', 'distinctive local features', 'historical attractions' and 'waterside location' are among the cluster of attributes featured here.

Visitor satisfaction with Castlefield

The consideration of attribute *importance* in the evaluation of Castlefield's 'product' has meant that the destination's qualities have been examined within the context of a general day-trip framework. The general importance of certain attributes may not, however, be relevant in the specific case of this urban heritage park and the decision-making process relating to it. For example, consumers may not expect certain qualities such as nightlife, or outcomes such as excitement and may be prepared to overlook the absence of certain elements like quality shopping facilities because they are compensated for by other desirable components such as a museum or a theme park. Therefore, in an effort to examine the particular qualities of the destination from the consumer perspective, the subjects' level of satisfaction with the visit, their intention to both return to Castlefield and recommend the place to others through word-of-mouth communication, and all related variables, were examined. Cross tabulations of subjects' level of satisfaction with socio-economic class, gender, date of last visit to Castlefield, frequency of previous visits to the destination and exposure to promotional literature prior to the visit showed only low levels of association between the variables.

Table 1 shows the results of the cross tabulation of the subjects' level of satisfaction, on a Likert-type scale ranging from 'very dissatisfied' (1) to 'very satisfied' (5), with their intention to repeat visit. Overall, 99 subjects (31.9%) were either very satisfied or satisfied with their visit and the majority (84.8%) of these people intended to return to Castlefield. A further 41 subjects (13.2%) also intended to return to the destination despite being less satisfied with their visit. By comparison, 81 subjects (26.1%) were either very dissatisfied or dissatisfied with their visit and overall, the majority (59.7%) of subjects did not intend to repeat visit; 30% of all subjects indicated that they were neither satisfied nor dissatisfied with the destination and would not return.

Intention to recommend Castlefield was considered to be a more critical variable than intention to repeat visit with respect to identifying the significant variables which underpin satisfaction, in that subjects must have felt sufficiently confident to be willing to recommend the destination's attributes, and because 71 subjects (22.8%) said that they would recommend Castlefield but would not repeat visit. The post-visit interviews revealed that many of these subjects felt that they had seen all that they had wanted to in one visit, were satisfied with their experience and were therefore intending to recommend the destination to others.

This part of the analysis then focused on two segments from the sample. The first segment comprised of subjects who were either satisfied or very satisfied and intended to recommend Castlefield to others (n = 94) – the 'satisfied/recommendation segment'. The second segment consisted of subjects who were either dissatisfied or very dissatisfied and would not be recommending the destination to others (n = 72) – the 'dissatisfied/no recommendation' segment.

Table 2 shows the cross tabulation of the subjects' level of satisfaction with their intention to recommend the destination. One hundred and ninety subjects (60.9%) said they would recommend Castlefield to others. Ninety-four of these (49.5%) were either satisfied or very satisfied. It is interesting to note that 87 (66.4%) of the subjects who were neither satisfied nor dissatisfied with Castlefield still intended to recommend the destination.

Table 1 Subjects' Level of Satisfaction with Castlefield Urban Heritage Park by Intention to Repeat Visit

	Repeat Visit	No Repeat Visit	Total
Very Satisfied	13 (4.2%)	2 (0.7%)	15 (4.8%)
Satisfied	71 (22.9%)	13 (4.2%)	84 (27.1%)
Neither Satisfied Nor Dissatisfied	37 (11.9%)	93 (30.0%)	130 (41.9%)
Dissatisfied	4 (1.3%)	71 (22.9%)	75 (24.2%)
Very Dissatisfied	0 (0.0%)	6 (1.9%)	6 (1.9%)
Total	125 (40.3%)	185 (59.7%)	310 (100%) *

* 2 subjects were undecided about their intention to repeat visit.

Satisfaction and the factors of significance from the visitor perspective

In order to reduce the data to more manageable proportions, identify the key dimensions of Castlefield's 'product', from the visitor perspective, and attempt to determine the factors of significance in the 'satisfied/recommendation' segment's attitude towards Castlefield, the subjects' post-visit ratings of the destination were subjected to principal components analysis. The 'satisfied/recommendation' segment's ratings were then examined with respect to their highest rated attribute loadings on the principal components.

The 'internal consistency' of the scale was determined using Cronbach's alpha coefficient. A score of 0.89 indicated a satisfactory level of reliability. The standardized item and split-half alpha coefficients, together with the Spearman Brown and Guttman split-half coefficients also confirmed the reliability of the matrices. A sphericity test statistic of 946.15412 (significance: .000) was obtained, there was a high correlation between each variable and at least one other variable in the set, and the proportion of large coefficients in the anti-image covariance matrix was low. This indicates that the model was appropriate. The Kaiser-Meyer-Olkin (KMO) measure of sampling adequacy was 0.725. This represents a 'middling' score (Kaiser, 1974), which also suggests that the model was an appropriate one to use.

Table 2 Subjects' Level of Satisfaction with Castlefield Urban Heritage Park by Intention to Recommend the Destination

	Recommendation	No Recommendation	Total
Very Satisfied	13 (4.2%)	2 (0.6%)	15 (4.8%)
Satisfied	81 (25.9%)	4 (1.3%)	85 (27.2%)
Neither Satisfied Nor Dissatisfied	87 (27.9%)	44 (14.11%)	131 (42.0%)
Dissatisfied	9 (2.9%)	66 (21.2%)	75 (24.0%)
Very Dissatisfied	0 (0.0%)	6 (1.9%)	6 .* (1.9%)
Total	190 (60.9%)	122 (39.1%)	312 (100%)

The principal components analysis produced 22 components with eigenvalues greater than 1, which explained 70.00% of the variance in the data. The communality data showed that a high proportion of the variance was accounted for by the common components indicating that there were no singularly important unique variables and that the relationship between the variables was complex. The component matrix obtained in the extraction phase of the analysis was subjected to a Varimax orthogonal rotation with Kaiser normalization in order to facilitate its interpretation. However, the Varimax rotation failed to converge in either 25 (0.15856) or 35 (0.09096) iterations. The unrotated matrix showed that many of the variables had moderate-size correlations with several components. Consequently, the identification of meaningful principal components was difficult. Eleven were labelled; they accounted for 72.38% of the variance explained by the first 22 principal components and 50.67% of the total variance in the correlation matrix. The labelled principal components, their associated attribute loadings and the variance in the data accounted for by each component (given in parentheses after each label) are given in Table 3.

Component 1 is a 'general factor' (Child, 1970) and accounts for the largest contribution (13.00%) to the total variance. Consequently, it correlates quite highly with a large number of variables. In addition to an emphasis on the comprehensive range of attractions and facilities, this principal component has a social element. It was, therefore, labelled 'extensive leisure provision and social opportunities'. Component 2 is correlated with attributes which seem to describe an 'entertainment and conviviality' dimension. By contrast, Component 3 consists of items relating to the heritage of the destination and its interest and educational value. It was therefore labelled 'history and education'. Component 4 is a 'bipolar factor'; in geometric terms, some of the test vectors have been resolved in one direction, others in opposite quadrants, thereby giving rise to both positive and negative values which seem to describe an 'undemanding recreation'. Component 5 seems to explain the behaviour of items relating to both the environment of Castlefield and the destination's communication with the public; it was labelled, 'quality of the site and its promotion'. The variables which have the highest loadings on Component 6 relate to 'amusement and comfort' and the Component 7 relates to 'safety' both in the sense of personal security and from the perspective of being a destination offering a low risk of disappointment particularly for 'older people'. 'Safety for seniors' was therefore considered to be appropriate. Component 8 is another a 'bipolar factor' which relates to 'wet weather facilities' whilst Component 9 consists of a range of attributes which have a common theme of 'special interests'. 'Peace and quiet' describes the variables which correlate with Component 10 and Component 11 is positively correlated with 'good value for money' and negatively correlated with 'familiarity with the destination'. It was therefore labelled as 'good value and different'. Principal components 12 to 22 were characterized by low positive and negative correlations with a large number of variables and as such, were not labelled.

Table 3 The Principal Components Derived from the Post-visit Attribute Ratings

1. **'Extensive Leisure Provision and Social Opportunities'** (13.00% Variance): 'many interesting things to do' (0.69), 'something for everyone' (0.66), 'a good atmosphere' (0.60), 'opportunities to meet people' (0.58), 'good picnic sites' (0.58), 'a busy place' (0.54), 'good tourist signposting' (0.54), 'enhancing togetherness' (0.54), 'availability of toilets' (0.51), 'enhancing wellbeing' (0.51), 'clean toilets' (0.49), 'beautiful gardens' (0.49), 'a lot going on' (0.48), 'variety of eating facilities' (0.46), 'appeal to young people' (0.46), 'good cafes' (0.45), 'green areas' (0.45), 'a place that friends and family could go' (0.44).

2. **'Entertainment and Conviviality'** (6.42%): 'an exciting place to visit' (0.61), 'entertainment' (0.55), 'a friendly place to visit' (0.53), 'good eating and drinking facilities' (0.51), 'wet weather facilities' (0.46), 'a convenient location' (0.45), 'good public houses' (0.42), 'quality attractions' (0.42).

3. **'History and Education'** (5.52%): 'heritage trails and information' (0.60), 'adequate healthcare in emergencies' (0.54), 'educational value' (0.46), 'an all year round attraction' (0.44), 'historical attractions' (0.43), 'distinctive local features' (0.40).

4. **'Undemanding Recreation'** (4.31%): 'not over commercialized' (0.43), 'opportunities for walking' (0.42), 'clean toilets' (-0.42), 'adequate healthcare in emergencies' (-0.41), 'quality of shopping facilities' (-0.37), 'historical attractions' (-0.34).

5. **'Quality of the Site and its Promotion'** (4.18%): 'green areas' (0.61), 'the quality of promotional literature' (0.54), 'appeals to younger people' (-0.42), 'appeals to older people' (0.41), 'quality of tourist information' (0.38), 'open spaces' (0.38), 'beautiful gardens' (0.32), 'convenient layout' (0.30), 'good picnic sites' (0.30).

6. **'Amusement and Comfort'** (3.51%): 'fairground rides' (0.42), 'opportunities for relaxation' (0.39), 'dry weather facilities' (0.35), 'facilities for the disabled' (0.31), 'toilet facilities' (0.31).

7. **'Safety for Seniors'** (3.40%): 'a safe place to visit' (0.56), 'good car parking facilities' (0.51), 'appeals to older people' (0.38), 'opportunities for sight seeing' (0.35), 'weather conditions during the visit' (0.34), 'historical attractions' (0.31).

8. **'Wet Weather Facilities'** (2.80%): 'a wet weather place' (0.36), 'an any weather place' (0.32), 'uncongested roads' (-0.46), 'a clean environment' (-0.41), 'scenic beauty' (-0.41).

9. **'Special Interests'** (2.71%): 'a waterside location' (0.38), 'markets' (0.38), 'special interests e.g. museums' (0.37), 'attractive buildings' (0.34), 'quality shopping facilities' (0.32).

10. **'Peace and Quiet'** (2.48%): 'not overcrowded' (0.37), 'opportunities for relaxation' (0.31), 'organized events' (-0.31).

11. **'Good Value and Different'** (2.34%): 'good value for money' (0.31), 'familiarity with a destination' (-0.45).

The principal components analysis has demonstrated that there are a large number of dimensions to the visitor experience of Castlefield. Notwithstanding the significance of the 'extensive leisure provision and social opportunities' component in terms of the proportion of the variance explained, components two and three reflect the two main attractions at the destination: Granada Studios Tour and the Greater Manchester Museum of Science and Industry. Low key recreation, the quality of the site, amusement and comfort, the provision of wet weather facilities, special interests, peace and quiet and value for money are also significant dimensions. Clearly, a wide range of variables, with both psychological and functional orientations, are influential in this context.

The 'satisfied/recommendation' segment's 10 highest post-visit attribute ratings on the 7-point Likert-type scale were 'special interests' (5.64), 'dry weather facilities' (5.61), 'convenient location' (5.60), 'educational value' (5.54), 'heritage trails and information' (5.53), 'historic attractions' (5.43), 'wet weather facilities' (5.35), 'opportunities for walking' (5.24), 'quality attractions' (5.20) and 'good public transport' (5.20). These variables loaded on the 'history and education' component, to a large extent and on the 'special interests', 'amusement and comfort', 'undemanding recreation' and 'entertainment and conviviality' principal components, to a lesser degree (Table 3).

The qualitative data analysis

The results from this part of the analysis were then supported with qualitative data in the form of the 'satisfied/recommendation' and 'dissatisfied/no recommendation' segments' particular 'likes' and 'dislikes' about the destination, obtained in the post-visit phase of the study. The frequency profiles of the two segments' particular 'likes' and 'dislikes' are given in Table 4. It is not surprising that the 'satisfied/recommendation' segment's most frequently listed 'likes' feature the historical and educational aspects of Castlefield – 'history' (80.9%), 'educational/informative' (64.9%), 'science museum' (55.3%), 'interesting' (38.3%). The destination's 'variety' (64.9%), including Granada Studios Tour (38.3%), its 'convenient location (41.5%), 'different' quality (40.4%), 'clean' state (36.2%) and 'value for money' (22.3%) are also particularly liked. These features, together with the destination's 'family orientation', were also listed by the 'dissatisfied/no recommendation' segment. The features were listed less frequently, however, and there is a marked change in their rank order. Notably, Granada Studios Tour is ranked first with 27.8% of the segment listing it as a particular 'like'.

Table 4 Frequency Profile of Particular 'Likes' and 'Dislikes' of the 'Satisfied/
Recommendation' and 'Dissatisfied/No recommendation' Segments

'Satisfied/Recommendation' Segment (n = 94)		'Dissatisfied/No Recommendation' Segment (n = 72)	
'Likes'	*Frequency*	*'Likes'*	*Frequency*
History	76 (80.9%)	Granada Studios Tour	20 (27.8%)
Variety/lots to do	61 (64.9%)	Educational/ informative	14 (19.4%)
Educational/informative	54 (57.4%)	Clean	14 (19.4%)
Science Museum	52 (55.3%)	Family orientation	11 (15.3%)
Convenient location	39 (41.5%)	Convenient location	11 (15.3%)
Different	38 (40.4%)	History	10 (13.9%)
Interesting	36 (38.3%)	Variety/lots to do	7 (9.7%)
Granada Studios Tour	36 (38.3%)	Quiet	6 (8.3%)
Clean	34 (36.2%)		
Good value for money	21 (22.3%)		
Quiet	12 (12.8%)		
'Dislikes'	*Frequency*	*'Dislikes'*	*Frequency*
Pubs/bars (too few)	15 (16.0%)	Not an exciting place	32 (44.4%)
Eating places (too few)	12 (12.8%)	Roman Fort	27 (37.5%)
Roman Fort	5 (5.3%)	Pubs/bars (too few)	22 (30.6%)
Site (too spread out)	4 (4.3%)	Not a young persons place	17 (23.6%)
		Not a safe place	16 (22.2%)
		Site (too spread out)	14 (19.4%)
		A boring place	9 (12.5%)
		Science Museum	5 (6.9%)

The frequency profile of the 'dissatisfied/no recommendation' segment's 'dislikes' shows that many of them (44.4%) do not consider Castlefield to be an exciting place. The first rank of Granada Studios Tour in their 'likes' also suggests that 'excitement' is an important attribute for this segment. Other prominent dislikes include the reconstructed Roman fort (37.5%) and the lack of pubs and bars on the site (30.6%). The latter criticism may be linked with the perception that Castlefield is not a young person's place (23.6%). Safety is also thought to be an issue by just over one fifth of this segment whilst just under one fifth consider the attractions on the site to be too remote from each other. Some of these dislikes are echoed by the 'satisfied/recommendation' segment but, not surprisingly, they were listed less frequently.

Summary

The results from the analysis of both the importance and evaluative components of consumer attitudes towards Castlefield Urban Heritage Park have shown that a wide range of attributes were considered, by subjects, to be relevant to both day-trip destination choice and the evaluation of Castlefield Urban Heritage Park. They have also demonstrated the complexity of the relationship between the variables and the importance of the combined effect of a large number of attributes. Together with the 'primary' elements of place, both the 'secondary' features and 'psychological aspects' of destinations are considered to be important from the consumer perspective.

The results from the importance versus perception analysis indicate that although Castlefield appears to have many strengths, it has weaknesses in key areas which are considered to be important in day-trip destination choice. This is supported by the fact that only one third of subjects were either very satisfied or satisfied with their visit to the destination and were prepared to recommend it to others. This 'satisfied/ recommendation' segment's highest rated Castlefield attributes were most highly correlated with the 'history and education' principal component. Their 'particular likes' also highlighted the destination's heritage resources and educational value together with many of the strengths identified by the analysis of the importance and perception data such as its variety of attractions, convenient location and good value for money. Clearly, this is a key segment for Castlefield in terms of its interest in the extant product, satisfaction level and intention to both repeat visit and recommend the destination to others.

It was also clear from the importance and perception data analysis that although the 'satisfied/recommendation' segment consider Castlefield's heritage and educational value to be strengths, these features are not considered to be important in day-trip destination choice by the majority of subjects. It is therefore not surprising that nearly 60% of subjects did not intend to return to the destination. The weaknesses highlighted by the analysis of the importance and perception data and the 'particular dislikes' of the 'dissatisfied/no recommendation' segment suggest that the lack of nightlife, quality shopping facilities and opportunities to meet people should be addressed if this destination is to compete in the day-trip market. Previous studies have shown that the majority of visitors to heritage visitor attractions require a 'quick fix' or 'potted history' rather than a detailed account of an area's past and its historic associations (Davies, 1988) and that a destination's heritage is only one of many elements in a visitor's overall experience of a place (Light, 1995). Should the findings from further on-going research, using a larger sample, reveal similar results, it is recommended that Castlefield's product development strategy should focus on the issues which have been highlighted here, particularly the destination's weaknesses, whilst attempting to retain both the interest of the segment which the destination is currently satisfying and the perception that Castlefield is a place that is 'different'.

References

Bojanic, D.C. (1991) The use of advertising in managing destination images. *Tourism Management* 12 (4), 352-355.

Calantone, R.J. and Johar, J.S. (1984) Seasonal segmentation of the tourist market using a benefit segmentation framework. *Journal of Travel Research* 23(2), 14-24.

Child, D. (1970) *The Essentials of Factor Analysis.* Holt, Rinehart and Winston, London.

Chon, K.S. (1991) Tourist destination image modification process: marketing implications. *Tourism Management* 12(1), 68-72.

Davies, G. (1988) Potted history. *Marxism Today* 47(1), 23-29.

Driscoll, A., Lawson, R. and Niven, B. (1994) Measuring tourists' destination perceptions. *Annals of Tourism Research* 21(3), 499-511.

Eagly, A.H. and Chaiken, S. (1993) *The Psychology of Attitude.* Harcourt Brace Jovanovich, Forth Worth.

Echtner, C.M. and Ritchie, J.R.B. (1993) The measurement of destination images: an empirical assessment. *Journal of Travel Research* 3(1), 3-12.

Edwards, J.A. (1989) Historic sites and their local environments. In: Herbert, D.T., Prentice, R.C. and Thomas, C.J. (eds.) *Heritage Sites: Strategies for Marketing and Development.* Avebury, Aldershot, pp. 271-292.

Fishbein, M. (1967) A consideration of beliefs, and their role in attitude measurement. In: Fishbein, M. (ed.) *Readings in Attitude Theory and Measurement.* Wiley, New York, pp. 257-266.

Fishbein, M. and Ajzen, I. (1975) *Belief, Attitude, Intention, Behaviour: An Introduction to Theory and Research.* Addison-Wesley, Reading, MA.

Gartner, W.C. (1986) Temporal influences on image change. *Annals of Tourism Research* 13(1), 635-644.

Glasson, J. (1994) Oxford: a heritage city under pressure. *Tourism Management* 15(2), 137-144.

Goodrich, J.N. (1977) Differences in perceived similarity of tourism regions: a spatial analysis. *Journal of Travel Research* 16(1), 10-13.

Gunn, C. (1972) *Vacationscape: Designing Tourist Regions.* Bureau of Business Research, University of Texas, Austin, Texas.

Gunn, C. (1988) *Tourism Planning,* 2nd edn. Taylor and Francis, New York.

Haahti, A.J. (1986) Finland's competitive positioning as a destination. *Annals of Tourism Research* 13(1), 11-26.

Haywood, K.M. and Muller, T. (1988) The urban tourist experience: measuring satisfaction. *Hospitality Research and Education Journal* 12(2), 453-459.

Howard, J.A. and Sheth, J.N. (1969) *The Theory of Buyer Behaviour.* Wiley, New York.

Jefferson, A. and Lickorish, L. (1988) *Marketing Tourism: A Practical Guide.* Longman, Harlow.

Johnson, P. and Thomas, B. (1990) Measuring local employment impact of tourist attractions. *Regional Studies* 24, 395-403.

Kaiser, H.F. (1974) An index of factorial simplicity. *Psychometrika* 39, 31-36.

Kelly, G.A. (1955) *The Psychology of Personal Constructs.* Norton, New York.

La Page, W.F. and Cormier, P.L. (1977) Images of camping – barriers to participation. *Journal of Travel Research* 15(4), 21-25.

Light, D. (1995) Heritage as informal education. In: Herbert, D.T. (ed.) *Heritage, Tourism and Society.* Belhaven, London, pp. 118-145.

Lowenthal, D. (1985) *The Past is a Foreign Country.* Cambridge University Press, Cambridge, Mass.

Middleton, V.T.C. (1994) *Marketing in Travel and Tourism,* 2nd edn. Heinemann, London.

Pearce, P.L. (1982) *The Social Psychology of Tourist Behaviour.* Pergamon Press, Oxford.

Perry, M., Izraeli, D. and Perry, A. (1976) Image change as a result of advertising. *Journal of Advertising Research* 16(1), 45-50.

Pizam, A., Neuman, Y. and Reichel, A. (1978) Dimensions of tourist satisfaction with a destination area. *Annals of Tourism Research* 5(3), 314-322.

Reilly, M.D. (1990) Free elicitation of descriptive adjectives for tourism image assessment. *Journal of Travel Research* 28(1), 21-26.

Ryan, C. (1991) *Recreational Tourism: A Social Science Perspective.* Routledge, London.

Ryan, C. (1995) *Researching Tourist Satisfaction: Issues, Concepts, Problems.* Routledge, London.

Scott, D.R., Schewe, C.D. and Frederick, D.G. (1978) A multibrand/multiattribute model of tourist state choice. *Journal of Travel Research* 17(1), 23-29.

Schofield, P. (2000) Deciphering day trip destination choice using a tourist expectation/satisfaction construct. In: Woodside, A.G., Crouch, G.I., Mazanec, J.A., Oppermann, M. and Sakai, M.Y. (eds.) *Consumer Psychology of Travel, Hospitality and Leisure.* CAB International, Wallingford.

Shih, D. (1986) VALS as a tool of tourism market research: the Pennsylvania experience. *Journal of Travel Research* 24(4), 2-10.

Sternquist-Witter, B. (1985) Attitudes about a resort area: a comparison of tourists and local retailers. *Journal of Travel Research* 24(1), 14-19.

Thomas, C.J. (1989) The roles of historic sites and reasons for visiting. In: Herbert, D.T., Prentice, R.C. and Thomas, C.J. (eds.) *Heritage Sites: Strategies for Marketing and Development.* Avebury, Aldershot, pp. 62-93.

Tourism Canada (1988) *Pleasure Travel Markets to North America – Switzerland, Hong Kong, Singapore – Highlights Report.* March, Prepared by Market Facts of Canada, Tourism Canada, Ottawa, Ontario.

Um, S. and Crompton, J.L. (1990) Attitude determinants in pleasure travel destination choice. *Annals of Tourism Research* 17(2), 432-448.

Var, T., Beck, R.A.D. and Loftus, P. (1977) Determination of touristic attractiveness of the touristic areas in British Columbia. *Journal of Travel Research* 15(3), 23-29.

Yi, Y. (1990) A critical review of consumer satisfaction. In: Zeithaml, V.A. (ed.) *Review of Marketing.* American Marketing Association.

Chapter nineteen
A Critical Review of Approaches to Measure Satisfaction with Tourist Destinations

Metin Kozak
School of Leisure and Food Management
Sheffield Hallam University
Sheffield S1 1WB, UK

Introduction

It is a feature of assessing services that because of their intangibility, the assessment has to be measured through customer feedback (Quelch and Ash, 1981). As customers are viewed as an extremely important dimension in the marketing of tourism services, marketing activities start and end with the extent to which they are satisfied or dissatisfied. Grönroos (1978) reports that customers are taking an active part in shaping the service offered as a result of the interaction between production and consumption. Deming (1982) points out that the customer has a significant place in the definition of quality and suggests businesses try to understand what the customer (market) needs and wants both at the moment and in the future. In doing so, products and services could be designed to satisfy these needs and wants. Zairi (1996) mentions the importance of asking customers about their needs and expectations and collecting feedback regularly about the level of service they have received in order to serve them better.

   Whilst much has been done in customer satisfaction-dissatisfaction (CS/D) research, it is sometimes unclear which model is most applicable and suited to a particular situation. This paper therefore critically examines to what extent the existing CS/D theories are applicable for the measurement of satisfaction with tourist destinations along with their strengths and weaknesses by reviewing previous literature within the related area. Among the approaches to be examined, which have been adopted into tourism research for the measurement of satisfaction with tourist destinations, are 'expectation-performance', 'importance-performance', 'disconfirmation' and 'performance-only'. This study also aims to emphasize main points which need to be developed further in a destination-based CS survey. Implications and recommendations are drawn for the use of the CS measurement process in the investigation of destination satisfaction research.

What is Customer Satisfaction?

The concept of CS has been used by consumer behaviour and marketing researchers. Researchers consider CS as a part of consumer behaviour whereas practitioners treat it as a focal point for designing successful marketing strategies. The majority of approaches view CS as a cognitive process (e.g. Bloemer and Poiesz, 1989). The widespread approach to the definition of CS is therefore that it is 'the accumulated experience of a customer's purchase and consumption experiences' (Andreassen, 1995, p. 33). Klaus (1985, p. 21) defines satisfaction as 'the customer's subjective evaluation of a consumption experience based on some relationship between the customer's perceptions and objective attributes of the product'. Thus, CS is treated as 'an abstract and theoretical phenomenon, it can be measured as a weighted average of multiple indicators' (Johnson and Fornell, 1991, in Andreassen, 1995, p. 33). In line with the theory of expectation and performance, Pizam *et al.* (1978, p. 315) define tourist satisfaction as 'the result of the interaction between a tourist's experience at the destination area and the expectations he/she had about that destination'.

Despite the fact that the definition varies, the common factor is that satisfaction is a post-consumption evaluative judgement (Westbrook and Oliver, 1991). This feature distinguishes CS research from attitude research as the former is a post-consumption construct and the latter is a pre-decision construct which does not require any direct experience with the object (LaTour and Peat, 1979). Although the relationship between customer satisfaction and attitude theories is not yet clear (Czepiel *et al.*, 1974), it is a fact that both concepts are interrelated (Figure 1). Satisfaction is believed to strengthen beliefs and attitudes whereas dissatisfaction may create negative beliefs and attitudes towards the object (Assael, 1987). A revised attitude appears as a result of satisfaction or dissatisfaction with the experience (Mayo and Jarvis, 1981; Oliver, 1981; Mountinho, 1987). The result would be an increase or decrease in the likelihood of repeat business for the destination. Moreover, the intensity of an attitude may also influence the level of satisfaction with an object. In other words, if the attitude is positive, satisfaction results. Similarly, dissatisfaction is expected when the attitude is negative. As such, as stated earlier, satisfaction or dissatisfaction with a previous experience is crucial because it may affect expectations for the next purchase (Westbrook and Newman, 1978). The next difference could be that attitude formation does not require any direct experience with the object, but satisfaction or dissatisfaction are a direct result of experience.

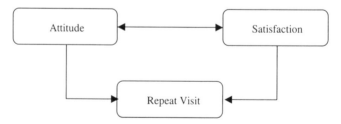

Figure 1 Relationship between Attitude, Satisfaction and Repeat Visit Intentions

Review of Customer Satisfaction Measurement Approaches

The measurement of CS has been extensively researched during the last three decades (e.g. Cardozo, 1965; LaTour and Peat, 1979; Oliver, 1980; Westbrook, 1980; Churchill and Suprenant, 1982; Woodruff *et al.,* 1983; Tse and Wilton, 1988). Since the early 1970s, the volume of CS research has been impressive. Though numerous theoretical structures have been proposed and empirically tested to examine the antecedents of satisfaction, a consensus approach has not yet been reached. As can be seen later, some believe that CS is a reflection of either positive or negative gaps between expectations and perceptions whereas others assert that it is an outcome solely of the perceptions. In addition, there has been extensive debate in the marketing literature regarding the nature and determinants of CS and how it is best measured (Oh and Parks, 1997). For instance, Peterson and Wilson (1992, p. 69) concluded that

> 'it is probably not possible to measure true satisfaction. True satisfaction is probably so intertwined with both interpersonal characteristics and methodological considerations that it may never be possible to disentangle them.'

Despite the fact that a variety of models have been posited and empirically tested, those widely accepted are disconfirmation, expectation-performance, importance-performance, and performance only models.

Specifically, the marketing literature has referred mainly to two approaches for use in CS research. The American school, led by Parasuraman *et al.* (1985, 1988, 1991), considers CS as a negative or positive outcome resulting from a comparison process between initial expectations and perceived performance of products and services (gap analysis). The Nordic school, led by Grönroos (1984), brings a completely different perspective to measuring CS by stating that it is only an outcome of the actual quality of performance and its perception by the customer (performance-only approach). It is beyond the scope of this chapter to present outcomes of all possible CS approaches, therefore discussion is limited to the most widely used models.

Expectation-performance approach

This approach, also believed to be similar to the contrast theory and aspiration theory, suggests that customers should have a knowledge about the product or service prior to commencing the consumption stage (Oliver, 1979). The idea in this theory basically comes from the evaluation of differences between perceived performance of a product or service and perceived importance of the same product or service (Cardozo, 1965; Olshavsky and Miller, 1972; Swan and Combs, 1976; Engledow, 1977). This approach proposes that customers are likely to make predictions regarding the future performance of an attribute or item (expectations). They then intend to mentally compare the performance to their expectations either during the purchasing stage or in the succeeding days.

Customers are expected to be dissatisfied if obtained performance is less than expected. Similarly, they are expected to be satisfied when expectations are met or exceeded. It is stated that measuring expectations and perceptions separately presents valuable implications for the service providers particularly when scores for certain items decline significantly from one period to another (Parasuraman *et al.,* 1994). By assessing whether outcomes are due to higher expectations or lower perceptions or both, customer perceptions of service quality in an encounter could be easily observed.

Importance-performance approach

The context of importance-performance analysis has been basically adapted from the expectation-performance approach, suggesting four conditions as 'high expectations-high performance', 'high expectations-low performance', 'low expectations-high performance' and 'low expectations-low performance' (Olshavsky and Miller, 1972). The main purpose of importance-performance analysis is to determine which attributes tourists consider most important and how well the destination performs in attributes that are considered important to customers. Poor performance on important attributes may have negative results for the destination (Leong and Tan, 1992; Go and Zhang, 1997). One of the simplest ways of discovering the importance of any destination attribute is to ask customers to identify dimensions that are taken into account when selecting destinations and to indicate their importance. At the same time, customers are requested to give their opinions regarding the performance of those destination dimensions. The relationship between the levels of importance and performance of a destination is categorized (Ryan, 1995, p. 76). High importance and low performance scores indicate that important attributes are perceived not to be present in the destination. Low importance and low performance scores refer to the unimportant attributes perceived not to be present in the destination. High importance and high performance scores show that important attributes are perceived to be present in the destination. Lastly, low importance and high performance scores are an indicator of the presence of unimportant attributes in the destination.

Among the advantages of using this method are to present significant marketing and management implications for decision-makers and help management focus on developing marketing strategies (Martilla and James, 1977), in particular attributes in the area where high importance and low performance appear could be moved into the area of critical strengths by improving customer services and products (Barksy and Labagh, 1992). The importance-performance approach has been found to be critical for evaluating the level of customers' satisfaction with a product or their holiday experiences in any area.

A different application of importance-performance analysis called the Fishbein-type choice-attitude model is suggested by Fishbein (1967). This model proposes that attitude towards a product or service can be calculated by multiplying beliefs (importance or motivations) and evaluations (perceived quality or performance). An empirical investigation by Goodrich (1978) was one of the first pieces of research introducing the Fishbein-type choice-attitude model to the body of tourism and travel literature. He investigated how perceptions influenced the choice of a vacation destination by comparing nine destinations. Although results confirmed that there was a strong relationship between customer perceptions of a destination and intention to choose it, it was suggested that perception itself was not the only predictor of selecting a holiday destination. Barsky (1992) posited a model, derived from disconfirmation paradigm and expectancy-value theory, that is like the Fishbein-type model. The only difference is that 'performance' was replaced by 'expectations met'.

Disconfirmation approach

Disconfirmation approach, derived from the adaptation level theory postulated by Helson (1964), considers that a customer's satisfaction with the outcome of a purchase would be determined by the discrepancy between the outcome (service or product performance versus expectations) and a standard of comparison known as the comparison level (Thibaut and Kelley, 1959). It is proposed that outcomes that confirm expectations (confirmation [as expected]) and are above the comparison level (positive discrepancies [better than expected]) will be satisfaction items whereas those below the comparison level (negative discrepancies [worse than expected]) will be dissatisfaction items (Oliver, 1980; Churchill and Suprenant, 1982).

Criticism of CS measurement in tourism on the basis of expectations

The measurement of satisfaction with destinations on the basis of expectations is critical because of the following reasons:

1. There appears to be a disagreement in the literature regarding the correct definition of expectations. Several forms of comparison used for setting expectations are suggested. Some researchers define them as predictions of future performance (Oliver, 1980), others as desires or goals (Spreng and Olshavsky, 1993) and some others in terms of norms based on past experiences (Cadotte *et al.*, 1987). In all these respects, for products and services which are frequently used, it is much easier to have baseline standards and every experience could update the direction of standards. In a tourism service where customers may usually take one or two vacations a year, it is unlikely for a customer to establish accurate standards concerning either particular destinations or taking vacations overall. The time interval between the time when a summer vacation is taken and the time when the next will be taken is much longer than for some other products or service consumption. People may change their expectations, evaluation of standards and even may forget how satisfied they were with the previous vacation.

2. It is pointed out that CS is an active and dynamic process (Fournier and Mick, 1999). Expectations may be influenced by advertising and other sales promotion methods (Cardozo, 1965). One shortcoming of the expectation-perception or the disconfirmation model is therefore that customers may update their expectations once they receive further information about the destination when there is a long delay between booking and taking a holiday (Boulding *et al.*, 1993). Given the fact that there is no possibility of displaying or testing a holiday destination in advance (intangibility), it is impossible for travellers to know what to expect since so many components (organizations) shape tourist experiences. The mismatch between the presence and promotion of a destination into a targeted potential market and what the destination really offers can not only affect the extent to which this promotion campaign is reliable but will also widen the gap between expectations and perceptions

(Laws, 1995). Thus, customers' direct experiences might become a significant factor on upgrading expectations (Nolan and Swan, 1984).

3. When the product is new and there has been no prior direct experience of it, the customer could tend to evaluate the actual performance of the product by using their previous holiday experiences with other brands, products or destinations (Cadotte *et al.,* 1987; Tse and Wilton, 1988; Erevelles and Leavitt, 1992). It is not reasonable to expect that customers visiting a new destination will have any previous confident expectations from the different attributes of the destination. They may have general expectations, but they cannot anticipate, for instance, the level of cleanliness. Any negative experience with the latest destination could be linked to prior positive experiences with former destinations. It is also claimed that customers' experiences with other brands or products can be affective while evaluating standards (Cadotte *et al.,* 1987).

4. Tourists may have difficulty in distinguishing between expectations and perceived performances during or after the holiday (Meyer and Westerbarkey, 1996). One reason for that could be the length of time spent at a destination. This is much longer than time spent at supermarkets, department stores, cafes and restaurants and so on. It is known that tourists have plenty of opportunity for contact with a number of people throughout their holiday. This interaction could occur between tourists and people working for the resort airport, local transportation, accommodation, tour, independent food and beverage outlets, entertainment, medical and photography services as well as with other tourists and the members of the host community (Ryan, 1995; Baum, 1997). As a consequence, views presented by Laws (1991) could be the fourth reason for understanding why the gap between expectations and perceptions may widen. Laws states that tourists discuss their holiday experiences with their friends and relatives, either while they are still on holiday or just afterwards, which in return changes their opinions. Tourists may also tend to discuss their holiday with managers, staff and other tourists within the destination. The feedback received from these people may influence tourists' opinions again and may alter their expectations or perceptions of service standards on a permanent or temporary basis.

5. Expectations are assumed to differ from one person to another (Miller, 1977). Cultural differences in attitudes and behaviour and social class may influence expectations and perceptions (Mayo and Jarvis, 1981). Tourist destinations attract tourists from different cultures and countries, whose level of satisfaction may depend more on their country of origin than on the performance of the destination. In a multi-cultural tourism experience, tourists' expectation and satisfaction levels can be influenced by their personality, lifestyle, motivations, previous experience with and knowledge of the destination, marketing method and image of the destination (Ryan, 1997). People with lower incomes were likely to be less critical about accommodation services than their counterparts with higher income levels. It is argued that higher income groups probably had more experience of travel and therefore higher expectations (Robinson and

Berl, 1979).

6. From the methodological point of view, the shortcoming of the Fishbein-type model of importance-performance measurement is that it does not pay attention to distinguishing differences between high importance and low performance scores. In other words, it is difficult to say that an average score of high importance and low performance of any attribute can be accepted as much the same as those of low importance and high performance of another element. For instance, say that the importance of accommodation is 6 and its perceived quality is 4. Similarly, say that the importance of food is 4 and its perceived quality is 6. The overall calculated attitude, according to the Fishbein model, will be 24 for both. Though they are equal in numerical value, the former attribute performs worse than the latter due to the negative gap between importance and perceived performance of the attribute. Another criticism is that respondents can confuse or overlap their perceptions of importance and performance level of any attribute when both surveys are conducted at the same time.

7. Finally, as a methodological point of view, it is hardly possible to keep the expectations and performance sample constant (Kozak and Nield, 1998). In other words, the number of questionnaires included for the analysis of results for arrival and departure surveys may not be equal as some of the respondents who take part in the first survey either could not be reached for the second part or refuse to take part in the study again. All these issues must also be addressed while undertaking research by using the importance-performance approach.

Performance-only approach

For the reasons given above, the performance-only approach avoids the use of expectations within the measurement of CS (Churchill and Suprenant, 1982; Cronin and Taylor, 1992; Erevelles and Leavitt, 1992). It is proposed that regardless of the existence of any previous expectations, the customer is likely to be satisfied when a product or service performs at a desired level (Czepiel *et al.,* 1974). It has been empirically supported that the performance-only approach had higher reliability and validity values than did other approaches such as expectation versus performance and disconfirmation where customer expectations were considered and also had the best correlation with the evaluation of both future behaviour and overall satisfaction (Prakash, 1984). In specific reference to its application into the tourism and hospitality fields, the performance-only approach gave higher correlation coefficient values in a research setting of visitor satisfaction with festivals (Crompton and Love, 1995). Yet, some researchers disagree with the application of the performance-only approach (Parasuraman *et al.,* 1985). Emphasizing the importance of expectations, they claim that, by using this approach, it is impossible to understand where expectations are higher and where perceptions are lower and how the former relates to the latter.

An Overview of Tourist Satisfaction Research

As in general marketing research, there is no consensus on how to measure CS in tourism or hospitality research. The traditional approaches have also been applied to researching CS within tourism and travel. For example, Parasuraman *et al.*'s (1985) expectation-perception gap model (Duke and Persia, 1996), Oliver's expectancy disconfirmation theory (Pizam and Milman, 1993), Sirgy's congruity model (Chon and Olsen, 1991), and performance-only model (Pizam *et al.*, 1978) have all been used in order to measure tourist satisfaction with specific destinations. An extensive literature review demonstrates that the existing literature on the measurement of tourist satisfaction with destinations has several weaknesses which need careful attention. Some of these studies are summarized in Table 1. It is possible to categorize major points into eight groups: scale development, attribute generation, quality of life, sample selection, consideration of multiple members' opinions, asking summary questions, consideration of differences between first-time and repeat tourists, and data collection. Each is briefly discussed below.

Scales

As a measure of consumer behaviour, the tourist satisfaction literature has mainly used the quantitative research method to collect and analyse primary sources of data. The quantitative research method is suggested as suitable for measuring CS because it is difficult to quantify qualitative data and personal bias would affect the analysis of the findings (Pizam *et al.*, 1979). In most previous destination satisfaction research, a five-point satisfaction scale was used (Pizam *et al.*, 1978; Pizam and Milman, 1993; Weber, 1997; Cho, 1998; Tribe and Snaith, 1998). Though this seems to be acceptable, further research should employ instruments with larger scales, e.g. a seven-point or ten-point scale to carry out an effective comparison analysis and clearly show the differences between scores. This will directly encourage researchers to raise the number of the sample population to increase the validity of the empirical findings as it is suggested that the number of the sample population needs to be higher as the number of items increases and a higher point scale is used (Hair *et al.*, 1995).

Attributes

Differences are observed in respect of the number and the context of destination attributes and the size of sampling. The number of attributes is usually between 14 and 56. Most studies do not use a significant sample size, restricting themselves to less than 200 respondents. This makes the reliability and the validity of the research findings questionable. Sampling error is expected to decrease as the size of the sample increases (Uhl and Schoner, 1969). The literature suggests a positive relationship between the number of items and the sample size, representing a ratio of at least 1:4 (Tinsley and Tinsley, 1987) or 1:5 (Hinkin *et al.*, 1997) or more acceptably, 1:10 (Hair *et al.*, 1995). A large sample population is helpful for generating better results from factor analysis as well as from the survey in general.

Quality of life (QOL)

The concept of the QOL determines people's priorities in their life. Different elements contribute to the QOL, e.g. self-esteem or self-actualization through job satisfaction, availability of leisure time and access to leisure activities, participation in community activities, friendships, family life, environment and so on (Headey, 1983). There are some examples in the marketing literature which attempted to explore the relationship between the QOL and the level of CS (Westbrook, 1980). Yet, the existing literature is limited to the assessment of tourist satisfaction only with destination-based attributes. There has been little empirical research applied to the investigation of the relationship between the level of tourists' satisfaction and their perceptions of the QOL although it is conceptually suggested that the overall quality of life could be one of the determinants of the evaluation of CS (Barksy, 1992; Fournier and Mick, 1999). Given these, one could suggest that the QOL of tourists from different backgrounds may utilize different satisfaction perceptions regardless of satisfactory or dissatisfactory destination products. It was found by van Raaij and Francken (1984) that tourists from lower socio-economic groups and from higher age brackets are all likely to have lower expectations. They might therefore consider, for example, a summer vacation abroad to be a luxury consumption, resulting in higher levels of vacation satisfaction. It might be worth mentioning that the reliability of tourist satisfaction studies will probably be increased if the QOL indicators can be identified and their impacts on the level of satisfaction can be established methodologically. A substantial amount of work is needed for this to be achieved.

Sampling

A further point to be taken into account while carrying out destination satisfaction research is that tourist destinations attract customers from different cultures and countries; therefore it is not reasonable to examine the satisfaction level of only one specific group of customers. Those who come from other main generating countries also need to be included in this type of research. The level of spoken and written language at the destination may be very good for one group, but it may not seem so for those who speak another language. This example also applies to food consumption patterns of customers and so on. It seems likely that previous research did not extensively consider the comparison of satisfaction levels of those who are from different countries, but visiting the same destination. There is an increasing number of studies in other areas of consumer behaviour research such as attitude, perception or expectations dealing with cross-cultural comparison (Richardson and Crompton, 1988; Luk *et al.*, 1993; Armstrong *et al.*, 1997). The types of the sample population and the sample destination are also homogeneous, sampling respondents represent only one country and those visiting only one destination. These areas of tourist satisfaction research need to be improved. The comparative analysis of tourist satisfaction measures may help to reinforce the validity and generalization of the findings and may also assist destination authorities to establish the positioning strategies and explore their core competencies for each group.

Multiple members

There is a clear gap in the literature in relation to the lack of consideration of opinions of other members travelling in the same party, e.g. partners, children, friends. Surveys are usually given to only one member of a group or a family selecting one partner or one in a group of friends as the sample and ignoring other members' opinions and their possible influence on future behaviour. Fournier and Mick (1999) emphasize the fact that satisfaction levels of other friends or relatives in the party may be additional factors contributing to the formation of individual CS. For example, assume that children and one partner are dissatisfied while another partner is felt to be highly satisfied. In such a case, it is difficult to claim that this party is either satisfied or dissatisfied and is likely or unlikely to come back in the future. It is therefore necessary to include the opinions of other members in the survey by asking such questions as how satisfied they are as a family or how likely to consider a visit in the future.

Summary questions

The summary questions refer to the assessment of the relationship between individual attributes and overall satisfaction, between satisfaction and repeat behaviour or between satisfaction and the intention to recommend a resort. It is important to identify and measure CS with each component of the destination, since CS/D with one of the components leads to CS/D with the destination itself (Pizam *et al.,* 1978). As general dis/satisfaction is the result of evaluating positive and negative experiences, the relative importance of each component to the general impression should be investigated (Rust *et al.,* 1996). Only a small number of researchers employed summary questions relating to the level of overall satisfaction and future behaviour (e.g. Danaher and Arweiler, 1996; Cho, 1998; Kozak and Rimmington, 2000). An investigation of each attribute's impact on the general level of satisfaction and future intentions could demonstrate the strengths and weaknesses of destinations by assessing individual performance levels. The strongest items would be those where the destination has competitive advantage whereas the weakest items would be those which need to be developed further.

First-time and repeat tourists

Several marketing researchers have attempted to establish an association between the extent of past visits and the level of CS. Of these, some failed (Thirkell and Vredendurg, 1982; Jurowski *et al.,* 1995-96) while others believed that they succeeded in confirming the existence of an association (Westbrook and Newman, 1978). It was found that customers with past experience had greater satisfaction levels than did those without. It is speculated that the level of tourists' satisfaction may be coloured by their past experiences and, as a result, either higher or lower satisfaction scores might appear in comparison with those of first-time tourists. Therefore, Crompton and Love (1995) suggest that satisfaction analysis relating to both groups should be performed separately. However, with a single exception (Kozak and Rimmington, 2000), there has been limited investigation into tourist destinations. This part of the research needs to be investigated further and be introduced into the destination satisfaction literature as a new dimension of the tourist satisfaction measurement approach.

Data collection

Previous research indicates that different decisions have been made regarding when to measure tourist satisfaction. These include comparing pre-holiday expectations and post-holiday perceptions (e.g. Chon and Olsen, 1991; Pizam and Milman, 1993; Duke and Persia, 1996), monitoring during the holiday (e.g. Pizam *et al.,* 1978; Tribe and Snaith, 1998), upon completing the tour (e.g. Pearce, 1980; Loundsbury and Hoopes, 1985; Chon and Olsen, 1991) and just before completing a holiday (e.g. Danaher and Arweiler, 1996; Qu and Li, 1997). As explained in detail above, the use of the disconfirmation-based measurement approach and its variants seem not to be reasonable for tourist destinations. The performance-only approach has potential to ease the designation and management of the research process and analyse its findings along with those of other research projects to be administered in other destinations. The literature on CS/D suggests that satisfaction is a function of overall post-purchase evaluation (Fornell, 1992) and CS should be measured immediately after purchase (Peterson and Wilson, 1992). A study could therefore attempt to measure tourist satisfaction by distributing questionnaires while tourists are still at the destination airport and waiting for departure in order to obtain fresh feedback about perceptions of their holidays. By so doing, tourists have the benefit of the entire holiday to assess their satisfaction perceptions of resort facilities, attractions and customer services. The experience will still be fresh in their minds.

Conclusion

This chapter has highlighted the fact that the measurement of customer or tourist satisfaction is important in carrying out destination performance research due to the close relationship between the level of CS/D with vacation experiences and future behaviour. In line with the overview of major attempts to measure CS and the examination of previous research findings primarily focused on tourist destinations, this chapter has suggested that the measurement and management of CS within the context of destination marketing should consider the methodological weaknesses of previous research and their potential to improve. An investigation of these issues could provide a better understanding of CS with destinations and provide a more comprehensive picture of destinations than the present one.

References

Andreassen, T.W. (1995) Dissatisfaction with public services: The case of public transportation. *Journal of Services Marketing* 9(5), 30-41.

Armstrong, R.W., Mok, M., Go, F. and Chan, G. (1997) The importance of cross-cultural expectations in the measurement of service quality perceptions in the hotel industry. *International Journal of Hospitality Management* 16(2), 181-190.

Assael, H. (1987) *Consumer Behaviour and Marketing Action,* 3rd edn. PWS-KENT

Publishing Company, Boston.

Barksy, J.D. (1992) Customer satisfaction in the hotel industry: meaning and measurement. *Hospitality Research Journal* 16(1), 51-73.

Barsky, J.D. and Labagh, R. (1992) Strategy for customer satisfaction. *Cornell Hotel and Restaurant Administration Quarterly* 33, 32-40.

Baum, T. (1997) Making or breaking the tourist experience: the role of human resource management. In: Ryan, C. (ed.) *The Tourist Experience*. Cassell, London, pp. 92-111.

Bloemer, J.M. and Poiesz, T.B.C. (1989) The illusion of customer satisfaction. *Journal of Consumer Satisfaction, Dissatisfaction and Complaining Behaviour* 2, 43-48.

Boulding, W., Kalra, A., Staeling, R. and Zeithaml, V.A. (1993) A dynamic process model of service quality: from expectations to behavioural intentions. *Journal of Marketing Research* 30, 7-27.

Cadotte, E.R., Woodruff, R.B. and Jenkins, R.L. (1987) Expectations and norms in models of consumer satisfaction. *Journal of Marketing Research* 24, 305-314.

Cardozo, R.N. (1965) An experimental study of customer effort, expectation and satisfaction. *Journal of Marketing Research* 11, 244-249.

Cho, B. (1998) Assessing tourist satisfaction: An exploratory study of Korean youth tourists in Australia. *Tourism Recreation Research* 23(1), 47-54.

Chon, K.S. and Olsen, M.D. (1991) Functional and symbolic approaches to consumer satisfaction/dissatisfaction in tourism. *Journal of the International Academy of Hospitality Research* 28, 1-20.

Churchill, G.A. and Suprenant, C. (1982) An investigation into the determinants of customer satisfaction. *Journal of Marketing Research* 29, 491-504.

Crompton, J.L. and Love, L.L. (1995) The predictive validity of alternative approaches to evaluating quality of a festival. *Journal of Travel Research* 34(1), 11-25.

Cronin, J. and Taylor, S.A. (1992) Measuring service quality: A reexamination and extension. *Journal of Marketing* 56, 55-68.

Czepiel, J.A., Rosenberg, L.J. and Akerele, A. (1974) Perspectives on consumer satisfaction. In: Curhan, R.C. (ed.) 1974 Combined Proceedings Series nr. 36. American Marketing Association, Chicago, pp. 119-123.

Danaher, P.J. and Arweiler, N. (1996) Customer satisfaction in the tourist industry: A case study of visitors to New Zealand. *Journal of Travel Research* 35, 89-93.

Deming, W.E. (1982) *Quality, Productivity and Competitive Position*. Institute of Technology, Center for Advanced Engineering Study, Cambridge, Massachusetts.

Duke, C.R. and Persia, M.A. (1996) Consumer-defined dimensions for escorted tour industry segment: Expectations, satisfactions and importance. *Journal of Travel and Tourism Marketing* 5(1-2), 77-99.

Engledow, J.L. (1977) Was customer satisfaction a pig in a poke? *Business Horizons* 20(2), 87-94.

Erevelles, S. and Leavitt, C. (1992) A comparison of current models of consumer satisfaction/dissatisfaction. *Journal of Consumer Satisfaction, Dissatisfaction and Complaining Behavior* 5, 104-114.

Fishbein, M. (1967) A behavior theory approach to the relations between beliefs about an object and the attitude toward the object. In: Fishbein, M. (ed.) *Readings in Attitude Theory and Measurement*. Wiley, New York, pp. 389-400.

Fornell, C. (1992) A National Customer Satisfaction Barometer: The Swedish

Experience. *Journal of Marketing* 56, 6-21.

Fournier, S. and Mick, D.G. (1999) Rediscovering satisfaction. *Journal of Marketing* 63, 5-23.

Go, F. and Zhang, W. (1997) Applying importance-performance analysis to Beijing as an international meeting destination. *Journal of Travel Research* 36, 42-49.

Goodrich, J.N. (1978) The relationship between preferences for and perceptions of vacation destinations: Application of a choice model. *Journal of Travel Research* 17, 8-13.

Grönroos, C. (1978) A service-oriented approach to marketing of services. *European Journal of Marketing* 12(8), 588-601.

Grönroos, C. (1984) A service quality model and its marketing implications. *European Journal of Marketing* 18(4), 36-44.

Hair, J.F., Anderson, R.E., Tatham, R.L. and Black, W.C. (1995) *Multivariate data analysis with readings*, 4th edn. Prentice-Hall International, New Jersey.

Headey, B. (1983) Quality of life studies: Their implications for social and market researchers. *European Research* April, 56-67.

Helson, H. (1964) *Adaptation-level Theory*. Harper and Row, New York.

Hinkin, T.R., Tracey, J.B. and Enz, C.A. (1997) Scale construction: Developing reliable and valid measurement instruments. *Journal of Hospitality and Tourism Research* 21(1), 100-120.

Johnson, M.D. and Fornell, C. (1991) A framework for comparing customer satisfaction across individuals and product categories. *Journal of Economic Psychology* 12, 267-286.

Jurowski, C., Cumbow, M.W., Uysal, M. and Noe, F.P. (1995-96) The effects of instrumental and expressive factors on overall satisfaction in a park environment. *Journal of Environmental Systems* 24(1), 47-68.

Klaus, P. (1985) Quality epiphenomenon: The conceptual understanding of quality in face-to-face service encounters. In: Czepiel, J.A., Solomon, M.R., Suprenant, C.L. and Guttman, E.G. (eds.) *The Service Encounter: Managing Employee Customer Interaction in Service Business.* Lexington Books, Lexington, MA, pp. 17-33.

Kozak, M. and Nield, K. (1998) Importance-performance analysis and cultural perspectives in Romanian Black Sea resorts. *Anatolia: An International Journal of Tourism and Hospitality Research* 9(2), 99-116.

Kozak, M. and Rimmington, M. (2000) Tourist satisfaction with Mallorca, Spain, as an off-season holiday destination. *Journal of Travel Research* 39(February), 260-269.

LaTour, S.A. and Peat, N.C. (1979) Conceptual and methodological issues in consumer satisfaction research. In: Wilkie, W.L. (ed.) *Advances in Consumer Research Vol.6. Proceedings of the Association for Consumer Research Ninth Annual Conference.* Florida, pp. 431-437.

Laws, E. (1991) *Tourism marketing: Service and Quality Management Perspectives.* Stanley Thornes Ltd., Cheltenham.

Laws, E. (1995) *Tourist Destination Management: Issues, Analysis and Policies.* Routledge, New York.

Leong, S.M. and Tan, C.T. (1992) Assessing national competitive superiority: An importance-performance matrix approach. *Marketing Intelligence and Planning* 10(1), 42-48.

Loundsbury, J.W. and Hoopes, L.L. (1985) An investigation of factors associated with vacation satisfaction. *Journal of Leisure Research* 17, 1-13.

Luk, S.T.K., deLeon, C.T., Leong, F.W. and Li, E.L. (1993) Value segmentation of tourists' expectations of service quality. *Journal of Travel and Tourism Marketing* 2(4), 23-38.

Martilla, J. and James, J. (1977) Importance-performance analysis. *Journal of Marketing* 41, 77-79.

Mayo, E.J. and Jarvis, L.P. (1981) *The Psychology of Leisure Travel: Effective Marketing and Selling of Travel Services*. CBI Publishing Company, Boston.

Meyer, A. and Westerbarkey, P. (1996) Measuring and managing hotel guest satisfaction. In: Olsen, M.D., Teare, R. and Gummesson, E. (eds.) *Service Quality in Hospitality Organisations*. Cassell, London, pp. 185-203.

Miller, J.A. (1977) Studying satisfaction, modifying models, eliciting expectations, posing problems and making meaningful measurements. In: Hunt, H.K. (ed.) *Conceptualization and Measurement of Consumer Satisfaction and Dissatisfaction*. Marketing Science Institute, Cambridge, Massachusetts.

Moutinho, L. (1987) Consumer behaviour in tourism. *European Journal of Marketing* 21(1), 5-44.

Nolan, J.J. and Swan, J.E. (1984) Rising expectation: Do expectations increase with experience? In: Hunt, H.K. and Day, R.L. (eds.) *Combined Proceedings of the Eighth Conference and the Ninth Conference, Louisiana and Arizona 1984-1985*. Indiana University, Indianapolis, pp. 17-22.

Oh, H. and Parks, S.C. (1997) Customer satisfaction and service quality: A critical review of the literature and research implications for the hospitality industry. *Hospitality Research Journal* 20(3), 35-64.

Oliver, R.L. (1979) Conceptualizing and measurement of disconfirmation perceptions in the prediction of consumer satisfaction. In: Hunt, H.K. and Day, R.L. (eds.) *Refining Concepts and Measures of Consumer Satisfaction and Complaining Behavior: Papers from the Fourth Annual Conference on Consumer Satisfaction, Dissatisfaction and Complaining Behavior*. Bloomington, Indiana, pp. 2-6.

Oliver, R.L. (1980) A cognitive model for the antecedents and consequences of satisfaction decisions. *Journal of Marketing Research* 27, 460-469.

Oliver, R.L. (1981) Measurement and evaluation of satisfaction processes in retail settings. *Journal of Retailing* 57(3), 25-48.

Olshavsky, R.W. and Miller, J.A. (1972) Consumer expectations, product performance and perceived product quality. *Journal of Marketing Research* 9, 19-21.

Parasuraman, A., Zeithaml, V.A. and Berry, L.L. (1985) A conceptual model of service quality and its implications for future research. *Journal of Marketing* 49, 41-50.

Parasuraman, A., Zeithaml, V.A. and Berry, L.L. (1988) Servqual: A multiple item scale for measuring consumer perceptions of service quality. *Journal of Retailing* 64(1), 12-37.

Parasuraman, A., Zeithaml, V.A. and Berry, L.L. (1991) Refinement and reassessment of the servqual scale. *Journal of Retailing* 67(4), 421-450.

Parasuraman, A., Zeithaml, V.A. and Berry, L.L. (1994) Reassessment of expectations as a comparison standard in measuring service quality: Implications for further research. *Journal of Marketing* 58, 121 ff.

Pearce, P.L. (1980) A favorability-satisfaction model of tourists' evaluations. *Journal of*

Travel Research 19, 13-17.

Peterson, R.A. and Wilson, W.R. (1992) Measuring customer satisfaction: Fact and artifact. *Journal of the Academy of Marketing Science* 20(1), 61-71.

Pizam, A. and Milman, A. (1993) Predicting satisfaction among first time visitors to a destination by using the expectancy disconfirmation theory. *International Journal of Hospitality Management* 12(2), 197-209.

Pizam, A., Neumann, Y. and Reichel, A. (1978) Dimensions of tourist satisfaction area. *Annals of Tourism Research* 5, 314-322.

Pizam, A., Neumann, Y. and Reichel, A. (1979) Tourist satisfaction: Uses and misuses. *Annals of Tourism Research* 6, 195-197.

Prakash, V. (1984) Validity and reliability of the confirmation of expectations paradigm as a determinant of consumer satisfaction. *Journal of the Academy of Marketing Science* 12(4), 63-76.

Qu, H. and Li, I. (1997) The characteristics and satisfaction of Mainland Chinese visitors to Hong Kong. *Journal of Travel Research* 36, 37-41.

Quelch, J.A. and Ash, S.B. (1981) Consumer satisfaction with professional services. In: Donnely, J.H. and George, W.R. (eds.) *Marketing of Services.* American Marketing Association, Illinois, pp. 82-85.

Richardson, S.L. and Crompton, J. (1988) Vacation patterns of French and English Canadians. *Annals of Tourism Research* 15(4), 430-448.

Robinson, L.M. and Berl, R.L. (1979) What about compliments: A follow-up study on customer complaints and compliments. In: Hunt, H.K. and Day, R.L. (eds.) *Refining Concepts and Measures of Consumer Satisfaction and Complaining Behavior: Papers from the Fourth Annual Conference on Consumer Satisfaction, Dissatisfaction and Complaining Behavior.* Bloomington, Indiana, pp. 144-147.

Rust, R.T., Zahonik, A.J. and Keiningham, T.L. (1996) *Service Marketing.* Harper Collins Publishers, New York.

Ryan, C. (1995) *Researching Tourist Satisfaction.* Routledge, London.

Ryan, C. (1997) From motivation to assessment. In: Ryan, C. (ed.) *The Tourist Experience.* Cassell, London, pp. 48-72.

Spreng, R.A. and Olshavsky, R.W. (1993) A desires congruency model of consumer satisfaction. *Journal of the Academy of Marketing Science* 21(Summer), 169-177.

Swan, J.E. and Combs, L.J. (1976) Product performance and consumer satisfaction: A new concept. *Journal of Marketing* 40(April), 25-33.

Thibaut, J.W. and Kelley, H.H. (1959) *The Social Psychology of Groups.* Wiley, New York.

Thirkell, P. and Vredenburg, H. (1982) Prepurchase information search and postpurchase product satisfaction: The effects of different sources. In: Walker, B.L. (ed.) *An Assessment of Marketing Thought and Practice.* American Marketing Association, Chicago.

Tinsley, H.O. and Tinsley, D. (1987) Uses of factor analysis in counselling psychology research. *Journal of Counseling Psychology* 34, 414-424.

Tribe, J. and Snaith, T. (1998) From servqual to Holsat: Holiday satisfaction in Varadero, Cuba. *Tourism Management* 19(1), 25-34.

Tse, D.K. and Wilton, P.C. (1988) Models of consumer satisfaction formation: An extension. *Journal of Marketing Research* 25(May), 204-212.

Uhl, K.P. and Schoner, B. (1969) *Marketing Research: Information Systems and*

Decision Making. Wiley, New York.

van Raaij, V. and Francken, F.A. (1984) Vacation decisions, activities and satisfactions. *Annals of Tourism Research* 11, 101-112.

Weber, K. (1997) Assessment of tourist satisfaction using the expectancy disconfirmation theory: A study of German travel market in Australia. *Pacific Tourism Review* 1, 35-45.

Westbrook, R.A. (1980) A rating scale for measuring product/service satisfaction. *Journal of Marketing* 44, 68-72.

Westbrook, R.A. and Newman, J.W. (1978) An analysis of shopper dissatisfaction for major household appliances. *Journal of Marketing Research* 15(August), 456-466.

Westbrook, R.A. and Oliver, R.L. (1991) The dimensionality of consumption emotion patterns and consumer satisfaction. *Journal of Consumer Research* 18, 84-91.

Woodruff, R.B., Cadotte, E.R. and Jenkins, R.I. (1983) Modeling consumer satisfaction processes using experience-based norms. *Journal of Marketing Research* 20, 296-304.

Zairi, M. (1996) *Benchmarking for Best Practice: Continuous Learning through Sustainable Innovation.* Butterworth-Heinemann, Oxford.

Table 1 Overview of previous tourist destination satisfaction research

Author(s)	Method	Scale	Nr. of Items	Timing	Summary Questions	Sample Size	Sample Population	Sample Destination
Danaher and Arweiler 1996	• Disconfirmation • Performance only	• 3-point better/ worse than expected • 11-point satisfaction scale	28	At the destination airport while departing	Overall satisfaction, intention to recommend	189	Mixed	New Zealand
Cho 1998	• Disconfirmation • Expectation- performance	• 7-point (better/ worse than expected) • 5-point	22	On the first and on the last day of each tour	Overall satisfaction, intention to recommend, intention to return	83	Korean	Australia
Pizam *et al.* 1978	• Performance only	• 5-point satisfaction scale	32	During the course of holiday at the sample destination	-------	685	American	US (Cape Cod)
Chon and Olsen 1990	• Expectation- performance	• 7-point D-T scale • 5-point Face scale • Non-verbal graphic scale	15	After tourists have completed their holiday experiences (by sending postal questionnaires)	-------	192	American	US (Virginia)
Qu and Li 1997	• Performance only	• 4-point satisfaction scale	33	While leaving the destination	Intention to return	100	Chinese	Hong Kong

Author(s)	Method	Scale	Nr. of Items	Timing	Summary Questions	Sample Size	Sample Population	Sample Destination
Tribe and Snaith 1998	• Expectation-performance	• 5-point Likert scale	56	During the course of holiday at the sample destination (in the hotel)	------	102	British	Cuba
Weber 1997	• Expectation-performance	• 5-point scale	14	On the first and on the last day of vacation	Overall satisfaction	69	German	Australia
Pizam and Milman 1993	• Expectation-performance	• 5 point Likert scale	21	Prior to holiday and after completion	Overall satisfaction	181	American	Spain
Kozak and Rimmington 2000	• Performance only	• 7-point D-T scale	38	At the destination airport while leaving	Overall satisfaction Intention to return Intention to recommend	220	British	Spain

Chapter twenty
A Review of Comparison Standards Used in Service Quality and Customer Satisfaction Studies: Some Emerging Issues for Hospitality and Tourism Research

Yüksel Ekinci, Michael Riley
School of Management Studies for the Service Sector
University of Surrey, Guildford GU2 5XH, UK

Joseph S. Chen
Department of Hospitality and Tourism Management
Virginia Polytechnic Institute and State University, Blacksburg, VA 24061-0429, USA

Abstract

This paper reviews the literature on comparison standards in service quality and satisfaction research. We identify various comparison standards, which include expectations, desires, equity and experiences employed and critically review their application. We draw out issues which arise and put forwards ways in which these can be explored in the future.

Introduction

The use of comparisons is central to our understanding of both service quality and customer satisfaction. This brings to the notion of comparison standards – what is being used as a reference comparison when evaluation takes place? This question has important implications for methodology. Although several comparison standards have been introduced into the literature from different perspectives, their utilization often triggers methodological problems in the measurement of service quality, mainly vague conceptualization and misinterpretation. Moreover, methodological problems have arisen when a single comparison standard is expected to be generic for every situation. Although these issues were addressed in generic marketing literature, the studies of comparison standard in hospitality and tourism literature are limited and the existing ones made a little impact in making a good progress. For example, customers give high scores on the expectation scale if their normative expectations are measured. When this score is used as a comparison standard against perceived performance, it is evident that perceived quality always accounts as negative (Parasuraman *et al.,*1991).

Recognizing the deficiencies on service quality research, this paper aims to first explore the nature of comparison standard and then to draw guidelines to measure service quality and customer satisfaction in the hospitality, tourism arena. To this end, the study first provides in-depth discussion on the dimensions that have been used to measure the service quality and customer satisfaction in the extant literature and then goes on to make recommendations to expand research in this area. The discussion involves an examination of four concepts closely associated with the comparisons; expectations, equity, experience, and desires.

Comparison Standards

Expectations

Expectations are widely employed as a comparison standard in the majority of customer satisfaction and service quality studies. According to expectancy value theory, consumers compare their expected level of performance with the perceived service performance in order to reach satisfaction or quality decision. However, Liljander and Strandvic (1993a, p. 12) argue that the use of expectations in those researches is itself usually vague and therefore it has to be refined in order to improve interpretation of the measurement data:

'The term expectations in service quality literature has a different meaning for different authors and the meaning is not always made clear to the reader, who reads into the word his/her own interpretation. Some research reports do not even mention how expectations were operationalized, thus making it difficult for the reader to draw any conclusion from the results'.

Definitions of expectations have varied from narrow to broad perspectives. A narrow view of expectations would see them as belief about the future performance of a product or service. This may be gained through various sources such as previous experiences, personal needs, and word-of-mouth promotions. Despite the fact that using narrow type of expectations is popular and reduces the confusion in responding to questions, this approach limits our understanding of the complex nature of expectations concept and how the consumer's evaluation mechanism works in assessing service quality and the cognitive processes involved in evaluation. For example confusion arises when expectations fail to predict customer satisfaction. LaTour and Peat (1979) argue that consumers can still be satisfied with products although they do not meet consumer's expectations when the product is better than anything else currently available. Hence early customer satisfaction scholars attempted to explore the nature of expectations in detail.

A broader definition of expectation implies that expectations are associated with different *levels of performance*. Miller's (1977) conceptualization of expectations is notable. Figure 1 shows the hierarchical model of expectations devised by Miller.

According to his description, expectations are classified into *ideal, expected, minimum tolerable,* and *deserved* categories. The ideal is the 'wished for' level. The ideal reflects what the respondents feel performance of the product, or service 'can be'.

The 'expected' is based on what respondent's objective calculation of probability of performance 'will be'. This is also known as *predictive* expectation. The 'minimum tolerable' is concerned with the least acceptable performance level. This is 'better than nothing' and reflects what the minimum level the respondent feels performance 'must be'. The 'deserved' level is determined by the individual's evaluation of 'rewards and costs'. Hence, it reflects what individuals in the light of their 'investments, feels that the performance "ought to be" or "should be"' (Miller, 1977, p. 76). Expectations are structured in a hierarchical order and related with different level of satisfaction. The desired expectation stands at the top of this hierarchy whereas minimum tolerable stands at the bottom. The position of the expected and deserved service may exchange according to situational factors (e.g. consumers' investment of product and the degree of feeling).

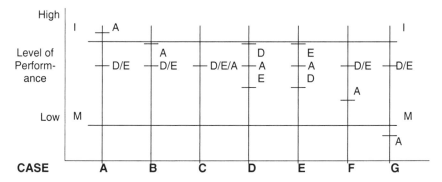

A = Actual Performance, I = Ideal Performance, E= Expected Probable Performance, D = Deserved Performance, M = Minimum Tolerable Performance,
Source: Miller (1977)
Figure 1 Types of expectations and levels of performance

The notion of expectations has also been a great interest to the Nordic American School of thought. Parasuraman *et al.* (1988) initially stated that the 'should' type of expectation is appropriate to measure service quality. This was actually based on the customer belief probabilities and reflects their *desires* and *wants*. For practical purposes, it is assumed that that expectation will be related to levels of satisfaction, that is, the 'should' means a degree of satisfaction. However, in a subsequent study, Parasuraman *et al.* (1991) report that the 'should' type of expectation is not useful in measuring service quality, since as expectation (E) is subtracted from perception (P) in the gap equation the mean value of expectation is usually higher than the perception and the gap score is always concluded as negative. Then, they introduced the idea of the normative expectation changing the statement from a 'Company should have...' statement to an 'Excellent company will have...' statement. In order to clarify what the excellent service means, Parasuraman *et al.* (1991, pp. 3-4) state that an excellent service is similar to the 'ideal' standard used in the satisfaction literature. However, the concept of an ideal point is problematic. In gap scoring, the perceived quality might decline as perception increasingly exceeds the ideal point in some situations. A considerable proportion of those sampled interpreted the meaning of the ideal point differently. In other words, even when experience is shared, people's interpretation of where the norm lies can vary (Teas, 1993, 1994).

According to their subsequent research, two types of expectations were proposed: desired service, and adequate service. Figure 2 shows Zeithaml *et al.*'s expectation model. Desired service defined, as the level of service that customers hope to receive, is a mixture of what customers believe the level of performance 'can be' and 'should be.' This measure associates with service quality. The adequate service expectation is defined as the lower level of performance that the consumers will accept. They also note that this level of expectation is comparable to Miller's minimum tolerable expectation (Zeithaml *et al.*, 1993, p. 6). Furthermore, the minimum tolerable expectation refers to predictive expectation and this associates with customer satisfaction. Adequate service is a minimum level of service that consumers are willing to accept. The area between desired service and adequate service is called 'the zone of tolerance' (ZOT). ZOT represents the range of service performance customers would tolerate.

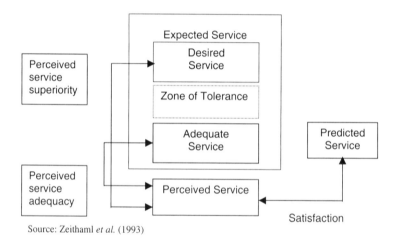

Source: Zeithaml *et al.* (1993)

Figure 2 Zeithaml *et al.*'s Expectation Model

By this conceptualization the two concepts, satisfaction and service quality, are rather distinct. Also service quality is superior and subordinate to customer satisfaction. A consumer may be satisfied as long as the perceived service performance meets customers' predicted expectations, but this does not ensure desired service quality. In turn, perceived service quality ensures consumer satisfaction (Zeithaml *et al.*, 1993, p. 9). Zeithaml *et al.* (1993, pp. 1-12) call the *desired* minus *perceived* and *adequate* minus *perceived* comparisons *service superiority* and *service adequacy* respectively. Service quality increases as a function of the gap between perceived service and the desired or adequate service and the actual perceived performance.

However, according to Zeithaml *et al.*'s study, desired service is mixed with Miller's ideal service and deserved service. Although they argue that adequate service is comparable to Miller's minimum tolerable level that is better than nothing. He notes that dissatisfaction occurs even if the perceived performance is below the expected or deserved but above the minimum tolerable level.

'… consumer experience dissatisfaction. He may attempt to remedy the situation and probably won't purchase that brand (continue patronising that store) but will switch to another. If no alternative is available, he will probably continue to use the product as long as it "satisfies" or fills a need'. (Miller 1977, p.79)

Based on the above statement, performing above the minimum tolerable level does not ensure satisfaction as Parasuraman *et al.* proposed. More importantly consumers are not tolerant of a level of performance that is equal to the minimum-tolerable level. Taking into account Miller's definition, consumers may only tolerate when the actual performance is below the ideal but equal to predictive and deserved service performance. A zone of tolerance may occur when the actual performance is below the expected (predicted) but equal to the deserved level. According to Miller's conceptualization, consumers may be disappointed at this level of performance and they feel some weak dissatisfaction but this situation can best be described as 'unsatisfaction' rather than 'dissatisfaction'. On the contrary, if performance is between minimum tolerable expectation and the deserved expectation level as being located on the top, consumers encounter dissatisfaction. Hence, the bottom line of satisfaction occurs where the actual performance is levelled to the *deserved expectation*.

Testing of Zeithaml *et al.*'s service expectation model has been an interest to another research team. Although there are some measurement problems involved, Dion *et al.* (1998) demonstrate that respondents can distinguish *adequate* and *desired* service. These two measures were found to be distinct from the perceived and predicted service. In other words, the conceptual proposition of a 'zone of tolerance'(ZOT) was confirmed. They advocate that the range of the ZOT influences perceived service quality but not satisfaction. Moreover, customers with larger ZOT tend to have a more favourable view of service quality. Service satisfaction on the other hand, is not concerned with the boundaries of the ZOT in a comparison process and this should not be affected by changes in the size of the ZOT. Their study also suggests that the desired service is less variable compared with adequate service (Dion *et al.*, 1998, p. 82). Customer's desired service level may move down in order to maintain the ZOT. Furthermore, the study not only supports the relationship between service superiority (desired vs. perceived service, r = .37) and service quality but also between service adequacy and service quality (adequate vs. perceived service r = .18). The correlation between service quality and service superiority also reveals that service superiority is a determinant of service quality compared to service adequacy.

A pragmatic argument raised by Johnston (1987) emphasizes that customers' expectations are dynamic and continue to change before, during or even after the visit period. Therefore, expectations are difficult to measure in a particular point in time. The previous studies suggest that expectations may be valuable when assessed at a different consumption period (e.g. pre- or post-consumption stages). Despite the fact that perceived performance, alone, was found to be a strong variable in predicting service quality in empirical studies, it is still abstract and provides limited information to enhance our understanding of service quality and satisfaction concepts. Hence, assessing desired and deserved expectations may be valuable to locate the level of service performance. This information provides additional information to managers to improve existing performance. Alternative ideal or deserved service level may be used as internal *benchmarks* or *standards* in order to adjust what the future performance level of organization should be. In addition, assessing expectations at the pre-consumption can be a valuable tool for market segmentation.

As the *deserved* service expectations are mixed with *desired* services in the previous studies, the relationship between these two concepts needs further elaboration. Although Dion *et al.*'s (1998, p. 81) study shows that 'buyers are willing to accept a minimal service level significantly lower than predicted (expected service) service level', whether or not this level of service is above the deserved service level recommended by Miller's model is not known. Because they did not measure *deserved* service.

Equity

Equity theory has been applied to the study of customer dis/satisfaction within different consumption situations (Oliver and DeSarbo, 1988). Equity theory postulates that a person involved in social (or exchange) relationships compares his input/outcome ratios with others' input/outcome ratios. The equity theory suggests that parties in the exchange relationship are satisfied when they feel they had been treated fairly. Inequity occurs when the perceived inputs and/or outcome ratio are believed to be inconsistent with the perceived inputs and/or outcome of other parties (Huppertz *et al.*, 1978). In line with this view, equity theory is a bipolar concept similar to the expectancy-disconfirmation paradigm. However, the distinction between these two theories is specific to the kind of comparative factors or evaluative outcomes (Oliver, 1997, p. 209). For example, in equity theory, one measures the perception of other's inputs and outcomes as opposed to expectation or norms that are employed by the expectancy-disconfirmation theory. Furthermore, each situation leads to a different emotional outcome (e.g. positive equity may cause embarrassment, guilt or glee whereas positive disconfirmation causes delight and elation).

Although the use of equity theory as a comparison standard is recommended to assess satisfaction between the two parties, its support was controversial in empirical studies. For example, Tse and Wilton's (1988) study shows that equity was not a good comparison standard; however, Liljander (1995, p. 148) argues that the discouraging result might be obtained due to poor measurement.

Experience-based norms

It is proposed that consumers employ their previous experiences as a comparison standard for the evaluation of performance before arriving at satisfaction decision. Consumer's experiences may be gathered from more than one source and eventually constitute norms that establish what a focal brand should be able to achieve. Woodruff *et al.* (1983) claim that the experience-based norm differs from that of customer expectations in the sense that it is derived through the experience of focal or different brands and thus, not attainable ideals. Furthermore, 'experience-based norms reflect desired performance in meeting needs/wants. They are constrained by the performance consumer believe is possible as indicated by the performance of known brands' (Cadotte *et al.*, 1987, p. 306).'

No direct experience is necessary for evaluation of focal brand (belief on what a focal brand should achieve) and experiences with other brands in the evoked set, similar product categories or brand attitude might be employed as a norm. Therefore experience brand norm may share some common core with other brands and similar products. In line with this, the experience based-norm can be operationalized in three possible forms including a best brand norm, a brand-based norm, and a product-based norm.

In a comparative study of various alternative standards, Cadotte *et al.* (1987) show that inferred disconfirmation models with the best brand norm or product type norm explain more of the variation in satisfaction than the focal brand as a norm. Moreover, across three-service situation, the expectation model (belief standard) was not supported for predicting satisfaction. The study suggests that there is no single comparison standard that best explains customer satisfaction, rather it varies across situations.

Liljander and Strandvik (1993b) classify the available comparison standards into the four categories: transaction, relationship, industry standards and ideal. The transaction standard focuses perceived quality of a specific transaction. The predictive expectation (will happen) and equity are the main pillars of this group. The relationship group refers to image and brand norm where consumer's relationship with company is taken into account over time. The industry standards contain the *best brand norm*, *product norm*, and *adequate standard*. The latter may be compiled through consumer's experiences from other companies within the industry. Although the ideal expectation may represent excellent service as in the form of desired service, it is not necessarily connected with any existing service currently used. Their study suggests that the brand norm is the most effective comparison standard whereas the best brand norm was found to be the least effective one in assessing service quality.

Desires

The theoretical arguments employing values (desires, needs or wants) as a comparison standard is compelling, because values occupy the focal point of human perception and evaluation (Rokeach, 1973). The means-end models imply that product attributes are linked to consumer values. The consequences of this evaluation are the desired outcome (Gutman, 1982; Olshavsky and Spreng, 1989). Although the early empirical studies reveal little support for using values as the standard, this result is controversial and likely to be caused by methodological problems (Westbrook and Reilly, 1983). It was also demonstrated that the formulation of desired expectation as 'should expectation' causes serious measurement problems in the gap model (Teas, 1994).

However, Spreng *et al.* (1996) offer an alternative model by considering the previous methodological problems. They employed values as a comparison standard by redefining the roles of desires, expectations, and performance in the process of satisfaction formation. The results indicated that the desired congruency between what a person desires and what they get, had a significant effect on attribute satisfaction, information satisfaction, and overall satisfaction. However, the findings were limited due to the fact that the study was based on experimental research design. Therefore, the concept of value and its relationship with service quality and customer satisfaction may need further elaboration.

Multiple comparison standard

The polarity of expectations and experience based criteria highlights probability of multiple standards being used by consumers in arriving at the satisfaction of services. The same idea also introduces the switching behaviours of comparison standards from person to person as well as from situation to situation. Woodruff *et al.* (1983, p. 299) note that:

> 'One person may have considerable experience with only one brand, whereas another may have experiences with an assortment of brands. Moreover, the same person may apply different norms in different use situations. For instance, one kind of norm may be used to determine satisfaction with restaurant visited for a special occasion, whereas another might be applied when the family goes out for a meal'.

Woodruff *et al.* (1991) note that if a customer uses multiple comparison standards at the time of measurement, the identification of the right standard may be difficult due to the factors involved with limited memory (e.g. accessibility, product type, life style etc.). Although this may be overcome by providing as many standards as possible, service quality scholars refer this issue as a continuing debate that has to be addressed by a further study (Parasuraman *et al.*, 1994a)

An alternative argument emphasizes that consumers recall different evaluation strategies for post-purchase evaluation relative to pre-purchase evaluation (Gardial *et al.*, 1994). This reinforces the idea that the standard may be constructed at the time of appraisal rather than recalled from prior experience. Furthermore, the comparison standard used by consumers may not only shift from single to multiple before and after evaluation but also change by type. If one accepts that customers use multiple comparison standards, a further issue has arisen in order to identify the right pair and their relationship with evaluation of service quality.

Which Comparison Standard is Better?

Liljander (1994) argues that if the nature of comparison standard can be articulated it may shed a light on the conceptual distinction between satisfaction and service quality. Hence, the question of which comparison standard is most likely to influence satisfaction or service quality was addressed but the findings have diverged according to the researchers' interpretation of service quality and satisfaction. Tse and Wilton (1988) examine this possibility by using three types of comparison standards: expectations, ideal, and equity. The results indicate that customers use two types of comparison standards expectation and brand norm simultaneously in satisfaction formation, but not equity. However, Liljander (1994) pinpoints that *deserved service* is the best determinant of satisfaction with service among the other seven alternatives including *service excellence, best brand norm, product type norm, brand norm, adequate service, predicted service, and equity*. Although deserved service has been very seldom used, mis-specified or mixed with other standards in previous studies, this is in a sense what customers get as a benefit as a result of interaction with an organization. In fact, the use of comparison standard is recommended to be situational and consumers may use one or more comparison standards at the same time. For example, Spreng *et al.* (1996)

produced first evidence that consumers use multiple standards in making satisfaction decisions. Their study reveals that both expectations and desired congruency influence satisfaction. However, their model proposes that while both standards are important, the effective use of comparison standard may be reduced under different conditions, such as the amount of information received or the type of product in evaluation.

Discussion and Conclusion

In the light of the examination above it is possible to make a number of suggestions for future research. One issue emerging from the discussion is that the level of expectation is proposed to be dynamic. In which case it may be more meaningful to measure the customers' pre-purchase expectations in order to gain a better understanding of how the customer perceives tourism and hospitality products/services from the beginning. This measurement should be based on customers' ideal expectations (Martin and Simmons, 1999). We argue that the decision-making process and post-purchase evaluation are likely to be affected by ideal expectations that may be consequent upon goals. Achieving or failing one's goals critically affects evaluation of services. Furthermore, marketing communication may use this information to influence customer's decision-making process.

Having suggested that pre-purchase expectations are essential, from a service quality and satisfaction point of view it may be more meaningful to measure customers' post-purchase expectations in order to determine what the critical factors, from the customer perspective are. We argue that *predictive* expectations and *deserved* expectations are crucial in forming satisfaction and service quality judgement.

In turning to the issue of comparison standards, it may be possible, in methodological terms, to illuminate the differences between satisfaction and quality by measuring them against different comparison standards. Such research would reveal the antecedents of constructs from both concepts. Hence, the degree of difference in antecedents would be one way of differentiating the concepts.

In a sense there is a case for suggesting that there is an issue of overlap between expectations, satisfaction, and service quality. They can be seen in terms of a shared mental script. That is, that predictive expectation provides a mental framework or script that describes a range of attributes that have to be satisfied. The question is – does this range over the evaluation of service quality? This idea has certain practical implications. Management can not control service quality but they can influence customer satisfaction during the service encounter. If research can discover customer's predictive expectations, then assuming the 'shared script' scenario it follows that managers should be able to control satisfaction in order to improve perceived quality, if one accepts that satisfaction is an antecedent of service quality.

The diversity and multiple components of hospitality and tourism activities make it a complex and unique product. Customers often experience new products and environments in their visits of service areas (visiting a hotel or destination for holiday). Accordingly, the unpredictable nature of new environment causes frustration as well as stresses on consumers. Understanding customers' predictive expectations helps managers to establish appropriate scripts to avoid possible confusion and disappointments in service operations (Shoemaker, 1996). Furthermore, by comparing customers' predictive expectations to their ideal expectations may help them to understand customers better. Hence, with the above comparisons, the needed marketing message can be formulated effectively in order to provide a realistic cognitive script.

Finally, in addition to the above conceptual and methodological ramifications, researchers might consider exploring the following six critical issues in relation to other comparison standards and their utilization in order to advance the theories involving service quality and customer satisfaction, helping provide hospitality and tourism practitioners and researchers better insights on utilizing the comparison standards.

1. What is the relationship between other comparison standards and different types of expectations?
2. Would customers' perception of service quality and satisfaction differ if they had different types of expectation? Although Anderson (1973) proposed four theories deeply rooted in cognitive psychology in order to understand the consumer's evaluation of the disconfirmation process and satisfaction decision (e.g. Cognitive Dissonance Theory, Contrast Theory, Generalized Negativity Theory, and Assimilation Contrast Theory), there is a lack of empirical research in this area.
3. What is the relationship between the different types of expectations and brand norm?
4. Do customers' zones of tolerance (ZOT) differ according to product and service type? What is the range of ZOT? Does this vary according to market segments and the type of hospitality or tourism product?
5. Is there a relationship between customer's ZOT and post-purchase behaviours (e.g. intention to recommend and intention to visit)?
6. What type of comparison standard is more relevant to service quality and customer satisfaction?

References

Anderson, R.E. (1973) Consumer dissatisfaction: the effects of disconfirmed expectancy on perceived product performance. *Journal of Marketing Research* 10, 38-44.

Cadotte, E.R., Woodruff, R.B. and Jenkins, R.L. (1987) Expectations and norms in models of consumer satisfaction. *Journal of Marketing Research* 24, 305-314.

Dion, P.A., Javalgi, R. and Dilorenzo-Aiss, J. (1998) An Empirical assessment of the Zeitmanl, Berry and Parasuraman service expectation model. *The Service Industries Journal* 18(4), 66-86.

Gardial, S.F., Clemons, D.S., Woodruff, R.B., Schumann, D.W. and Burns, M.J. (1994) Comparing consumers' recall of prepurchase and postpurchase product evaluation experiences. *Journal of Consumer Research* 20, 548-560.

Gutman, J. (1982) A means-end chain model based on consumer categorization process. *Journal of Marketing* 46, 60-72.

Huppertz, J.W., Arenson S.J. and Evans, R.H. (1978) An application of equity theory to buyer-seller exchange situations. *Journal of Marketing Research* 15, 250-260.

Johnston, R. (1987) A framework for developing quality strategy in a customer processing operation. *Journal of Quality and Reliability Management* 4, 37-45.

LaTour, S.A. and Peat, N.C. (1979) Conceptual and methodological issues in consumer satisfaction research. In: William, L.W. (eds.) *Advances In Consumer Research*. Association for Consumer Research, Ann Arbor, MI, pp. 431-437.

Liljander, V. (1994) Modeling perceived service quality using different comparison standard. *Journal of Consumer Satisfaction and Dissatisfaction* 7, 126-142.

Liljander, V. (1995) Introducing deserved service and equity into service quality models. In: Kleinaltenkamp, M. (ed.) *Dienstleistungsmarketing: Konzeptionen und Anwendungen*. Betriebswirstschaftlicher Verlag. Wiesbaden, Germany, pp. 143-168.

Liljander, V. and Strandvik, T. (1993a) Different comparison standard as determinants of service quality. *Journal of Consumer Satisfaction and Dissatisfaction* 6, 118-132.

Liljander, V. and Strandvik, T. (1993b) Estimating zones of tolerance in perceived service quality and perceived service value. *International Journal of Service Industry Management* 4(2), 6-28.

Martin, D. and Simmons, P. (1999) Customer expectations: a conceptual model for understanding the expectations continuum. *Journal of Hospitality and Leisure Marketing* 6(1), 67-81.

Miller, J.A. (1977) Studying satisfaction: modifying models, eliciting expectations, posing problems and making meaningful measurements. In: Hunt, H.K. (ed.) *Conceptualizations and Measurement of Consumer Satisfaction and Dissatisfaction*. Indiana University, School of Business, Bloomington, pp. 72-91.

Oliver, R.L. (1997) *Satisfaction: A Behavioral Perspective On The Consumer*. McGraw-Hill Company, London.

Oliver, R.L. and DeSarbo, W.S. (1988) Response determinants in satisfaction judgement. *Journal of Consumer Research* 14, 495-507.

Oliver, R.L. and Swan, J.E. (1989) Equity and disconfirmation perceptions as influences on merchant and product satisfaction. *Journal of Consumer Research* 16, 372-383.

Olshavsky, R.W. and Spreng, R.A. (1989) A desires as standard model of consumer satisfaction. *Journal of Consumer Satisfaction, Dissatisfaction and Complaining Behaviour* 2, 49-54.

Parasuraman, A., Zeithaml, V.A. and Berry, L.L. (1988) SERVQUAL a multiple-item scale for measuring consumer perception of service quality. *Journal of Retailing* 64, 13-40.

Parasuraman, A., Berry, L.L. and Zeithaml, V.A. (1991) Refinement and reassessment of the SERVQUAL scale. *Journal of Retailing* 67, 421-450.

Parasuraman, A., Zeithaml, V.A. and Berry, L.L. (1994a) Alternative scales for measuring service quality: a comparative assessment based on psychometric and diagnostic criteria. *Journal of Retailing* 70 (3), 193-199.

Rokeach, M. (1973) *The Nature of Human Values*. The Free Press, New York.

Shoemaker, S. (1996) Scripts: precursor of customer expectations. *Cornell Hotel and Restaurant Administration Quarterly* 37, 42-53.

Spreng, R.A. and Mackoy, R.D. (1996) An empirical examination of a model of perceived service quality and satisfaction. *Journal of Retailing* 72(2), 201-214.

Spreng, R.A., MacKenzie, S.B. and Olshavsky, R.W. (1996) A re-examination of the determinants of consumer satisfaction. *Journal of Marketing* 60, 15-32.

Teas, R.K. (1993) Expectations, performance evaluation, and consumers' perceptions of quality. *Journal of Marketing* 57, 18-34.

Teas, R.K. (1994) Expectations as a comparison standard in measuring service quality. *Journal of Marketing* 58, 132-139.

Tse, D.K. and Wilton, P.C. (1988) Models of consumer satisfaction formation, an extension. *Journal of Marketing Research* 25, 204-212.

Westbrook, R.A. and Reilly, M.D. (1983) Value-precept disparity: an alternative to the disconfirmation of expectations theory of consumer satisfaction. In: Bagozzi, R.P. and Tybout, A.M. (eds.) *Advances in Consumer Research*. Association for Consumer Research, Ann Arbor, MI, pp. 256-261.

Woodruff, R.B., Cadotte, E.R. and Jenkins, R.L. (1983) Modeling consumer satisfaction processes using experiences-based norms. *Journal of Marketing Research* 20, 296-304.

Woodruff, R.B., Clemons, S.D., Schumann, D.W., Gardial, S.F. and Burns, M.J. (1991) The standard issue in cs/d research: a historical perspective. *Journal of Consumer Satisfaction, Dissatisfaction and Complaining Behavior* 4, 103-109.

Zeithaml, V.A., Berry, L.L. and Parasuraman, A. (1993) The nature and determinants of customer expectations of service. *Journal of Academy of Marketing Science* 24(1), 1-12.

Chapter twenty-one
The Antecedents and Consequences of Vacationers' Dis/satisfaction: Tales from the Field

Alain Decrop
Department of Business Administration, University of Namur, Belgium

Abstract

In this paper, vacationers' post-experience processes are revisited from an interpretive perspective. Propositions regarding the antecedents and consequences of dis/satisfaction are generated based on the grounded analysis of empirical material about the vacation decision-making process of 25 Belgian households. On one hand, dis/satisfaction judgments appear to result from the intervention of emotions or from comparison, attribution and distribution processes. On the other hand, it is shown that satisfaction (dissatisfaction) does not always lead to repeat purchase (behavioural change) but may sometimes result in attitudinal and behavioural change (repeat purchase). Different theories are used to comment on those emerging findings. This multidimensional nature of vacationers' dis/satisfaction challenges the prevalence of the classical disconfirmation model as a basis for both understanding and measuring dis/satisfaction.

Introduction

Vacationers' dis/satisfaction processes are the focus of interest of this paper. Many researchers in consumer behaviour have stressed the importance of considering post-purchase assessment: decision making does not cease once a purchase is consumed. Product evaluation takes place and this reinforces further behaviour. This has obvious implications for marketing strategy. It is not surprising then that dis/satisfaction has grown to one of the most popular topics in the marketing literature. The systematic study of tourist dis/satisfaction is a more recent endeavour which still entails some grey areas. Ritchie (1994) points out the need for 'research related to post-experience feelings and behaviour with a view to understanding the impact of previous travel experience on future choice behaviour' (p.11). In this paper, vacationers' post-experience processes are revisited from an interpretive perspective. The following findings are part of a Ph.D. dissertation about judgements and decision making by vacationers (Decrop, 1999b). Dis/satisfactions may be seen as one major type of judgments such as perceptions or preferences. This study strives toward a deep understanding and interpretation of vacationers' dis/satisfaction judgments. We respectively deal with their antecedents, i.e. how they come about, and their consequences, i.e. what they result in. This double focus of interest is both theoretically and practically relevant: 'First, to improve the understanding of satisfaction judgments, it is important to identify the causes and correlates of consumer satisfaction or dissatisfaction. Second, to improve predictions and managerial decisions, it is critical to consider various post-choice behaviours, such as complaint behaviour and repeat vacation' (Mazursky, 1989, p. 333).

The overall tourist's decision-making process has been investigated in several papers and monographs in the two last decades (for reviews, see Ross, 1994; Decrop, 1999a). A few authors have focused their research on the formation of tourist dis/satisfaction. Dis/satisfaction was first described as an attributional problem. Following equity theory, Francken and van Raaij (1981) postulate that 'the attribution of inequality is an important factor in determining dissatisfaction' (p. 110). This means that the service that is offered by the provider should sufficiently justify the amount of money that was paid for the service. If this is not the case, then this will lead to dissatisfaction. The implication is that dissatisfaction should arise only if negative feelings about the vacation are attributed to factors external to the vacationer (supply variables such as accommodation, transportation and food), not if they are seen as the result of internal factors (such as attitudes, expectations and intrinsic rewards). This theory has further been developed (van Raaij and Francken, 1984; Zalatan, 1994) and empirically supported (Gitelson and Crompton, 1984; Lounsbury and Hoopes, 1985; Botterill, 1987).

Other authors refer to the classical disconfirmation theory when studying post-experience travel evaluation. Pizam et al. (1978) were the first to conceptualize tourist satisfaction as the result of the interaction between a tourist's experience at a destination area and his/her prior expectations. Chon (1989) further explains that tourist satisfaction depends upon 'the goodness of fit between his/her expectation about the destination and the perceived evaluative outcome of the experience at the destination' (p. 5). He defines expectation as all traveller's previous images of the destination. These images are compared against what he/she actually sees, feels and achieves during his/her stay at the destination. In later studies (Chon, 1990, 1992; Chon et al., 1994), Chon adapts the classical expectancy disconfirmation model using Sirgy's evaluative congruity theory and brings empirical support for it. Four mental states, or evaluative congruities, are distinguished, resulting from the comparison process between the perceived image of the destination and its perceived reality. Each state is translated into a degree of tourist (dis)satisfaction. Mazursky (1989) somewhat qualifies the disconfirmation theory by showing that past experience (reflected by norms) is determinant in shaping satisfaction and by then future tourism decisions. He further argues that norms form another baseline standard, which does not necessarily coincide with the expectational baseline.

It is remarkable that this disconfirmation paradigm has been dominating satisfaction research for the past 15 years (Schofield, 1999). Research by Duke and Persia (1996a, 1996b), Ryan and Cliff (1997), Weiermair and Fuchs (1999) all are within this tradition. In addition, the comparison between expectation and actual product performance has been extensively used for measurement. In importance-performance analysis (Martilla and James, 1977), the relative importance of various attributes and the performance of the firm in providing those attributes are combined for strategic analysis and planning, i.e. to identify areas for service quality improvements (see Hudson and Shephard, 1998). In SERVQUAL models (Parasuraman *et al.*, 1988), a measure of service quality is obtained for each attribute by deducting the expectation rating from the perception rating for that attribute (see Ryan and Cliff, 1997; Weiermair and Fuchs, 1999). Finally, pre- and post-purchase/experience measurement of judgments is used in image modification studies (e.g. Pearce, 1982; Phelps, 1986; Chon, 1987; Sussmann and Unel, 1999). The omnipresence of the disconfirmation model has been challenged in the past few years. Among other authors, Ryan (1999) warns that 'the apparent ease of [satisfaction] measurement makes us blind to the real nature of the experience tourists seek and often find' (p. 267). There is a need for a deeper and wider understanding of how dis/satisfaction arises and what its consequences are. That is why we will go and listen to the field in order to develop propositions inductively instead of testing stereotypical and stringent hypotheses. An inductive interpretive approach is chosen where the focus is on understanding and not on prediction.

Methodology

This paper is the result of a doctoral research (Decrop, 1999b) where the actual vacation decision-making process of 25 Belgian households was followed for a whole year. Informants were recruited according to theoretical sampling, i.e. looking for cases who were likely to yield rich and varied information in order to maximize theory development (Strauss and Corbin, 1990). Having some intention to go on summer vacation that year (i.e. 1996) was the only criterion to be eligible for the study. A distinction was made between four basic types of vacation decision-making units (DMUs): singles (representing tourists who decide on their own), couples (married or non-married), families with children and groups of friends. Those 25 DMUs were interviewed in depth two or three times before the summer vacation (i.e. in February, April and June) in such a way that their plans, judgements, and decisions could be followed. They were interviewed once again after the vacation (i.e. in November) for post-experience thoughts, feelings and evaluations. Most results of this paper actually emerge from this last series of interviews. This real situation longitudinal design helps understanding the actual nature of dis/satisfaction judgments. These interview data were triangulated with observation data collected at the Brussels Travel Trade Fair and in two travel agencies. The analysis and interpretation of the interview and observation transcripts are based on the grounded theory approach (Glaser and Strauss, 1967), which is 'a qualitative research method that uses a systematic set of procedures to develop an inductively derived grounded theory about a phenomenon' (Strauss and Corbin, 1990, p. 24). These procedures include:

- the concurrent collection and analysis of data,
- the enhancement of theoretical sensitivity,
- categories, patterns, and propositions emerge from the coding process of the data (rather than being imposed beforehand) and are permanently called into question.

Coding is made at three levels (i.e. open, axial, and selective coding) from the most descriptive to the most interpretative, from the most concrete to the most abstract, from the most analytical to the most holistic.

The Antecedents of Dis/satisfaction

When identifying the antecedents of informants' dis/satisfaction judgments, three major explanations emerge from the data. First, there is a comparison process between the just lived vacation/destination and previous vacation/destination experiences. Relative performances are compared with kinds of norms resulting from previous experience. This comparison may have some bearing on the destination in general or on specific attributes of it, such as illustrated by the two following quotes:

> *Paul*: I am personally satisfied but I would not start it over again, I would not start again. I will never go to Malta again, that's certain, whereas I would gladly return to Greece. I do not know whether you grasp the distinction.
> *Paul*: The only reproach I would make: I found that there were not many big unusual sights in Cyprus in comparison with Sicily, Crete, etc. where actually there were much more things to see. At least regarding monuments, I did not see anything… There are a few churches but these are not …

The previous finding is related to experienced-based norms theory (Woodruff *et al.*, 1983; Cadotte *et al.*, 1987), which suggests that consumers are comparing actual product performances against performance norms. Performance norms are based on experience and may take the form of another product brand (for instance, the preferred brand, or the standard brand). Besides performance norms, Woodruff and his fellows propose two other experienced-based standards of comparison, i.e. brand attitudes and expectations. This introduces the second emerging finding about the antecedents of satisfaction.

Satisfaction may result from a direct comparison process between expectation (based on previous experience, or other sources of information) and performance on specific attributes. The level of expectation, and the matching probability that post-experience assessment results in dis/satisfaction is very dependent on the destination itself:

> *Michèle*: To some extent, having rain in Ireland is less serious than having rain at the Côte d'Azur because you do not go there for… You go there for… But I personally know some people… For example, it seems that in some southern destinations, in Spain or in Provence, this summer the weather was not that nice: even cloudier and rainier than here. Actually those people were extremely disappointed and others even have shortened their vacation wondering 'what did we come here for?' [laugh]. In Ireland, you will not pack up and go just because it rains. Because actually, I guess one knows it, it is risky…

Based on this comparison process, there are three possible resulting moods
1 Disappointment: vacationers are dissatisfied because (some of) their expectations have not been met.
2 Surprise: vacationers are satisfied because destination performance goes beyond expectations, enjoyable unexpected things have occurred.
3 Indifference: vacationers are neither satisfied, nor dissatisfied, since (positive

or negative) expected aspects were found in the real vacation experience.
This is in line[1] with the classical expectancy disconfirmation model (Oliver, 1980; Churchill and Surprenant, 1982), which postulates that consumers enter into purchase with expectations of how the product will actually perform. Once the product is purchased and used, outcomes (actual product performances) are compared against those expectations. This comparison process results in either confirmation (performance equals expectations) or disconfirmation (positive if performance is better than expected; negative if it is worse). Positive disconfirmation leads to satisfaction while negative disconfirmation results in dissatisfaction. Simple confirmation implies a more neutral response. However, there are more indications in the data that vacationers are more likely to be satisfied in that case (see later). As it has already been pointed out above, disconfirmation theory has been widely used to explain tourist dis/satisfaction (e.g. Chon's studies).

Finally, it is worth noticing that informants often simply mention the difference between vacation expectations and performances, without any evaluation. This is interpreted as post-experience beliefs or perception judgments and leads to the proposition that the comparison process expected vs. actual performance is not a sufficient condition for (dis)satisfaction. This is not even a necessary condition since (dis)satisfaction does not always result from the product itself but may be the consequence of an attributional process. By this we mean that, in certain situations, informants locate the origin of their (dis)satisfaction in other factors than the product and the experience itself. 'It's my fault', 'it's his fault' are typical replies. In the first case, we could speak of internal attribution or of 'mea culpa' behaviour. The vacationer is (dis)satisfied simply because of his/her own decisions and behaviour. In the following quote, the father of a family explains that they are dissatisfied about their last vacation in Brittany just because they did lack knowledge of the destination:

> *Jean*: We are still happy with our agency. They did not make any failure or whatever. No, that was right. But maybe we have made an unwise choice regarding the geographical location. Because one always starts with some lack of knowledge.

In the second case ('other's fault'), we speak of external attribution. Possible sources of external attribution for (dis)satisfaction are people (tourist intermediaries, parents and friends, even some members of the DMU), hazard (e.g. an unexpected truck strike has caused big traffic jams), information sources (guides, brochures, travel agents). The distribution of attribution is asymmetrical: external attribution is more frequent in satisfaction judgments while internal attribution occurs more frequently in dissatisfaction judgments. To some extent, this phenomenon, which is interpreted as dissonance or altruism, is in contradiction with van Raaij and Francken (1984). These authors postulate that vacationers who attribute their dissatisfaction to external factors are more dissatisfied than vacationers who attribute their dissatisfaction to themselves. This emerging attributional framework may be related to the attribution theory perspective on consumer dis/satisfaction (Folkes, 1984). Attribution theory postulates that consumers use three bases to classify and to understand why a product does not perform as expected, i.e. stability (are the causes temporary or permanent?), locus (are the causes consumer- or marketer-related?), and controllability (are the causes under volitional control or are they constrained by external factors?). The two latter conditions are found in our data (see the previous quotation). Attributional frameworks have already been used to examine tourist satisfaction such as illustrated in the introduction of this paper.

The previous emerging explanations of vacationer dis/satisfaction share the same utilitarian view. In contrast, some chunks in the data show that (dis)satisfaction may have a more hedonistic and emotional background. Mental states like post-vacation depression, the joy of coming back home (because of home sickness or risk aversion), or pride in having broken with the past (because of innovation) are not directly related to the destination itself and utilities to the vacationers. This suggests that post-experience feelings and emotions should be added to the cognitive approach to consumer dis/satisfaction. This affective perspective is supported by Westbrook (1980, 1987), and Westbrook and Oliver (1991). Our data give empirical evidence to Westbrook's (1980) proposition that dis/satisfaction partly results from personality traits or enduring attitudes (an optimistic vacationer is more likely to be satisfied than a pessimistic vacationer, whatever the destination performance), and momentary moods such as joy, depression or harmony.

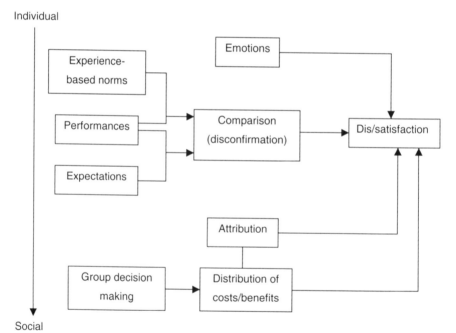

Figure 1 The antecedents of vacationers' dis/satisfaction

There is a last aspect that needs to be mentioned about the antecedents of dis/satisfaction. Vacation dis/satisfaction is seldom equally distributed among the different members of the DMU. This is particularly the case in families where parents are satisfied with a vacation item, while children declare that they are somewhat dissatisfied, and vice versa. The mother of a newly made family evaluates their camping experience as follows:

> *Anne*: Oh yes, the children like it: it's much funnier. Moreover it is a closed-in place where they can do whatever they want: it is safe. It is definitely less comfortable for the parents but for them, it is a dream vacation. As soon as they arrive, the kids, the girls make up a group of friends because it is rather a family, at least in the summertime, family [camping]. And the little boy too: he has found a little neighbour…

Distribution conflicts is a major emerging aspect of group decision making, which may be connected with equity theory (see above). A vacationer will be dissatisfied if she/he perceives inequalities in the distribution of the costs and benefits of the vacation experience in his/her disfavour. In contrast, s/he will be satisfied if the exchange is fair or in his/her favour. This is in line[1] with literature by Oliver and Swan (1989), and Francken and van Raaij (1981).

The previous findings suggest different explanations of vacationers' dis/satisfaction. These are combined in Figure 1. Theories are presented following a continuum on the left side, which represents the individual vs. social nature of the explanation. Emotions lie on the individual side as they by nature are person-related. Experience-based norms theory and the classical disconfirmation approach also basically involve the individual but pertain to the product, whereas attribution and distribution of costs/benefits theories are rather concerned with the group.

Consequences of Dis/satisfaction

After the antecedents, the consequences of (dis)satisfaction judgments are now considered. Different situations emerge from the data. First, experience leads through (dis)satisfaction to perceptual and attitudinal change. On one hand, experience contributes to changing perception judgments, to breaking down preconceived ideas about particular destination attributes. For example, after several visits to Spain, someone realizes that 'they [the Spanish people] become a little bit more friendly.' In the same way, a teacher of history is completely reconsidering her lectures after visiting countries (i.e. Turkey, Morocco or Italy) which were often associated with negative clichés. On the other hand, one comes across attitudinal or preferential change. As a result of dissatisfaction, most vacationers are willing to change destination, i.e. they exclude the just visited destination from future consideration sets ('you will never get me there again'). Repeated dissatisfaction resulting from several missed vacation experiences reinforces the willingness to a radical change (e.g. summer vacation is left out for winter ski vacation). This willingness to change does not always stem from dissatisfaction but may also arise when vacationers are satisfied. This is either explained by the desire to break with routine or by emotional factors. For example, while being satisfied with her last vacation, an old widow does not want to go on vacation anymore because she felt even more depressed after the vacation experience. Variety seeking is another major explanation.

Findings indicate that discovering new things or acquiring broader knowledge is one of the major reasons for variety seeking. Another reason is the fear of being disappointed by a second experience at a place which is connected with (very) good memories. Experience causes an upward shift in the expectation level (see later), which results in a higher risk of not being as satisfied as before. Westbrook and Newman (1978) suggest that high levels of satisfaction with a previously owned brand are often accompanied by some dissatisfaction following repurchase. This is in line with Oliver's (1980) expectancy disconfirmation model. A rise in the expectation level means that negative disconfirmation (i.e. product performance is worse than expected) is more likely to occur. Avoiding painful memories associated with particular destinations is also mentioned: 'I systematically refuse the destinations where I went with my husband in the past because I think that it is useless to torture yourself for the enjoyment'. Further, personal factors come into play: variety seeking is an expression of status; it is used to reveal an adventurous, unstable, or prospective nature, and to enhance self-image. Finally, some variety seekers have no other justification than a question of principle, a rule of thumb: 'And then we have a principle, never go twice to the same place. No, because the world is too small... actually too big to waste our time going twice to the same place'.

While dissatisfaction most of the time leads to attitudinal and behavioural change, satisfaction results in brand loyalty and repeat purchase. When satisfied, the vacationer is loyal ('we must go back there'), they desire to go back to the same destination and to live the same vacation experiences again. The father of a mid-life family declares that they will return to the same destination (France) until they are no longer satisfied:

Patrick: But we did it already tell you: we like to go back to places which we enjoyed. It is about the same as when people are going to a restaurant because they enjoy being there and because it is usually good. And then it happens once that they are less well served and they don't go there anymore. And I personally think it's about what happens : you have good memories and you want to go back there. Maybe you will go there again in another context and you will say 'well, we now did go round it.' And actually it is not because you did go round it, it's simply because parameters will not have been as enjoyable or positive as before, and then you will go somewhere else.

For a few 'masochists', dissatisfaction also results in brand loyalty. This is explained by the following reasons:

- Destination evaluation happens in a compensatory way: attributes are given different weights, and the weakness of one attribute can be offset by the strength of (an)other more important and enduring attribute(s). For instance, a mother is dissatisfied about her last vacation in Switzerland because of the climate but nevertheless she is ready to go back there because her satisfaction on other attributes (i.e. the tourist infrastructure and the Swiss mentality) is higher.
- The vacationer is resigned, as there is no real alternative to the chosen way. For

example, dissatisfaction about a crowded destination, or organized tours (which allow too little time to visit) results in repeated behaviour because those vacationers cannot afford to visit that destination in the off-season, or by themselves.

- The informant realizes that they are dissatisfied because they have missed important aspects of the destination: 'And while coming back in the airplane, I was even saying to myself, well, I'd like to go back again, just to make the [day] trips I did not make.'

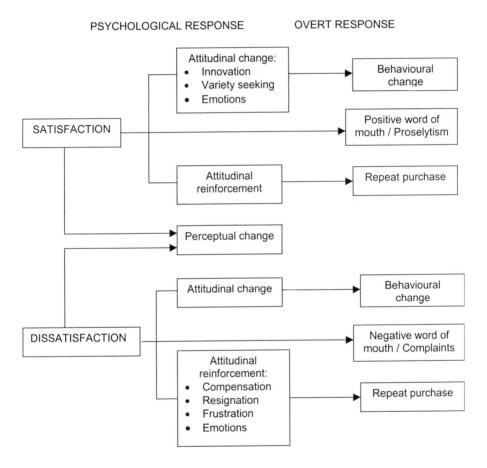

Figure 2 The consequences of vacationers' dis/satisfaction

- Other informants themselves find it hard to explain why they are likely to repeat their behaviour while being dissatisfied. Emotional drives towards the destination seem to prevail over rational considerations: 'And even the first time I went to the Vatican, I found it too big. I was crushed. However just after it, I wanted to return there; that's very strange.'

Another important consequence of vacationers' dis/satisfaction is information giving and, more particularly, word of mouth. A feeling of satisfaction results in advising relatives to visit the destination ('you must go there'), and giving a lot of information about its attributes. For a few informants, this kind of proselytism is very pronounced:

> *Anne*: And for example in Hungary, I tried to send a number of friends there: I am a bit contagious like that.
> *Peter*: Converter.
> *Anne*: Converter, yes. When I find a place I like (and I like everywhere that I go), I like telling other people to go there.

In contrast, dissatisfaction leads to negative word of mouth to relatives and friends. This is rather holistic (less detailed information is given) or focuses on only one attribute: 'take care of your money if you are going to France.' An even more severe response to dissatisfaction is complaint behaviour. For example, an older single woman writes a letter to the local tourism office, while another one gives a phone call to the travel agent. Complaints may also occur on the vacation spot (an older female widow succeeds in moving hotel after complaining to the tour-operator's representative). However, data show that only a small minority of unsatisfied vacationers starts active complaining behaviour after the vacation experience. This is in line with empirical findings by Andreasen and Best (1977). The set of previous emerging propositions regarding the consequences of vacationers' dis/satisfaction is summarized in Figure 2. A distinction is made between psychological responses, which occur inside the person and overt responses, which are the observable consequences in the outside world.

Related phenomena

In addition to the antecedents and consequences of tourist dis/satisfaction, four related phenomena deserve close attention. First, *cognitive dissonance* (Festinger, 1957) occurs very often. Informants are used to put some decisions and choices into question, and to express post-experience regret: 'And also when I think about it again, I say, well, we should have gone to see that.' As a consequence, vacationers make efforts to reduce those dissonant elements by justifying that they actually made the good choice ('I do not regret it at all'), that they wanted to avoid saturation ('it's like when eating pastry, there is a time when it does not lust anymore'), that the good choice is only postponed, or that although it was not a good choice, there was no alternative solution. Informants are looking for having good conscience. It is much less likely that they acknowledge having made an unwise decision. Another, but much less occurring dimension of cognitive dissonance is attribution (see above). Finally, it is worth noticing that dissonance results in information collection. Most of the time in our data, post-experience dissonance results in an active search of supportive evidence that the right (wrong) choice has been made. After coming back home, a dissatisfied informant looks for and gets confirmation from several information sources that she indeed made a poor financial choice. Most often, post-experience information is related to price and product performance but it may also pertain to the number or perceived performance of rejected alternatives. After realizing that they missed interesting spots in Paris due to a lack of information, an older couple bought two guides for 'the next time.' There is a kind of information catch-up effect. A last finding indicates that the vacation experience itself constitutes new information, as thoughts and conversations that occurred during the trip may be the source of dissonance.

Prolonged involvement is a second emerging interpretation of post-experience information collection. After visiting a particular destination, there seems to be a growing sensitivity to any information regarding that destination. There is a voluntary search or a more or less automatic bias in selective perception. When listening to the news, the informant's ears are pricking up as the destination region or country is mentioned:

> *Roger*: In 1964, we went there and we came back in love with the place. It was magical. As a result, one of our main interests is Turkey or anything to do with Turkey. We will read a book about Turkey much more easily than we would read a book about Peru. If we see a program on the television or hear one on the radio, we will always be attentive to it. Why? Because there is a little place in our hearts which is Turkish. Because it truly was ...
> *Jacqueline*: An enchantment.

This phenomenon is confirmed by the observation data of the Brussels Vacation Fair. Visitors automatically were attracted by information stands of destinations that they had experienced before. Prolonged involvement is also related to hedonic consumption. Post-experience information search prolongs and extends the emotions and moods triggered off by the vacation experience:

> *Anne*: Yes, it is very nice to get to know a bit of the town and then to read a novel about the place where, for example, someone discovers the town after us, even if Denis wrote a novel before we had read it, but it was translated just a few years ago. And then we can feel again the same way the author did about the place.

Thirdly, reading through the interview transcripts creates the impression that informants are generally much *more satisfied than dissatisfied*. This is in line with the results of many academic, government, and business surveys, which show that the overall level of consumer satisfaction is high (Wilkie, 1990). However, this impression should be balanced. Generic satisfaction[2] indeed occurs more often than generic dissatisfaction (83/13 quotes). However, positive evaluations do no longer prevail when considering the destination in particular: about equal numbers (170/155 quotes) of satisfaction and dissatisfaction judgments are observed.

Finally, there is a clear tendency to evaluate the destination in a global way. Informants evaluate the destination as being good, and then it is good for all aspects, or as being not good, and then it is not good for any aspect. This phenomenon is called the *'halo' effect.* Positive halo effect is much more salient than negative halo effect. It is characterized by those typical sentences: 'everything is beautiful there', 'it seems that everything matches there', 'I dislike nothing in this destination.' Again this may be explained by the natural human tendency towards optimism, and by cognitive dissonance (if everything is good, there is no dissonant element).

Conclusion

In this paper, vacationers' post-experience processes have been revisited from a naturalistic interpretive perspective. Theoretical propositions regarding the antecedents and consequences of dis/satisfaction have been developed. These propositions have emerged from the analysis of empirical material about the actual decision-making process of 25 Belgian households. Different theories may be used to explain the formation of dis/satisfaction judgments, i.e. the intervention of emotions, the comparison process of performances with expectations or experience-based norms, and the attribution or the distribution of costs/benefits among the different members of the vacation DMU. Those theories can be classified according to whether they have an individual or a social nature and are person- or product-related. In the second part of the paper, the consequences of dis/satisfaction judgments have been examined. It has been shown that satisfaction does not always lead to repeat purchase but may sometimes result in attitudinal and behavioural change when the vacationer is driven by emotions, variety seeking or innovation will. In the same way, a behavioural change is not the only possible consequence of dissatisfaction. A dissatisfied vacationer may be induced to repeat his/her purchase because of compensation, resignation or frustration. Both satisfaction and dissatisfaction result in perceptual change and word of mouth.

The multidimensional nature of vacationers' dis/satisfaction has been put into light through this paper. Findings suggest that the prevalence of the classical expectancy disconfirmation model should be challenged. Although it can be used to describe the formation of satisfaction in certain cases, it is not always the right explanation. Alternative theories that include emotional and social components should be considered as a basis for both understanding and measuring dis/satisfaction.

Endnotes

[1] However, it should be noted that the use of equity theory to explain consumer dis/satisfaction first pertains to the relationships between sellers and buyers, and not to the members of a decision-making unit.
[2] Generic satisfaction is concerned with the overall evaluation of the vacation experience. Typical text chunks are: 'we liked it very much', 'it was a nice vacation', 'going away did me good'.

References

Andreasen, A.R. and Best, A. (1977) Consumers complain: Does business respond? *Harvard Business Review* July-August, 94-104.
Botterill, T.D. (1987) Dissatisfaction with a construction of satisfaction. *Annals of*

Tourism Research 14, 139-141.

Cadotte, E.R., Woodruff, R.B. and Jenkins, R.L. (1987) Expectations and norms in models of consumer satisfaction. *Journal of Marketing Research* 24, 305-314.

Chon, K. (1987) An assessment of images of Korea as a tourist destination by American tourists. *Hotel and Tourism Management Review* 3, 155-170.

Chon, K.S. (1989) Understanding recreational traveler's motivation, expectation, satisfaction. *Revue de tourisme* 44(1), 3-7.

Chon, K.S. (1990) The role of destination image in tourism: a review and discussion. *Revue de Tourisme* 45(2), 2-9.

Chon, K.S. (1992) The role of destination image in tourism: an extension. *Revue de Tourisme* 47(2), 2-9.

Chon, K.S., Christianson, D.J. and Lee, C.L. (1994) Contemporary research issues related tourist satisfaction and dissatisfaction. In: Gasser, R.V. and Weiermair, K. (eds.) *Spoilt for Choice. Decision Making Processes and Preference Changes of Tourist – Intertemporal and Intercountry Perspectives.* Thaur: Kulturverlag, pp. 149-160.

Churchill, G.A. and Surprenant, C. (1982) An investigation into the determinants of customer satisfaction. *Journal of Marketing Research* 19, 491-504.

Decrop, A. (1999a) Tourists' decision making and behaviour processes. In: Pizam, A. and Mansfeld, Y. (eds.) *Consumer Behaviour in Travel and Tourism.* The Haworth Press, New York.

Decrop, A. (1999b) *Commitments and Opportunities: Judgment and Decision Making by Vacationers.* Universitaires de Namur, Presses, Namur.

Duke, C.R. and Persia, M.A. (1996a) Consumer-defined dimensions for the escorted tour industry segment: Expectations, satisfactions, and importance. *Journal of Travel and Tourism Marketing* 5(1/2), 77-99.

Duke, C.R. and Persia, M.A. (1996b) Performance-importance analysis of escorted tour evaluations. *Journal of Travel and Tourism Marketing* 5(3), 207-223.

Festinger, L. (1957) *A Theory of Cognitive Dissonance.* Stanford University Press, Stanford, CA.

Folkes, V.S. (1984) Consumer reactions to product failure: An attributional approach. *Journal of Consumer Research* 10, 398-409.

Francken, D.A. and van Raaij, W.F. (1981) Satisfaction with leisure time activities. *Journal of Leisure Research* 13, 337-352.

Gitelson, R.J. and Crompton, J.L. (1984) Insights into the repeat vacation phenomenon. *Annals of Tourism Research* 11, 199-217.

Glaser, B. and Strauss, A. (1967) *The Discovery of Grounded Theory.* Aldine, Chicago.

Hudson, S. and Shephard, G.W. (1998) Measuring service quality at tourist destinations: An application of importance-performance analysis to an alpine ski resort. *Journal of Travel and Tourism Marketing* 7(3), 61-77.

Lounsbury, J.W. and Hoopes, L.L. (1985) An investigation of factors associated with vacation satisfaction. *Journal of Leisure Research* 17, 1-13.

Martilla, J.A. and James, J.C. (1977) Importance-performance analysis. *Journal of Marketing* 41(1), 13-17.

Mazursky, D. (1989) Past Experience and Future Tourism Decisions. *Annals of Tourism Research* 16, 333-344.

Oliver, R.L. (1980) A cognitive model of the antecedents and consequence of satisfaction decisions. *Journal of Marketing Research* 17, 460-469.

Oliver, R.L. and Swan, J.E. (1989) Consumer perceptions of interpersonal equity and satisfaction in transactions: a field survey approach. *Journal of Marketing* 53, 21-35.

Parasuraman, A., Zeithaml, V.A. and Berry, L.L. (1988) SERVQUAL: A multiple-item scale for measuring consumer perceptions of service quality. *Journal of Retailing* 64, 12-43.

Pearce, P.L. (1982) *The Social Psychology of Tourist Behaviour.* Pergamon Press, Oxford.

Phelps, A. (1986) Holiday destination image – the problem of assessment: An example developed in Menorca. *Tourism Management* 7,168-180.

Pizam, A., Neuman, Y. and Reichel, A. (1978) Dimensions of tourist satisfaction with a destination area. *Annals of Tourism Research* 5, 314-322.

Ritchie, J.R.B. (1994) Research on leisure behaviour and tourism – state of the art. In: Gasser, R.V. and Weiermair, K. (eds.) *Spoilt for Choice. Decision Making Processes and Preference Change of Tourists: Intertemporal and Intercountry Perspectives.* Thaur, Kulturverlag, pp. 2-27.

Ross, G.F. (1994) *The Psychology of Tourism.* Hospitality Press, Melbourne.

Ryan, C. (1999) From the psychometrics of SERVQUAL to sex: Measurements of tourist satisfaction. In: Pizam, A. and Mansfeld, Y. (eds.) *Consumer Behaviour in Travel and Tourism.* The Haworth Hospitality Press, New York, pp. 267-286.

Ryan, C. and Cliff, A. (1997) Do travel agencies measure up to customer expectations? An empirical investigation of travel agencies service quality as measured by SERVQUAL. *Journal of Travel and Tourism Marketing* 6(2), 1-32.

Schofield, P. (1999) Developing a day trip expectation/satisfaction construct: A comparative analysis of scale construction techniques. *Journal of Travel and Tourism Marketing* 8(3), 101-110.

Strauss, A. and Corbin J. (1990) *Basics of Qualitative Research: Grounded Theory Procedures and Techniques.* Sage, Newbury Park.

Sussmann, S. and Unel, A. (1999) Destination image and its modification after travel: An empirical study on Turkey. In: Pizam, A. and Mansfeld, Y. (eds.) *Consumer Behaviour in Travel and Tourism.* The Haworth Hospitality Press, New York, pp. 207-226.

Van Raaij, W.F. and Francken, D.A. (1984) Vacations decisions activities and satisfaction. *Annals of Tourism Research* 11, 101-112.

Weiermair, K. and Fuchs, M. (1999) Measuring tourist judgment on service quality. *Annals of Tourism Research* 26, 1004-1021.

Westbrook, R.A. (1980) Interpersonal influences on customer satisfaction with products. *Journal of Consumer Research* 7, 49-53.

Westbrook, R.A. (1987) Product consumption based affective purchases and postpurchase processes. *Journal of Marketing Research* 24, 258-270.

Westbrook, R.A. and Newman, J.W. (1978) An analysis of shopper dissatisfaction for major household appliances. *Journal of Marketing Research* 15, 456-466.

Westbrook, R.A. and Oliver, R. (1991) The dimensionality of consumption emotion patterns and consumer satisfaction. *Journal of Consumer Research* 18, 84-91.

Wilkie, W.L. (1990) *Consumer Behaviour.* John Wiley and Sons, New York.

Woodruff, R.B., Cadotte, E.R. and Jenkins, R.L. (1983) Modeling consumer satisfaction processes using experience-based norms. *Journal of Marketing Research* 20, 296-304.

Zalatan, A. (1994) Tourist satisfaction: A predetermined model. *Revue de Tourisme* 1, 9-13.

Index

Note:
Page numbers in *italics* refer to definitions.

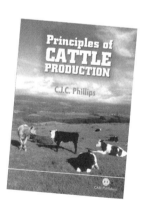

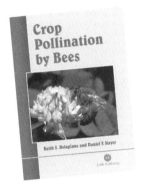

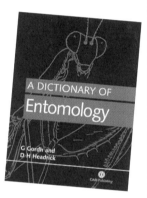